Better Homes and Gardens®

BIGGEST BOOK OF DIABETIC RECIPES

WILEY

John Wiley & Sons, Inc.

Our Better Homes and Gardens®
Test Kitchen seal on the back cover
of this book assures you that every
recipe in *Biggest Book of Diabetic
Recipes* has been tested in the Better
Homes and Gardens® Test Kitchen.
This means that each recipe is
practical and reliable, and meets our
high standards of taste appeal. We
guarantee your satisfaction with this
book for as long as you own it.

TABLE OF CONTENTS

DIABETES: THE BASICS

By Kristi Thomas, R.D.

An estimated 18.2 million people in the United States, or 8.7% of the U.S. adult population, have diabetes. Of those, only 13 million have been diagnosed, leaving 5.2 million people (or nearly one-third) unaware that they have the disease.*

*U.S. Department of Health and Human Services, Centers for Disease Control and Prevention, 2003

Understanding diabetes and how to prevent its complications gives you a better chance of controlling your disease. Fortunately, managing diabetes has come a long way in a short time, and research for new medicines and tools is ongoing. It pays to learn all you can, then develop a plan that fits your lifestyle. After all, you—not your doctor, dietitian, or other health professional—play the most important role in keeping yourself healthy.

DEFINE YOUR DIABETES

Your health-care team will work with you to develop a personalized plan, consisting of healthful foods, physical activity, and, if necessary, the medication that's right for you, your lifestyle, and your type of diabetes (type 1, type 2, or gestational). The difference among the types is distinct, but the general treatment plans have similarities. Type 1 or type 2 can occur in both adults and children.

Type 1 diabetes: In people with this form of the disease, the pancreas doesn't produce insulin, which makes it impossible to control blood glucose. Type 1 diabetics need insulin injections to live. A typical treatment plan for type 1 diabetes begins with an individualized meal plan, guidelines for physical activity, and self-blood glucose testing several times a day. Insulin therapy, consisting of multiple daily insulin injections, is then integrated into the person's usual lifestyle and coincides with the time and amount of food eaten.

Type 2 diabetes: In type 2 diabetics, either the pancreas doesn't produce enough insulin or the body doesn't respond to the insulin that is produced. Because the insulin can't deliver glucose to the cells, too much glucose remains in the blood. Many people control type 2 diabetes without medication by following a specially designed meal plan and engaging in routine physical activity. Because 8 out of 10 people are overweight when diagnosed with type 2 diabetes, the typical meal plan may be designed for weight loss. The right plan also helps to achieve healthy blood cholesterol and blood pressure levels. Self-blood glucose testing and often oral medications and/or insulin play a role in treating type 2 diabetes. Type 2 is a progressive disease and, as the disease progresses, treatment changes. This involves combining lifestyle strategies with oral medications, oral medications with insulin, or insulin alone.

Gestational diabetes: This type of diabetes develops only during pregnancy. Like type 2 diabetes, it occurs more often in African Americans, Native Americans, Hispanic Americans, and in women with a family history of diabetes. Women who've had gestational diabetes may develop type 2 diabetes.

DEVELOP YOUR MEAL PLAN

Adhering to a healthful meal plan remains one of the most important measures you can take to keep your blood glucose under control. In years past, people with diabetes were expected to follow a strict diet regimen that had little regard for individual likes or dislikes. Today diabetes experts realize that a one-size-fits-all approach doesn't work and isn't necessary. Work with your dietitian to design a meal plan that reflects your individual needs and preferences. There's no reason to buy special "diabetic" food products. Your plan should be built around foods that you enjoy and:

- Include fruits, vegetables, and whole grains.
- Reduce the amount of saturated fat and cholesterol you eat.

- Minimize the amount of salt/sodium you eat.

- Incorporate a moderate amount of sugar, because some sugar can be part of a healthful diabetes meal plan.

- Help you maintain or achieve an ideal weight.

FOLLOW YOUR MEAL PLAN

As you start using your meal plan, you'll see that it tells you what, how much, and when to eat, but you have to be comfortable with the foods it suggests. Your meal plan will also guide you in eating the right amounts of three major nutrients—carbohydrates, protein, and fat. It should be nutritionally balanced to provide the vitamins, minerals, and fiber you need. And if you need to lose weight, it should indicate the appropriate number of calories to help you lose at a safe and attainable pace.

While that may sound complicated, it can be simple, especially if you use either of a couple of important techniques to keep track of what you're eating. Two well-known meal planning systems for diabetics are the Exchange Lists for Meal Planning and carbohydrate counting. To make either system easy for you to follow, every recipe in this book provides you with nutritional information and the number of exchanges in each serving. (See page 7 for information on how we calculate nutrition content and how to keep track of exchanges and carbohydrates.)

TRACK THE EXCHANGES

If you use the Exchange Lists for Meal Planning, a system designed by the American Diabetes Association and the American Dietetic Association, your dietitian will work with you to develop a pattern of food exchanges—or a meal plan—suited to your specific needs. You'll then be able to keep track of the number of exchanges from various food groups that you eat each day. You'll tally those numbers and match the total to the daily allowance set in your meal plan.

THE CARBOHYDRATE QUESTION

Although the calories from all three major nutrients affect your blood glucose level, carbohydrates affect it the most. So why not just avoid carbohydrates altogether? While carbohydrates may be the main nutrient that raises blood glucose, you should not cut them out of your diet. Foods that contain

MONITOR YOUR BLOOD GLUCOSE

No matter what type of diabetes you have, it's important to test your blood glucose, especially if you're taking insulin shots or oral medication. Usually you test blood glucose before each meal to determine whether it's in the high, low, or normal range. Your health-care providers will teach you how to measure your blood glucose with a simple finger-prick test, as well as how to adjust your food intake, physical activity, and/or medication when your blood glucose is too high or too low. Good diabetes control means keeping your blood glucose level as close to normal as possible. The normal range before eating is less than 100 milligrams per deciliter. Your health-care providers will discuss what the best goals are for you. To keep your blood glucose at a healthy level, follow these five important guidelines:

- Eat about the same amount of food each day.

- Eat meals and snacks at about the same times each day.

- Do not skip meals or snacks.

- Take medicines at the same times each day.

- Do physical activity at about the same times each day.

carbohydrates are among the healthiest foods available—vegetables, fruits, whole grains, and low-fat or fat-free dairy foods. Eliminating these foods from your diet actually could compromise your health.

HOW SWEET IT IS

For many years, people with diabetes were told to shun sugar because it was thought that sugar caused blood glucose to soar out of control. More than a dozen studies have shown that sugars in foods do not cause blood glucose to spike any higher or faster than do starches, such as those in potatoes and bread. As a result, the American Diabetes Association's recommendations regarding sugar have changed. They now say "scientific evidence has shown that the use of sucrose (table sugar) as part of the meal plan does not impair blood glucose control in individuals with type 1 or type 2 diabetes."

However, sugar is not a "free food." It still contains calories and offers no nutritional value beyond providing energy. So when you eat foods that contain sugar, you must substitute them for other carbohydrate foods in your meal plan. If you have a sweet tooth, ask your dietitian to help you work sugar into your meal plan so that you won't be tempted to use sugar with abandon.

COUNT CARBOHYDRATES

Carbohydrate counting is the method diabetes educators prefer for keeping tabs on what you eat. Carbohydrate counting makes sense because the carbohydrate content of foods and beverages has the greatest effect on blood glucose levels. If you focus on carbohydrate content, you can eat a variety of foods and still control your blood glucose.

When counting carbohydrates, you can tally the number of carbohydrate grams you eat each day. Or you can figure the number of carbohydrate choices and keep track of those (this allows you to work with smaller numbers).

Basic carbohydrate counting relies on eating about the same amount of carbohydrates at the same times each day to keep blood glucose levels in your target range. It's a good meal-planning method if you have type 2 diabetes and don't take any daily oral diabetes medications. It's also a good method for those who take 1 or 2 shots of insulin per day.

Advanced carbohydrate counting is more complex than basic carbohydrate counting. It's appropriate for individuals who take multiple insulin injections daily or use an insulin pump. The advantage lies in having greater flexibility in meal planning. With advanced counting, you estimate the amount of carbohydrates you'll be eating and adjust your mealtime insulin dose based on your insulin-to-carbohydrate ratio. For advanced carbohydrate counting, seek the assistance of a registered dietitian or certified diabetes educator.

INCREASE YOUR ACTIVITY

Because being overweight stands out as a major culprit for the increase in type 2 diabetes, physical activity is a must. Physical activity leads to better blood glucose control in type 2 diabetes by helping your body use insulin efficiently and burn calories, which makes it easier to achieve or maintain a healthy weight. In type 1, the benefits of physical activity lie in reducing the risk for cardiovascular disease, rather than controlling blood glucose.

How much activity is enough? The National Academy of Science's Institute of Medicine recommends one hour of moderate activity each day. Health experts agree that you can reap benefits from as little as 30 minutes of moderate activity on most—and preferably all—days. However, if you've been sedentary, any increase in activity is better than none. It's OK to accumulate your daily total in 10-minute chunks if that works better for you. Check in with your doctor about your plans to increase activity, and start slowly if you haven't been active. For example, taking a 10-minute walk after dinner a few nights a week is a good start.

STAY INVOLVED AND INFORMED

Getting physical activity, eating healthfully, and monitoring blood glucose levels are principal factors in keeping diabetes in check—all easier to do if you follow the plans you've developed with your health-care providers. Update your providers on your progress and let them know if you want to change something that's not working for you. Additionally, stay informed about diabetes to have more power over the disease and a better quality of life. Remember—you're the only one who can monitor your progress day by day.

Kristi Thomas, R.D., is the author of *Better Homes and Gardens® New Diabetic Cookbook* and *Better Homes and Gardens® Easy Diabetic Meals for 2 or 4 Servings.*

BE A SUGAR SLEUTH

Learning the different forms and names of sugar can make life sweeter. Remember that sugar content is included in the total grams listed for carbohydrates.

Sucrose: appears in table sugar, molasses, beet sugar, brown sugar, cane sugar, powdered sugar, raw sugar, turbinado, and maple syrup.

Other "-ose" sugars: glucose (or dextrose), fructose, lactose, and maltose.

Sugar alcohols: sorbitol, xylitol, and mannitol. Limit these sugars, as they can cause diarrhea, gas, and cramping.

Fructose and sugar alcohols affect blood glucose less than sucrose or other carbohydrates and can be used in moderate amounts, but large amounts of fructose may increase blood fat levels.

USING OUR NUTRITION INFORMATION

With each recipe in this book, we give important nutrition information to help you control your diabetes. Below, you'll find out how we calculate our nutrition analyses and how you can make sure our recipes fit into your meal plan.

1 NUTRITION INFORMATION WITH EVERY RECIPE

For each serving, you'll find the amount of calories (cal.), fat, saturated (sat.) fat, cholesterol (chol.), sodium, total carbohydrates (carbo.), fiber, and protein (pro.). In addition, we list the number of servings of diabetic exchanges for each serving in case you prefer that method to keep track of what you're eating.

2 RECIPE OPTIONS AND ALTERNATIVES

In calculating our nutrition information, we've made some decisions about what's included and what's not, especially when we're offering some flexibility in our recipes. Here are the guidelines we use when analyzing recipes that list ingredient options or serving suggestions:

- When ingredient choices appear in a recipe (such as butter or margarine), we use the first one mentioned for our analysis.
- When we offer a range in the number of servings, we use the smaller number of servings as the basis for our calculations.
- When an ingredient is listed as optional, such as a garnish or flavoring, we don't include that ingredient in our analysis.

3 INTERPRETING THE NUMBERS

Our nutrition analyses can help you keep track of the nutritional value of the foods you eat, but it's important that you and your dietitian have worked out a meal plan that's right for you first. That plan should give you set amounts of nutrients or the number of diabetic exchanges or carbohydrate choices you can eat each day. Keep those numbers handy inside your kitchen cabinet door and in your purse or briefcase. Then use our nutrition analyses to keep a running tally of what you're eating. At the end of each day, see how your numbers compare to the goals set in your meal plan.

4 DIABETIC EXCHANGES

Using diabetic exchanges is one way of monitoring what you eat. To use the exchange system correctly, follow the meal plan recommended for you by your dietitian, which should indicate the number of servings to have from each exchange group in a day. The exchanges listed with our recipes include the following food groupings: starch, fruit, milk, other carbohydrates, nonstarchy vegetables, meat and meat substitutes, fat, and free foods.

5 CARBOHYDRATE COUNTING

You can keep track of carbohydrates with one of two methods—counting grams of carbohydrates or tallying carbohydrate choices. The amount of total carbohydrates is listed in grams with each recipe. If you want to tally carbohydrate choices, have a registered dietitian or certified diabetes educator show you how to do these calculations. (The benefit of this system is that you're keeping track of smaller numbers, which may make your counting simpler.) Remember, even though a high-carbohydrate recipe may look like one portion on your plate, it may contain enough carbohydrates to count as two or more carbohydrate choices.

WEEKDAY MENUS (1-7)

These menus will take the guesswork out of tracking your carb intake and planning meals. Depending upon your individual needs, choose from the 1,500-calorie-per-day, 1,800-calorie-per-day, or 2,000-calorie-per-day options.

MENU #1

Breakfast:

Almond-Orange Granola (pg. 50)	⅓ cup
Plain low-fat yogurt	6-oz. carton
Mixed berries	1½ cups
Tea or coffee	

Breakfast totals: 315 calories, 57 g carbo., 3 g fat, 12 g protein

Lunch:

Turkey-Tomato Wraps (pg. 263)	1 serving
Baby carrots	1 cup
Apple	1 small
Low-fat milk	1 cup

Lunch totals: 410 calories, 61 g carbo., 5 g fat, 29 g protein

Supper:

Spicy Ginger Fish (pg. 168)	1 serving
Oven-Roasted Vegetables (pg. 368)	1 serving
Whole wheat roll	1 small
Soft, non-hydrogenated margarine	2 tsp.
Mixed green salad	2 cups
Reduced-fat salad dressing	2 Tbsp.
Mocha Cake with Berries (pg. 385)	1 serving
Coffee or tea	

Supper totals: 621 calories, 67 g carbo., 24 g fat, 34g protein

Evening snack:

Peanut-Packed Munch Mix (pg. 33)	½ cup
Coffee, tea, or water	

Snack totals: 153 calories, 17 g carbo., 9 g fat, 5g protein

1,500-calorie day totals:
1,499 calories, 202 g carbo., 41 g fat, 80 g protein

Afternoon snack:

Banana-Oat Muffins (pg. 67)	1 muffin
Soft, non-hydrogenated margarine	2 tsp.
Apple juice	½ cup

Snack totals: 324 calories, 42 g carbo., 15 g fat, 5 g protein

1,800-calorie day totals:
1,823 calories, 244 g carbo., 56 g fat, 85 g protein

Morning snack:

English muffin	½ muffin
Peanut butter	1 Tbsp.

Snack totals: 180 calories, 15 g carbo., 8 g fat, 10g protein

2,000-calorie day totals:
2,003 calories, 259 g carbo., 64 g fat, 95 g protein

MENU #2

Breakfast:

Bacon 'n' Egg Pockets (pg. 54)	1 serving
Honeydew melon	1½ cups cubes
Tea or coffee	

Breakfast totals: 242 calories, 40 g carbo., 4 g fat, 13 g protein

Lunch:

Grilled Tomato & Mozzarella Salad (pg. 256)	1 serving
Whole grain pita bread	1 pita
Purchased hummus	2 Tbsp.
Banana	1 small
Tea, coffee, or water	

Lunch totals: 479 calories, 59 g carbo., 17 g fat, 23 g protein

Supper:

Chicken with Broccoli & Garlic (pg. 139)	1 serving
Cooked brown rice	⅔ cup
Tomato, sliced	1 small
Pear, canned	½ cup
Tea, coffee, or water	

Supper totals: 503 calories, 71 g carbo., 11 g fat, 30 g protein

Evening snack:

Whole wheat crackers	6 crackers
Flavored tub-style light cream cheese	2 Tbsp.
Low-fat milk	1 cup

Snack totals: 230 calories, 27 g carbo., 9 g fat, 11 g protein

1,500-calorie day totals:
1,454 calories, 197 g carbo., 40 g fat, 77 g protein

Afternoon snack:

Scones with Currants (pg. 62)	1 scone
Soft, non-hydrogenated margarine	2 tsp.
Water, tea, or coffee	

Snack totals: 292 calories, 32 g carbo., 16 g fat, 4 g protein

1,800-calorie day totals:
1,746 calories, 229 g carbo., 55 g fat, 81 g protein

Morning snack:

Low-fat fruit yogurt	6-oz. carton
Lunch Box Oatmeal Cookies (pg. 395)	1 cookie

Snack totals: 255 calories, 42 g carbo., 6 g fat, 3 g protein

2,000-calorie day totals:
2,001 calories, 271 g carbo., 61 g fat, 84 g protein

MENU #3

Breakfast:

Banana-Stuffed French Toast (pg. 57)	1 serving
Light syrup	2 Tbsp.
Low-fat milk	1 cup
Tea or coffee	

Breakfast totals: 360 calories, 61 g carbo., 4 g fat, 17 g protein

Lunch:
Black Bean-Tortilla Soup
  (pg. 211)   1 serving
Shredded Monterey
  Jack cheese   2 Tbsp.
Grapes   about 17 grapes or 3 oz.
Tea, coffee, or water
Lunch totals: 281 calories,
46 g carbo., 8 g fat, 12 g protein

Supper:
Mixed green salad   1 cup
Reduced-fat salad dressing 2 Tbsp.
Top Sirloin with Onion-Mushroom
  Medley (pg. 78)   1 serving
Cooked couscous
       ⅔ cup with 2 tsp. olive oil
Steamed green beans   1 cup
Brownie Cookies
  (pg. 397)   1 cookie
Tea, coffee, or water
Supper totals: 666 calories,
74 g carbo., 23 g fat, 40 g protein

Evening snack:
Whole grain bagel   ½ bagel
Flavored tub-style light
  cream cheese   2 Tbsp.
Low-fat milk   1 cup
Snack totals: 230 calories,
27 g carbo., 7 g fat, 11 g protein

1,500-calorie day totals:
1,537 calories, 208 g carbo.,
42 g fat, 80 g protein

Afternoon snack:
Savory Nuts (pg. 35)   ¼ cup
Apple   1 small
Water, tea, or coffee
Snack totals: 319 calories,
20 g carbo., 27 g fat, 3 g protein

1,800-calorie day totals:
1,856 calories, 228 g carbo.,
69 g fat, 83 g protein

Morning snack:
Lovin' Lemon Swirl Dip
  (pg. 43)   1 serving
Fresh strawberries   1¼ cups
Snack totals: 113 calories,
28 g carbo., 1 g fat, 2 g protein

2,000-calorie day totals:
1,969 calories, 256 g carbo.,
70 g fat, 85 g protein

MENU #4
Breakfast:
Tango Mango Smoothies
  (pg. 46)   1 serving
Breakfast Pizza (pg. 338) 1 serving
Tea or coffee
Breakfast totals: 363 calories,
52 g carbo., 11 g fat, 18 g protein

Lunch:
Terrific Tortellini Salad
  (pg. 354)   1 serving
Grated Parmesan cheese   2 Tbsp.
Low-fat milk   1 cup
Fresh blueberries   ¾ cup
Tea, coffee, or water
Lunch totals: 350 calories,
49 g carbo., 9 g fat, 21 g protein

Supper:
Tomato juice   ½ cup
Lamb with Roasted-Pepper Bulgur
  (pg. 153)   1 serving
Greens (collard, mustard, kale
  or spinach), steamed   1 cup
Peaches, canned   ½ cup
Mocha Meringue Stars
  (pg. 399)   2 cookies
Tea, coffee, or water
Supper totals: 458 calories,
71 g carbo., 7 g fat, 32 g protein

Evening snack:
Spiced Popcorn (pg. 29)   2 cups
Almonds   1 oz.
Low-fat fruit yogurt 6 oz. carton
Snack totals: 408 calories,
50 g carbo., 17 g fat, 8 g protein

1,500-calorie day totals:
1,579 calories, 222 g carbo.,
43 g fat, 78 g protein

Afternoon snack:
Mediterranean Walnut Spread
  (pg. 42)   2 Tbsp.
Melba toast   4 slices
Baby carrots and
  celery sticks   1 cup total
Snack totals: 243 calories,
33 g carbo., 8 g fat, 9 g protein

1,800-calorie day totals:
1,822 calories, 255 g carbo.,
51 g fat, 87 g protein

Morning snack:
Date-Nut Bread (pg. 64)   1 serving
Soft, non-hydrogenated
  margarine   2 tsp.
Snack totals: 209 calories,
22 g carbo., 13 g fat, 3 g protein

2,000-calorie day totals:
2,031 calories, 277 g carbo.,
64 g fat, 90 g protein

MENU #5
Breakfast:
Southwestern Breakfast Tostadas
  (pg. 274)   1 serving
Nectarine   1 small
Plain low-fat yogurt 6-oz. carton
Tea or coffee
Breakfast totals: 365 calories,
51 g carbo., 9 g fat, 23 g protein

Lunch:
Roast Beef Sandwiches with
  Horseradish Slaw
  (pg. 265)   1 serving
Fruit cocktail, canned   ½ cup
Tea, coffee, or water
Lunch totals: 363 calories,
45 g carbo., 10 g fat, 22 g protein

Supper:
Mixed green salad   1 cup
Reduced-fat salad dressing 2 Tbsp.
Toasted nuts (for salad)   2 Tbsp.
Creole-Style Shrimp & Grits
  (page 186)   1 serving
Honey-Apricot Frozen Yogurt
  (pg. 394)   1 serving
Vanilla Bean Biscotti
  (pg. 401)   1 cookie
Tea, coffee, or water
Supper totals: 540 calories,
61 g carbo., 21 g fat, 32 g protein

Evening snack:
Chunky Apple-Pumpkin Muffins
  (pg. 337)   1 muffin
Soft, non-hydrogenated
  margarine   2 tsp.
Low-fat milk   1 cup
Snack totals: 311calories,
35 g carbo., 14 g fat, 11 g protein

1,500-calorie day totals:
1,579 calories, 192 g carbo.,
52 g fat, 88 g protein

Afternoon snack:
Fruit Cups with Strawberry
  Dressing (pg. 355)   1 serving
Lunch Box Oatmeal Cookies
  (pg. 395)   1 cookie
Snack totals: 195 calories,
38 g carbo., 5 g fat, 4 g protein

1,800-calorie day totals:
1,774 calories, 230 g carbo.,
57 g fat, 92 g protein

Morning snack:
Soda crackers   6 crackers
Cheese   1 oz.
Dates   3
Snack totals: 240 calories,
30 g carbo., 9 g fat, 10 g protein

2,000-calorie day totals:
2,014 calories, 260 g carbo.,
65 g fat, 102 g protein

MENU #6

Breakfast:
Maple-Glazed Pears & Cereal
  (pg. 49)   1 serving
Whole wheat toast   1 slice
Peanut butter   1 Tbsp.
Low-fat milk   1 cup
Tea or coffee
Breakfast totals: 419 calories,
57 g carbo., 11 g fat, 21 g protein

Lunch:
Cheesy Ham Quesadillas
  (pg. 349)   1 serving
Kiwifruit   2
Chocolate Chip-Yogurt Drops
  (pg. 396)   1 cookie
Tea, coffee, or water
Lunch totals: 441 calories,
70 g carbo., 13 g fat, 14 g protein

Supper:
Herbed Pasta Primavera
  (pg. 229)   1 serving
Grated Parmesan cheese 2 Tbsp.
Summer Berries with Almond-Sour
  Cream Sauce (pg. 393) 1 serving
Tea, coffee, or water
Supper totals: 399 calories,
60 g carbo., 11 g fat, 20 g protein

Evening snack:
Fruit Bread
  (pg. 63)   1 serving
Soft, non-hydrogenated
  margarine   2 tsp.
Low-fat milk   1 cup
Snack totals: 308 calories,
36 g carbo., 14 g fat, 10 g protein

1,500-calorie day totals:
1,566 calories, 223 g carbo.,
48 g fat, 65 g protein

Afternoon snack:
Honey-Mustard Snack Mix
  (pg. 32)   1 cup
Low-fat milk   1 cup
Snack totals: 292 calories,
34 g carbo., 10 g fat, 14 g protein

1,800-calorie day totals:
1,858 calories, 257 g carbo.,
58 g fat, 79 g protein

Morning snack:
Sugar-free pudding made
  with low-fat milk   ½ cup
Mandarin oranges, canned   ¾ cup
Snack totals: 140 calories,
30 g carbo., 0 g fat, 4 g protein

2,000-calorie day totals:
1,998 calories, 287 g carbo.,
58 g fat, 83 g protein

MENU #7
(COMPANY MENU)

Breakfast:
Asparagus & Potato Skillet
  (pg. 55)   1 serving
Turkey-Apple Sausage Patties
  (pg. 68)   1 serving
Orange juice   ½ cup
Tea or coffee
Breakfast totals: 303 calories,
34 g carbo., 9 g fat, 23 g protein

Lunch:
Stir-Fried Beef & Apple Salad
  (pg. 249)   1 serving
Seven-Grain Bread (pg. 65) 1 slice
  or whole wheat pita   1 pita
Marinated Strawberries
  (pg. 392)   1 serving
Tea, coffee, or water

Lunch totals: 453 calories,
59 g carbo., 15 g fat, 23 g protein

Supper:
Grilled Salmon with
  Orange-Pineapple Salsa
  (pg. 176)   1 serving
Rice Pilaf with Toasted Pecans
  (pg. 362)   1 serving
Steamed fresh broccoli   ½ cup
Mocha Custards
  (pg. 381)   1 serving
Tea, coffee, or water
Supper totals: 546 calories,
60 g carbo., 17 g fat, 36 g protein

Evening snack:
Three-B Muffins (pg. 66) 1 muffin
Soft, non-hydrogenated
  margarine   2 tsp.
Cantaloupe   1 cup cubes
Snack totals: 287 calories,
38 g carbo., 14 g fat, 4 g protein

1,500-calorie day totals:
1,588 calories, 191 g carbo.,
55 g fat, 86 g protein

Afternoon snack:
Carrot Hummus
  (pg. 40)   4 Tbsp. (¼ cup)
Thin, crisp breadsticks   4
Celery sticks   1 cup
Snack totals: 205 calories,
36 g carbo., 4 g fat, 9 g protein

1,800-calorie day totals:
1,793 calories, 227 g carbo.,
59 g fat, 95 g protein

Morning snack:
Chocolate-Cherry Biscotti
  (pg. 400)   1 cookie
Fresh dark sweet cherries   12
Low-fat milk   ½ cup
Snack totals: 183 calories,
33 g carbo., 3 g fat, 6 g protein

2,000-calorie day totals:
1,976 calories, 260 g carbo.,
62 g fat, 101 g protein

APPETIZERS

1

THAI SPINACH DIP

PREP:
15 minutes
CHILL:
2 to 24 hours
MAKES:
*about
2½ cups dip*

4

carbs per
serving

Exchanges:
½ High-Fat Meat

1	cup chopped fresh spinach
1	8-ounce carton light dairy sour cream
1	cup plain low-fat yogurt
¼	cup snipped fresh mint
¼	cup finely chopped peanuts
¼	cup peanut butter
1	tablespoon honey
1	tablespoon reduced-sodium soy sauce
1	to 2 teaspoons crushed red pepper

Chopped peanuts (optional)

Fresh mint leaves (optional)

Assorted vegetable dippers
(such as peeled baby carrots, zucchini slices, pea pods, yellow
summer squash sticks, and/or red sweet pepper strips)

1 In a medium bowl combine spinach, sour cream, and yogurt. Stir in the snipped mint, the ¼ cup chopped peanuts, the peanut butter, honey, soy sauce, and crushed red pepper. Cover and chill for at least 2 hours or up to 24 hours. If desired, garnish with additional chopped peanuts and fresh mint leaves. Serve with vegetable dippers.

Nutrition Facts per 2 tablespoons dip: 56 cal., 4 g total fat (1 g sat. fat), 4 mg chol., 61 mg sodium, 4 g carbo., 0 g fiber, 3 g pro.

LAYERED SOUTHWESTERN APPETIZER PLATTER

2   cups shredded lettuce

1   15-ounce can black beans, rinsed and drained

½   cup chopped green sweet pepper

2   tablespoons bottled chopped red jalapeño chile peppers
    or canned diced green chile peppers

1   8-ounce carton fat-free dairy sour cream

1   8-ounce jar chunky salsa

½   cup shredded reduced-fat cheddar cheese (2 ounces)

2   tablespoons chopped pitted ripe olives (optional)

1   recipe Homemade Tortilla Chips

1 Line a 12-inch platter with shredded lettuce. In a medium bowl stir together black beans, sweet pepper, and chile peppers. Spoon bean mixture over lettuce, leaving a border of lettuce. Spoon sour cream over bean mixture; gently spread into a smooth layer, leaving a border of bean mixture.

2 Drain excess liquid from salsa. Spoon salsa over the sour cream layer, leaving a border of sour cream. Sprinkle cheese over salsa. If desired, top with olives. If desired, cover and chill for up to 6 hours. Serve with Homemade Tortilla Chips.

HOMEMADE TORTILLA CHIPS: Cut each of eight 7- to 8-inch flour tortillas into 6 wedges. Arrange wedges in a single layer on ungreased baking sheets. Bake in a 350° oven for 5 to 8 minutes or until dry and crisp, rotating baking sheets once. Makes 48 chips.

Nutrition Facts per serving: 92 cal., 2 g total fat (1 g sat. fat), 3 mg chol., 229 mg sodium, 15 g carbo., 2 g fiber, 5 g pro.

PREP:
30 minutes
BAKE:
5 minutes (chips)
OVEN:
350°F
MAKES:
16 servings

15
carbs per serving

Exchanges:
1 Starch
½ Very Lean Meat

BLACK BEAN SALSA

PREP:
25 minutes
CHILL:
4 to 24 hours
MAKES:
about
3¹/₂ cups salsa

1	15-ounce can black beans, rinsed and drained
1	medium cucumber, peeled, seeded, and chopped
1	medium tomato, seeded and chopped
¹/₂	cup sliced green onions
¹/₄	cup lime juice
1	tablespoon snipped fresh cilantro
1	tablespoon olive oil
¹/₂	teaspoon ground cumin
¹/₈	teaspoon salt
¹/₈	teaspoon cayenne pepper
	Baked tortilla chips

6
carbs per serving

❶ In a medium bowl combine black beans, cucumber, tomato, green onions, lime juice, cilantro, oil, cumin, salt, and cayenne pepper. Cover; chill for at least 4 hours or up to 24 hours. Use a slotted spoon to serve. Serve with baked tortilla chips.

Nutrition Facts per ¹/₄ cup salsa: 35 cal., 1 g total fat (0 g sat. fat), 0 mg chol., 98 mg sodium, 6 g carbo., 2 g fiber, 2 g pro.

Exchanges:
¹/₂ Starch

TOMATO & BASIL CHÈVRE SPREAD

⅓ cup dried tomatoes (not oil-packed)
   Boiling water

4 ounces soft goat cheese (chèvre)

½ of an 8-ounce package reduced-fat cream cheese (Neufchâtel), softened

¼ cup snipped fresh basil or 2 teaspoons dried basil, crushed

3 cloves garlic, minced

⅛ teaspoon black pepper

2 to 3 tablespoons fat-free milk
   Miniature toasts and/or assorted reduced-fat crackers

1 In a small bowl cover dried tomatoes with boiling water; let stand for 10 minutes. Drain tomatoes, discarding liquid. Finely snip tomatoes.

2 In a medium bowl stir together snipped tomatoes, goat cheese, cream cheese, basil, garlic, and pepper. Stir in enough of the milk to reach spreading consistency. Cover and chill for at least 2 hours or up to 8 hours. Serve with miniature toasts and/or crackers.

Nutrition Facts per 2 tablespoons spread: 67 cal., 5 g total fat (3 g sat. fat), 14 mg chol., 126 mg sodium, 2 g carbo., 0 g fiber, 4 g pro.

PREP:
15 minutes
STAND:
10 minutes
CHILL:
2 to 8 hours
MAKES:
1¼ cups spread

2
carbs per serving

Exchanges:
½ Medium-Fat Meat
½ Fat

CRANBERRY-CHUTNEY BITES

PREP:
20 minutes
STAND:
10 minutes
CHILL:
2 to 24 hours
MAKES:
20 appetizers

9
carbs per appetizer

Exchanges:
½ Other Carbo.

½ cup dried cranberries
  Boiling water
¾ cup purchased mango chutney
1½ teaspoons grated fresh ginger
½ of an 8-ounce package reduced-fat cream cheese (Neufchâtel), softened
20 water crackers
¼ cup chopped walnuts, toasted (optional)

1 In a small bowl cover dried cranberries with boiling water; let stand for 10 minutes. Drain.

2 Snip any large pieces of mango chutney. In a small bowl stir together chutney, drained cranberries, and ginger. Cover and chill for at least 2 hours or up to 24 hours.

3 For each appetizer, spread about 1 teaspoon of the cream cheese on a water cracker. Top with about 2 teaspoons of the chutney mixture. If desired, sprinkle with walnuts. Serve immediately.

Nutrition Facts per appetizer: 54 cal., 2 g total fat (1 g sat. fat), 4 mg chol., 68 mg sodium, 9 g carbo., 1 g fiber, 1 g pro.

HERBED CHEESE MINI PEPPERS

10   red, yellow, and/or orange miniature sweet peppers
(6 to 8 ounces total)

1   8-ounce package reduced-fat cream cheese (Neufchâtel), softened

1   to 2 tablespoons snipped fresh oregano, rosemary, tarragon,
or thyme or ½ to 1 teaspoon dried oregano, rosemary, tarragon,
or thyme, crushed

    Finely shredded lemon peel (set aside)

1   tablespoon lemon juice

1   tablespoon fat-free milk

    Fresh oregano leaves (optional)

1 Halve each sweet pepper lengthwise. Remove the seeds; set peppers aside.

2 In a small bowl stir together cream cheese, the snipped or dried herb, lemon juice, and milk. Stir in additional milk, if needed, to reach piping consistency.

3 Pipe or spoon cream cheese mixture into pepper halves. Sprinkle cream cheese mixture with lemon pee. Cover and chill for up to 4 hours. If desired, garnish with oregano leaves.

Nutrition Facts per appetizer: 32 cal., 3 g total fat (2 g sat. fat), 9 mg chol., 46 mg sodium, 1 g carbo., 0 g fiber, 1 g pro.

START TO FINISH:
25 minutes
MAKES:
20 appetizers

1

carb per appetizer

Exchanges:
½ Fat

GREEK-STYLE STUFFED MUSHROOMS

PREP:
25 minutes
BAKE:
*5 minutes +
8 minutes*
OVEN:
425°F
MAKES:
20 appetizers

2

carbs per
appetizer

Exchanges:
Free

20	large fresh mushrooms, 1½ to 2 inches in diameter (about 1½ pounds)
	Nonstick cooking spray
1	cup finely chopped broccoli
1	medium onion, chopped
2	cloves garlic, minced
2	teaspoons snipped fresh oregano or ½ teaspoon dried oregano, crushed
⅛	teaspoon salt
⅛	teaspoon black pepper
3	tablespoons crumbled feta cheese
2	tablespoons fine dry bread crumbs

❶ Clean mushrooms. Remove stems from mushrooms. Set stems aside. Lightly coat the rounded side of each mushroom cap with nonstick cooking spray. Place mushroom caps, stem sides down, in a 15×10×1-inch baking pan. Bake in a 425° oven for 5 minutes. Carefully place mushroom caps, stem sides down, on a double thickness of paper towels to drain while preparing filling.

❷ Meanwhile, for filling, chop enough of the mushroom stems to make 1 cup. Coat an unheated large nonstick skillet with nonstick cooking spray. Preheat over medium heat. Add the 1 cup chopped mushroom stems, the broccoli, onion, garlic, dried oregano (if using), salt, and pepper to hot skillet. Cook and stir for 5 to 10 minutes or just until tender and most of the liquid is evaporated. Stir in 2 tablespoons of the feta cheese, the bread crumbs, and fresh oregano (if using).

❸ Place mushroom caps, stem sides up, in the same baking pan. Spoon the broccoli mixture into mushroom caps. Bake in the 425° oven for 8 to 10 minutes more or until heated through. Sprinkle with the remaining 1 tablespoon feta cheese.

Nutrition Facts per appetizer: 19 cal., 1 g total fat (0 g sat. fat), 1 mg chol., 51 mg sodium, 2 g carbo., 0 g fiber, 2 g pro.

DEVILED EGGS WITH CURRIED CRAB

8   hard-cooked eggs

¼   cup light mayonnaise dressing or salad dressing

1   tablespoon finely chopped green onion

1   to 2 teaspoons flavored mustard
(such as Dijon-style mustard or horseradish mustard)

¼   teaspoon salt

¼   teaspoon cayenne pepper

1   to 2 tablespoons purchased mango chutney

3   tablespoons light mayonnaise dressing or salad dressing

½   teaspoon curry powder

½   cup cooked crabmeat (about 2¾ ounces)

     Desired garnishes
(such as paprika, finely chopped sweet pepper, snipped fresh chives, sliced or chopped toasted almonds, and/or cracked black pepper) (optional)

1 Halve the hard-cooked eggs lengthwise and remove yolks. Set whites aside. In a quart-size resealable plastic bag combine egg yolks, the ¼ cup mayonnaise dressing, the green onion, mustard, ⅛ teaspoon of the salt, and ⅛ teaspoon of the cayenne pepper. Seal bag. Gently squeeze the bag to mix ingredients until smooth. Snip off one corner of the bag; pipe egg yolk mixture into egg white halves. (Or in a small bowl combine egg yolks, the ¼ cup mayonnaise dressing, the green onion, mustard, ⅛ teaspoon of the salt, and ⅛ teaspoon of the cayenne pepper; mash and stir with a fork until well mixed. Spoon into a decorating bag fitted with a star tip; pipe into egg white halves.)

2 Cut up any large pieces of chutney. In a small bowl combine chutney, the 3 tablespoons mayonnaise dressing, curry powder, remaining ⅛ teaspoon salt, and remaining ⅛ teaspoon cayenne pepper. Gently fold in crabmeat. Top each deviled egg with a spoonful of the crab mixture. Cover and chill for at least 1 hour or up to 2 hours. If desired, garnish with desired garnishes.

TO MAKE AHEAD: The egg yolk mixture may be made a day ahead and stored, covered, in the refrigerator. Wrap and chill egg white halves separately.

Nutrition Facts per appetizer: 70 cal., 5 g total fat (1 g sat. fat), 113 mg chol., 142 mg sodium, 2 g carbo., 0 g fiber, 4 g pro.

PREP:
20 minutes
CHILL:
1 to 2 hours
MAKES:
16 appetizers

2
carbs per appetizer

Exchanges:
½ Medium-Fat Meat
½ Fat

SWEET PEAR & CHEESE CROSTINI

START TO FINISH:
15 minutes
MAKES:
16 appetizers

16 ⅜-inch-thick slices baguette-style French bread

4 ounces Gorgonzola cheese or other blue cheese, crumbled

1 small ripe pear, halved, cored, and very thinly sliced

2 tablespoons flavored honey (such as French lavender honey) or regular honey

   Fresh mint sprigs (optional)

1 Place bread slices on a large baking sheet. Broil 4 to 5 inches from the heat for 30 to 60 seconds or until bread is lightly toasted. Turn bread slices over; top with Gorgonzola cheese. Broil for 30 to 60 seconds more or until cheese is bubbly and bread is toasted.

2 Top bread slices with pear slices. Lightly drizzle pear slices with honey. If desired, garnish with mint sprigs. Arrange bread slices on a serving platter. Serve immediately.

Nutrition Facts per appetizer: 72 cal., 2 g total fat (1 g sat. fat), 5 mg chol., 175 mg sodium, 10 g carbo., 1 g fiber, 3 g pro.

10 carbs per appetizer

Exchanges:
1 Starch

MINI SPINACH CALZONES

Nonstick cooking spray

½ of a 10-ounce package frozen chopped spinach, thawed and well drained

½ of an 8-ounce package reduced-fat cream cheese (Neufchâtel), softened

3 tablespoons grated Parmesan cheese

2 tablespoons chopped green onion

¼ teaspoon black pepper

1 13.8-ounce package refrigerated pizza dough (for 1 crust)

1 egg white

1 tablespoon water

PREP:
30 minutes
BAKE:
8 minutes per batch
OVEN:
400°F
MAKES:
25 appetizers

1 Line 2 baking sheets with foil; lightly coat the foil with nonstick cooking spray. Set baking sheets aside. For filling, in a medium bowl stir together spinach, cream cheese, 2 tablespoons of the Parmesan cheese, the green onion, and pepper. Set aside.

2 Unroll pizza dough on a lightly floured surface; roll dough into a 15-inch square. Using a pizza cutter or sharp knife, cut into twenty-five 3-inch squares. Spoon a slightly rounded teaspoon of the filling onto the center of each square. In a small bowl use a fork to beat together egg white and the water. Brush edges of dough squares with egg white mixture. Lift a corner of each square and stretch dough over filling to opposite corner, making a triangle. Press edges with the tines of a fork to seal.

3 Arrange the calzones on prepared baking sheets. Prick tops of calzones with fork. Brush tops of calzones with egg white mixture. Sprinkle with the remaining 1 tablespoon Parmesan cheese. Bake one sheet at a time in a 400° oven for 8 to 10 minutes or until calzones are golden brown. Cool slightly on baking sheets. Serve warm.

TO MAKE AHEAD: Prepare spinach filling as directed in step 1. Cover and chill for up to 24 hours. Before using, let filling stand at room temperature for 30 minutes to soften, if necessary. Continue as directed in steps 2 and 3.

Nutrition Facts per appetizer: 56 cal., 2 g total fat (1 g sat. fat), 4 mg chol., 125 mg sodium, 8 g carbo., 0 g fiber, 2 g pro.

8

carbs per appetizer

Exchanges:
½ Starch
½ Fat

WHITE BEAN & TOMATO BRUSCHETTA

2 tablespoons oil-packed dried tomatoes

½ cup snipped watercress or fresh flat-leaf parsley

2 tablespoons pine nuts, toasted

1 cup canned white kidney beans (cannellini beans), rinsed and drained

1 tablespoon fat-free milk

2 to 3 teaspoons lemon juice

1 teaspoon snipped fresh thyme or ¼ teaspoon dried thyme, crushed

¼ teaspoon salt

¼ teaspoon black pepper

2 cloves garlic, cut up

12 ½-inch-thick slices baguette-style French bread

Watercress sprigs (optional)

11
carbs per
appetizer

Exchanges:
1 Starch

❶ Drain tomatoes, reserving oil; finely snip tomatoes. In a small bowl combine snipped tomatoes, 1 teaspoon of the reserved oil, the ½ cup watercress or parsley, and the pine nuts; set tomato mixture aside.

❷ In a food processor or blender combine another 1 teaspoon of the reserved oil, the beans, milk, lemon juice, thyme, salt, pepper, and garlic. Cover and process or blend until smooth. Set bean mixture aside.

❸ Place bread slices on a baking sheet. Broil 4 inches from the heat for 1½ to 2 minutes or until bread is lightly toasted, turning once. Remove from oven; cool slightly.

❹ Place about 1 tablespoon of the bean mixture on each of the toasted bread slices, spreading evenly to edges. Broil 4 inches from heat about 1 minute or until bean mixture is warm. Remove from oven. Top each with some of the tomato mixture. If desired, garnish with watercress sprigs. Serve immediately.

TO MAKE AHEAD: Prepare as directed through step 3. Cover and chill tomato and bean mixtures separately for up to 24 hours. Place toasted bread slices in an airtight container; store at room temperature for up to 24 hours. Continue as directed in step 4.

Nutrition Facts per appetizer: 75 cal., 2 g total fat (0 g sat. fat), 0 mg chol., 184 mg sodium, 11 g carbo., 1 g fiber, 3 g pro.

HERBED SEAFOOD BRUSCHETTA

24 ¼-inch-thick slices baguette-style French bread

2 teaspoons snipped fresh chives

2 teaspoons snipped fresh basil or ½ teaspoon dried basil, crushed

2 teaspoons lemon juice

1 teaspoon snipped fresh mint

1 teaspoon olive oil

1 clove garlic, minced

¼ teaspoon salt

¾ cup chopped, seeded plum tomatoes

3 ounces frozen crabmeat, thawed and drained, or ½ of a 6-ounce can crabmeat, drained, flaked, and cartilage removed (½ cup)

4 ounces peeled, cooked shrimp, coarsely chopped (½ cup)

¼ cup finely chopped onion

¼ teaspoon black pepper

1 Arrange bread slices on a baking sheet. Broil 3 to 4 inches from heat for 1 to 2 minutes or until toasted, turning once. Cool on wire racks.

2 In a medium bowl stir together chives, basil, lemon juice, mint, oil, garlic, and salt. Add tomatoes, crabmeat, shrimp, and onion; toss to coat.

3 Arrange toasted bread on a serving platter; spoon seafood mixture on each slice. Sprinkle with pepper. Serve immediately.

TO MAKE AHEAD: Prepare seafood mixture as directed in step 2. Cover and chill seafood mixture for up to 24 hours. Stir seafood mixture. Broil bread slices as directed in step 1; continue as directed in step 3.

Nutrition Facts per appetizer: 25 cal., 0 g total fat (0 g sat. fat), 13 mg chol., 74 mg sodium, 3 g carbo., 0 g fiber, 2 g pro.

START TO FINISH:
25 minutes
MAKES:
24 appetizers

3
carbs per appetizer

Exchanges:
½ Other Carbo.

GINGER SHRIMP SKEWERS

PREP:
30 minutes
MARINATE:
1 to 2 hours
MAKES:
8 appetizers

2
carbs per
appetizer

Exchanges:
1 Very Lean Meat

16	fresh or frozen large shrimp in shells (about 12 ounces)
1	teaspoon finely shredded orange peel
3	tablespoons orange juice
1	tablespoon white wine vinegar
1	teaspoon toasted sesame oil or olive oil
1	teaspoon grated fresh ginger or ½ teaspoon ground ginger
⅛	teaspoon salt
⅛	teaspoon cayenne pepper
1	clove garlic, minced
16	fresh pea pods
8	canned mandarin orange sections
	Reduced-sodium soy sauce (optional)

1 Thaw shrimp, if frozen. Peel and devein shrimp, leaving tails intact (if desired). In a large saucepan cook shrimp in a large amount of boiling water for 1 to 3 minutes or until shrimp are opaque. Drain. Rinse shrimp with cold water; drain.

2 Place shrimp in a resealable plastic bag set in a shallow bowl. For marinade, in a small bowl combine orange peel, orange juice, vinegar, oil, ginger, salt, cayenne pepper, and garlic. Pour over shrimp. Seal bag; turn to coat shrimp. Marinate in the refrigerator for at least 1 hour or up to 2 hours.

3 Place pea pods in a steamer basket over boiling water. Cover and steam for 2 to 3 minutes or just until tender. Rinse with cold water; drain.

4 Drain shrimp, discarding marinade. Wrap each shrimp with a pea pod. On each of eight 6-inch skewers, thread 2 wrapped shrimp and 1 mandarin orange section. If desired, serve with soy sauce.

Nutrition Facts per appetizer: 44 cal., 1 g total fat (0 g sat. fat), 48 mg chol., 58 mg sodium, 2 g carbo., 0 g fiber, 7 g pro.

SNACKS

VEGETABLE PITA PIZZAS

PREP:
10 minutes
BAKE:
5 minutes +
8 minutes
OVEN:
400°F
MAKES:
4 servings

20
carbs per
serving

Exchanges:
½ Vegetable
1 Starch
½ Fat

2   large whole wheat pita bread rounds
    Nonstick cooking spray

½   cup assorted fresh vegetables
    (such as small broccoli or cauliflower florets, red sweet pepper strips,
    sliced fresh mushrooms, and/or chopped carrot)

¼   cup pizza sauce

¼   cup shredded mozzarella cheese (1 ounce)

❶ Place pita bread rounds on a baking sheet. Bake in a 400° oven for
5 minutes.

❷ Meanwhile, coat an unheated small nonstick skillet with nonstick
cooking spray. Preheat over medium heat. Add the assorted vegetables;
cook and stir until crisp-tender.

❸ Spread pizza sauce on pita bread rounds; sprinkle with cooked vegetables
and cheese. Bake for 8 to 10 minutes more or until light brown. Cut in half and
serve warm.

Nutrition Facts per serving: 113 cal., 2 g total fat (1 g sat. fat), 4 mg chol., 291 mg sodium, 20 g carbo.,
3 g fiber, 5 g pro.

POTATO SKINS

6   large baking potatoes (such as russet or long white)

2   teaspoons cooking oil

1   to 1½ teaspoons chili powder

⅛   teaspoon salt

     Several drops bottled hot pepper sauce

⅔   cup chopped Canadian-style bacon or low-fat cooked boneless ham

⅔   cup finely chopped, seeded tomato (1 medium)

2   tablespoons finely chopped green onion

¾   cup shredded reduced-fat cheddar cheese (3 ounces)

½   cup light dairy sour cream (optional)

1 Scrub potatoes and prick with a fork. Bake in a 425° oven for 40 to 45 minutes or until tender; cool.

2 Cut each potato lengthwise into 4 wedges. Scoop out the inside of each potato wedge. Cover and chill the leftover potato pulp for another use.

3 In a small bowl combine oil, chili powder, salt, and hot pepper sauce. Using a pastry brush, brush the insides of the potato wedges with the oil mixture. Place the potato wedges in a single layer on a large baking sheet. Sprinkle wedges with Canadian bacon, tomato, and green onion; top with cheese.

4 Bake about 10 minutes or until cheese melts and potatoes are heated through. If desired, serve with sour cream.

TO MAKE AHEAD: Prepare as directed through step 3. Cover and chill assembled potato wedges for up to 24 hours. Continue as directed in step 4.

Nutrition Facts per wedge: 48 cal., 1 g total fat (1 g sat. fat), 5 mg chol., 97 mg sodium, 7 g carbo., 1 g fiber, 2 g pro.

PREP:
30 minutes
BAKE:
40 minutes +
10 minutes
OVEN:
425°F
MAKES:
24 wedges

7

carbs per wedge

Exchanges:
½ Starch

GRANOLA BARS

PREP:
20 minutes
BAKE:
25 minutes
OVEN:
325°F
MAKES:
24 bars

1	cup low-fat granola
1	cup rolled oats
½	cup mixed nuts
½	cup all-purpose flour
½	cup raisins
1	beaten egg or ¼ cup refrigerated or frozen egg product, thawed
3	tablespoons packed brown sugar
3	tablespoons cooking oil
3	tablespoons honey
½	teaspoon ground cinnamon

15
carbs per
bar

❶ Line an 8×8×2-inch baking pan with foil. Grease the foil; set pan aside. In a large bowl combine granola, rolled oats, nuts, flour, and raisins. In a small bowl stir together egg, brown sugar, oil, honey, and cinnamon. Add to granola mixture, stirring until well coated. Press evenly into the prepared pan.

❷ Bake in a 325° oven for 25 to 30 minutes or until lightly browned around the edges. Cool in pan on a wire rack. Use foil to remove from pan. Cut into bars.

Nutrition Facts per bar: 99 cal., 4 g total fat (1 g sat. fat), 9 mg chol., 14 mg sodium, 15 g carbo., 1 g fiber, 2 g pro.

Exchanges:
1 Other Carbo.
½ Fat

SPICED POPCORN

½ teaspoon ground cumin
½ teaspoon chili powder
¼ to ½ teaspoon salt
    Dash cayenne pepper
    Dash ground cinnamon
12 cups air-popped popcorn
    Nonstick cooking spray

START TO FINISH:
10 minutes
MAKES:
12 cups

1 In a small bowl stir together cumin, chili powder, salt, cayenne pepper, and cinnamon.

2 Spread popped popcorn evenly in a large shallow baking pan. Lightly coat popcorn with nonstick cooking spray. Sprinkle the cumin mixture evenly over popcorn; toss to coat.

Nutrition Facts per 1-cup serving: 31 cal., 0 g total fat (0 g sat. fat), 0 mg chol., 50 mg sodium, 6 g carbo., 1 g fiber, 1 g pro.

INDIAN SPICED POPCORN: Prepare as directed, except omit cumin, chili powder, cayenne pepper, and cinnamon and instead use ½ teaspoon curry powder, ½ teaspoon garam masala, ¼ teaspoon ground turmeric, and ¼ teaspoon black pepper.

Nutrition Facts per 1-cup serving: 31 cal., 0 g total fat (0 g sat. fat), 0 mg chol., 49 mg sodium, 6 g carbo., 1 g fiber, 1 g pro.

6
carbs per serving

Exchanges:
½ Starch

MAPLE-MUSTARD CRUNCH

PREP:
10 minutes
BAKE:
45 minutes
OVEN:
300°F
MAKES:
5 cups

Nonstick cooking spray

3 cups bite-size rice square cereal

2 cups bite-size shredded wheat biscuits

¾ cup shelled pumpkin seeds

¼ cup maple-flavored syrup

2 tablespoons Dijon-style mustard

½ teaspoon garlic powder

15
carbs per
serving

1 Lightly coat a 13×9×2-inch baking pan with nonstick cooking spray. In prepared pan combine rice square cereal, shredded wheat biscuits, and pumpkin seeds; set aside. In a small bowl stir together syrup, mustard, and garlic powder. Drizzle over cereal mixture; toss to coat.

2 Bake in a 300° oven for 45 minutes, gently stirring 3 times. Spread baked mixture on foil; cool completely.

TO MAKE AHEAD: Prepare as directed. Store in an airtight container at room temperature for up to 2 weeks.

Nutrition Facts per ⅓-cup serving: 118 cal., 5 g total fat (1 g sat. fat), 0 mg chol., 163 mg sodium, 15 g carbo., 1 g fiber, 5 g pro.

Exchanges:
1 Starch
1 Fat

FRUIT & NUT SNACK MIX

10	cups air-popped popcorn
	Nonstick cooking spray
1	tablespoon taco seasoning mix
1	cup peanuts
1	cup golden raisins
½	cup shelled pumpkin seeds, toasted

1 Remove uncooked kernels from popped corn. Place popped corn in a very large bowl; lightly coat popcorn with nonstick cooking spray. Sprinkle popcorn with taco seasoning mix; stir lightly to coat. Stir in peanuts, raisins, and pumpkin seeds.

Nutrition Facts per ¾-cup serving: 128 cal., 7 g total fat (1 g sat. fat), 0 mg chol., 93 mg sodium, 15 g carbo., 2 g fiber, 4 g pro.

START TO FINISH:
15 minutes
MAKES:
12 cups

15
carbs per serving

Exchanges:
½ Fruit
½ Starch
1 Fat

HONEY-MUSTARD SNACK MIX

PREP:
10 minutes
BAKE:
20 minutes
OVEN:
300°F
MAKES:
7 cups

2	cups crispy corn and rice cereal
1½	cups bite-size shredded wheat biscuits
¾	cup peanuts
3	tablespoons honey mustard
2	tablespoons butter or margarine, melted
1	teaspoon Worcestershire sauce
¼	teaspoon garlic powder
⅛	teaspoon cayenne pepper
3	cups air-popped popcorn

11
carbs per serving

1 Line a 13×9×2-inch baking pan with foil. In prepared pan combine cereal, shredded wheat biscuits, and peanuts; set aside. In a small bowl combine honey mustard, butter, Worcestershire sauce, garlic powder, and cayenne pepper. Drizzle over cereal and nut mixture in pan, tossing gently to coat.

2 Bake in a 300° oven for 20 minutes, gently stirring after 10 minutes. Stir in popcorn. Use foil to remove baked mixture from pan; cool completely.

Nutrition Facts per ½-cup serving: 101 cal., 6 g total fat (1 g sat. fat), 5 mg chol., 114 mg sodium, 11 g carbo., 1 g fiber, 3 g pro.

Exchanges:
½ Starch
1½ Fat

PEANUT-PACKED MUNCH MIX

5 cups bite-size shredded wheat biscuits

¾ cup unsalted peanuts

¼ cup creamy peanut butter

2 tablespoons butter or margarine

1 tablespoon honey

½ cup mixed dried fruit bits or raisins

1 In a 13×9×2-inch baking pan combine shredded wheat biscuits and peanuts. Set aside.

2 In a small saucepan cook and stir peanut butter, butter, and honey over low heat until peanut butter and butter are melted. Drizzle over cereal mixture, tossing to coat.

3 Bake in a 350° oven for 10 minutes, stirring twice. Cool in pan on a wire rack about 10 minutes. Stir in mixed dried fruit bits. Cool completely.

TO MAKE AHEAD: Prepare as directed. Place in a tightly covered container. Store at room temperature for up to 1 week.

Nutrition Facts per about ½-cup serving: 153 cal., 9 g total fat (2 g sat. fat), 5 mg chol., 42 mg sodium, 17 g carbo., 2 g fiber, 5 g pro.

PREP:
10 minutes
BAKE:
10 minutes
COOL:
10 minutes
OVEN:
350°F
MAKES:
about 6½ cups

17
carbs per
serving

Exchanges:
½ Starch
½ High-Fat Meat
½ Other Carbo.
1 Fat

ROSEMARY ROASTED NUTS

PREP:
10 minutes
BAKE:
15 minutes
OVEN:
350°F
MAKES:
about 3 cups

4
carbs per
serving

Exchanges:
4 Fat

Nonstick cooking spray

1 egg white

2 teaspoons snipped fresh rosemary or 1 teaspoon dried rosemary, crushed

½ teaspoon salt

½ teaspoon coarsely ground black pepper

3 cups walnut pieces, hazelnuts (filberts), and/or whole almonds

1 Line a 13×9×2-inch baking pan with foil; lightly coat foil with nonstick cooking spray. Set aside. In a medium bowl beat egg white with a fork until frothy. Add rosemary, salt, and pepper, beating with the fork until combined. Add nuts; toss to coat.

2 Spread nut mixture evenly in prepared pan. Bake in a 350° oven for 15 to 20 minutes or until golden brown, stirring once.

3 Use foil to remove nuts from pan; cool completely. Break up any large pieces.

TO MAKE AHEAD: Prepare as directed. Place nuts in an airtight container. Freeze for up to 1 month.

Nutrition Facts per ¼-cup serving: 198 cal., 20 g total fat (2 g sat. fat), 0 mg chol., 102 mg sodium, 4 g carbo., 2 g fiber, 4 g pro.

SAVORY NUTS

2 cups macadamia nuts, broken walnuts, and/or unblanched almonds

2 tablespoons Worcestershire sauce for chicken

1 tablespoon olive oil

½ teaspoon dried thyme, crushed

¼ teaspoon salt

¼ teaspoon dried rosemary, crushed

⅛ teaspoon cayenne pepper

1 Spread nuts in a 13×9×2-inch baking pan. In a small bowl combine Worcestershire sauce, olive oil, thyme, salt, rosemary, and cayenne pepper; drizzle over nuts. Toss to coat.

2 Bake in a 350° oven for 12 to 15 minutes or until nuts are toasted, stirring occasionally. Spread on foil; cool completely.

TO MAKE AHEAD: Prepare as directed. Place nuts in an airtight container. Store at room temperature for up to 2 weeks.

Nutrition Facts per ¼-cup serving: 259 cal., 27 g total fat (4 g sat. fat), 0 mg chol., 106 mg sodium, 5 g carbo., 3 g fiber, 3 g pro.

PREP:
10 minutes
BAKE:
12 minutes
OVEN:
350°F
MAKES:
2 cups

5
carbs per serving

Exchanges:
½ High-Fat Meat
4½ Fat

HERBED SOY NUTS & SEEDS

PREP:
10 minutes
BAKE:
15 minutes
OVEN:
350°F
MAKES:
1 cup

2	teaspoons olive oil or cooking oil
½	teaspoon chili powder
½	teaspoon dried basil, crushed
¼	teaspoon dried oregano, crushed
⅛	teaspoon garlic powder
⅔	cup salted roasted soy nuts*
¼	cup shelled pumpkin seeds
¼	cup dried vegetables (such as carrots, corn, and/or peas)

13
carbs per
serving

1 In a small bowl stir together oil, chili powder, basil, oregano, and garlic powder. Add soy nuts and pumpkin seeds; toss to coat. Spread in a shallow baking pan.

2 Bake in a 350° oven for 15 to 20 minutes or until soy nuts are toasted, stirring after 10 minutes. Stir in dried vegetables.

*NOTE: If using unsalted roasted soy nuts, add a little salt to the chili powder mixture.

Nutrition Facts per ¼-cup serving: 195 cal., 12 g total fat (2 g sat. fat), 0 mg chol., 79 mg sodium, 13 g carbo., 3 g fiber, 11 g pro.

Exchanges:
1 Starch
1 High-Fat Meat
½ Fat

TEX-MEX PEA MEDLEY

1	cup sliced green onions or finely chopped onion
¾	cup finely chopped red or green sweet pepper
1	4-ounce can diced green chile peppers, drained
½	cup purchased salsa
½	cup bottled reduced-calorie Italian salad dressing
2	cloves garlic, minced
⅛	teaspoon black pepper
	Few dashes bottled hot pepper sauce
1	15-ounce can black-eyed peas, rinsed and drained*
	Assorted vegetable dippers or baked tortilla chips

1 In a large bowl combine green onions or onion, sweet pepper, chile peppers, salsa, Italian salad dressing, garlic, black pepper, and hot pepper sauce.

2 Add black-eyed peas, stirring gently to combine. Cover and chill for at least 3 hours or up to 24 hours. Serve with assorted vegetable dippers or baked tortilla chips.

***NOTE:** You can substitute ½ of a 16-ounce package frozen black-eyed peas (about 1⅔ cups) for the canned black-eyed peas. Cook the peas according to package directions. Drain and rinse in colander.

Nutrition Facts per ¼ cup vegetable mixture: 34 cal., 0 g total fat (0 g sat. fat), 1 mg chol., 223 mg sodium, 6 g carbo., 1 g fiber, 2 g pro.

PREP:
15 minutes
CHILL:
3 to 24 hours
MAKES:
about 3½ cups vegetable mixture

6
carbs per serving

Exchanges:
½ Other Carbo.

ROASTED RED PEPPER DIP

PREP:
10 minutes
CHILL:
4 to 24 hours
MAKES:
1¼ cups dip

1	8-ounce carton fat-free or light dairy sour cream
¼	cup chopped roasted red sweet peppers (about ¼ of a 7-ounce jar)
2	tablespoons sliced green onion
1	tablespoon snipped fresh basil or ½ teaspoon dried basil, crushed
1	clove garlic, minced
¼	teaspoon salt
	Assorted vegetable dippers or baked tortilla chips

4

carbs per serving

1 In a small bowl stir together sour cream, roasted red peppers, green onion, basil, garlic, and salt. Cover and chill for at least 4 hours or up to 24 hours to allow flavors to blend.

2 Stir before serving. Serve with assorted vegetable dippers or baked tortilla chips.

Nutrition Facts per 2 tablespoons dip: 23 cal., 0 g total fat (0 g sat. fat), 0 mg chol., 73 mg sodium, 4 g carbo., 0 g fiber, 1 g pro.

Exchanges:
Free

HERBED FETA CHEESE SPREAD

2 ounces feta cheese, crumbled

2 ounces reduced-fat cream cheese (Neufchâtel), softened

2 tablespoons fat-free milk

1 clove garlic, minced

¼ teaspoon dried Italian seasoning, crushed

Assorted fresh vegetables
(such as green sweet pepper pieces, carrot strips, pea pods,
zucchini slices, and/or yellow summer squash slices)

1 In a small bowl combine feta cheese, cream cheese, milk, garlic, and Italian seasoning. Stir until nearly smooth (mixture will thicken as it is stirred).

2 Cover and chill for at least 2 hours or up to 24 hours. Serve with assorted fresh vegetables.

Nutrition Facts per 2 tablespoons spread: 77 cal., 6 g total fat (4 g sat. fat), 23 mg chol., 216 mg sodium, 2 g carbo., 0 g fiber, 4 g pro.

PREP:
15 minutes
CHILL:
2 to 24 hours
MAKES:
½ cup spread

2
carbs per serving

Exchanges:
½ Medium-Fat Meat
1 Fat

CARROT HUMMUS

PREP:
15 minutes
CHILL:
1 hour
MAKES:
2 cups dip

1   cup chopped carrots
1   15-ounce can garbanzo beans (chickpeas), rinsed and drained
¼   cup tahini (sesame seed paste)
2   tablespoons lemon juice
2   cloves garlic, quartered
½   teaspoon ground cumin
¼   teaspoon salt
2   tablespoons snipped fresh parsley
    Assorted dippers
    (such as toasted whole wheat pita bread triangles, vegetable sticks, and/or whole-grain crackers)

8
carbs per
serving

Exchanges:
½ Starch
½ Fat

1 In a covered small saucepan cook carrots in a small amount of boiling water for 6 to 8 minutes or until tender; drain. In a food processor combine cooked carrots, garbanzo beans, tahini, lemon juice, garlic, cumin, and salt. Cover and process until mixture is smooth. Transfer to a small serving bowl. Stir in parsley.

2 Cover and chill for at least 1 hour. If too thick, stir in enough water, 1 tablespoon at a time, to reach dipping consistency. Serve with dippers.

TO MAKE AHEAD: Prepare spread as directed in step 1. Cover and chill for up to 3 days. Continue as directed in step 2.

Nutrition Facts per 2 tablespoons dip: 60 cal., 2 g total fat (0 g sat. fat), 0 mg chol., 124 mg sodium, 8 g carbo., 2 g fiber, 2 g pro.

SPICY BROCCOLI SPREAD

2 cups broccoli florets
½ cup chopped onion
1 tablespoon olive oil
2 tablespoons grated Parmesan cheese
¼ to ½ teaspoon crushed red pepper
   Assorted vegetable dippers, baked tortilla chips, or assorted crackers

1 In a covered medium saucepan cook broccoli in a small amount of boiling salted water about 10 minutes or until tender. Drain well, reserving cooking liquid.

2 In a small skillet cook onion in hot oil for 8 to 10 minutes or until onion is tender. In a food processor or blender combine broccoli, onion, Parmesan cheese, and crushed red pepper. Cover and process or blend until nearly smooth. If mixture seems dry and thick, stir in enough of the reserved cooking liquid, 1 tablespoon at a time, to reach a spreading consistency. Cover and chill for at least 3 hours or up to 24 hours.

3 Serve with vegetable dippers, baked tortilla chips, or assorted crackers.

Nutrition Facts per 2 tablespoons spread: 32 cal., 2 g total fat (0 g sat. fat), 1 mg chol., 26 mg sodium, 3 g carbo., 1 g fiber, 1 g pro.

PREP:
25 minutes
CHILL:
3 to 24 hours
MAKES:
1 cup spread

3
carbs per serving

Exchanges:
½ Fat

MEDITERRANEAN WALNUT SPREAD

START TO FINISH:
10 minutes
MAKES:
about ⅔ cup spread

1	cup canned garbanzo beans (chickpeas), rinsed and drained
½	cup chopped walnuts
½	cup lightly packed fresh basil leaves
¼	cup water
4	teaspoons lemon juice
¼	teaspoon salt
⅛	teaspoon black pepper
	Pita bread rounds, cut into wedges

13 carbs per serving

❶ In a blender or food processor combine beans, walnuts, basil leaves, the water, lemon juice, salt, and pepper. Cover and blend or process until nearly smooth, scraping down side of container occasionally. If too thick, stir in additional water, 1 tablespoon at a time, to reach a spreading consistency.

❷ Serve spread on pita wedges.

TO MAKE AHEAD: Prepare spread as directed. Place spread in an airtight container and chill for up to 3 days.

Nutrition Facts per about 2 tablespoons spread: 138 cal., 8 g total fat (1 g sat. fat), 0 mg chol., 261 mg sodium, 13 g carbo., 3 g fiber, 4 g pro.

Exchanges:
1 Starch
1 Fat

LOVIN' LEMON SWIRL DIP

1   cup vanilla low-fat yogurt

¼   teaspoon finely shredded lemon peel

1   tablespoon lemon juice

     Dash ground cinnamon

     Dash ground ginger

3   tablespoons strawberry jam or preserves

3   cups assorted fresh fruit
     (such as apple and/or pear wedges,* plum slices, strawberries,
     raspberries, and/or seedless grapes)

1 In a medium bowl stir together yogurt, lemon peel, lemon juice, cinnamon, and ginger. Cover and chill for at least 1 hour or up to 24 hours.

2 To serve, transfer yogurt mixture to a serving bowl. Drop small spoonfuls of jam over yogurt mixture. Using a thin knife or spatula, gently swirl jam into yogurt mixture. Serve fruit with swirled yogurt mixture.

*NOTE: To prevent apples and pears from turning brown, place the sliced fruit in a bowl. Add 2 tablespoons lemon juice and 2 tablespoons water; toss to coat. Drain. If desired, pat dry with paper towels.

Nutrition Facts per serving: 63 cal., 1 g total fat (0 g sat. fat), 2 mg chol., 30 mg sodium, 13 g carbo., 0 g fiber, 2 g pro.

PREP:
10 minutes
CHILL:
1 to 24 hours
MAKES:
6 servings

13
carbs per
serving

Exchanges:
1 Other Carbo.

FRUIT KABOBS

PREP:
20 minutes
CHILL:
*30 to
60 minutes*
MAKES:
8 servings

¾   cup bite-size cantaloupe chunks

¾   cup bite-size honeydew melon chunks

¾   cup small fresh strawberries, hulled

¾   cup bite-size fresh pineapple chunks

1   small banana cut into 1-inch-thick slices

1   cup orange juice

¼   cup lime juice

1   6-ounce carton vanilla low-fat or fat-free yogurt

2   tablespoons frozen orange juice concentrate, thawed

     Ground nutmeg or ground cinnamon (optional)

14
carbs per
serving

1 On eight 6-inch skewers, alternately thread cantaloupe, honeydew melon, strawberries, pineapple, and banana. Place kabobs in a glass baking dish. In a small bowl combine orange juice and lime juice; pour evenly over kabobs. Cover; chill kabobs for at least 30 minutes or up to 60 minutes, turning occasionally.

2 Meanwhile, for dip, in a small bowl stir together yogurt and orange juice concentrate. Cover and chill until ready to serve.

3 To serve, arrange kabobs on a serving platter; discard juice mixture. If desired, sprinkle nutmeg or cinnamon over kabobs. Serve with dip.

Exchanges:
1 Fruit

Nutrition Facts per serving: 62 cal., 0 g total fat (0 g sat. fat), 1 mg chol., 20 mg sodium, 14 g carbo., 1 g fiber, 2 g pro.

TROPICAL FRUIT POPS

½ cup boiling water
1 4-serving-size package sugar-free lemon-, mixed fruit-, or strawberry-flavored gelatin
1 15¼-ounce can crushed pineapple (juice pack)
2 medium bananas, cut into chunks

1 In a 1- or 2-cup glass measure stir together boiling water and gelatin until gelatin dissolves. Pour into a blender. Add undrained pineapple and banana chunks. Cover and blend until smooth.

2 Pour a scant ½ cup of the fruit mixture into each of eight 5- to 6-ounce paper or plastic drink cups. (Or pour a scant ⅓ cup into each of twelve 3-ounce paper cups.) Cover each cup with foil. Using the tip of a knife, make a small hole in the foil over each cup. Insert a wooden stick into the cup through the hole. Freeze about 6 hours or until firm.

3 To serve, quickly dip the cups in warm water to slightly soften fruit mixture. Remove foil and loosen sides of pops from drink cups. Tear off the paper or plastic.

Nutrition Facts per ½-cup pop: 65 cal., 0 g total fat (0 g sat. fat), 0 mg chol., 29 mg sodium, 15 g carbo., 1 g fiber, 1 g pro.

PREP:
15 minutes
FREEZE:
6 hours
MAKES:
8 or 12 pops

15
carbs per
pop

Exchanges:
1 Fruit

TANGO MANGO SMOOTHIES

START TO FINISH:
10 minutes
MAKES:
6 (6-ounce) servings

2	ripe bananas, chilled
⅔	cup peeled, sliced mango
1	12-ounce can mango, peach, apricot, or other fruit nectar, chilled
1	cup plain fat-free yogurt
1	tablespoon honey (optional)
	Assorted cut-up fresh fruit (such as bananas, peeled kiwifruit, and/or peeled mango) (optional)

24 carbs per serving

Exchanges:
1 Fruit
½ Milk

1 Cut bananas into chunks. In a blender combine bananas, sliced mango, fruit nectar, yogurt, and, if desired, honey.

2 Cover and blend until smooth. Pour into 6 chilled glasses. If desired, garnish with cut-up fresh fruit.

Nutrition Facts per serving: 108 cal., 0 g total fat (0 g sat. fat), 1 mg chol., 33 mg sodium, 24 g carbo., 1 g fiber, 3 g pro.

BREAKFAST

OATMEAL BRUNCH CASSEROLE

PREP:
15 minutes
BAKE:
10 minutes +
5 minutes
OVEN:
350°F
MAKES:
4 servings

36
carbs per serving

Exchanges:
½ Milk
1 Fruit
1 Starch
1½ Fat

Nonstick cooking spray

2 cups fat-free milk

1 tablespoon butter or margarine

1 cup regular rolled oats

1 cup chopped apple or pear

⅓ cup dried tart cherries or golden raisins

¼ cup coarsely chopped walnuts, toasted

½ teaspoon vanilla

¼ teaspoon salt

1 tablespoon packed brown sugar

Milk (optional)

1 Lightly coat a 1½-quart casserole with nonstick cooking spray; set aside. In a medium saucepan bring the 2 cups milk and the butter to boiling. Slowly stir in oats. Stir in apple or pear, cherries or golden raisins, walnuts, vanilla, and salt. Cook and stir until bubbly. Cook and stir for 2 minutes more. Pour into the prepared casserole.

2 Bake in a 350° oven for 10 minutes. Sprinkle with brown sugar. Bake about 5 minutes more or until bubbly around the edge. Cool slightly. If desired, serve the warm oatmeal with additional milk.

Nutrition Facts per serving: 256 cal., 10 g total fat (2 g sat. fat), 11 mg chol., 225 mg sodium, 36 g carbo., 4 g fiber, 8 g pro.

MAPLE-GLAZED PEARS & CEREAL

4   ripe medium pears
⅓   cup desired dried fruit
     (such as dried cranberries, cherries, snipped apricots, or raisins)
1   tablespoon light pancake and waffle syrup product
½   cup pear nectar or apple juice
3   cups cooked oatmeal or multigrain cereal*
3   tablespoons chopped walnuts, toasted

PREP:
20 minutes
BAKE:
20 minutes
OVEN:
350°F
MAKES:
8 servings

❶ Cut pears in half, leaving stems intact on 4 of the halves. Remove cores. Arrange pears, cut sides up, in a 3-quart baking dish. Top pears with desired dried fruit. Drizzle with syrup product. Add the pear nectar or apple juice to the baking dish.

❷ Cover and bake in a 350° oven for 20 to 25 minutes or until pears are tender, spooning cooking liquid over pears occasionally. Serve warm pear halves and dried fruit with hot cereal; sprinkle with walnuts. Drizzle with any remaining cooking liquid.

30
carbs per serving

*NOTE: To make 3 cups cooked oatmeal or multigrain cereal, in a medium saucepan heat 3 cups water to boiling; stir in 1⅔ cups regular rolled oats or 2½ cups multigrain cereal. Cook for 5 to 7 minutes for oats or 1 to 2 minutes for multigrain cereal or until most of the liquid is evaporated, stirring occasionally. Let oats or multigrain cereal stand, covered, for 3 minutes.

Nutrition Facts per serving: 149 cal., 3 g total fat (0 g sat. fat), 0 mg chol., 9 mg sodium, 30 g carbo., 5 g fiber, 3 g pro.

Exchanges:
1 Fruit
1 Starch

ALMOND-ORANGE GRANOLA

PREP:
15 minutes
BAKE:
30 minutes
OVEN:
325°F
MAKES:
4 cups

23
carbs per
serving

Exchanges:
1 Starch
½ Other Carbo.
½ Fat

Nonstick cooking spray
2½ cups regular rolled oats
1 cup wheat flakes
⅓ cup Grape Nuts® or whole bran cereal
⅓ cup sliced almonds or pecan pieces
⅓ cup orange juice
2 tablespoons honey
¼ teaspoon ground allspice
¼ teaspoon ground cinnamon
Low-fat yogurt, fat-free milk, and/or fresh fruit (optional)

1 Coat a 15×10×1-inch baking pan with nonstick cooking spray; set aside. In a large bowl stir together oats, wheat flakes, Grape Nuts® or whole bran cereal, and nuts. In a small saucepan stir together orange juice, honey, allspice, and cinnamon. Cook and stir just until boiling. Remove from heat. Pour over oat mixture, tossing just until coated.

2 Spread oat mixture evenly in prepared pan. Bake, uncovered, in a 325° oven for 30 to 35 minutes or until oats are lightly browned, stirring twice. Remove from oven. Immediately turn out onto a large piece of foil; cool completely. If desired, serve with yogurt, milk, and/or fresh fruit.

TO MAKE AHEAD: Prepare as directed. Store in an airtight container in the refrigerator for up to 2 weeks or in the freezer for up to 3 months.

Nutrition Facts per ⅓ cup granola: 136 cal., 3 g total fat (0 g sat. fat), 0 mg chol., 39 mg sodium, 23 g carbo., 3 g fiber, 4 g pro.

TOMATO-BROWN RICE FRITTATA

6   egg whites

3   eggs

¼   teaspoon salt

⅛   teaspoon black pepper

½   cup cooked brown rice

    Nonstick cooking spray

¼   cup chopped onion

1   clove garlic, minced

2   cups packed fresh mustard greens, stems trimmed, torn into 1-inch pieces

1   medium tomato, seeded and chopped

⅓   cup shredded fontina, provolone, or Gruyère cheese

START TO FINISH:
25 minutes
MAKES:
4 servings

10 carbs per serving

1 In a medium bowl combine egg whites, eggs, salt, and pepper. Beat with a wire whisk or rotary beater. Stir in brown rice; set aside. Coat an unheated large broilerproof skillet with nonstick cooking spray. Preheat over medium heat. Cook onion and garlic in hot skillet until tender. Stir in mustard greens; cook and stir about 2 minutes or until wilted. Stir in tomato and cook for 1 minute more.

2 Pour egg mixture into skillet over vegetables; do not stir. Cook over medium-low heat. As mixture sets, run a spatula around edge of the skillet, lifting the egg mixture so that the uncooked portion flows underneath. Continue cooking and lifting edge until the egg mixture is nearly set (top will be moist). Sprinkle with cheese. Place skillet under broiler so the top of frittata is 4 to 5 inches from heat. Broil for 1 to 2 minutes or just until top is set and cheese melts.

Nutrition Facts per serving: 168 cal., 8 g total fat (3 g sat. fat), 171 mg chol., 377 mg sodium, 10 g carbo., 2 g fiber, 15 g pro.

Exchanges:
1 Vegetable
½ Starch
1 Very Lean Meat
1 Medium-Fat Meat

RANCH EGGS

PREP:
25 minutes
BAKE:
20 minutes
STAND:
5 minutes
OVEN:
400°F
MAKES:
6 servings

7

carbs per
serving

Exchanges:
1 Vegetable
1 Medium-Fat Meat
½ Fat

Nonstick cooking spray

1   large onion, halved and thinly sliced

1   14½-ounce can diced tomatoes, drained

1   fresh jalapeño chile pepper, seeded and chopped*

1   clove garlic, minced

½   teaspoon chili powder

6   eggs

¼   teaspoon salt

⅛   teaspoon black pepper

⅓   cup reduced-fat shredded Monterey Jack or cheddar cheese

1   tablespoon snipped fresh cilantro

6   6-inch corn tortillas, warmed according to package directions (optional)

1 Coat an unheated large ovenproof skillet with nonstick cooking spray. Preheat skillet over medium-high heat. Add onion to hot skillet. Cook about 5 minutes or until tender, stirring occasionally. Remove from heat.

2 Meanwhile, in a small bowl stir together drained tomatoes, chile pepper, garlic, and chili powder. Pour tomato mixture over onion in skillet; spread evenly. Break one of the eggs into a measuring cup or custard cup. Carefully slide egg onto tomato mixture. Repeat with remaining eggs, spacing eggs as evenly as possible. Sprinkle eggs with salt and black pepper.

3 Bake, uncovered, in a 400° oven about 20 minutes or until eggs are set. Remove from oven. Sprinkle with cheese; let stand for 5 minutes. Sprinkle with cilantro. If desired, serve with warmed tortillas.

*NOTE: Because chile peppers contain volatile oils that can burn your skin and eyes, avoid direct contact with them as much as possible. When working with chile peppers, wear plastic or rubber gloves. If your bare hands do touch the peppers, wash your hands and nails well with soap and warm water.

Nutrition Facts per serving: 121 cal., 7 g total fat (3 g sat. fat), 217 mg chol., 367 mg sodium, 7 g carbo., 2 g fiber, 9 g pro.

BAKED BRIE STRATA

2   small zucchini, cut crosswise into ¼-inch-thick slices (about 2 cups)
Nonstick cooking spray

6   cups crusty sourdough bread torn into bite-size pieces (6 ounces)

1   4.4-ounce package Brie cheese

1   cup halved grape tomatoes or cherry tomatoes

4   slightly beaten eggs or 1 cup refrigerated or frozen egg product, thawed

⅔   cup evaporated fat-free milk

⅓   cup sliced green onions

3   tablespoons snipped fresh dill or 1 tablespoon dried dill

½   teaspoon salt

⅛   teaspoon black pepper

PREP:
25 minutes
CHILL:
4 to 24 hours
BAKE:
30 minutes +
25 minutes
STAND:
10 minutes
OVEN:
325°F
MAKES:
6 servings

21
carbs per serving

Exchanges:
½ Vegetable
1 Starch
1½ Medium-Fat Meat
½ Fat

1 In a covered medium saucepan cook zucchini in a small amount of boiling lightly salted water for 2 to 3 minutes or just until tender. Drain zucchini. Set aside.

2 Meanwhile, coat a 2-quart rectangular baking dish with nonstick cooking spray. Arrange 4 cups of the bread pieces in the prepared baking dish. If desired, remove and discard rind from cheese. Cut cheese into ½-inch cubes. Sprinkle cheese evenly over bread in baking dish. Arrange zucchini and tomatoes on top. Sprinkle with remaining 2 cups bread pieces.

3 In a medium bowl combine eggs, evaporated fat-free milk, green onions, dill, salt, and pepper. Pour evenly over mixture in baking dish. Lightly press down layers with back of spoon. Cover with plastic wrap; chill for at least 4 hours or up to 24 hours.

4 Remove plastic wrap from strata; cover with foil. Bake in a 325° oven for 30 minutes. Uncover; bake for 25 to 30 minutes more or until a knife inserted near the center comes out clean. Let stand for 10 minutes before serving.

Nutrition Facts per serving: 231 cal., 10 g total fat (5 g sat. fat), 163 mg chol., 581 mg sodium, 21 g carbo., 2 g fiber, 14 g pro.

BACON 'N' EGG POCKETS

START TO FINISH:
15 minutes
MAKES:
4 servings

18
carbs per serving

Exchanges:
1 Starch
1½ Very Lean Meat
½ Fat

2   eggs
4   egg whites
3   ounces Canadian-style bacon, chopped
3   tablespoons water
2   tablespoons sliced green onion (optional)
⅛   teaspoon salt
    Nonstick cooking spray
2   large whole wheat pita bread rounds, halved crosswise
½   cup shredded reduced-fat cheddar cheese (2 ounces) (optional)

1 In a medium bowl combine eggs, egg whites, Canadian bacon, the water, green onion (if desired), and salt. Beat with a wire whisk or rotary beater until well mixed.

2 Lightly coat an unheated large nonstick skillet with nonstick cooking spray. Preheat over medium heat. Add egg mixture to skillet. Cook, without stirring, until mixture begins to set on the bottom and around edge. Using a spatula or a large spoon, lift and fold the partially cooked eggs so that the uncooked portion flows underneath. Continue cooking about 2 minutes more or until egg mixture is cooked through but is still glossy and moist. Remove from heat immediately.

3 Fill pita halves with egg mixture. If desired, sprinkle with cheese.

Nutrition Facts per serving: 162 cal., 4 g total fat (1 g sat. fat), 118 mg chol., 616 mg sodium, 18 g carbo., 2 g fiber, 13 g pro.

ASPARAGUS & POTATO SKILLET

8 ounces tiny new potatoes, cut into ¼-inch-thick slices

1 cup fresh asparagus cut into ½-inch pieces
   Nonstick cooking spray

3 slightly beaten eggs or 1½ cups refrigerated
   or frozen egg product, thawed

1 tablespoon snipped fresh parsley

1 teaspoon snipped fresh rosemary

¼ teaspoon onion powder

¼ teaspoon salt

¼ teaspoon black pepper

2 small tomatoes, seeded and coarsely chopped

1 tablespoon finely shredded Parmesan cheese

START TO FINISH:
30 minutes
MAKES:
4 servings

15
carbs per serving

Exchanges:
½ Vegetable
1 Starch
½ Medium-Fat Meat

1 In a covered large nonstick skillet cook potatoes in a small amount of boiling water for 5 minutes. Add asparagus. Cook, covered, for 5 to 7 minutes more or until vegetables are tender. Drain vegetables in a colander. Cool and dry the skillet. Lightly coat the skillet with nonstick cooking spray. Return vegetables to the skillet.

2 In a small bowl combine eggs, parsley, rosemary, onion powder, salt, and pepper. Pour over vegetables in the skillet; do not stir. Cook over medium heat. As mixture sets, run a spatula around the edge of the skillet, lifting egg mixture so that the uncooked portion flows underneath. Continue cooking and lifting edge until egg mixture is nearly set (top will be moist).

3 Remove skillet from heat. Let stand, covered, for 3 to 4 minutes or until top is set. Sprinkle with tomatoes and Parmesan cheese.

Nutrition Facts per serving: 127 cal., 4 g total fat (2 g sat. fat), 160 mg chol., 223 mg sodium, 15 g carbo., 2 g fiber, 8 g pro.

BLUEBERRY BLINTZES

PREP:
30 minutes
BAKE:
15 minutes
OVEN:
400°F
MAKES:
8 servings

31
carbs per
serving

Exchanges:
1½ Fruit
½ Starch
1½ Lean Meat
½ Fat

2	eggs or ½ cup refrigerated or frozen egg product, thawed
1⅓	cups fat-free milk
¾	cup whole wheat flour
1	tablespoon cooking oil
¼	teaspoon salt
1	15-ounce carton part-skim ricotta cheese
2	cups blueberries
¼	cup packed brown sugar
1½	teaspoons finely shredded orange peel
1	cup orange juice
1	tablespoon cornstarch
1	tablespoon granulated sugar
¼	teaspoon ground cardamom

1 For crepes, in a medium bowl combine eggs, milk, whole wheat flour, oil, and salt; beat with a wire whisk or rotary beater until well mixed. Heat a lightly greased 6-inch skillet over medium heat; remove from heat. Spoon in 2 tablespoons of the egg mixture; lift and tilt skillet to spread egg mixture. Return to heat; cook on one side only for 1 to 2 minutes or until brown. Invert over clean white paper towels; remove crepe. Repeat with the remaining egg mixture, lightly greasing skillet occasionally.

2 For filling, in another medium bowl combine ricotta cheese, 1 cup of the blueberries, the brown sugar, and 1 teaspoon of the orange peel. Fill each crepe, browned side down, with a rounded tablespoon of the filling. Roll up.

3 Place blintzes in a 3-quart rectangular baking dish. Bake, uncovered, in a 400° oven for 15 to 20 minutes or until heated through.

4 Meanwhile, for sauce, in a small saucepan stir together the remaining ½ teaspoon orange peel, the orange juice, cornstarch, granulated sugar, and cardamom. Cook and stir until thickened and bubbly. Cook and stir for 2 minutes more. Stir in the remaining 1 cup blueberries. Spoon the sauce over warm blintzes.

Nutrition Facts per serving: 229 cal., 8 g total fat (3 g sat. fat), 70 mg chol., 181 mg sodium, 31 g carbo., 2 g fiber, 11 g pro.

BANANA-STUFFED FRENCH TOAST

Nonstick cooking spray

2 eggs or ½ cup refrigerated or frozen egg product, thawed

½ cup fat-free milk

½ teaspoon vanilla

⅛ teaspoon ground cinnamon

4 1-inch-thick slices French bread

⅔ cup thinly sliced banana

Sifted powdered sugar, light pancake and waffle syrup product, or maple syrup (optional)

1 Line a baking sheet with foil; lightly coat foil with nonstick cooking spray. Set aside. In a shallow bowl combine eggs, milk, vanilla, and cinnamon. Beat with a wire whisk or rotary beater until well mixed. Set aside.

2 Using a serrated knife, cut a pocket in each bread slice, cutting horizontally from the top crust almost to, but not through, the bottom crust. Fill bread pockets with sliced banana.

3 Dip bread slices into egg mixture, coating both sides of each slice. Place on the prepared baking sheet. Bake in a 500° oven for 10 to 12 minutes or until golden brown, turning once. If desired, sprinkle with powdered sugar or serve with syrup.

Nutrition Facts per serving: 210 cal., 4 g total fat (1 g sat. fat), 107 mg chol., 352 mg sodium, 34 g carbo., 2 g fiber, 9 g pro.

PREP:
20 minutes
BAKE:
10 minutes
OVEN:
500°F
MAKES:
4 servings

34 carbs per serving

Exchanges:
1½ Starch
½ Other Carbo.
½ Medium-Fat Meat

BUTTERMILK OAT PANCAKES

PREP:
20 minutes
COOK:
3 minutes
per batch
MAKES:
8 servings
(about
16 pancakes)

36
carbs per
serving

Exchanges:
2 Starch
½ Other Carbo.
1 Fat

1¼	cups regular rolled oats
¾	cup all-purpose flour
½	cup whole wheat flour
1	tablespoon baking powder
¼	teaspoon salt
3	egg whites
2¼	cups buttermilk or sour milk*
2	tablespoons cooking oil
1	tablespoon honey
1	teaspoon vanilla
	Nonstick cooking spray
	Light pancake syrup and waffle syrup product (optional)

1 In a large bowl combine oats, all-purpose flour, whole wheat flour, baking powder, and salt. Make a well in the center of the flour mixture; set aside.

2 In a medium bowl beat the egg whites with a fork; stir in buttermilk, oil, honey, and vanilla. Add egg white mixture all at once to flour mixture. Stir just until moistened (batter should be lumpy). If you prefer softened oats, cover batter and allow to stand at room temperature for 15 minutes.

3 Coat an unheated griddle or heavy nonstick skillet with nonstick cooking spray. Preheat over medium-high heat. For each pancake, pour about ¼ cup of the batter onto the hot griddle or skillet. Spread batter into a circle about 4 inches in diameter. Cook over medium heat for 3 to 4 minutes or until the pancakes are golden brown, turning to cook second sides when pancakes have bubbly surfaces and edges are slightly dry. If desired, serve pancakes with syrup.

*NOTE: To make 2¼ cups sour milk, place 7 teaspoons lemon juice or vinegar in a 4-cup glass measuring cup. Add enough milk to make 2¼ cups liquid; stir. Let the mixture stand for 5 minutes before using.

Nutrition Facts per serving: 237 cal., 6 g total fat (1 g sat. fat), 3 mg chol., 257 mg sodium, 36 g carbo., 4 g fiber, 10 g pro.

PUMPKIN WAFFLES

- 2 cups all-purpose flour
- 2 tablespoons packed brown sugar
- 1 tablespoon baking powder
- ½ teaspoon salt
- ½ teaspoon pumpkin pie spice
- 1½ cups fat-free milk
- 1 cup canned pumpkin
- 2 slightly beaten eggs or ½ cup refrigerated or frozen egg product, thawed
- 2 tablespoons cooking oil
  Orange sections (optional)

1 In a medium bowl stir together flour, brown sugar, baking powder, salt, and pumpkin pie spice. Make a well in the center of the flour mixture.

2 In another medium bowl combine milk, pumpkin, eggs, and oil. Add milk mixture all at once to flour mixture. Stir just until moistened (batter should be lumpy).

3 Pour about ¾ cup batter onto grid of a preheated, lightly greased waffle baker. Close lid quickly; do not open lid until waffle is done. Bake according to manufacturer's directions. When done, use a fork to lift waffle off grid. Repeat with remaining batter. Serve warm. If desired, top with orange sections.

Nutrition Facts per serving: 155 cal., 4 g total fat (1 g sat. fat), 43 mg chol., 221 mg sodium, 24 g carbo., 1 g fiber, 5 g pro.

PREP:
10 minutes
BAKE:
per waffle baker directions
MAKES:
10 servings

24
carbs per serving

Exchanges:
1 Starch
½ Other Carbo.
½ Fat

WALNUT WAFFLES WITH BLUEBERRY SAUCE

PREP:
15 minutes
BAKE:
per waffle
baker directions
MAKES:
8 servings

33
carbs per
serving

Exchanges:
1 Starch
1 Other Carbo.
1½ Fat

1	cup all-purpose flour
1	cup whole wheat flour
¼	cup coarsely ground toasted walnuts
2	teaspoons baking powder
1	teaspoon baking soda
4	egg whites
1¼	cups buttermilk or sour milk*
2	tablespoons cooking oil
1	recipe Blueberry Sauce

1 In a large bowl stir together all-purpose flour, whole wheat flour, walnuts, baking powder, and baking soda. Make a well in the center of the flour mixture; set aside. In a large mixing bowl beat the egg whites with an electric mixer on medium speed until very foamy. Stir in buttermilk and oil. Add egg white mixture all at once to the flour mixture. Stir just until moistened (batter should be slightly lumpy).

2 Pour 1 cup of the batter onto grids of a preheated, lightly greased waffle baker. Close lid quickly; do not open lid until waffle is done. Bake according to manufacturer's directions. When done, use a fork to lift waffle off grids. Repeat with remaining batter. Serve waffles warm with Blueberry Sauce.

BLUEBERRY SAUCE: In a medium saucepan combine 1 cup fresh or frozen blueberries, ¼ cup white grape juice, and 1 tablespoon honey. Heat just until bubbles form around edge. Cool slightly. Transfer to a blender. Cover and blend until smooth. Transfer sauce to a serving bowl. Stir in 1 cup fresh or frozen blueberries. Makes about 1⅔ cups sauce.

*NOTE: To make 1¼ cups sour milk, place 4 teaspoons lemon juice or vinegar in a glass measuring cup. Add enough milk to make 1¼ cups liquid; stir. Let the mixture stand for 5 minutes before using.

Nutrition Facts per serving: 224 cal., 7 g total fat (1 g sat. fat), 3 mg chol., 359 mg sodium, 33 g carbo., 4 g fiber, 8 g pro.

SPICED FAN BISCUITS

Nonstick cooking spray
2 cups all-purpose flour
4 teaspoons baking powder
½ teaspoon cream of tartar
¼ teaspoon salt
¼ cup shortening
¾ cup fat-free milk
2 tablespoons sugar
1 teaspoon ground cinnamon

1 Coat twelve 2½-inch muffin cups with nonstick cooking spray; set aside. In a large bowl stir together flour, baking powder, cream of tartar, and salt. Using a pastry blender, cut in shortening until mixture resembles coarse crumbs. Make a well in the center of the flour mixture; add milk. Stir just until dough clings together.

2 Turn out dough onto a lightly floured surface. Knead dough by folding and gently pressing dough for 10 to 12 strokes or until nearly smooth. Divide dough in half. Roll one half into a 12×10-inch rectangle. In a small bowl combine sugar and cinnamon. Sprinkle half of the sugar mixture over the rectangle.

3 Cut rectangle into five 12×2-inch strips. Stack the strips on top of each other; cut into six 2-inch-square stacks. Place each stack, cut side down, in a prepared muffin cup. Repeat with remaining dough and sugar mixture.

4 Bake in a 450° oven for 10 to 12 minutes or until golden brown. Serve warm.

Nutrition Facts per biscuit: 121 cal., 4 g total fat (1 g sat. fat), 0 mg chol., 190 mg sodium, 18 g carbo., 1 g fiber, 3 g pro.

PREP:
20 minutes
BAKE:
10 minutes
OVEN:
450°F
MAKES:
12 biscuits

18 carbs per serving

Exchanges:
1 Starch
1 Fat

SCONES WITH CURRANTS

PREP:
15 minutes
BAKE:
10 minutes
OVEN:
400°F
MAKES:
8 scones

2	cups all-purpose flour
¼	cup sugar
1½	teaspoons baking powder
⅛	teaspoon salt
⅛	teaspoon ground nutmeg
¼	cup cold butter, cut up
¼	cup dried currants or raisins
2	beaten egg whites
⅓	cup fat-free milk
	Fat-free milk
1	recipe Strawberry Cream Cheese (optional)

32
carbs per
serving

Exchanges:
1 Starch
1 Other Carbo.
1 Fat

1 In a medium bowl stir together flour, sugar, baking powder, salt, and nutmeg. Using a pastry blender, cut in butter until mixture resembles coarse crumbs. Stir in currants. Make a well in the center of flour mixture.

2 In a small bowl stir together egg whites and the ⅓ cup milk. Add milk mixture all at once to flour mixture. Stir just until moistened. Turn out dough onto a lightly floured surface. Knead dough by folding and gently pressing dough for 10 to 12 strokes or until nearly smooth.

3 Divide dough in half. Roll or pat each dough half into a 5-inch circle. Cut each circle into 4 wedges. Place wedges on a baking sheet. Brush with additional milk. Bake in a 400° oven for 10 to 12 minutes or until bottoms are browned. Serve warm. If desired, serve with Strawberry Cream Cheese.

TO MAKE AHEAD: Prepare as directed. Wrap cooled scones in foil and place in an airtight freezer container. Seal, label, and freeze for up to 3 months. To serve, place foil-wrapped scones in a 350°F oven and bake about 10 minutes or until heated through.

Nutrition Facts per scone: 202 cal., 6 g total fat (3 g sat. fat), 16 mg chol., 144 mg sodium, 32 g carbo., 1 g fiber, 4 g pro.

STRAWBERRY CREAM CHEESE: In a small bowl combine ½ of an 8-ounce tub fat-free cream cheese and 2 tablespoons low-calorie strawberry spread.

FRUIT BREAD

1   cup all-purpose flour
½   cup sugar
¼   cup whole wheat flour
1½   teaspoons baking powder
½   teaspoon salt
¼   teaspoon pumpkin pie spice
1   beaten egg or ¼ cup refrigerated or frozen egg product, thawed
½   cup applesauce
2   tablespoons cooking oil
½   cup snipped dried apricots

1 Grease and lightly flour one 7½×3½×2-inch, two 5¾×3×2-inch, or four 4½×2½×1½-inch individual loaf pan(s); set aside.

2 In a medium bowl combine all-purpose flour, sugar, whole wheat flour, baking powder, salt, and pumpkin pie spice. In a small bowl combine egg, applesauce, and oil. Add egg mixture all at once to flour mixture. Stir just until moistened. Fold in dried apricots. Pour into prepared pan(s).

3 Bake in a 350° oven for 45 to 50 minutes for the 7½×3½×2-inch pan (20 to 25 minutes for smaller pans) or until a toothpick inserted near the center(s) comes out clean. Cool in pan(s) on a wire rack for 10 minutes. Remove from pan(s). Cool on wire rack. Wrap in plastic wrap and store overnight before slicing.

TO MAKE AHEAD: Prepare as directed. Wrap cooled bread in foil and place in plastic freezer bag(s). Seal, label, and freeze for up to 3 months. Thaw overnight before serving.

Nutrition Facts per serving: 128 cal., 3 g total fat (1 g sat. fat), 18 mg chol., 135 mg sodium, 24 g carbo., 1 g fiber, 2 g pro.

PREP:
15 minutes
BAKE:
45 minutes
(for 7½×3½×2-inch pan);
20 minutes
(for smaller pans)
OVEN:
350°F
MAKES:
12 servings

24 carbs per serving

Exchanges:
½ Fruit
½ Starch
½ Other Carbo.
½ Fat

DATE-NUT BREAD

PREP:
15 minutes
STAND:
20 minutes
BAKE:
50 minutes
OVEN:
350°F
MAKES:
1 loaf
(16 servings)

22
carbs per
serving

Exchanges:
½ Fruit
1 Starch

1½   cups boiling water
1   8-ounce package pitted whole dates, snipped
1   cup all-purpose flour
1   cup whole wheat flour
1   teaspoon baking soda
1   teaspoon baking powder
½   teaspoon salt
1   egg or ¼ cup refrigerated or frozen egg product, thawed
1   teaspoon vanilla
½   cup sliced almonds, toasted and coarsely chopped

❶ In a medium bowl pour the boiling water over dates. Let stand about 20 minutes or until dates are softened and mixture has cooled slightly.

❷ Lightly grease bottom and ½ inch up sides of an 8×4×2-inch loaf pan; set aside. In a large bowl stir together all-purpose flour, whole wheat flour, baking soda, baking powder, and salt. In a small bowl beat together egg and vanilla with a fork; stir into the cooled date mixture. Add date mixture and almonds to flour mixture; stir until well mixed (mixture will be thick).

❸ Spoon batter into prepared pan, spreading evenly. Bake in a 350° oven for 50 to 55 minutes or until a toothpick inserted near the center comes out clean. Cool in pan on a wire rack for 10 minutes. Remove from pan. Cool completely on a wire rack. Wrap in plastic wrap and store overnight before slicing.

Nutrition Facts per serving: 119 cal., 3 g total fat (0 g sat. fat), 13 mg chol., 182 mg sodium, 22 g carbo., 3 g fiber, 3 g pro.

SEVEN-GRAIN BREAD

¾ to 1¼ cups all-purpose flour

½ cup seven-grain cereal

1 package active dry yeast

⅔ cup water

⅓ cup applesauce

2 tablespoons honey

1 teaspoon salt

1 egg or ¼ cup refrigerated or frozen egg product, thawed

1¾ cups whole wheat flour

⅓ cup shelled sunflower seeds

1 In a large mixing bowl stir together ¾ cup of the all-purpose flour, the cereal, and yeast; set aside.

2 In a medium saucepan combine the water, applesauce, honey, and salt; heat and stir just until warm (120°F to 130°F). Add applesauce mixture and egg to flour mixture. Beat with an electric mixer on low to medium speed for 30 seconds, scraping side of bowl constantly. Beat on high speed for 3 minutes. Using a wooden spoon, stir in the whole wheat flour, sunflower seeds, and as much of the remaining all-purpose flour as you can.

3 Turn out dough onto a lightly floured surface. Knead in enough of the remaining all-purpose flour to make a moderately stiff dough that is smooth and elastic (6 to 8 minutes total). Shape dough into a ball. Place in a lightly greased bowl; turn once to grease surface of dough. Cover; let rise in a warm place until double in size (1 to 1½ hours).

4 Punch down dough. Turn out onto a lightly floured surface; cover and let rest for 10 minutes. Lightly grease an 8×4×2-inch loaf pan.

5 Shape dough into loaf. Place in prepared pan. Cover and let rise in a warm place until nearly double (30 to 45 minutes).

6 Bake in a 375° oven for 40 to 45 minutes or until bread sounds hollow when lightly tapped. (If necessary to prevent overbrowning, cover loosely with foil for the last 10 minutes of baking.) Immediately remove bread from pan. Cool on a wire rack.

Nutrition Facts per serving: 111 cal., 2 g total fat (0 g sat. fat), 13 mg chol., 151 mg sodium, 20 g carbo., 2 g fiber, 4 g pro.

PREP:
30 minutes
RISE:
1 hour + 30 minutes
BAKE:
40 minutes
OVEN:
375°F
MAKES:
1 loaf (16 servings)

20 carbs per serving

Exchanges:
1½ Starch

THREE-B MUFFINS
(BUCKWHEAT, BLUEBERRY & BUTTERNUT)

PREP:
20 minutes
BAKE:
15 minutes
OVEN:
400°F
MAKES:
12 muffins

23
carbs per
muffin

Exchanges:
½ Fruit
1 Starch
½ Fat

Nonstick cooking spray
1⅓ cups all-purpose flour
¾ cup buckwheat flour
¼ cup sugar
1½ teaspoons baking powder
1 teaspoon ground cinnamon
½ teaspoon baking soda
½ teaspoon salt
2 slightly beaten eggs or ½ cup refrigerated or frozen egg product, thawed
1 cup mashed cooked butternut squash
½ cup fat-free milk
½ teaspoon finely shredded orange peel
¼ cup orange juice
2 tablespoons cooking oil
¾ cup fresh or frozen blueberries
Rolled oats

1 Coat twelve 2½-inch muffin cups with nonstick cooking spray or line with paper bake cups; set pan aside. In a medium bowl combine the all-purpose flour, buckwheat flour, sugar, baking powder, cinnamon, baking soda, and salt. Make a well in the center of the flour mixture; set aside.

2 In a medium bowl combine eggs, squash, milk, orange peel, orange juice, and oil. Add the egg mixture all at once to the flour mixture. Stir just until moistened (batter should be lumpy). Fold in blueberries.

3 Spoon batter into the prepared muffin cups, filling each almost full. Sprinkle with oats. Bake in a 400° oven for 15 to 20 minutes or until the muffins are light brown. Cool in muffin cups on wire rack for 5 minutes. Remove from muffin cups; serve warm.

Nutrition Facts per muffin: 137 cal., 4 g total fat (1 g sat. fat), 36 mg chol., 217 mg sodium, 23 g carbo., 2 g fiber, 4 g pro.

BANANA-OAT MUFFINS

2¼	cups regular rolled oats
¾	cup whole wheat flour
⅓	cup sugar
1	teaspoon baking powder
1¼	teaspoons apple pie spice or ground cinnamon
½	teaspoon baking soda
½	teaspoon salt
1	cup buttermilk or sour milk*
1	large ripe banana, mashed
2	slightly beaten eggs or ½ cup refrigerated or frozen egg product, thawed
2	tablespoons butter, melted
1	teaspoon vanilla
1	tablespoon butter

1 Line twelve 2½-inch muffin cups with paper bake cups. Place 2 cups of the rolled oats in a food processor or blender; cover and process or blend until fine. Transfer oats to a large bowl; stir in whole wheat flour, sugar, baking powder, ¾ teaspoon of the apple pie spice, the baking soda, and salt. Make a well in the center of the flour mixture; set aside.

2 In a medium bowl whisk together buttermilk, banana, eggs, the 2 tablespoons melted butter, and vanilla. Add buttermilk mixture all at once to flour mixture; stir just until moistened. Spoon batter into muffin cups.

3 For topping, stir together the remaining ¼ cup oats and the remaining ½ teaspoon apple pie spice. Using a pastry blender, cut in the 1 tablespoon butter until mixture is crumbly. Sprinkle topping over batter in muffin cups.

4 Bake in a 350° oven for 20 to 22 minutes or until a toothpick inserted in centers of muffins comes out clean.

TO MAKE AHEAD: Prepare as directed. Cool muffins; store in an airtight container at room temperature for up to 3 days or freeze for up to 1 month.

*NOTE: To make 1 cup sour milk, place 1 tablespoon lemon juice or vinegar in a glass measuring cup. Add enough milk to make 1 cup liquid; stir. Let the mixture stand for 5 minutes before using.

Nutrition Facts per muffin: 174 cal., 5 g total fat (2 g sat. fat), 44 mg chol., 225 mg sodium, 27 g carbo., 3 g fiber, 6 g pro.

PREP:
20 minutes
BAKE:
20 minutes
OVEN:
350°F
MAKES:
12 muffins

27
carbs per muffin

Exchanges:
1½ Starch
½ Other Carbo.
½ Fat

TURKEY-APPLE SAUSAGE PATTIES

PREP:
15 minutes
BROIL:
10 minutes
MAKES:
4 servings

4

carbs per
serving

Exchanges:
2 Very Lean Meat
1 Fat

½ cup shredded, peeled apple
¼ cup finely chopped almonds or pecans
1½ teaspoons snipped fresh sage or ½ teaspoon dried sage, crushed
¼ teaspoon black pepper
⅛ teaspoon salt
⅛ teaspoon paprika
⅛ teaspoon cayenne pepper
   Dash ground nutmeg
8 ounces uncooked ground turkey breast
   Nonstick cooking spray

1 In a large bowl combine apple, nuts, sage, black pepper, salt, paprika, cayenne pepper, and nutmeg. Add ground turkey; mix well. Shape mixture into four ½-inch-thick patties.

2 Lightly coat the unheated rack of a broiler pan with nonstick cooking spray. Arrange patties on rack. Broil 4 to 5 inches from the heat about 10 minutes or until no longer pink (165°F),* turning once halfway through broiling time. (Or coat an unheated large skillet with nonstick cooking spray. Preheat over medium heat. Add patties to hot skillet. Cook for 8 to 10 minutes or until no longer pink [165°F],* turning once halfway through cooking time. If patties brown too quickly, reduce heat.)

*NOTE: The internal color of a turkey patty is not a reliable doneness indicator. A turkey patty cooked to 165°F is safe, regardless of color. To measure the doneness of a patty, insert an instant-read thermometer through the side of the patty to a depth of 2 to 3 inches.

Nutrition Facts per serving: 116 cal., 5 g total fat (1 g sat. fat), 23 mg chol., 113 mg sodium, 4 g carbo., 1 g fiber, 15 g pro.

BEEF & PORK

CAJUN-STYLE STEAKS

PREP:
20 minutes
COOK:
30 minutes
MAKES:
4 servings

2	tablespoons all-purpose flour
4	4-ounce beef cubed steaks
2	teaspoons cooking oil
1	14½-ounce can diced tomatoes, undrained
1	cup low-sodium tomato sauce
1½	teaspoons dried oregano, crushed, or 2 teaspoons snipped fresh oregano
1	teaspoon salt-free Cajun seasoning or blackened steak seasoning*
¼	teaspoon salt
2	small green sweet peppers, cut into strips
1	small onion, sliced and separated into rings
2	cups hot cooked brown rice

38
carbs per
serving

Exchanges:
2 Vegetable
2 Starch
3 Lean Meat

1 Place the flour in a shallow dish. Dip steaks into flour, coating both sides. In a large skillet heat oil over medium heat. Cook steaks, half at a time, in hot oil until brown, turning once (add additional oil if necessary).

2 Add undrained tomatoes, tomato sauce, oregano, Cajun seasoning, and salt to steaks in skillet. Bring to boiling; reduce heat. Cover and simmer for 25 minutes, stirring occasionally. Add sweet peppers and onion. Cover and simmer for 5 to 7 minutes more or until steaks and vegetables are tender. Skim fat from juices. Serve with hot cooked rice.

*NOTE: To make your own blackened seasoning, in a small bowl combine ½ teaspoon onion powder; ½ teaspoon garlic powder; ½ teaspoon white pepper; ½ teaspoon cayenne pepper; ½ teaspoon black pepper; ½ teaspoon dried thyme, crushed; and ⅛ teaspoon salt. Store, tightly covered, in a cool place for up to 6 months. Makes 1 tablespoon.

Nutrition Facts per serving: 363 cal., 9 g total fat (2 g sat. fat), 66 mg chol., 398 mg sodium, 38 g carbo., 4 g fiber, 29 g pro.

PEPPERCORN STEAK WITH VEGETABLES

2   6-ounce boneless beef ribeye steaks, cut 1 inch thick
1   tablespoon multicolor peppercorns, crushed
½   teaspoon salt
2   tablespoons butter or margarine, softened
2   teaspoons mild-flavored molasses
¼   teaspoon finely shredded lemon peel
1   teaspoon lemon juice
2   cups fresh sugar snap peas
½   cup carrot cut into thin bite-size strips

PREP:
20 minutes
BROIL:
12 minutes
MAKES:
4 servings

1 Trim fat from steaks. Press peppercorns and salt into both sides of steaks. Place steaks on the unheated rack of broiler pan. Broil 3 to 4 inches from heat until desired doneness, turning once halfway through broiling time. Allow 12 to 14 minutes for medium-rare doneness (145°F) or 15 to 18 minutes for medium doneness (160°F).

2 Meanwhile, in a small bowl combine butter, molasses, lemon peel, and lemon juice (mixture will appear curdled).

3 In a covered medium saucepan cook snap peas and carrot in a small amount of boiling salted water for 2 to 4 minutes or until crisp-tender; drain. Stir in 1 tablespoon of the molasses mixture.

4 To serve, top steaks with remaining molasses mixture. Thinly slice steaks; toss with vegetable mixture.

Nutrition Facts per serving: 247 cal., 12 g total fat (6 g sat. fat), 66 mg chol., 418 mg sodium, 13 g carbo., 3 g fiber, 20 g pro.

13 carbs per serving

Exchanges:
1 Vegetable
2½ Lean Meat
½ Other Carbo.
1 Fat

RIBEYE STEAKS WITH CARAMELIZED ONIONS

PREP:
25 minutes
GRILL:
11 minutes
MAKES:
4 servings

5
carbs per
serving

Exchanges:
3½ Very Lean Meat
1½ Fat

¾ teaspoon coarse salt

¾ teaspoon cracked black pepper

½ teaspoon mustard seeds, crushed

2 boneless beef ribeye steaks, cut 1 inch thick (1 to 1¼ pounds total)
   Nonstick cooking spray

1 medium sweet onion (such as Vidalia, Maui, or Walla Walla),
   halved lengthwise and thinly sliced

¼ cup chopped red sweet pepper

1 fresh jalapeño chile pepper, seeded and finely chopped*

1 clove garlic, minced

1 tablespoon balsamic vinegar

½ teaspoon dried sage, crushed, or 1½ teaspoons snipped fresh sage

1 In a small bowl combine salt, black pepper, and mustard seeds; divide mixture in half. Cut each steak into 2 portions. Rub half of the mustard seed mixture onto one side of the steaks; set aside.

2 Coat an unheated large nonstick skillet with nonstick cooking spray. Preheat over medium heat. Add onion to hot skillet. Cook and stir about 5 minutes. Add sweet pepper, chile pepper, and garlic; cook and stir about 5 minutes more or until onion is golden brown and peppers are tender. Add balsamic vinegar, sage, and remaining half of the mustard seed mixture; cook and stir for 1 minute more. Remove from heat. Cover and keep warm.

3 Place steaks on the rack of an uncovered grill directly over medium coals. Grill until desired doneness, turning once halfway through grilling time. Allow 11 to 15 minutes for medium-rare doneness (145°F) or 14 to 18 minutes for medium doneness (160°F). Serve with onion mixture.

***NOTE:** Because chile peppers contain volatile oils that can burn your skin and eyes, avoid direct contact with them as much as possible. When working with chile peppers, wear plastic or rubber gloves. If your bare hands do touch the peppers, wash your hands and nails well with soap and warm water.*

Nutrition Facts per serving: 194 cal., 7 g total fat (3 g sat. fat), 54 mg chol., 423 mg sodium, 5 g carbo., 1 g fiber, 25 g pro.

SALSA STEAK

1	1- to 1½-pound boneless beef round steak, cut ½ inch thick
¼	teaspoon salt
⅛	teaspoon black pepper
	Nonstick cooking spray
2	teaspoons olive oil or cooking oil
1½	cups sliced fresh mushrooms
¾	cup green sweet pepper strips
1	small onion, sliced
1	8-ounce can tomato sauce
2	to 3 teaspoons chili powder

❶ Trim fat from steak. Sprinkle both sides of steak with salt and black pepper. Cut into 4 to 6 serving-size pieces. Coat an unheated large nonstick skillet with nonstick cooking spray. Preheat over medium heat. Brown steak on both sides in hot skillet. Transfer to a 2-quart square baking dish.

❷ Add oil to same skillet. Add mushrooms, sweet pepper, and onion to hot oil. Cook and stir over medium heat for 5 to 8 minutes or until tender. Stir in tomato sauce and chili powder. Cook and stir until bubbly.

❸ Pour mushroom mixture over steak in baking dish. Cover and bake in a 350° oven about 45 minutes or until steak is tender.

TEST KITCHEN TIP: Another time, opt for an Italian-flavored dish by substituting 1 to 1½ teaspoons dried Italian seasoning, crushed, for the chili powder.

Nutrition Facts per serving: 192 cal., 6 g total fat (1 g sat. fat), 64 mg chol., 472 mg sodium, 7 g carbo., 2 g fiber, 28 g pro.

PREP:
20 minutes
BAKE:
45 minutes
OVEN:
350°F
MAKES:
4 to 6 servings

7
carbs per serving

Exchanges:
1 Vegetable
4 Very Lean Meat
½ Fat

GINGER-BEEF STIR-FRY

8 ounces beef top round steak

½ cup reduced-sodium beef broth

3 tablespoons reduced-sodium soy sauce

2½ teaspoons cornstarch

1 teaspoon sugar

½ teaspoon grated fresh ginger

Nonstick cooking spray

12 ounces fresh asparagus, trimmed and cut into 1-inch-long pieces

1½ cups sliced fresh mushrooms

1 cup small broccoli florets

4 green onions, bias-sliced into 1-inch pieces

2 teaspoons cooking oil

2 cups hot cooked brown rice

31
carbs per serving

Exchanges:
2 Vegetable
1½ Starch
2 Very Lean Meat

1 Trim fat from steak. Thinly slice steak across the grain; cut into bite-size strips. Set aside. For sauce, in a small bowl stir together beef broth, soy sauce, cornstarch, sugar, and ginger; set aside.

2 Lightly coat an unheated wok or large nonstick skillet with nonstick cooking spray. Preheat over medium-high heat. Add asparagus, mushrooms, broccoli, and green onions to hot wok or skillet. Cook and stir for 3 to 4 minutes or until vegetables are crisp-tender. Remove vegetables from wok or skillet.

3 Carefully add oil to the hot wok or skillet. Add meat. Stir-fry for 2 to 3 minutes or until meat is slightly pink in center. Push meat from center of wok or skillet. Stir sauce; add to the center of wok or skillet. Cook and stir until thickened and bubbly.

4 Return cooked vegetables to wok or skillet. Stir vegetables and meat together to coat with sauce. Cook and stir about 2 minutes more or until heated through. Serve with hot cooked rice.

Nutrition Facts per serving: 250 cal., 6 g total fat (1 g sat. fat), 32 mg chol., 528 mg sodium, 31 g carbo., 4 g fiber, 20 g pro.

PEPPER OF A STEAK

2 boneless beef top loin steaks, cut 1 inch thick (1 to 1¼ pounds total)
½ teaspoon salt
½ teaspoon cracked black pepper
2 teaspoons olive oil
1 cup red, green, and/or yellow sweet pepper strips
1 clove garlic, minced
1 to 1½ teaspoons snipped fresh oregano or ¼ teaspoon dried oregano, crushed

1 Cut each steak in half. Sprinkle steaks with salt. Press pepper onto steaks.

2 Place steaks on the unheated rack of a broiler pan. Broil 3 to 4 inches from the heat until desired doneness, turning once halfway through broiling time. Allow 12 to 14 minutes for medium-rare doneness (145°F) or 15 to 18 minutes for medium doneness (160°F).

3 Meanwhile, in a large skillet heat oil over medium heat. Add sweet pepper strips and garlic. Cook and stir until tender. Stir in oregano. Spoon sweet pepper mixture over meat.

Nutrition Facts per serving: 189 cal., 8 g total fat (2 g sat. fat), 66 mg chol., 349 mg sodium, 3 g carbo., 1 g fiber, 25 g pro.

PREP:
10 minutes
BROIL:
12 minutes
MAKES:
4 servings

3
carbs per serving

Exchanges:
½ Vegetable
3½ Very Lean Meat
1 Fat

HERBED STEAK WITH BALSAMIC SAUCE

START TO FINISH:
20 minutes
MAKES:
4 servings

2 carbs per serving

Exchanges:
3½ Lean Meat
½ Fat

2	teaspoons dried Italian seasoning, crushed
1	teaspoon garlic powder
1	teaspoon cracked black pepper
¼	teaspoon salt
2	boneless beef top loin steaks, cut ¾ inch thick
1	tablespoon olive oil
½	cup reduced-sodium beef broth
1	tablespoon balsamic vinegar
1	tablespoon butter
2	tablespoons snipped fresh flat-leaf parsley

1 In a small bowl combine Italian seasoning, garlic powder, cracked pepper, and salt. Sprinkle evenly over both sides of each steak; rub in with your fingers.

2 In a heavy large skillet heat oil over medium-low to medium heat. Add steaks; cook until desired doneness, turning once halfway through cooking time. Allow 10 to 13 minutes for medium-rare doneness (145°F) to medium doneness (160°F). Remove steaks from skillet, reserving drippings in the skillet. Keep steaks warm.

3 For sauce, carefully add beef broth and balsamic vinegar to the skillet; stir to scrape up any crusty brown bits from bottom of skillet. Bring to boiling. Boil gently, uncovered, about 4 minutes or until sauce is reduced by half. Remove from heat; stir in butter.

4 Divide sauce among 4 dinner plates. Cut each steak in half. Place a piece of meat on top of sauce on each plate; sprinkle with parsley.

Nutrition Facts per serving: 217 cal., 11 g total fat (4 g sat. fat), 75 mg chol., 281 mg sodium, 2 g carbo., 0 g fiber, 25 g pro.

MEDITERRANEAN BEEF KABOBS

1½   pounds boneless beef top sirloin steak, cut 1½ inches thick

3   green onions, thinly sliced

3   tablespoons olive oil

3   tablespoons lemon juice

2   tablespoons snipped fresh tarragon or 2 teaspoons dried tarragon, crushed

4   cloves garlic, minced

2   teaspoons snipped fresh oregano or ¾ teaspoon dried oregano, crushed

¼   teaspoon black pepper

4   Meyer lemons, halved, or 2 small oranges, quartered

8   baby zucchini

8   miniature yellow sweet peppers

Fresh baby spinach (optional)

1 Trim fat from meat. Cut meat into 1½-inch pieces. Place meat in a resealable plastic bag set in a large bowl.

2 For marinade, in a small bowl combine green onions, olive oil, lemon juice, tarragon, garlic, oregano, and pepper. Pour over meat. Seal bag; turn to coat meat. Marinate in the refrigerator for at least 4 hours or up to 24 hours, turning bag occasionally. If using wooden skewers, soak skewers in water for 30 minutes before grilling.

3 Drain meat, discarding marinade. On eight 8-inch skewers, alternately thread meat, lemon halves, zucchini, and sweet peppers, leaving a ¼-inch space between pieces. Place skewers on the rack of an uncovered grill directly over medium coals. Grill for 12 to 15 minutes or until meat is desired doneness, turning occasionally. If desired, serve over a bed of baby spinach.

TO BROIL: Place skewers on the unheated rack of a broiler pan. Broil 4 to 5 inches from the heat for 12 to 15 minutes or until meat is desired doneness, turning occasionally.

Nutrition Facts per serving: 136 cal., 5 g total fat (1 g sat. fat), 40 mg chol., 49 mg sodium, 4 g carbo., 1 g fiber, 19 g pro.

PREP:
25 minutes
MARINATE:
4 to 24 hours
GRILL:
12 minutes
MAKES:
8 servings

4
carbs per serving

Exchanges:
1 Vegetable
2½ Very Lean Meat
½ Fat

TOP SIRLOIN WITH ONION-MUSHROOM MEDLEY

START TO FINISH:
35 minutes
MAKES:
4 servings

17
carbs per serving

Exchanges:
1½ Vegetable
3½ Very Lean Meat
½ Other Carbo.
½ Fat

2	tablespoons dried tomatoes
	Boiling water
1	cup fresh shiitake mushrooms* (2½ ounces)
¾	cup fresh oyster mushrooms* (1½ ounces)
1¼	cups fresh button mushrooms (3 ounces)
	Nonstick cooking spray
1	large sweet onion (such as Vidalia, Maui, or Walla Walla), halved crosswise and thinly sliced (2 cups)
1	tablespoon balsamic vinegar
¼	teaspoon salt
⅛	teaspoon black pepper
2	boneless beef top sirloin steaks, cut 1 inch thick (1 to 1¼ pounds total)
¼	teaspoon salt
⅛	teaspoon black pepper

1 In a small bowl cover tomatoes with boiling water. Cover and let stand for 5 minutes. Drain and snip tomatoes. Set aside.

2 Remove stems from shiitake and oyster mushrooms; discard stems. Coarsely chop shiitake and oyster mushrooms; slice button mushrooms. Coat an unheated large nonstick skillet with nonstick cooking spray. Preheat over medium-low heat. Add onion to hot skillet. Cover and cook for 10 minutes, stirring occasionally.

3 Add mushrooms to onion in skillet. Cook for 8 to 10 minutes more or until onion is golden brown and most of the liquid is evaporated.

4 Stir in snipped tomatoes, balsamic vinegar, ¼ teaspoon salt, and ⅛ teaspoon pepper; heat through.

5 Meanwhile, cut each steak into 2 portions. Place on the unheated rack of a broiler pan. Sprinkle with ¼ teaspoon salt and ⅛ teaspoon pepper. Broil 3 to 4 inches from heat until desired doneness, turning once halfway through broiling time. Allow 15 to 17 minutes for medium-rare doneness (145°F) or 20 to 22 minutes for medium doneness (160°F). Spoon onion mixture over steaks to serve.

*NOTE: You can use an additional 4 ounces fresh button mushrooms instead of the shiitake and oyster mushrooms.

Nutrition Facts per serving: 223 cal., 6 g total fat (2 g sat. fat), 69 mg chol., 388 mg sodium, 17 g carbo., 3 g fiber, 27 g pro.

SPICY SIRLOIN STEAKS

8	cloves garlic, peeled
¾	teaspoon salt
1	tablespoon chili powder
1	tablespoon five-spice powder
2	teaspoons ground ginger
1	teaspoon black pepper
2	boneless beef top sirloin steaks, cut 1 inch thick (1 to 1¼ pounds total)

1 Chop garlic with salt on a cutting board; press with side of large knife to form a chunky paste. In a small bowl combine garlic paste, chili powder, five-spice powder, ginger, and pepper; set aside.

2 Cut each steak into 2 portions. Sprinkle garlic mixture over both sides of meat; rub in with your fingers. Place meat in a large resealable plastic bag; seal bag. Chill for 2 hours.

3 Place meat on the rack of an uncovered grill directly over medium coals. Grill until desired doneness. Allow 14 to 18 minutes for medium-rare doneness (145°F) or 18 to 22 minutes for medium doneness (160°F), turning once halfway through grilling time.

Nutrition Facts per serving: 166 cal., 5 g total fat (1 g sat. fat), 53 mg chol., 518 mg sodium, 5 g carbo., 1 g fiber, 25 g pro.

PREP:
20 minutes
CHILL:
2 hours
GRILL:
14 minutes
MAKES:
4 servings

5 carbs per serving

Exchanges:
3½ Very Lean Meat
1 Fat

CITRUS GRILLED SIRLOIN STEAK

PREP:
25 minutes
GRILL:
14 minutes
MAKES:
6 servings

8
carbs per
serving

Exchanges:
1½ Vegetable
3 Very Lean Meat
1½ Fat

1	teaspoon finely shredded lemon peel
¼	cup lemon juice
2	tablespoons olive oil
3	cloves garlic, minced
1	teaspoon cracked black pepper
¾	teaspoon salt
3	small yellow or green sweet peppers, quartered
3	small zucchini, sliced lengthwise into 3 planks
1½	pounds boneless beef top sirloin steak, cut 1 to 1¼ inches thick

1 For dressing, in a small bowl combine lemon peel, lemon juice, oil, garlic, pepper, and salt. In a glass baking dish toss 2 tablespoons of the dressing with sweet peppers and zucchini; set aside. Reserve 2 tablespoons of the dressing. Brush steak with some of the remaining dressing.

2 Place steak on the rack of an uncovered grill directly over medium coals. Grill until desired doneness, turning once and brushing with dressing halfway through grilling time. Allow 14 to 18 minutes for medium-rare doneness (145°F) or 18 to 22 minutes for medium doneness (160°F). Discard remainder of dressing used as brush-on.

3 Place vegetables on grill around meat for the last 10 minutes of grilling time. Grill vegetables, turning once.

4 With kitchen shears, cut zucchini into bite-size pieces. In a medium bowl toss vegetables with the reserved 2 tablespoons dressing. Slice steak; serve with vegetables.

Nutrition Facts per serving: 214 cal., 9 g total fat (2 g sat. fat), 54 mg chol., 359 mg sodium, 8 g carbo., 1 g fiber, 26 g pro.

CURRIED BEEF WITH APPLE COUSCOUS

1	pound boneless beef top sirloin steak, cut 1 inch thick
¼	teaspoon salt
⅛	teaspoon black pepper
	Nonstick cooking spray
2	medium red and/or green sweet peppers, seeded and cut into thin bite-size strips
1	medium onion, coarsely chopped
1	tablespoon curry powder
1	cup water
¾	cup apple juice or apple cider
2	teaspoons instant beef bouillon granules
1	cup quick-cooking couscous
1	medium tart green apple (such as Granny Smith), cored and coarsely chopped
⅓	cup chopped peanuts

PREP:
25 minutes
GRILL:
14 minutes
MAKES:
6 servings

36
carbs per serving

Exchanges:
½ Vegetable
½ Fruit
1½ Starch
2½ Lean Meat

1 Trim fat from steak. Lightly sprinkle steak with salt and black pepper.

2 Place steak on the rack of an uncovered grill directly over medium coals. Grill until desired doneness, turning once halfway through grilling time. Allow 14 to 18 minutes for medium-rare doneness (145°F) or 18 to 22 minutes for medium doneness (160°F).

3 Meanwhile, coat an unheated large nonstick skillet with nonstick cooking spray. Preheat over medium heat. Add sweet peppers and onion to hot skillet; cook and stir for 5 minutes. Add curry powder. Cook and stir for 1 minute. Add the water, apple juice, and bouillon granules. Bring to boiling. Stir in couscous and apple; remove from heat. Cover and let stand about 5 minutes or until liquid is absorbed.

4 To serve, fluff couscous mixture with a fork. Thinly slice steak across the grain. Serve steak slices over couscous mixture. Sprinkle with peanuts.

TO BROIL: Place steak on the unheated rack of a broiler pan. Broil 3 to 4 inches from the heat until desired doneness, turning once halfway through broiling time. Allow 15 to 17 minutes for medium-rare doneness (145°F) or 20 to 22 minutes for medium doneness (160°F).

Nutrition Facts per serving: 303 cal., 7 g total fat (2 g sat. fat), 36 mg chol., 422 mg sodium, 36 g carbo., 4 g fiber, 23 g pro.

GRILLED FIVE-SPICE STEAK

PREP:
15 minutes
MARINATE:
4 to 6 hours
GRILL:
14 minutes
MAKES:
6 servings

6   boneless beef top sirloin steaks, cut 1 inch thick (1½ to 2 pounds total)

½   cup reduced-sodium soy sauce

2   tablespoons finely chopped fresh ginger

6   cloves garlic, minced

1   tablespoon cooking oil

1   tablespoon cider vinegar

2   teaspoons five-spice powder

1   teaspoon crushed red pepper

1
carb per serving

1 Trim fat from steaks. Place steaks in a resealable plastic bag set in a deep bowl. In a small bowl combine soy sauce, ginger, garlic, oil, cider vinegar, five-spice powder, and crushed red pepper; pour over steaks. Seal bag; turn to coat steaks. Marinate in the refrigerator for at least 4 hours or up to 6 hours, turning bag occasionally.

2 Drain steaks; discard marinade. Place steaks on the rack of an uncovered grill directly over medium coals. Grill until desired doneness, turning once halfway through grilling time. Allow 14 to 18 minutes for medium-rare doneness (145°F) or 18 to 22 minutes for medium doneness (160°F).

Nutrition Facts per serving: 151 cal., 5 g total fat (1 g sat. fat), 53 mg chol., 153 mg sodium, 1 g carbo., 0 g fiber, 25 g pro.

Exchanges:
4 Very Lean Meat
½ Fat

SIRLOIN WITH MUSTARD & CHIVES

4	boneless beef top sirloin or ribeye steaks, cut about ¾ inch thick (1 to 1¼ pounds total)
1½	teaspoons garlic-pepper seasoning
¼	cup light dairy sour cream
1	tablespoon Dijon-style mustard
2	teaspoons snipped fresh chives

1 Sprinkle both sides of steaks with 1¼ teaspoons of the seasoning. Place steaks on the rack of an uncovered grill directly over medium coals. Grill until desired doneness, turning once halfway through grilling time. Allow 12 to 16 minutes for medium-rare doneness (145°F) or 16 to 20 minutes for medium doneness (160°F). Transfer steaks to a serving platter.

2 Meanwhile, in a small bowl combine sour cream, mustard, chives, and remaining ¼ teaspoon seasoning. Spoon sour cream mixture over steaks.

Nutrition Facts per serving: 164 cal., 5 g total fat (2 g sat. fat), 59 mg chol., 265 mg sodium, 2 g carbo., 0 g fiber, 26 g pro.

PREP:
10 minutes
GRILL:
12 minutes
MAKES:
4 servings

2
carbs per serving

Exchanges:
4 Very Lean Meat
½ Fat

GARLIC & SPICE BRISKET

PREP:
15 minutes
BAKE:
3½ hours
OVEN:
325°F
MAKES:
10 servings

1	3- to 3½-pound fresh beef brisket
¾	cup water
2	tablespoons cider vinegar
1	tablespoon Worcestershire sauce
2	teaspoons celery seeds
1	teaspoon onion salt
1	teaspoon black pepper
3	cloves garlic, minced

1 Place meat in a 13×9×2-inch baking pan. In a small bowl combine the water, vinegar, Worcestershire sauce, celery seeds, onion salt, pepper, and garlic. Pour mixture over meat. Cover with foil.

2 Bake in a 325° oven for 3½ to 4 hours or until tender. Thinly slice meat across the grain to serve. If desired, spoon cooking juices over meat.

Nutrition Facts per serving: 192 cal., 7 g total fat (2 g sat. fat), 78 mg chol., 281 mg sodium, 1 g carbo., 0 g fiber, 29 g pro.

1
carb per
serving

Exchanges:
4 Very Lean Meat
1 Fat

LEMON-SOY MARINATED FLANK STEAK

1   1- to 1¼-pound beef flank steak

2   green onions, sliced

¼   cup water

¼   cup dry red wine

¼   cup reduced-sodium soy sauce

3   tablespoons lemon juice

2   tablespoons cooking oil

2   cloves garlic, minced

½   teaspoon celery seeds

½   teaspoon black pepper

⅛   teaspoon salt

1 Score both sides of steak in a diamond pattern by making shallow diagonal cuts at 1-inch intervals. Place steak in a resealable plastic bag set in a shallow dish. For marinade, in a small bowl combine green onions, the water, wine, soy sauce, lemon juice, oil, garlic, celery seeds, pepper, and salt. Pour over meat. Seal bag; turn to coat meat. Marinate in the refrigerator for at least 6 hours or up to 24 hours, turning bag occasionally.

2 Drain steak, discarding marinade. Place steak on the rack of an uncovered grill directly over medium coals. Grill for 17 to 21 minutes or until medium doneness (160°F), turning once halfway through grilling time. Thinly slice steak diagonally across the grain.

Nutrition Facts per serving: 207 cal., 10 g total fat (4 g sat. fat), 46 mg chol., 281 mg sodium, 1 g carbo., 0 g fiber, 25 g pro.

PREP:
15 minutes
MARINATE:
6 to 24 hours
GRILL:
17 minutes
MAKES:
4 servings

1
carb per serving

Exchanges:
3½ Very Lean Meat
½ Fat

PEPPER STEAK WITH HORSERADISH SAUCE

PREP:
20 minutes
GRILL:
17 minutes
MAKES:
6 servings

2
carbs per
serving

Exchanges:
3½ Very Lean Meat
½ Fat

¼ cup light mayonnaise dressing or salad dressing

1 tablespoon vinegar

2 teaspoons snipped fresh parsley

2 to 3 teaspoons prepared horseradish

1½ pounds beef flank steak or boneless beef top sirloin steak, cut 1 inch thick

2 teaspoons cracked black pepper

1 For sauce, in a small bowl stir together mayonnaise dressing, vinegar, parsley, and horseradish. Set aside.

2 Trim fat from steak. If using flank steak, score both sides of steak in a diamond pattern by making shallow diagonal cuts at 1-inch intervals. Sprinkle both sides of steak with cracked black pepper; gently press into surface.

3 Place steak on the rack of an uncovered grill directly over medium coals. Grill for 17 to 21 minutes or until medium doneness (160°F), turning once halfway through grilling time.

4 To serve, thinly slice steak diagonally across the grain. Serve with sauce.

TO BROIL: Place steak on the unheated rack of a broiler pan 3 to 4 inches from the heat for 15 to 18 minutes or until medium doneness (160°F), turning once halfway through broiling time.

Nutrition Facts per serving: 213 cal., 11 g total fat (4 g sat. fat), 49 mg chol., 126 mg sodium, 2 g carbo., 0 g fiber, 25 g pro.

SPINACH-STUFFED FLANK STEAK

1   1-pound beef flank steak

¼   teaspoon salt

⅛   teaspoon black pepper

½   of a 10-ounce package frozen chopped spinach, thawed and well drained

¼   cup grated Parmesan cheese

2   tablespoons snipped fresh basil or 2 teaspoons dried basil, crushed

PREP:
20 minutes
BROIL:
12 minutes
MAKES:
4 servings

1 Score both sides of steak in a diamond pattern by making shallow diagonal cuts at 1-inch intervals. Place steak between 2 pieces of plastic wrap. Using the flat side of a meat mallet, pound steak into a 12×8-inch rectangle. Remove plastic wrap. Sprinkle steak with salt and pepper.

2 Spread spinach over steak. Sprinkle with Parmesan cheese and basil. Starting from a short side, roll up steak. Secure with wooden toothpicks at 1-inch intervals, starting ½ inch from one end. Cut between the toothpicks to make eight 1-inch-thick slices.

1 carb per serving

3 Place slices, cut sides down, on the unheated rack of a broiler pan. Broil 3 to 4 inches from the heat for 12 to 16 minutes or until medium doneness (160°F). To serve, remove toothpicks.

Nutrition Facts per serving: 207 cal., 9 g total fat (4 g sat. fat), 50 mg chol., 331 mg sodium, 1 g carbo., 1 g fiber, 28 g pro.

Exchanges:
4 Very Lean Meat
1½ Fat

SOUTHWESTERN TRI-TIP ROAST

PREP:
15 minutes
CHILL:
6 to 24 hours
ROAST:
30 minutes
STAND:
15 minutes
OVEN:
425°F
MAKES:
6 to 8 servings

1 carb per serving

Exchanges:
3 Very Lean Meat
1 Fat

1	tablespoon dried chipotle chile peppers, seeded and finely chopped*
1	tablespoon snipped fresh oregano or 1 teaspoon dried oregano, crushed
1	tablespoon olive oil
1	teaspoon ground cumin
½	teaspoon salt
2	cloves garlic, minced
1	1½- to 2-pound boneless beef tri-tip roast (bottom sirloin)

1 For rub, in a small bowl combine chipotle peppers, oregano, oil, cumin, salt, and garlic. Spread evenly over surface of roast; rub in with plastic glove-covered hands. Cover and chill for at least 6 hours or up to 24 hours.

2 Place roast on a rack in a shallow roasting pan. Insert an oven-going meat thermometer in center of roast. Roast in a 425° oven until desired doneness. Allow 30 to 35 minutes for medium-rare doneness (140°F) or 40 to 45 minutes for medium doneness (155°F). Cover with foil and let stand for 15 minutes before carving. The temperature of the meat after standing should be 145°F for medium-rare doneness or 160°F for medium doneness.

*NOTE: Because chile peppers contain volatile oils that can burn your skin and eyes, avoid direct contact with them as much as possible. When working with chile peppers, wear plastic or rubber gloves. If your bare hands do touch the peppers, wash your hands and nails well with soap and warm water.

Nutrition Facts per serving: 156 cal., 7 g total fat (2 g sat. fat), 45 mg chol., 248 mg sodium, 1 g carbo., 0 g fiber, 21 g pro.

SPICED POT ROAST WITH ROOT VEGETABLES

1	3-pound boneless beef chuck pot roast
3½	teaspoons garam masala
¾	teaspoon salt
	Nonstick cooking spray
1	cup reduced-sodium beef broth
¼	cup dry red wine or reduced-sodium beef broth
30	small carrots with tops (about 12 ounces) or 2 cups packaged peeled baby carrots
1	pound round red potatoes, quartered
2	medium parsnips, peeled and cut into ½-inch-thick slices
1	medium rutabaga, peeled and cut into 1-inch pieces
1	red onion, cut into wedges
2	tablespoons cornstarch
2	tablespoons cold water
1	cup plain low-fat yogurt
⅛	teaspoon black pepper

1 Trim fat from roast. For rub, in a small bowl stir together 2½ teaspoons of the garam masala and ½ teaspoon of the salt. Sprinkle evenly over roast; rub in with your fingers. Coat an unheated 4-quart Dutch oven with nonstick cooking spray. Preheat over medium heat. Cook roast in hot Dutch oven until browned, turning to brown evenly on all sides. Drain off fat.

2 Pour the 1 cup beef broth and the wine or additional beef broth over roast. Bring to boiling; reduce heat. Cover and simmer for 1¼ hours.

3 Add carrots, potatoes, parsnips, rutabaga, and red onion to Dutch oven. Return to boiling; reduce heat. Cover and simmer for 25 to 30 minutes or until beef and vegetables are tender. Transfer beef and vegetable mixture to a serving platter, reserving cooking liquid; cover and keep warm.

4 Skim fat from cooking liquid. Strain cooking liquid. Measure 1½ cups of the cooking liquid; return to the Dutch oven. Discard remaining cooking liquid. In a small bowl stir together cornstarch, the cold water, and the remaining 1 teaspoon garam masala. Add to liquid in Dutch oven. Cook and stir over medium heat until thickened and bubbly. Cook and stir for 2 minutes more. Stir in yogurt, the remaining ¼ teaspoon salt, and the pepper; heat through but do not boil. Serve yogurt mixture with meat and vegetables.

Nutrition Facts per serving: 271 cal., 6 g total fat (2 g sat. fat), 82 mg chol., 363 mg sodium, 20 g carbo., 4 g fiber, 32 g pro.

PREP:
30 minutes
COOK:
*1¼ hours +
25 minutes*
MAKES:
10 servings

20
carbs per serving

Exchanges:
1 Vegetable
½ Starch
4 Very Lean Meat
½ Other Carbo.
½ Fat

GRILLED PORK & PEPPER SKEWERS

PREP:
20 minutes
MARINATE:
4 to 6 hours
GRILL:
12 minutes
MAKES:
4 servings

14
carbs per
serving

Exchanges:
1 Vegetable
½ Milk
2½ Lean Meat

12 ounces boneless pork top loin roast

2 medium red sweet peppers, cut into 1-inch squares

1 medium red onion, cut into 1-inch pieces

1 cup plain low-fat yogurt

3 green onions, thinly sliced

2 canned chipotle peppers in adobo sauce, finely chopped*

2 tablespoons snipped fresh parsley

1 tablespoon grated fresh ginger

2 cloves garlic, minced

1 teaspoon sugar

1 teaspoon ground coriander

¼ teaspoon salt

⅛ teaspoon black pepper

Hot cooked brown rice (optional)

❶ Trim fat from roast. Cut roast into 1-inch pieces. In a medium bowl combine meat, sweet peppers, and red onion.

❷ For marinade, in a small bowl stir together yogurt, green onions, chipotle peppers, parsley, ginger, garlic, sugar, coriander, salt, and black pepper. Pour over meat mixture, stirring to coat. Cover and marinate in the refrigerator for at least 4 hours or up to 6 hours, stirring occasionally. If using wooden skewers, soak skewers in water for 30 minutes before grilling.

❸ On eight 6- to 8-inch skewers, alternately thread meat, sweet peppers, and red onion, leaving a ¼-inch space between pieces.

❹ Place skewers on the rack of an uncovered grill directly over medium coals. Grill for 12 to 14 minutes or until meat is slightly pink in the center, turning once halfway through grilling time. If desired, serve kabobs with rice.

*NOTE: Because chile peppers contain volatile oils that can burn your skin and eyes, avoid direct contact with them as much as possible. When working with chile peppers, wear plastic or rubber gloves. If your bare hands do touch the peppers, wash your hands and nails well with soap and warm water.

Nutrition Facts per serving: 184 cal., 3 g total fat (1 g sat. fat), 53 mg chol., 298 mg sodium, 14 g carbo., 2 g fiber, 24 g pro.

CARIBBEAN PORK WITH SWEET POTATOES

4   tablespoons Pickapeppa sauce*

2   cloves garlic, minced

1   teaspoon snipped fresh thyme or ¼ teaspoon dried thyme, crushed

1   2-pound boneless pork loin roast (single loin)

2   large sweet potatoes, peeled and cut into ¾-inch pieces (1 to 1¼ pounds total)

1   recipe Mango-Jicama Salsa

    Fresh cilantro (optional)

PREP:
30 minutes
ROAST:
*45 minutes +
30 minutes*
STAND:
15 minutes
OVEN:
325°F
MAKES:
8 servings

24 carbs per serving

1 In a small bowl combine 3 tablespoons of the Pickapeppa sauce, the garlic, and thyme; set aside.

2 Trim fat from roast. Brush garlic mixture on all sides of roast. Place roast on a rack in a shallow roasting pan. Insert an oven-going meat thermometer into center of roast. Roast in a 325° oven for 45 minutes.

3 Meanwhile, in a medium saucepan cook sweet potatoes in boiling, lightly salted water about 8 minutes or just until tender; drain. Toss sweet potatoes with remaining 1 tablespoon Pickapeppa sauce. Place sweet potatoes around roast in pan. Continue roasting for 30 to 45 minutes more or until internal temperature registers 155°F. Cover meat with foil and let stand on a wire rack for 15 minutes. The temperature of the meat after standing should be 160°F.

4 To serve, slice roast. Serve with sweet potatoes and Mango-Jicama Salsa. If desired, garnish with cilantro.

Exchanges:
½ Fruit
1 Starch
3½ Very Lean Meat
½ Fat

MANGO-JICAMA SALSA: Drain one 8-ounce can pineapple tidbits (juice pack), reserving 2 tablespoons of the juice. In a medium bowl combine pineapple; reserved pineapple juice; 1 cup peeled, chopped jicama; 1 medium mango, peeled, seeded, and chopped; 1 large tomato, seeded and chopped; 1 green onion, sliced; 1 or 2 fresh jalapeño chile peppers, seeded and finely chopped;** 1 tablespoon lime juice; and ⅛ teaspoon salt. Cover and refrigerate until serving time or up to 24 hours.

*NOTE: If you can't find Pickapeppa sauce, substitute 3 tablespoons Worcestershire sauce mixed with a dash of bottled hot pepper sauce.

**NOTE: Because chile peppers contain volatile oils that can burn your skin and eyes, avoid direct contact with them as much as possible. When working with chile peppers, wear plastic or rubber gloves. If your bare hands do touch the peppers, wash your hands and nails well with soap and warm water.

Nutrition Facts per serving: 265 cal., 7 g total fat (2 g sat. fat), 62 mg chol., 151 mg sodium, 24 g carbo., 3 g fiber, 26 g pro.

CHILI-GLAZED PORK ROAST

PREP:
20 minutes
ROAST:
1¼ hours
STAND:
15 minutes
OVEN:
325°F
MAKES:
8 to 10 servings

2
carbs per serving

Exchanges:
3 Very Lean Meat
½ Fat

1   tablespoon packed brown sugar
1   tablespoon snipped fresh thyme or 1 teaspoon dried thyme, crushed
1   teaspoon chili powder
1   teaspoon snipped fresh rosemary or ¼ teaspoon dried rosemary, crushed
⅛   teaspoon cayenne pepper
1   2- to 2½-pound boneless pork top loin roast (single loin)

❶ In a small bowl combine brown sugar, thyme, chili powder, rosemary, and cayenne pepper. Sprinkle brown sugar mixture evenly over roast; rub in with your fingers.

❷ Place roast on a rack in a shallow roasting pan. Insert an oven-going meat thermometer into center of roast. Roast in a 325° oven for 1¼ to 1½ hours or until thermometer registers 155°F. Cover with foil and let stand for 15 minutes before carving. The temperature of the meat after standing should be 160°F.

TO MAKE AHEAD: Prepare as directed through step 1. Cover and chill for up to 24 hours. Continue as directed in step 2.

Nutrition Facts per serving: 134 cal., 4 g total fat (2 g sat. fat), 50 mg chol., 37 mg sodium, 2 g carbo., 0 g fiber, 20 g pro.

ORANGE-RUBBED PORK ROAST

1   2- to 2½-pound boneless pork top loin roast (single loin)
1   tablespoon finely shredded orange peel
1   teaspoon ground coriander
1   teaspoon paprika
½   teaspoon salt
½   teaspoon ground ginger
¼   teaspoon black pepper

1 Trim fat from roast. Rub orange peel onto all sides of roast. In a small bowl stir together coriander, paprika, salt, ginger, and pepper. Sprinkle evenly over roast. Place roast on a rack in a shallow roasting pan. Insert an oven-going meat thermometer into center of roast.

2 Roast in a 325° oven for 1 to 1½ hours or until thermometer registers 155°F. Cover with foil and let stand for 15 minutes before carving. The temperature of the meat after standing should be 160°F.

Nutrition Facts per serving: 171 cal., 6 g total fat (2 g sat. fat), 66 mg chol., 238 mg sodium, 1 g carbo., 0 g fiber, 27 g pro.

PREP:
15 minutes
ROAST:
1 hour
STAND:
15 minutes
OVEN:
325°F
MAKES:
6 to 8 servings

1
carb per serving

Exchanges:
4 Very Lean Meat
½ Fat

PORK TENDERLOIN OVER RED CABBAGE

PREP:
20 minutes
ROAST:
25 minutes
STAND:
10 minutes
OVEN:
425°F
MAKES:
4 servings

23
carbs per
serving

Exchanges:
1 Vegetable
½ Fruit
3 Lean Meat
½ Other Carbo.

1   12-ounce pork tenderloin
    Nonstick cooking spray
1   medium red onion, cut into thin wedges
3   cups shredded red cabbage
⅓   cup white wine vinegar
½   cup white wine vinegar
2   teaspoons packed brown sugar
1   cup reduced-sodium chicken broth
⅓   cup golden raisins
2   teaspoons snipped fresh thyme or ½ teaspoon dried thyme, crushed
1   tablespoon cornstarch
1   tablespoon cold water
¼   cup coarsely chopped nuts, toasted

❶ Place pork tenderloin on a rack in a shallow roasting pan. Sprinkle with salt and black pepper. Insert an oven-going meat thermometer into the center of pork tenderloin. Roast in a 425° oven for 25 to 35 minutes or until thermometer registers 155°F. Remove pork from oven. Cover with foil; let stand for 10 minutes. The temperature of the pork after standing should be 160°F.

❷ Meanwhile, coat an unheated large nonstick skillet with nonstick cooking spray. Preheat over medium heat. Cook onion in hot skillet about 4 minutes or until tender, stirring frequently. Add red cabbage. Cook for 5 minutes, stirring occasionally. Stir in the ⅓ cup vinegar, ¼ teaspoon salt, and ⅛ teaspoon black pepper. Bring to boiling; reduce heat to low. Cover and cook about 10 minutes or until the cabbage is tender, stirring occasionally.

❸ For sauce, in a small saucepan bring the ½ cup vinegar, the brown sugar, ¼ teaspoon salt, and ⅛ teaspoon black pepper to boiling. Boil gently, uncovered, about 6 minutes or until vinegar mixture is reduced by about half. Stir in chicken broth, golden raisins, and thyme. Bring to boiling; reduce heat. In a small bowl combine cornstarch and cold water; add to vinegar mixture. Cook and stir until thickened and bubbly. Cook and stir for 2 minutes more.

❹ To serve, slice pork diagonally into ½-inch-thick slices. Divide cabbage mixture among 4 dinner plates. Top with pork slices and drizzle with sauce. Sprinkle with nuts.

Nutrition Facts per serving: 253 cal., 7 g total fat (1 g sat. fat), 55 mg chol., 561 mg sodium, 23 g carbo., 3 g fiber, 21 g pro.

MUSTARD-ORANGE PORK TENDERLOIN

1   12-ounce pork tenderloin

2   tablespoons apricot preserves or orange marmalade

1   tablespoon Dijon-style mustard

     Nonstick cooking spray

2   cups sliced fresh mushrooms

½   cup sliced green onions

2   tablespoons orange juice

1 Trim fat from pork tenderloin. Place pork tenderloin in a shallow roasting pan. Insert an oven-going meat thermometer into center of pork tenderloin. Roast in a 425° oven for 10 minutes.

2 In a small bowl stir together apricot preserves or orange marmalade and mustard. Spoon 4 teaspoons of the mustard mixture over the pork tenderloin; set remaining mustard mixture aside. Roast for 15 to 20 minutes more or until meat thermometer registers 160°F.

3 Meanwhile, lightly coat an unheated medium saucepan with nonstick cooking spray. Preheat over medium heat. Add mushrooms and green onions to hot saucepan. Cook and stir for 2 to 3 minutes or until mushrooms are tender. Stir in orange juice and remaining mustard mixture. Cook and stir until heated through.

4 To serve, thinly slice meat. Spoon mushroom mixture over meat.

Nutrition Facts per serving: 151 cal., 3 g total fat (1 g sat. fat), 55 mg chol., 131 mg sodium, 11 g carbo., 1 g fiber, 20 g pro.

PREP:
10 minutes
ROAST:
10 minutes +
15 minutes
OVEN:
425°F
MAKES:
4 servings

11
carbs per
serving

Exchanges:
½ Vegetable
3 Very Lean Meat
½ Other Carbo.

MOLASSES-GLAZED PORK TENDERLOIN

START TO FINISH:
30 minutes
MAKES:
4 servings

48
carbs per serving

Exchanges:
2 Starch
3 Very Lean Meat
1 Other Carbo.
1 Fat

1   12-ounce pork tenderloin
2   slices turkey bacon, coarsely chopped
3   cups loose-pack frozen lima beans or Italian green beans
½   cup chopped onion
⅔   cup water
1   tablespoon olive oil
½   cup orange juice
3   tablespoons molasses
1   teaspoon cornstarch
½   teaspoon salt
¼   teaspoon black pepper
    Steamed fresh spinach or turnip greens (optional)
2   tablespoons snipped fresh parsley

1 Trim fat from meat. Cut meat into ½-inch-thick slices; set aside. In a large nonstick skillet cook bacon over medium heat until crisp. Drain bacon, discarding drippings. Set aside. In the same skillet combine frozen lima beans and onion; add the water. Cook according to bean package directions. Drain bean mixture; set aside.

2 In the same skillet heat oil over medium-high heat. Add meat to skillet. Cook for 5 to 7 minutes or until meat is barely pink in center, turning once.

3 Meanwhile, in a small bowl stir together orange juice, molasses, cornstarch, salt, and pepper. Add to meat in skillet. Cook and stir until thickened and bubbly. Cook and stir for 2 minutes more. Stir bean mixture into orange juice mixture; heat through.

4 To serve, if desired, arrange steamed spinach on 4 dinner plates. Spoon the meat mixture over spinach. Sprinkle with the bacon and parsley.

Nutrition Facts per serving: 376 cal., 8 g total fat (2 g sat. fat), 60 mg chol., 492 mg sodium, 48 g carbo., 8 g fiber, 29 g pro.

ADOBO PORK CHOPS

6   boneless pork top loin chops, cut ¾ inch thick
(1½ to 1¾ pounds total)

2   tablespoons packed brown sugar

2   tablespoons snipped fresh cilantro

2   tablespoons olive oil

2   tablespoons orange juice

1   tablespoon red wine vinegar or cider vinegar

2   teaspoons hot chili powder

1   teaspoon ground cumin

1   teaspoon dried oregano, crushed, or 1 tablespoon
snipped fresh oregano

½   teaspoon salt

¼   teaspoon cayenne pepper (optional)

¼   teaspoon ground cinnamon

3   cloves garlic, minced

1 Trim fat from chops. Place chops in a resealable plastic bag set in a shallow dish. For marinade, in a small bowl combine brown sugar, cilantro, oil, orange juice, vinegar, chili powder, cumin, oregano, salt, cayenne pepper (if desired), cinnamon, and garlic. Pour marinade over chops. Seal bag; turn to coat chops. Marinate in the refrigerator for at least 2 hours or up to 24 hours, turning bag occasionally.

2 Drain chops, discarding marinade. Place chops on the rack of an uncovered grill directly over medium coals. Grill for 12 to 15 minutes or until chops are done (160°F), turning once halfway through grilling time.

Nutrition Facts per serving: 189 cal., 7 g total fat (2 g sat. fat), 71 mg chol., 170 mg sodium, 3 g carbo., 0 g fiber, 25 g pro.

PREP:
15 minutes
MARINATE:
2 to 24 hours
GRILL:
12 minutes
MAKES:
6 servings

3
carbs per serving

Exchanges:
4 Very Lean Meat
1 Fat

PORK DIANE

START TO FINISH:
25 minutes
MAKES:
4 servings

1 tablespoon water

1 tablespoon Worcestershire sauce for chicken

1 teaspoon lemon juice

1 teaspoon Dijon-style mustard

4 3-ounce boneless pork top loin chops, cut ¾ to 1 inch thick

½ to 1 teaspoon lemon-pepper seasoning

1 tablespoon butter or margarine

1 tablespoon snipped fresh chives, parsley, or oregano

1 carb per serving

Exchanges:
3 Very Lean Meat
½ Fat

1 For sauce, in a small bowl stir together the water, Worcestershire sauce, lemon juice, and mustard; set aside.

2 Trim fat from chops. Sprinkle both sides of each chop with lemon-pepper seasoning. In a 10-inch skillet melt butter over medium heat. Add chops and cook for 8 to 12 minutes or until pork juices run clear (160°F), turning once halfway through cooking time. Remove from heat. Transfer chops to a serving platter; cover and keep warm.

3 Pour sauce into skillet; stir to scrape up any crusty browned bits from bottom of skillet. Stir chives into sauce. Pour sauce over chops.

Nutrition Facts per serving: 131 cal., 5 g total fat (2 g sat. fat), 55 mg chol., 377 mg sodium, 1 g carbo., 0 g fiber, 19 g pro.

POULTRY

HONEY-GLAZED CHICKEN

PREP:
15 minutes
ROAST:
60 minutes +
15 minutes
OVEN:
375°F
MAKES:
8 servings

13
carbs per
serving

Exchanges:
3½ Medium-Fat Meat
1 Other Carbo.

1	large lemon
¼	cup honey
2	tablespoons packed brown sugar
2	cloves garlic, minced
1	tablespoon grated fresh ginger
1	3½- to 4-pound whole broiler-fryer chicken
½	teaspoon salt
½	teaspoon black pepper

1 Halve lemon; cut one portion into wedges. Squeeze remaining half (should have about 2 tablespoons juice).

2 In a small bowl combine the lemon juice, honey, brown sugar, garlic, and ginger. Loosen skin from the breast of the chicken; spoon 2 tablespoons of the honey mixture under skin. Smooth skin and massage gently to evenly spread the honey mixture. Place lemon wedges in cavity of the chicken. Set remaining honey mixture aside.

3 Skewer neck skin to back of chicken; tie legs to tail. Twist wing tips under back. Place chicken, breast side up, on a rack in a foil-lined shallow roasting pan. Insert an oven-going meat thermometer into center of an inside thigh muscle. Sprinkle with salt and pepper. Roast, uncovered, in a 375° oven for 1 hour.

4 Spoon remaining honey mixture over bird. Return to oven and roast 15 to 45 minutes more or until drumsticks move easily in their sockets and meat thermometer registers 180°F.

Nutrition Facts per serving: 332 cal., 20 g total fat (6 g sat. fat), 101 mg chol., 223 mg sodium, 13 g carbo., 0 g fiber, 25 g pro.

SPICY BARBECUED CHICKEN

$\frac{1}{2}$	cup cider vinegar
2	tablespoons spicy brown mustard
1	tablespoon Worcestershire sauce or Worcestershire sauce for chicken
1	teaspoon paprika
$\frac{1}{2}$	teaspoon black pepper
$\frac{1}{4}$	teaspoon bottled hot pepper sauce
$\frac{1}{8}$	teaspoon celery seeds
$\frac{1}{8}$	teaspoon salt
$2\frac{1}{2}$	pounds meaty chicken pieces (breast halves, thighs, and drumsticks), skinned
$\frac{1}{4}$	teaspoon salt
$\frac{1}{4}$	teaspoon black pepper

1 For sauce, in a small saucepan combine vinegar, mustard, Worcestershire sauce, paprika, the $\frac{1}{2}$ teaspoon black pepper, the hot pepper sauce, celery seeds, and the $\frac{1}{8}$ teaspoon salt. Bring to boiling; reduce heat. Simmer, uncovered, for 5 minutes, stirring occasionally.

2 Sprinkle chicken with the $\frac{1}{4}$ teaspoon salt and the $\frac{1}{4}$ teaspoon black pepper. Brush chicken pieces with sauce. Place chicken pieces, bone sides up, on an uncovered grill directly over medium coals. Grill for 35 to 45 minutes or until no longer pink (170°F for breasts; 180°F for thighs and drumsticks), turning and brushing with remaining sauce halfway through grilling time. Discard any remaining sauce.

TO BROIL: Place chicken pieces, bone sides up, on the unheated rack of a broiler pan. Brush with sauce. Broil 4 to 5 inches from the heat about 20 minutes or until lightly browned. Turn chicken pieces over and brush with remaining sauce. Broil for 5 to 15 minutes more or until chicken is no longer pink (170°F).

Nutrition Facts per serving: 172 cal., 6 g total fat (2 g sat. fat), 77 mg chol., 317 mg sodium, 2 g carbo., 0 g fiber, 25 g pro.

PREP:
25 minutes
GRILL:
35 minutes
MAKES:
6 servings

2

carbs per serving

Exchanges:
3½ Very Lean Meat
1 Fat

PEPPER-LIME CHICKEN

PREP:
10 minutes
BROIL:
20 minutes +
5 minutes
MAKES:
6 servings

2
carbs per
serving

Exchanges:
3½ Very Lean Meat
1½ Fat

2½ pounds meaty chicken pieces (breast halves, thighs, and drumsticks), skinned

1 teaspoon finely shredded lime peel

¼ cup lime juice

1 tablespoon olive oil or cooking oil

1 teaspoon dried thyme or basil, crushed, or 1 tablespoon snipped fresh thyme or basil

2 cloves garlic, minced

½ to 1 teaspoon black pepper

¼ teaspoon salt

❶ Place chicken, bone sides up, on the unheated rack of a broiler pan. Broil 4 to 5 inches from the heat for 20 minutes.

❷ Meanwhile, for glaze, in a small bowl stir together lime peel, lime juice, oil, thyme or basil, garlic, pepper, and salt.

❸ Brush chicken with glaze. Turn chicken; brush with more glaze. Broil for 5 to 15 minutes more or until chicken is tender and no longer pink (170°F for breasts; 180°F for thighs and drumsticks), brushing with the remaining glaze during the last 5 minutes of broiling time.

Nutrition Facts per serving: 188 cal., 8 g total fat (2 g sat. fat), 77 mg chol., 167 mg sodium, 2 g carbo., 0 g fiber, 25 g pro.

LEMON CHICKEN WITH GARLIC & ROSEMARY

1   tablespoon snipped fresh rosemary or 1 teaspoon dried rosemary, crushed

1   teaspoon salt

1   teaspoon coarsely ground black pepper

2½   pounds meaty chicken pieces (breast halves, thighs, and drumsticks), skinned

1   tablespoon olive oil

1   teaspoon finely shredded lemon peel

1   tablespoon lemon juice

2   cloves garlic, minced

1 In a small bowl combine rosemary, salt, and pepper. Sprinkle rosemary mixture evenly over chicken pieces; rub in with your fingers. Place chicken pieces, bone sides up, in a lightly greased 13×9×2-inch baking pan.

2 In a small bowl combine oil, lemon peel, lemon juice, and garlic; drizzle over chicken.

3 Bake in a 425° oven for 20 minutes. Turn chicken pieces bone sides down; spoon pan juices over chicken. Bake 15 to 20 minutes more or until chicken is no longer pink (170°F for breasts; 180°F for thighs and drumsticks).

Nutrition Facts per serving: 184 cal., 8 g total fat (2 g sat. fat), 77 mg chol., 457 mg sodium, 1 g carbo., 0 g fiber, 25 g pro.

PREP:
15 minutes
BAKE:
20 minutes +
15 minutes
OVEN:
425°F
MAKES:
6 servings

1 carb per serving

Exchanges:
3½ Very Lean Meat
1½ Fat

HERBED MUSTARD CHICKEN

PREP:
15 minutes
GRILL:
50 minutes
MAKES:
8 servings

1	tablespoon snipped fresh parsley
1	tablespoon water
1	tablespoon light mayonnaise dressing or salad dressing
1	tablespoon Dijon-style mustard
1	teaspoon dried oregano, crushed, or 1 tablespoon snipped fresh oregano
⅛	teaspoon cayenne pepper
3	pounds meaty chicken pieces (breast halves, thighs, and drumsticks), skinned
¼	teaspoon salt
¼	teaspoon black pepper

1
carb per
serving

1 For sauce, in a small bowl combine parsley, the water, mayonnaise dressing, mustard, oregano, and cayenne pepper. Cover and refrigerate until ready to use. Sprinkle chicken with salt and black pepper.

2 Arrange medium-hot coals around a drip pan. Test for medium heat above pan. Place chicken pieces, bone sides down, on grill rack over drip pan. Cover and grill for 50 to 60 minutes or until chicken is no longer pink (170°F for breasts; 180°F for thighs and drumsticks), brushing occasionally with sauce during the last 10 minutes of grilling time.

Nutrition Facts per serving: 153 cal., 6 g total fat (2 g sat. fat), 70 mg chol., 192 mg sodium, 1 g carbo., 0 g fiber, 23 g pro.

Exchanges:
3½ Very Lean Meat
½ Fat

CITRUS CHICKEN WITH HERBS & SPICES

1 teaspoon coriander seeds

1 teaspoon fennel seeds

2½ pounds meaty chicken pieces (breast halves, thighs, and drumsticks), skinned

½ cup orange juice

¼ cup thinly sliced green onions

3 tablespoons honey

1 tablespoon snipped fresh thyme or 1 teaspoon dried thyme, crushed

1 tablespoon snipped fresh sage or 1 teaspoon dried sage, crushed

1 tablespoon snipped fresh rosemary or 1 teaspoon dried rosemary, crushed

½ teaspoon salt

½ teaspoon cracked black pepper

1 In a small skillet cook coriander seeds and fennel seeds over medium heat about 5 minutes or until seeds are fragrant and toasted, stirring constantly. Remove from heat; let cool. Crush spices with a mortar and pestle.

2 Place chicken in a resealable plastic bag set in a shallow dish. For marinade, in a small bowl combine orange juice, green onions, honey, thyme, sage, rosemary, salt, and pepper. Stir in crushed spices. Pour over chicken; seal bag. Marinate in the refrigerator for at least 4 hours or up to 8 hours, turning bag occasionally.

3 Drain chicken, discarding marinade. Arrange medium-hot coals around a drip pan. Test for medium heat above the pan. Place chicken pieces, bone sides up, on grill rack over drip pan. Cover and grill for 50 to 60 minutes or until chicken is no longer pink (170°F for breasts; 180°F for thighs and drumsticks), turning once halfway through grilling time.

Nutrition Facts per serving: 206 cal., 6 g total fat (2 g sat. fat), 77 mg chol., 265 mg sodium, 12 g carbo., 1 g fiber, 25 g pro.

PREP:
25 minutes
MARINATE:
4 to 8 hours
GRILL:
50 minutes
MAKES:
6 servings

12
carbs per serving

Exchanges:
3½ Very Lean Meat
1 Other Carbo.
½ Fat

CHICKEN IN SHIITAKE MUSHROOM SAUCE

PREP:
20 minutes
COOK:
40 minutes
MAKES:
8 servings

10
carbs per
serving

Exchanges:
1 Vegetable
3 Very Lean Meat
½ Other Carbo.
1 Fat

3 pounds meaty chicken pieces (breast halves, thighs, and drumsticks), skinned

½ teaspoon salt

¼ teaspoon black pepper

Nonstick cooking spray

8 ounces pearl onions

4 medium carrots, cut into 1-inch-long pieces

¼ cup dry vermouth or reduced-sodium chicken broth

1 14-ounce can reduced-sodium chicken broth

3 tablespoons snipped fresh parsley

1 tablespoon snipped fresh thyme or 1 teaspoon dried thyme, crushed

1 tablespoon snipped fresh rosemary or 1 teaspoon dried rosemary, crushed

8 ounces fresh shiitake or button mushrooms, halved

Fresh rosemary (optional)

1 Sprinkle chicken with salt and pepper. Coat an unheated 12-inch nonstick skillet with nonstick cooking spray. Preheat over medium heat. Cook chicken in hot skillet about 10 minutes or until chicken is golden brown, turning to brown evenly. Remove chicken.

2 Add pearl onions and carrots to skillet. Cook about 5 minutes or until onions are golden brown, stirring occasionally. Add vermouth or chicken broth, scraping up any crusty browned bits from bottom of skillet. Return chicken to skillet. Pour broth over chicken; sprinkle with parsley, thyme, and rosemary.

3 Bring to boiling; reduce heat. Cover and simmer about 40 minutes or until chicken is no longer pink (170°F for breasts; 180°F for thighs and drumsticks), adding mushrooms for the last 10 minutes of cooking. If desired, garnish with fresh rosemary.

Nutrition Facts per serving: 195 cal., 6 g total fat (2 g sat. fat), 69 mg chol., 350 mg sodium, 10 g carbo., 2 g fiber, 24 g pro.

BASQUE CHICKEN

2   tablespoons all-purpose flour

4   skinless, boneless chicken breast halves (1 to 1½ pounds total)
      Nonstick cooking spray

2   large green and/or yellow sweet peppers, cut into bite-size strips

1   large onion, halved lengthwise and thinly sliced

3   cloves garlic, minced

1   teaspoon paprika

⅛   teaspoon cayenne pepper

1   14½-ounce can diced tomatoes, undrained

¼   cup reduced-sodium chicken broth

¼   cup sliced pitted ripe olives

1   tablespoon snipped fresh oregano

2   cups hot cooked bulgur or barley pilaf (optional)

1 Place flour in a shallow dish. Dip chicken in flour to coat. Coat an unheated large nonstick skillet with nonstick cooking spray. Preheat over medium heat. Add chicken to hot skillet. Cook about 4 minutes or until chicken is brown, turning once. Remove chicken.

2 Add sweet peppers, onion, and garlic to hot skillet. Cook and stir for 3 to 4 minutes or until vegetables are nearly tender. Add paprika and cayenne pepper. Cook and stir for 1 minute more.

3 Stir in tomatoes, chicken broth, and olives. Bring to boiling. Return chicken to skillet, spooning tomato mixture over chicken. Reduce heat. Cover and simmer about 10 minutes or until chicken is tender and no longer pink.

4 Transfer chicken to a serving platter. Stir oregano into tomato mixture. Spoon the tomato mixture over chicken. If desired, serve with bulgur or barley pilaf.

Nutrition Facts per serving: 215 cal., 3 g total fat (1 g sat. fat), 66 mg chol., 344 mg sodium, 17 g carbo., 3 g fiber, 29 g pro.

PREP:
25 minutes
COOK:
10 minutes
MAKES:
4 servings

17
carbs per serving

Exchanges:
2 Vegetable
3½ Very Lean Meat
½ Other Carbo.
½ Fat

CHICKEN WITH CHUNKY VEGETABLE SAUCE

START TO FINISH:
40 minutes
MAKES:
4 servings

40
carbs per
serving

Exchanges:
1½ Vegetable
2 Starch
3½ Very Lean Meat

2   tablespoons all-purpose flour

4   skinless, boneless chicken breast halves (1 to 1½ pounds total)
    Nonstick cooking spray

1   cup finely chopped onion

2   cloves garlic, minced

1   14½-ounce can diced tomatoes, undrained

1   14-ounce can artichoke hearts, drained and halved

⅓   cup reduced-sodium chicken broth

1   tablespoon snipped fresh oregano or 1 teaspoon dried oregano, crushed

    Dash black pepper

2   teaspoons drained capers or 2 tablespoons chopped pitted ripe olives

2   cups hot cooked brown rice

1 Place flour in a shallow dish. Dip chicken in flour to coat. Set aside.

2 Coat an unheated large nonstick skillet with nonstick cooking spray. Preheat skillet over medium heat. Add onion to hot skillet. Cook and stir for 3 minutes. Stir in garlic; push onion mixture to side of skillet. Add chicken. Cook about 4 minutes or until chicken is brown, turning once halfway through cooking time. Add undrained tomatoes, artichoke hearts, chicken broth, dried oregano (if using), and pepper; stir just to combine.

3 Bring to boiling; reduce heat. Cover and simmer about 10 minutes or until chicken is tender and no longer pink. Remove chicken; cover and keep warm.

4 Simmer tomato mixture, uncovered, about 3 minutes or until reduced to desired consistency. Stir in capers or olives and, if using, fresh oregano. Serve chicken over hot cooked rice. Top with the tomato mixture.

Nutrition Facts per serving: 319 cal., 2 g total fat (1 g sat. fat), 66 mg chol., 639 mg sodium, 40 g carbo., 6 g fiber, 32 g pro.

ORANGE-SAUCED CHICKEN

4   skinless, boneless chicken breast halves (1 to 1½ pounds total)

¼   teaspoon salt

       Nonstick cooking spray

2   medium oranges

2   tablespoons orange marmalade

¼   teaspoon ground ginger

⅛   teaspoon crushed red pepper (optional)

START TO FINISH:
20 minutes
MAKES:
4 servings

❶ Sprinkle chicken with salt. Coat an unheated large nonstick skillet with nonstick cooking spray. Preheat skillet over medium heat. Add chicken to hot skillet; cook for 8 to 10 minutes or until chicken is no longer pink (170°F), turning once.

❷ Meanwhile, finely shred enough of the orange peel to measure ½ teaspoon; set aside. Peel oranges. Cut oranges in half lengthwise; cut crosswise into slices. In a small bowl combine orange peel and orange slices. Add orange marmalade, ginger, and, if desired, crushed red pepper; toss gently to coat.

❸ Remove cooked chicken from skillet; cover and keep warm. Reduce heat to low. Add orange mixture to the skillet. Cook and stir for 30 to 60 seconds or until marmalade is melted and mixture is heated through. Serve the orange mixture over chicken.

Nutrition Facts per serving: 167 cal., 2 g total fat (0 g sat. fat), 66 mg chol., 213 mg sodium, 10 g carbo., 1 g fiber, 27 g pro.

10 carbs per serving

Exchanges:
½ Fruit
4 Very Lean Meat

PEPPER & PEACH FAJITA CHICKEN

START TO FINISH:
30 minutes
MAKES:
4 servings

6
carbs per serving

Exchanges:
1 Vegetable
3½ Very Lean Meat

4   skinless, boneless chicken breast halves (1 to 1½ pounds total)
1½   teaspoons fajita seasoning
    Nonstick cooking spray
2   medium red and/or green sweet peppers, cut into thin bite-size strips
1   medium fresh peach or nectarine, halved, pitted, and cut into thin slices, or 1 cup frozen unsweetened sliced peaches, thawed

❶ Sprinkle both sides of chicken breast halves with the fajita seasoning. Coat an unheated large nonstick skillet with nonstick cooking spray. Preheat skillet over medium heat. Cook chicken in hot skillet for 12 to 15 minutes or until chicken is no longer pink (170°F), turning once halfway through cooking time. Transfer chicken to a serving platter; keep warm.

❷ Add sweet pepper strips to hot skillet. Cook and stir about 3 minutes or until crisp-tender. Gently stir in peach slices. Cook for 1 to 2 minutes more or until heated through. Spoon pepper strips and peaches over chicken.

Nutrition Facts per serving: 156 cal., 2 g total fat (0 g sat. fat), 66 mg chol., 138 mg sodium, 6 g carbo., 2 g fiber, 27 g pro.

TORTILLA-CRUSTED CHICKEN

Nonstick cooking spray

1 cup finely crushed tortilla chips

½ teaspoon dried oregano, crushed

¼ teaspoon ground cumin

¼ teaspoon black pepper

1 egg or ¼ cup refrigerated or frozen egg product, thawed

4 skinless, boneless chicken breast halves (1 to 1½ pounds total)

Purchased salsa (optional)

1 Coat a 15×10×1-inch baking pan with nonstick cooking spray; set aside. In a shallow dish combine tortilla chips, oregano, cumin, and pepper. In another shallow dish beat egg lightly with a fork. Dip chicken in egg, then coat with tortilla chip mixture.

2 Arrange chicken in the prepared baking pan. Bake in a 375° oven about 25 minutes or until chicken is no longer pink (170°F). If desired, serve the chicken with salsa.

Nutrition Facts per serving: 198 cal., 5 g total fat (1 g sat. fat), 119 mg chol., 133 mg sodium, 7 g carbo., 1 g fiber, 29 g pro.

PREP:
10 minutes
BAKE:
25 minutes
OVEN:
375°F
MAKES:
4 servings

7
carbs per serving

Exchanges:
½ Starch
4 Very Lean Meat
½ Fat

CREAMY CHICKEN ENCHILADAS

PREP:
45 minutes
BAKE:
20 minutes +
20 minutes
STAND:
5 minutes
OVEN:
350°F
MAKES:
6 servings

23

carbs per serving

Exchanges:
1 Vegetable
1 Starch
2 Very Lean Meat
1½ Fat

8	ounces skinless, boneless chicken breast halves
⅔	cup reduced-sodium chicken broth
¼	teaspoon black pepper
4	cups torn fresh spinach
2	tablespoons thinly sliced green onion
1¼	cups light dairy sour cream
2	tablespoons all-purpose flour
½	teaspoon salt
½	teaspoon ground cumin
½	cup fat-free milk
1	4-ounce can diced green chile peppers, drained
	Nonstick cooking spray
6	7-inch flour tortillas
½	cup shredded reduced-fat cheddar or Monterey Jack cheese (2 ounces)
	Chopped tomato or purchased salsa (optional)
	Thinly sliced green onions or snipped fresh cilantro (optional)

1 In a large skillet combine chicken, chicken broth, and black pepper. Bring to boiling; reduce heat. Cover and simmer for 12 to 14 minutes or until chicken is no longer pink. Drain well; cool slightly. When cool enough to handle, use 2 forks to shred chicken into bite-size pieces. (You should have about 1½ cups shredded chicken.) Set aside.

2 Place spinach in a steamer basket over boiling water. Reduce heat. Cover and steam for 3 to 5 minutes or until tender. Drain well.

3 For filling, in a large bowl combine shredded chicken, spinach, and the 2 tablespoons green onion; set aside. For sauce, in a small bowl combine sour cream, flour, salt, and cumin. Stir in milk and chile peppers. Stir half (about 1 cup) of the sauce into the chicken mixture; set remaining sauce aside.

4 Coat a 2-quart rectangular baking dish with nonstick cooking spray. Divide the filling among the tortillas. Roll up tortillas. Place tortillas, seam sides down, in the prepared dish. Spoon remaining sauce on top of tortillas.

5 Cover and bake in a 350° oven for 20 minutes. Uncover and bake about 20 minutes more or until heated through. Sprinkle with cheese; let stand for 5 minutes. If desired, garnish with chopped tomato or salsa and additional green onions or cilantro.

Nutrition Facts per serving: 251 cal., 9 g total fat (4 g sat. fat), 46 mg chol., 571 mg sodium, 23 g carbo., 1 g fiber, 18 g pro.

**DEVILED EGGS
WITH CURRIED CRAB**
Recipe on page 19

HONEY·MUSTARD SNACK MIX
Recipe on page 32

SPICY BROCCOLI SPREAD
Recipe on page 41

MAPLE·GLAZED PEARS & CEREAL
Recipe on page 49

BLUEBERRY BLINTZES
Recipe on page 56

**CURRIED BEEF
WITH APPLE COUSCOUS**
Recipe on page 81

**CARIBBEAN PORK
WITH SWEET POTATOES**
Recipe on page 91

PORK DIANE
Recipe on page 98

CREAMY CHICKEN ENCHILADAS
Recipe on page 112

BANGKOK STIR-FRY
Recipe on page 129

LAMB & PEPPERS
Recipe on page 156

**GRILLED BASS
WITH STRAWBERRY SALSA**
Recipe on page 169

**BAKED ORANGE ROUGHY
WITH CITRUS SALSA**
Recipe on page 170

SOY-LIME SCALLOPS WITH LEEKS
Recipe on page 179

SPICY JALAPEÑO·SHRIMP PASTA
Recipe on page 183

KALE, LENTIL & CHICKEN SOUP
Recipe on page 196

BANGKOK STIR-FRY

2 tablespoons fish sauce (nam pla)

1 tablespoon lime juice

2 teaspoons minced fresh lemongrass or 1 teaspoon finely shredded lemon peel

Nonstick cooking spray

1 medium red onion, halved lengthwise and sliced

3 cloves garlic, minced

1 small cucumber, cut into thin bite-size strips (about 1 cup)

¼ of a pineapple, peeled, cored, and cut into bite-size pieces

1 or 2 fresh jalapeño chile peppers, seeded and finely chopped*

12 ounces skinless, boneless chicken breast halves, cut into thin bite-size strips

1 cup sugar snap pea pods, trimmed

3 cups hot cooked brown, jasmine, or basmati rice

Snipped fresh cilantro or parsley (optional)

1 For sauce, in a small bowl stir together fish sauce, lime juice, and lemongrass or lemon peel; set aside.

2 Coat an unheated large nonstick wok or 12-inch nonstick skillet with nonstick cooking spray. Preheat wok or skillet over medium-high heat. Add red onion and garlic to hot wok or skillet; cook and stir for 2 minutes. Add cucumber, pineapple, and chile peppers. Cook and stir for 2 minutes more. Remove from wok or skillet.

3 Add chicken to hot wok or skillet. Cook and stir for 2 to 3 minutes or until chicken is tender and no longer pink. Return onion mixture to wok or skillet; add pea pods. Add sauce. Cook and stir about 1 minute or until heated through. Serve immediately over hot cooked rice. If desired, sprinkle with snipped cilantro or parsley.

*NOTE: Because chile peppers contain volatile oils that can burn your skin and eyes, avoid direct contact with them as much as possible. When working with chile peppers, wear plastic or rubber gloves. If your bare hands do touch the peppers, wash your hands and nails well with soap and warm water.

Nutrition Facts per serving: 327 cal., 3 g total fat (1 g sat. fat), 49 mg chol., 541 mg sodium, 49 g carbo., 5 g fiber, 26 g pro.

START TO FINISH:
25 minutes
MAKES:
4 servings

49
carbs per serving

Exchanges:
1 Vegetable
½ Fruit
2½ Starch
2½ Very Lean Meat

ORANGE-GINGER CHICKEN

PREP:
15 minutes
MARINATE:
2 to 6 hours
BAKE:
20 minutes
OVEN:
375°F
MAKES:
4 servings

31 carbs per serving

Exchanges:
1½ Starch
3½ Very Lean Meat
½ Other Carbo.
½ Fat

4	skinless, boneless chicken breast halves (1 to 1½ pounds total)
4	green onions, finely chopped
½	cup orange juice
1	tablespoon packed brown sugar
1	tablespoon finely chopped fresh ginger
1	tablespoon olive oil
2	cloves garlic, minced
1	teaspoon ground coriander
½	teaspoon paprika
¼	teaspoon salt
¼	teaspoon ground cinnamon
¼	teaspoon black pepper
	Nonstick cooking spray
2	cups hot cooked brown or basmati rice

1 Place chicken in a resealable plastic bag set in a shallow dish. For marinade, in a small bowl combine green onions, orange juice, brown sugar, ginger, oil, garlic, coriander, paprika, salt, cinnamon, and pepper. Pour over chicken. Seal bag; turn to coat chicken. Marinate in the refrigerator for at least 2 hours or up to 6 hours, turning bag occasionally. Drain chicken, reserving marinade.

2 Lightly coat a 2-quart rectangular baking dish with nonstick cooking spray. Arrange chicken in the prepared baking dish; pour marinade over chicken.

3 Bake, uncovered, in a 375° oven about 20 minutes or until chicken is tender and no longer pink. Transfer chicken to a serving platter. Strain the juices remaining in baking dish; stir juices into rice. Serve the chicken with rice.

Nutrition Facts per serving: 305 cal., 6 g total fat (1 g sat. fat), 66 mg chol., 217 mg sodium, 31 g carbo., 2 g fiber, 30 g pro.

CHICKEN PAELLA

Nonstick cooking spray

1   cup chopped onion

1   large red sweet pepper, cut into thin strips

12   ounces skinless, boneless chicken breast halves, cut into bite-size strips

1   clove garlic, minced

½   teaspoon paprika

¼   teaspoon ground turmeric

1¾   cups instant brown rice

1   14-ounce can reduced-sodium chicken broth

¼   cup water

¼   teaspoon salt

¼   teaspoon black pepper

2   medium tomatoes, seeded and chopped

1   cup loose-pack frozen peas

1 Coat an unheated large nonstick skillet with nonstick cooking spray. Preheat skillet over medium heat. Add onion and sweet pepper to hot skillet. Cook and stir about 4 minutes or until onion is tender.

2 Add chicken, garlic, paprika, and turmeric to skillet. Cook and stir until chicken is brown. Stir in uncooked rice, chicken broth, the water, salt, and black pepper.

3 Bring to boiling; reduce heat. Cover and simmer for 10 minutes. Remove from heat. Stir in tomatoes and peas. Cover and let stand for 5 minutes before serving.

Nutrition Facts per serving: 275 cal., 3 g total fat (0 g sat. fat), 49 mg chol., 478 mg sodium, 37 g carbo., 5 g fiber, 26 g pro.

PREP:
20 minutes
COOK:
10 minutes
STAND:
5 minutes
MAKES:
4 servings

37
carbs per serving

Exchanges:
1 Vegetable
2 Starch
2½ Very Lean Meat

ASIAN PRIMAVERA STIR-FRY

START TO FINISH:
35 minutes
MAKES:
4 servings

39
carbs per serving

Exchanges:
1 Vegetable
2 Starch
2½ Very Lean Meat

1	ounce dried shiitake mushrooms (1½ cups)
1	cup warm water
1	tablespoon cornstarch
4	ounces dried whole wheat fettuccine or linguine
12	ounces skinless, boneless chicken breast halves, cut into 1-inch pieces
2	tablespoons dry sherry
2	tablespoons reduced-sodium soy sauce
1	tablespoon grated fresh ginger
2	cloves garlic, minced
	Nonstick cooking spray
1	cup fresh sugar snap peas, strings and tips removed
1	cup carrots cut into thin bite-size strips
4	green onions, bias-sliced into 1-inch pieces

1 In a small bowl combine dried mushrooms and the warm water; let stand for 15 minutes. Drain mushrooms, reserving liquid. Squeeze mushrooms to remove excess liquid. Discard stems. Slice mushroom caps; set aside. For sauce, stir cornstarch into reserved mushroom liquid; set aside.

2 Meanwhile, cook pasta according to package directions, except omit any oil or salt. Drain. Return pasta to hot saucepan; cover and keep warm.

3 In a medium bowl stir together chicken, sherry, soy sauce, ginger, and garlic; set aside.

4 Coat an unheated large wok or large nonstick skillet with nonstick cooking spray. Preheat over medium-high heat. Add sugar snap peas and carrots to hot wok or skillet; cook and stir for 3 to 4 minutes or until crisp-tender. Add green onions; cook and stir for 1 minute more. Remove vegetables from wok or skillet.

5 Add chicken mixture to hot wok or skillet. Cook and stir for 3 to 4 minutes or until chicken is no longer pink. Push chicken from center of wok or skillet. Stir sauce; add to center of wok or skillet. Cook and stir until thickened and bubbly.

6 Return cooked vegetables to wok or skillet. Add mushrooms and cooked pasta. Stir all ingredients together to coat with sauce. Cook and stir about 1 minute more or until heated through. Serve immediately.

Nutrition Facts per serving: 285 cal., 2 g total fat (0 g sat. fat), 49 mg chol., 367 mg sodium, 39 g carbo., 3 g fiber, 27 g pro.

CILANTRO CHICKEN WITH PEANUTS

Nonstick cooking spray

1   pound skinless, boneless chicken breast halves, cut into 1-inch pieces

4   teaspoons reduced-sodium soy sauce

2   teaspoons rice vinegar

1   teaspoon toasted sesame oil

⅛   teaspoon crushed red pepper

1½   cups fresh cilantro leaves

4   cups finely shredded napa cabbage

¼   cup dry-roasted peanuts, coarsely chopped

1 Coat an unheated large nonstick skillet with nonstick cooking spray. Preheat over medium heat. Add chicken to skillet. Cook and stir for 3 to 4 minutes or until chicken is no longer pink.

2 Add soy sauce, rice vinegar, sesame oil, and crushed red pepper. Cook and stir for 1 minute more. Remove from heat. Stir in cilantro.

3 Spoon chicken mixture over cabbage and sprinkle with peanuts. Serve immediately.

Nutrition Facts per serving: 216 cal., 8 g total fat (1 g sat. fat), 66 mg chol., 350 mg sodium, 6 g carbo., 2 g fiber, 30 g pro.

START TO FINISH:
25 minutes
MAKES:
4 servings

6
carbs per serving

Exchanges:
1 Vegetable
4 Very Lean Meat
1 Fat

GRILLED PLUM CHICKEN KABOBS

PREP:
20 minutes
GRILL:
8 minutes
MAKES:
4 servings

1	pound skinless, boneless chicken breast halves, cut into 1-inch pieces
1½	teaspoons Jamaican jerk seasoning
1	cup fresh sugar snap peas or pea pods, strings and tips removed
1	cup fresh pineapple cubes
1	medium red sweet pepper, cut into 1-inch pieces
¼	cup plum preserves or jam

23 carbs per serving

❶ Sprinkle chicken with about half of the jerk seasoning; toss gently to coat. Cut any large snap peas in half crosswise. If using wooden skewers, soak skewers in water for 30 minutes before grilling.

❷ On 4 long or 8 short skewers, alternately thread chicken, sugar snap peas, pineapple, and sweet pepper, leaving a ¼-inch space between pieces. For sauce, in a small saucepan stir the remaining jerk seasoning into plum preserves. Cook and stir just until melted; set aside.

❸ Place skewers on the rack of an uncovered grill directly over medium coals. Grill for 8 to 12 minutes or until chicken is no longer pink and vegetables are tender, turning once and brushing occasionally with sauce during the last 3 minutes of grilling time.

TO BROIL: Place kabobs on the unheated rack of a broiler pan. Broil 4 to 5 inches from the heat for 8 to 12 minutes, turning once and brushing occasionally with sauce during the last 5 minutes of broiling time.

Nutrition Facts per serving: 221 cal., 2 g total fat (1 g sat. fat), 66 mg chol., 185 mg sodium, 23 g carbo., 2 g fiber, 27 g pro.

Exchanges:
½ Vegetable
½ Fruit
3½ Lean Meat
1 Other Carbo.

SPICED CHICKEN KABOBS

1   pound skinless, boneless chicken breast halves, cut into 1-inch pieces

2   tablespoons finely snipped fresh cilantro

1   tablespoon grated fresh ginger

2   cloves garlic, minced

1   fresh serrano chile pepper, seeded and finely chopped*

1   teaspoon cooking oil

½   teaspoon ground coriander

½   teaspoon ground cumin

¼   teaspoon salt

¼   teaspoon garam masala (optional)

⅛   teaspoon ground nutmeg

1   cup fresh pineapple cubes

½   of a medium red sweet pepper, cut into 1-inch pieces

½   of a medium green sweet pepper, cut into 1-inch pieces

PREP:
25 minutes
CHILL:
2 to 6 hours
GRILL:
8 minutes
MAKES:
4 servings

8
carbs per serving

Exchanges:
½ Fruit
3½ Very Lean Meat
½ Fat

1 Place chicken in a large resealable plastic bag set in a shallow dish. Add cilantro, ginger, garlic, chile pepper, oil, coriander, cumin, salt, garam masala (if desired), and nutmeg to bag. Seal bag. Turn and press bag to coat chicken. Chill for at least 2 hours or up to 6 hours. If using wooden skewers, soak skewers in water for 30 minutes before grilling.

2 On eight 10- to 12-inch skewers, alternately thread the chicken, pineapple, red sweet pepper, and green sweet pepper, leaving a ¼-inch space between pieces.

3 Place skewers on the rack of an uncovered grill directly over medium coals. Grill for 8 to 12 minutes or until chicken is no longer pink, turning occasionally to brown evenly.

TO BROIL: Place kabobs on the unheated rack of a broiler pan. Broil 4 to 5 inches from the heat for 8 to 12 minutes or until chicken is no longer pink, turning occasionally to brown evenly.

*NOTE: Because chile peppers contain volatile oils that can burn your skin and eyes, avoid direct contact with them as much as possible. When working with chile peppers, wear plastic or rubber gloves. If your bare hands do touch the peppers, wash your hands and nails well with soap and warm water.

Nutrition Facts per serving: 175 cal., 3 g total fat (1 g sat. fat), 66 mg chol., 212 mg sodium, 8 g carbo., 1 g fiber, 27 g pro.

MEDITERRANEAN CHICKEN & PASTA

START TO FINISH:
30 minutes
MAKES:
4 servings

1   6-ounce jar marinated artichoke hearts

Nonstick cooking spray

12   ounces skinless, boneless chicken breast halves, cut into ¾-inch cubes

3   cloves garlic, thinly sliced

¼   cup reduced-sodium chicken broth

¼   cup dry white wine or reduced-sodium chicken broth

1   tablespoon snipped fresh oregano or 1 teaspoon dried oregano, crushed

1   7-ounce jar roasted red sweet peppers, drained and cut into strips

¼   cup pitted kalamata olives

2   cups hot cooked whole wheat penne pasta

¼   cup crumbled feta cheese (optional)

27
carbs per serving

Exchanges:
½ Vegetable
1 Starch
3 Very Lean Meat
½ Other Carbo.
½ Fat

❶ Drain artichokes, reserving marinade. Set aside. Coat an unheated large nonstick skillet with nonstick cooking spray. Preheat over medium heat. Add chicken and garlic to hot skillet. Cook and stir until chicken is brown. Add the reserved artichoke marinade, the ¼ cup chicken broth, the wine or additional chicken broth, and, if using, dried oregano.

❷ Bring to boiling; reduce heat. Cover and simmer for 10 minutes. Stir in artichokes, roasted peppers, olives, and, if using, fresh oregano. Heat through.

❸ To serve, spoon the chicken mixture over pasta. If desired, sprinkle with feta cheese.

Nutrition Facts per serving: 255 cal., 6 g total fat (0 g sat. fat), 49 mg chol., 312 mg sodium, 27 g carbo., 3 g fiber, 25 g pro.

ASIAN CHICKEN KABOBS

¼ cup water

2 tablespoons reduced-sodium soy sauce

2 tablespoons dry sherry

1 teaspoon grated fresh ginger or ¼ teaspoon ground ginger

⅛ teaspoon crushed red pepper

8 skinless, boneless chicken thighs (about 1½ pounds total)

1 For marinade, in a small bowl combine the water, soy sauce, sherry, ginger, and crushed red pepper. Cut chicken into thin strips. On metal skewers, thread chicken, accordion-style, leaving a ¼-inch space between pieces. Place skewers in a resealable plastic bag set in a shallow dish. Pour marinade over chicken. Seal bag. Marinate in the refrigerator for at least 2 hours or up to 24 hours, turning bag occasionally.

2 Drain kabobs, discarding marinade. Place kabobs on the rack of an uncovered grill directly over medium coals. Grill for 12 to 15 minutes or until chicken is no longer pink, turning once halfway through grilling time.

Nutrition Facts per serving: 180 cal., 5 g total fat (1 g sat. fat), 115 mg chol., 407 mg sodium, 1 g carbo., 0 g fiber, 28 g pro.

PREP:
25 minutes
MARINATE:
2 to 24 hours
GRILL:
12 minutes
MAKES:
4 servings

1 carb per serving

Exchanges:
4 Very Lean Meat
1 Fat

GINGER CHICKEN

PREP:
35 minutes
COOK:
15 minutes
MAKES:
6 servings

1   tablespoon olive oil

6   skinless, boneless chicken thighs (about 18 ounces total)

1   large onion, halved and sliced

1   fennel bulb, thinly sliced (1 cup)

2   tablespoons grated fresh ginger

1   tablespoon sugar

1   14½-ounce can diced tomatoes, undrained

½   cup dry white wine or reduced-sodium chicken broth

1   tablespoon balsamic vinegar

¼   teaspoon black pepper

3   cups hot cooked brown rice

33
carbs per
serving

Exchanges:
1 Vegetable
1½ Starch
2 Very Lean Meat
½ Other Carbo.
½ Fat

❶ In a large skillet heat oil over medium heat. Add chicken; cook for 4 to 6 minutes or until lightly browned, turning once halfway through cooking time. Remove chicken from skillet; set aside.

❷ Add onion, fennel, and ginger to skillet; cook and stir about 4 minutes or until tender. Add sugar and cook and stir for 5 minutes more. Add undrained tomatoes, wine or chicken broth, balsamic vinegar, and pepper to skillet. Bring to boiling; return chicken to skillet. Reduce heat. Cover and simmer for 15 to 20 minutes or until chicken is tender and no longer pink. Serve over hot cooked brown rice.

Nutrition Facts per serving: 269 cal., 6 g total fat (1 g sat. fat), 57 mg chol., 187 mg sodium, 33 g carbo., 3 g fiber, 17 g pro.

CHICKEN WITH BROCCOLI & GARLIC

¼ cup all-purpose flour

½ teaspoon salt

¼ teaspoon black pepper

4 skinless, boneless chicken thighs (about 12 ounces total)

1 tablespoon olive oil

1 bulb garlic, separated into cloves, peeled, and sliced (about ¼ cup)

1 cup reduced-sodium chicken broth

3 tablespoons red wine vinegar

1 tablespoon honey

6 cups packaged shredded broccoli (broccoli slaw mix)

2 tablespoons chopped pecans, toasted

1 In a plastic bag combine flour, salt, and pepper. Add chicken; shake to coat.

2 In a large skillet heat oil over medium heat. Add chicken; cook for 12 to 15 minutes or until chicken is tender and no longer pink, turning once. Transfer chicken to a serving platter; cover and keep warm.

3 Add garlic to skillet. Cook and stir for 1 minute. Add chicken broth, vinegar, and honey. Bring to boiling; reduce heat. Simmer, uncovered, for 5 minutes. Stir in broccoli. Return to boiling; reduce heat. Cover and simmer for 5 to 8 minutes more or until broccoli is tender. Stir in pecans. Spoon the broccoli mixture over chicken.

Nutrition Facts per serving: 258 cal., 9 g total fat (2 g sat. fat), 68 mg chol., 531 mg sodium, 21 g carbo., 4 g fiber, 22 g pro.

START TO FINISH:
35 minutes
MAKES:
4 servings

21
carbs per serving

Exchanges:
1½ Vegetable
2½ Lean Meat
1 Other Carbo.

CARAWAY CHICKEN & VEGETABLE STEW

PREP:
45 minutes
COOK:
*40 minutes +
10 minutes*
MAKES:
6 servings

19
carbs per
serving

Exchanges:
3 Vegetable
3 Lean Meat

3   pounds bone-in chicken thighs and/or bone-in chicken breasts, skinned
3¾ cups water
2   teaspoons instant chicken bouillon granules
1   teaspoon caraway seeds, crushed
½   teaspoon salt
¼   teaspoon black pepper
8   ounces fresh green beans, trimmed and cut into 2-inch-long pieces
2   medium carrots, cut into ¾-inch chunks
2   stalks celery, bias-cut into ½-inch-thick slices
2   cups sliced fresh shiitake, cremini, oyster, and/or button mushrooms
1   cup pearl onions, peeled
¼   cup cold water
¼   cup all-purpose flour

1 In a 4-quart Dutch oven combine chicken, the 3¾ cups water, the bouillon granules, caraway seeds, salt, and pepper. Bring to boiling; reduce heat. Cover and simmer for 40 minutes. Stir in green beans, carrots, celery, mushrooms, and pearl onions. Return to boiling; reduce heat. Cover and simmer about 10 minutes or until chicken is tender.

2 Remove chicken pieces from Dutch oven; set aside to cool slightly. When cool enough to handle, remove chicken from bones; discard bones. Cut up the chicken; add to vegetable mixture in Dutch oven. In a small bowl combine the ¼ cup cold water and the flour; whisk until smooth. Add to stew. Cook and stir until thickened and bubbly. Cook and stir for 1 minute more.

Nutrition Facts per serving: 226 cal., 4 g total fat (1 g sat. fat), 90 mg chol., 604 mg sodium, 19 g carbo., 4 g fiber, 30 g pro.

CHICKEN-STUFFED ZUCCHINI

4 8-ounce zucchini

1½ cups chopped cooked chicken or turkey (about 8 ounces)

1 cup chopped steamed vegetables (such as sweet peppers, eggplant, and/or zucchini)

½ cup chopped tomato

6 tablespoons finely shredded Parmesan cheese

1 teaspoon Mediterranean seasoning or other herb seasoning blend

1 In a Dutch oven or large saucepan cook whole zucchini in a large amount of boiling, lightly salted water for 5 minutes; drain and cool slightly. Cut a lengthwise slice from the top of each zucchini. Using a spoon, carefully scoop out pulp, leaving about ¼-inch-thick shells.

2 For filling, in a medium bowl stir together cooked chicken, steamed vegetables, tomato, 4 tablespoons of the Parmesan cheese, and the Mediterranean seasoning. Spoon filling into zucchini shells. Place in a shallow baking pan. Sprinkle with the remaining 2 tablespoons Parmesan cheese.

3 Bake in a 400° oven for 10 to 15 minutes or until heated through.

Nutrition Facts per serving: 175 cal., 7 g total fat (3 g sat. fat), 53 mg chol., 267 mg sodium, 8 g carbo., 3 g fiber, 21 g pro.

PREP:
20 minutes
BAKE:
10 minutes
OVEN:
400°F
MAKES:
4 servings

8

carbs per serving

Exchanges:
1½ Vegetable
2½ Lean Meat

JERK-RUBBED TURKEY BREAST

PREP:
30 minutes
GRILL:
1¼ hours
STAND:
10 minutes
MAKES:
12 servings

2

carbs per serving

Exchanges:
4 Lean Meat

Nonstick cooking spray

1   large red onion, finely chopped

3   cloves garlic, minced

1   fresh jalapeño chile pepper, seeded and finely chopped*

1   teaspoon snipped fresh thyme or ¼ teaspoon dried thyme, crushed

½   teaspoon salt

½   teaspoon ground allspice

¼   teaspoon ground nutmeg

⅛   teaspoon ground cloves

¼   cup dark rum

2   tablespoons lime juice

1   4- to 5-pound whole turkey breast, split

1 Coat an unheated large nonstick skillet with nonstick cooking spray. Preheat skillet over medium heat. Add onion, garlic, and chile pepper to hot skillet; cook about 4 minutes or until tender. Add thyme, the ½ teaspoon salt, the allspice, nutmeg, and cloves. Cook and stir for 1 minute. Remove from heat; add rum and lime juice. Return to heat. Bring to boiling; reduce heat. Simmer, uncovered, for 1 to 2 minutes or until liquid is evaporated. Remove from heat and cool.

2 Starting at the edge of each turkey breast half, slip your fingers between the skin and the meat, loosening the skin to make a pocket. Using your hands or a spoon, spread onion mixture evenly under skin. Sprinkle outside of each turkey breast half with additional salt and black pepper. Insert an oven-going meat thermometer into thickest part of a turkey breast half, not touching bone.

3 Arrange medium-hot coals around a drip pan. Test for medium heat above pan. Place turkey breast halves, bone sides down, on grill rack over drip pan. Cover; grill for 1¼ to 2 hours or until meat thermometer registers 170°F.

4 Remove turkey breast halves from grill. Cover with foil; let stand for 10 minutes before carving.

*NOTE: Because chile peppers contain volatile oils that can burn your skin and eyes, avoid direct contact with them as much as possible. When working with chile peppers, wear plastic or rubber gloves. If your bare hands do touch the peppers, wash your hands and nails well with soap and warm water.

Nutrition Facts per serving: 217 cal., 9 g total fat (2 g sat. fat), 83 mg chol., 179 mg sodium, 2 g carbo., 0 g fiber, 28 g pro.

TURKEY SCALOPPINE WITH PEPPERS

1   12-ounce turkey breast tenderloin
½   cup thinly sliced leek
¼   cup thinly sliced red sweet pepper
1   tablespoon thinly sliced fresh serrano or Anaheim chile pepper*
¼   teaspoon salt
⅓   cup all-purpose flour
     Nonstick cooking spray
     Lime wedges

PREP:
20 minutes
COOK:
6 minutes
MAKES:
4 servings

1 Cut turkey breast tenderloin crosswise into 4 pieces; place each piece between 2 pieces of plastic wrap. Using the flat side of a meat mallet, lightly pound to ¼-inch thickness; remove top piece of plastic wrap. Sprinkle leek, sweet pepper, chile pepper, and salt on both sides of turkey; cover with plastic wrap. Lightly pound to ⅛-inch thickness; remove plastic wrap. Coat with flour, shaking off any excess.

2 Coat an unheated large nonstick skillet with nonstick cooking spray. Preheat skillet over medium-high heat. Cook turkey in hot skillet for 6 to 8 minutes or until no longer pink, turning once halfway through cooking time. (Turn down heat if necessary to prevent overbrowning.) Serve with lime wedges.

*NOTE: Because chile peppers contain volatile oils that can burn your skin and eyes, avoid direct contact with them as much as possible. When working with chile peppers, wear plastic or rubber gloves. If your bare hands do touch the peppers, wash your hands and nails well with soap and warm water.

Nutrition Facts per serving: 141 cal., 1 g total fat (0 g sat. fat), 51 mg chol., 188 mg sodium, 9 g carbo., 1 g fiber, 21 g pro.

9
carbs per
serving

Exchanges:
3 Very Lean Meat
½ Other Carbo.

SWEET & SPICY TURKEY SKILLET

START TO FINISH:
35 minutes
MAKES:
4 servings

18
carbs per serving

Exchanges:
½ Vegetable
½ Fruit
4 Very Lean Meat
½ Other Carbo.

2	turkey breast tenderloins (about 1 pound total)
½	cup apple juice or apple cider
¼	cup bottled hoisin sauce
1	teaspoon grated fresh ginger
¼	teaspoon salt
⅛	teaspoon cayenne pepper
	Nonstick cooking spray
1	medium red, green, or yellow sweet pepper, seeded and cut into thin bite-size strips
1	medium onion, cut into thin wedges
⅓	cup cold water
2	teaspoons cornstarch
1	medium apple or pear, peeled (if desired), cored, and cut into wedges

1 Split each turkey breast tenderloin in half horizontally to form a total of 4 turkey steaks; set aside. In a small bowl stir together apple juice, hoisin sauce, ginger, salt, and cayenne pepper; set aside.

2 Coat an unheated large nonstick skillet with nonstick cooking spray. Preheat skillet over medium heat. Add sweet pepper strips and onion wedges to hot skillet; cook for 4 to 5 minutes or until nearly tender. Remove vegetables from skillet. Add turkey to skillet. Cook until browned, turning once.

3 Return cooked vegetables to skillet. Add apple juice mixture. Bring to boiling; reduce heat. Cover and simmer for 8 to 10 minutes or until turkey is no longer pink (170°F).

4 Using a slotted spoon, transfer turkey and vegetables to a serving platter, reserving liquid in skillet. Cover and keep warm.

5 In a small bowl combine the cold water and cornstarch; add to liquid in skillet. Cook and stir until thickened and bubbly. Add apple or pear. Cover and cook about 3 minutes more or just until apple is slightly softened. Spoon apple mixture over turkey and vegetables.

Nutrition Facts per serving: 210 cal., 2 g total fat (1 g sat. fat), 68 mg chol., 425 mg sodium, 18 g carbo., 2 g fiber, 28 g pro.

INDIAN-SPICED TURKEY TENDERLOINS

2   turkey breast tenderloins (about 1 pound total)

1½ teaspoons ground cumin

1½ teaspoons coriander seeds, crushed

1   teaspoon finely shredded lime peel

¾   teaspoon salt

¾   teaspoon ground ginger

¼   to ½ teaspoon crushed red pepper

¼   cup light dairy sour cream

1   tablespoon lime juice

2
carbs per serving

1 Split each turkey breast tenderloin in half horizontally to form a total of 4 turkey steaks; set aside. In a small bowl combine cumin, coriander seeds, lime peel, salt, ginger, and crushed red pepper. Set aside ¼ teaspoon of the cumin mixture. Sprinkle remaining cumin mixture over the turkey steaks; rub in with your fingers.

2 Place turkey steaks on the rack of an uncovered grill directly over medium coals. Grill for 12 to 15 minutes or until no longer pink (170°F), turning once halfway through grilling time.

3 Meanwhile, in a small bowl combine sour cream, lime juice, and the reserved ¼ teaspoon cumin mixture. Serve sauce with grilled turkey steaks.

TO BROIL: Coat the unheated rack of a broiler pan with nonstick cooking spray. Place turkey steaks on prepared rack; broil 4 to 5 inches from the heat for 8 to 10 minutes or until no longer pink (170°F), turning once halfway through broiling time.

Nutrition Facts per serving: 158 cal., 3 g total fat (1 g sat. fat), 73 mg chol., 502 mg sodium, 2 g carbo., 1 g fiber, 28 g pro.

PREP:
15 minutes
GRILL:
12 minutes
MAKES:
4 servings

Exchanges:
4 Very Lean Meat
½ Fat

CRUNCHY PARMESAN TURKEY

PREP:
15 minutes
COOK:
6 minutes
MAKES:
4 servings

¼   cup seasoned fine dry bread crumbs

¼   cup toasted wheat germ

¼   cup grated Parmesan cheese

2   teaspoons sesame seeds or ¼ teaspoon dried Italian seasoning, crushed

1   egg or ¼ cup refrigerated or frozen egg product, thawed

¼   teaspoon seasoned salt, or ⅛ teaspoon salt plus ⅛ teaspoon black pepper

2   turkey breast tenderloins (about 1 pound total)

     Nonstick cooking spray

9

carbs per
serving

1 In a small shallow dish combine bread crumbs, wheat germ, Parmesan cheese, and sesame seeds or Italian seasoning.

2 In another small shallow dish beat together egg and seasoned salt. Split each turkey breast tenderloin in half horizontally to form a total of 4 turkey steaks. Dip turkey steaks into egg mixture, allowing excess to drain off. Coat with crumb mixture.

3 Coat an unheated large nonstick skillet with nonstick cooking spray. Preheat over medium heat. Cook turkey in hot skillet for 6 to 8 minutes or until turkey is no longer pink (170°F), turning once halfway through cooking time. (If turkey starts to brown too quickly, reduce heat to medium-low.)

Exchanges:
½ Starch
4½ Very Lean Meat
1 Fat

Nutrition Facts per serving: 231 cal., 6 g total fat (2 g sat. fat), 125 mg chol., 429 mg sodium, 9 g carbo., 1 g fiber, 34 g pro.

ASPARAGUS-STUFFED TURKEY ROLLS

2   turkey breast tenderloins (about 1 pound total)
16   thin fresh asparagus spears
     Nonstick cooking spray
½   cup reduced-sodium chicken broth
2   tablespoons lemon juice
¼   teaspoon salt
⅛   teaspoon black pepper

START TO FINISH:
30 minutes
MAKES:
4 servings

1 Split each turkey breast tenderloin in half horizontally to form a total of 4 turkey steaks. Place each steak between 2 pieces of plastic wrap. Using the flat side of a meat mallet, lightly pound to ¼-inch thickness. Trim asparagus spears, breaking off woody ends. Arrange 4 asparagus spears on the short end of each turkey piece. Roll up turkey. If necessary, secure with wooden toothpicks.

2 Coat an unheated large nonstick skillet with nonstick cooking spray. Preheat skillet over medium heat. Cook turkey rolls in hot skillet until browned, turning to brown evenly. Add broth, lemon juice, salt, and pepper. Bring to boiling; reduce heat. Cover and simmer for 8 to 10 minutes or until turkey is no longer pink.

3 Transfer turkey to serving platter; discard toothpicks. Cover and keep warm. Boil liquid in skillet, uncovered, for 2 to 3 minutes or until reduced to ½ cup. Spoon over turkey.

Nutrition Facts per serving: 142 cal., 2 g total fat (1 g sat. fat), 68 mg chol., 271 mg sodium, 3 g carbo., 1 g fiber, 28 g pro.

3

carbs per serving

Exchanges:
½ Vegetable
4 Very Lean Meat

SPICED JERK TURKEY WITH MANGO SALSA

START TO FINISH:
30 minutes
MAKES:
4 servings

10 carbs per serving

Exchanges:
½ Fruit
4 Very Lean Meat
½ Fat

4	teaspoons Jamaican jerk seasoning
1	teaspoon ground cumin
½	teaspoon salt
½	teaspoon ground ginger
⅛	teaspoon cayenne pepper
1	tablespoon olive oil
2	cloves garlic, minced
8	2-ounce turkey breast slices, cut ¼ to ⅜ inch thick
1	cup chopped, peeled mango, peeled peach, or nectarine
¼	cup finely chopped red sweet pepper
¼	cup finely chopped red onion
2	tablespoons snipped fresh cilantro
1	tablespoon lime juice
1	teaspoon finely chopped, seeded fresh serrano chile pepper*
	Nonstick cooking spray

1 In a small bowl combine jerk seasoning, cumin, salt, ginger, and cayenne pepper; reserve 1 teaspoon of the cumin mixture for the salsa. Add oil and garlic to the remaining cumin mixture. Use your fingers to rub mixture evenly onto both sides of each turkey slice. Set aside.

2 For salsa, in a small bowl stir together mango, sweet pepper, red onion, cilantro, lime juice, chile pepper, and reserved 1 teaspoon cumin mixture. Set aside.

3 Coat an unheated large nonstick skillet with nonstick cooking spray. Preheat over medium heat. Add half of the turkey slices to hot skillet; cook for 4 to 6 minutes or until turkey is no longer pink, turning once halfway through cooking time. Transfer turkey slices to a serving platter. Cover; keep warm. Repeat with remaining turkey slices. Serve turkey slices with salsa.

***NOTE:** Because chile peppers contain volatile oils that can burn your skin and eyes, avoid direct contact with them as much as possible. When working with chile peppers, wear plastic or rubber gloves. If your bare hands do touch the peppers, wash your hands and nails well with soap and warm water.

Nutrition Facts per serving: 200 cal., 5 g total fat (1 g sat. fat), 68 mg chol., 649 mg sodium, 10 g carbo., 1 g fiber, 27 g pro.

LAMB & VEAL

HARVEST LEG OF LAMB

PREP:
30 minutes
CHILL:
8 to 24 hours
ROAST:
1¾ hours
STAND:
15 minutes
OVEN:
325°F
MAKES:
*12 to
16 servings*

2
carbs per
serving

Exchanges:
3½ Very Lean Meat

1 5- to 7-pound whole lamb leg roast* (with bone)
6 cloves garlic, cut into thin slices
2 to 3 tablespoons lemon juice
3 tablespoons snipped fresh parsley
2 tablespoons olive oil or cooking oil
1 tablespoon dried Italian seasoning or dried oregano, crushed
1 teaspoon black pepper

❶ Trim fat from lamb. With the tip of a knife, cut ½-inch-wide slits into lamb at 1-inch intervals (approximately 36 holes); insert a thin slice of garlic into each slit. Brush lamb with lemon juice. In a small bowl stir together parsley, oil, Italian seasoning or oregano, and pepper. Pat parsley mixture onto lamb. Wrap tightly in plastic wrap; chill in the refrigerator for at least 8 hours or up to 24 hours.

❷ Place lamb, fat side up, on a rack in a shallow roasting pan. Insert an oven-going meat thermometer into center of meat, making sure thermometer does not touch bone. Roast in a 325° oven until desired doneness. Allow 1¾ to 2¼ hours for medium-rare doneness (140°F) or 2¼ to 2¾ hours for medium doneness (155°F). Transfer meat to serving platter. Cover meat with foil and let stand for 15 minutes before carving. The temperature of the meat after standing should be 145°F for medium-rare doneness or 160°F for medium doneness.

***NOTE:** To use two 1½- to 2-pound boneless lamb leg roasts, prepare as directed except roast 1 to 1¼ hours for medium-rare doneness (140°F) or 1¼ to 1½ hours for medium doneness (155°F).

Nutrition Facts per serving: 187 cal., 8 g total fat (3 g sat. fat), 79 mg chol., 68 mg sodium, 2 g carbo., 0 g fiber, 25 g pro.

BALSAMIC-MARINATED LEG OF LAMB

1 5- to 6-pound leg of lamb, boned, rolled, and tied

4 to 6 cloves garlic, sliced

⅔ cup balsamic vinegar

½ cup olive oil

2 tablespoons Dijon-style mustard

1 tablespoon sugar

2 teaspoons dried basil, crushed, or 2 tablespoons snipped fresh basil

4 cloves garlic, minced

1 teaspoon salt

½ teaspoon black pepper

❶ Trim fat from lamb. With the tip of a knife, cut 1-inch-wide pockets into lamb at 3-inch intervals; insert a slice of garlic into each of the pockets. Set aside.

❷ For marinade, in a small bowl combine balsamic vinegar, oil, mustard, sugar, basil, minced garlic, salt, and pepper. Place leg of lamb in a large resealable plastic bag. Pour marinade over lamb. Seal bag; turn to coat lamb. Marinate in the refrigerator for at least 8 hours or up to 24 hours, turning bag occasionally. Drain and discard marinade.

❸ Place lamb on a rack in a shallow roasting pan. Insert an oven-going meat thermometer into the thickest portion of the leg. Roast in a 325° oven until desired doneness. Allow 2 to 2½ hours for medium-rare doneness (140°F) or 2½ to 3 hours for medium doneness (155°F). Cover and let stand for 15 minutes before carving. The temperature of the meat after standing should be 145°F for medium-rare doneness or 160°F for medium doneness. Remove strings. Thinly slice lamb to serve.

Nutrition Facts per serving: 188 cal., 7 g total fat (3 g sat. fat), 87 mg chol., 126 mg sodium, 0 g carbo., 0 g fiber, 28 g pro.

PREP:
20 minutes
MARINATE:
8 to 24 hours
ROAST:
2 hours
STAND:
15 minutes
OVEN:
325°F
MAKES:
12 to 16 servings

0

carbs per serving

Exchanges:
4 Very Lean Meat
1 Fat

BAKED LAMB & VEGETABLES

PREP:
20 minutes
BAKE:
50 minutes
OVEN:
350°F
MAKES:
4 servings

4	6- to 7-ounce lamb shoulder chops, cut ¾ inch thick
1	cup thin onion wedges
⅔	cup peeled turnip cut into thin bite-size strips
½	cup carrot cut into thin bite-size strips
½	cup thinly sliced celery
¼	teaspoon garlic salt
¼	teaspoon dried thyme, crushed, or ½ teaspoon snipped fresh thyme
⅛	teaspoon black pepper
4	thin lemon slices

8

carbs per serving

Exchanges:
1½ Vegetable
2½ Lean Meat

1 Cut four 12-inch squares of heavy foil or cut eight 12-inch squares of regular foil. Trim fat from chops. Arrange a chop on each square of heavy foil or on a double layer of regular foil. Place onion, turnip, carrot, and celery on top of the chops.

2 Sprinkle garlic salt, thyme, and pepper evenly over vegetables and chops. Add lemon slices. Bring up 2 opposite edges of each foil square and seal with a double fold. Fold remaining ends to completely enclose chops and vegetables, leaving space for steam to build. Place packets in a shallow baking pan.

3 Bake in a 350° oven about 50 minutes or until chops are medium doneness (160°F) and vegetables are tender. Discard lemon slices before serving.

Nutrition Facts per serving: 180 cal., 7 g total fat (2 g sat. fat), 68 mg chol., 148 mg sodium, 8 g carbo., 2 g fiber, 21 g pro.

LAMB WITH ROASTED-PEPPER BULGUR

2	cups water
1	cup bulgur
½	cup chopped onion
4	lamb loin chops, cut 1 inch thick (about 1 pound total)
1½	teaspoons lemon-pepper seasoning
1	cup small fresh spinach leaves or shredded fresh spinach
1	7-ounce jar roasted red sweet peppers, drained and coarsely chopped

1 In a medium saucepan combine the water, bulgur, and onion. Bring to boiling; reduce heat. Cover and simmer for 12 to 15 minutes or until most of the liquid is absorbed. Drain. Cover and keep warm.

2 Meanwhile, trim fat from chops. Sprinkle chops with ½ teaspoon of the lemon-pepper seasoning. Place chops on the unheated rack of a broiler pan. Broil 3 to 4 inches from the heat until desired doneness, turning once halfway through broiling time. Allow 8 to 10 minutes for medium-rare doneness (145°F) or 10 to 15 minutes for medium doneness (160°F).

3 To serve, stir the remaining 1 teaspoon lemon-pepper seasoning, the spinach, and roasted peppers into bulgur mixture. Divide bulgur mixture among 4 dinner plates. Top with lamb chops.

Nutrition Facts per serving: 259 cal., 5 g total fat (2 g sat. fat), 60 mg chol., 181 mg sodium, 31 g carbo., 8 g fiber, 24 g pro.

PREP:
20 minutes
BROIL:
8 minutes
MAKES:
4 servings

31
carbs per serving

Exchanges:
1 Vegetable
1½ Starch
2½ Very Lean Meat
½ Fat

LAMB CHOPS WITH GARLIC MUSHROOMS

START TO FINISH:
30 minutes
MAKES:
4 servings

3
carbs per serving

Exchanges:
½ Vegetable
5½ Very Lean Meat
2 Fat

1 tablespoon olive oil

1 teaspoon dried oregano or thyme, crushed, or 2 teaspoons snipped fresh oregano or thyme

¼ teaspoon salt

¼ teaspoon black pepper

8 lamb loin chops, cut 1 inch thick (about 2 pounds total)
Nonstick cooking spray

1 medium shallot, thinly sliced

2 cups sliced fresh mushrooms

2 cloves garlic, minced

2 tablespoons dry white wine
Salt
Black pepper

1 In a small bowl combine oil, oregano, the ¼ teaspoon salt, and the ¼ teaspoon pepper. Brush herb mixture onto one side of each chop. Coat an unheated large nonstick skillet with nonstick cooking spray. Preheat over medium-high heat. Add chops to hot skillet. Cook until desired doneness, turning once halfway through cooking time. Allow 9 to 11 minutes for medium-rare doneness (145°F) to medium doneness (160°F). Transfer chops to a serving platter; keep warm. Reserve 1 tablespoon of the drippings in the skillet.

2 Stir shallot into drippings in skillet. Cook and stir for 30 seconds. Stir in mushrooms and garlic. Cook and stir about 3 minutes or until mushrooms are tender. Remove from heat; let cool for 30 seconds. Carefully add wine to skillet. Return to heat and bring to boiling. Cook until most of the wine has evaporated. Season mushroom mixture to taste with additional salt and pepper. Spoon mushroom mixture over chops.

Nutrition Facts per serving: 288 cal., 12 g total fat (4 g sat. fat), 119 mg chol., 311 mg sodium, 3 g carbo., 1 g fiber, 40 g pro.

MUSTARD-ROSEMARY GRILLED LAMB

8   lamb rib or loin chops, cut 1 inch thick (about 2 pounds total)

¼   cup stone-ground mustard

¼   cup thinly sliced green onions

2   tablespoons dry white wine

1   tablespoon balsamic vinegar or rice vinegar

3   cloves garlic, minced

1   teaspoon snipped fresh rosemary or ¼ teaspoon dried rosemary, crushed

1   teaspoon honey

½   teaspoon salt

½   teaspoon black pepper

PREP:
20 minutes
CHILL:
2 to 3 hours
GRILL:
12 minutes
MAKES:
4 servings

4 carbs per serving

1 Trim fat from chops. In a small bowl stir together mustard, green onions, wine, vinegar, garlic, rosemary, honey, salt, and pepper. Spread mixture evenly over both sides of each chop. Place chops on a large plate and cover loosely with plastic wrap. Chill for at least 2 hours or up to 3 hours.

2 Place chops on the rack of an uncovered grill directly over medium coals. Grill until desired doneness, turning once halfway through grilling time. Allow 12 to 14 minutes for medium-rare doneness (145°F) or 15 to 17 minutes for medium doneness (160°F).

Nutrition Facts per serving: 195 cal., 8 g total fat (3 g sat. fat), 64 mg chol., 713 mg sodium, 4 g carbo., 0 g fiber, 20 g pro.

Exchanges:
3 Very Lean Meat
½ Fat

LAMB & PEPPERS

START TO FINISH:
25 minutes
MAKES:
4 servings

3
carbs per serving

Exchanges:
1 Vegetable
3½ Very Lean Meat
1 Fat

8   lamb loin or rib chops, cut 1 inch thick (about 2 pounds total)
    Nonstick cooking spray

3   small green, red, and/or yellow sweet peppers, cut into 1-inch pieces

1   tablespoon snipped fresh oregano or 1 teaspoon dried oregano, crushed

2   cloves garlic, minced

¼   cup sliced pitted green olives or ripe olives
    Small whole chile peppers (optional)

1 Place chops on the unheated rack of a broiler pan. Broil 3 to 4 inches from heat for 10 to 15 minutes or until medium doneness (160°F), turning once halfway through broiling time. Transfer to a serving platter.

2 Meanwhile, coat an unheated large nonstick skillet with nonstick cooking spray. Preheat over medium heat. Add sweet peppers, oregano, and garlic to hot skillet. Cook and stir for 6 to 8 minutes or until sweet peppers are crisp-tender. Stir in olives; heat through. Spoon sweet pepper mixture over chops. If desired, garnish with whole chile peppers.

Nutrition Facts per serving: 194 cal., 8 g total fat (2 g sat. fat), 80 mg chol., 275 mg sodium, 3 g carbo., 1 g fiber, 26 g pro.

HERBED LAMB CHOPS

8   lamb rib chops, cut 1 inch thick (about 2 pounds total)

½   cup dry white wine

2   tablespoons snipped fresh oregano, basil, and/or thyme
or 2 teaspoons dried oregano, basil, and/or thyme, crushed

2   tablespoons olive oil

½   teaspoon salt

¼   teaspoon black pepper

2   cloves garlic, minced

PREP:
15 minutes
MARINATE:
4 to 24 hours
GRILL:
12 minutes
MAKES:
4 servings

1 Place chops in a resealable plastic bag set in a shallow dish. For marinade, in a small bowl combine wine, herb, oil, salt, pepper, and garlic. Pour over chops. Seal bag; turn to coat chops. Marinate in the refrigerator for at least 4 hours or up to 24 hours, turning bag occasionally.

2 Drain chops, discarding marinade. Place chops on the rack of an uncovered grill directly over medium coals. Grill until desired doneness, turning once halfway through grilling time. Allow 12 to 14 minutes for medium-rare doneness (145°F) or 15 to 17 minutes for medium doneness (160°F).

0

carbs per serving

TO BROIL: Place chops on the unheated rack of a broiler pan. Broil 3 to 4 inches from the heat until desired doneness, turning once halfway through broiling time. Allow 8 to 10 minutes for medium-rare doneness (145°F) or 10 to 15 minutes for medium doneness (160°F).

Nutrition Facts per serving: 186 cal., 11 g total fat (3 g sat. fat), 64 mg chol., 153 mg sodium, 0 g carbo., 0 g fiber, 20 g pro.

Exchanges:
3 Lean Meat
5 Fat

GINGER-MARINATED LAMB CHOPS

PREP:
20 minutes
MARINATE:
4 to 24 hours
GRILL:
12 minutes
MAKES:
4 servings

8	lamb rib chops, cut 1 inch thick (about 2 pounds total)
1	green onion, chopped
3	tablespoons reduced-sodium soy sauce
2	tablespoons rice vinegar
2	tablespoons cooking oil
2	tablespoons grated fresh ginger
¼	teaspoon salt
⅛	teaspoon crushed red pepper
1	clove garlic, minced

1
carb per
serving

1 Place chops in a resealable plastic bag set in a shallow dish. For marinade, in a small bowl combine green onion, soy sauce, rice vinegar, oil, ginger, salt, crushed red pepper, and garlic. Pour over chops. Seal bag; turn to coat chops. Marinate in the refrigerator for at least 4 hours or up to 24 hours, turning bag occasionally.

2 Drain meat, discarding marinade. Place chops on the rack of an uncovered grill directly over medium coals. Grill until desired doneness, turning once halfway through grilling time. Allow 12 to 14 minutes for medium-rare doneness (145°F) or 15 to 17 minutes for medium doneness (160°F).

Nutrition Facts per serving: 184 cal., 11 g total fat (3 g sat. fat), 64 mg chol., 250 mg sodium, 1 g carbo., 0 g fiber, 20 g pro.

Exchanges:
3 Very Lean Meat
½ Fat

VEAL WITH FENNEL-WINE SAUCE

1   small fennel bulb

4   veal cutlets (about 12 ounces total)

¼   teaspoon salt

⅛   teaspoon black pepper

1   tablespoon butter

1   clove garlic, minced

½   cup dry white wine

⅓   cup reduced-sodium chicken broth

⅛   teaspoon salt

      Dash black pepper

1 Remove feathery tops from fennel bulb; snip enough of the tops to measure 1 to 2 tablespoons. Set aside. Cut off and discard upper stalks. Remove any wilted outer layers and cut a thin slice from the fennel base. Cut fennel bulb into thin slices, removing the core; set aside.

2 Trim fat from veal; season veal with the ¼ teaspoon salt and the ⅛ teaspoon pepper. In a large skillet melt butter over medium-high heat. Cook veal, half at a time, in hot butter for 4 to 6 minutes or until browned and slightly pink in center, turning once. Transfer veal to a serving platter. Cover and keep warm.

3 Add the sliced fennel and garlic to hot skillet; cook and stir for 1 minute. Add wine and broth. Bring to boiling; reduce heat. Simmer, uncovered, for 4 to 5 minutes or until mixture is reduced by half. Stir in the ⅛ teaspoon salt and the dash pepper. Spoon fennel sauce over meat. Sprinkle with reserved snipped fennel tops.

Nutrition Facts per serving: 147 cal., 5 g total fat (2 g sat. fat), 74 mg chol., 343 mg sodium, 2 g carbo., 1 g fiber, 19 g pro.

START TO FINISH:
30 minutes
MAKES:
4 servings

2
carbs per serving

Exchanges:
½ Vegetable
2½ Very Lean Meat
1 Fat

VEAL CHOPS WITH TOMATO-PEPPER RELISH

START TO FINISH:
20 minutes
MAKES:
6 servings

Nonstick cooking spray

2   cloves garlic, minced

1   14½-ounce can diced tomatoes with Italian herbs, undrained

1   7-ounce jar roasted red sweet peppers, rinsed, drained, and chopped

¼   teaspoon crushed red pepper

4   veal loin chops, cut 1 inch thick (about 2 pounds total)

¼   teaspoon salt

1   tablespoon balsamic vinegar

8

carbs per serving

1 Coat an unheated medium nonstick saucepan with nonstick cooking spray. Preheat over medium heat. Add garlic and cook for 1 to 2 minutes or until golden brown. Add tomatoes, roasted red peppers, and crushed red pepper. Bring to boiling; reduce heat. Simmer, uncovered, about 12 minutes or until slightly thickened.

2 Meanwhile, sprinkle veal chops with salt. Heat a large nonstick skillet over medium-high heat until hot. Reduce heat to medium. Place veal chops in skillet; cook for 12 to 14 minutes or until medium doneness (160°F), turning once halfway through cooking time. Carefully cut meat from bones; thinly slice meat.

3 Stir balsamic vinegar into tomato mixture; serve with chops.

Nutrition Facts per serving: 138 cal., 3 g total fat (1 g sat. fat), 70 mg chol., 335 mg sodium, 8 g carbo., 1 g fiber, 18 g pro.

Exchanges:
1 Vegetable
2½ Very Lean Meat
½ Fat

VEAL CHOPS WITH EGGPLANT RELISH

2 cups Japanese eggplant cut into ½-inch cubes (6 ounces)

2 plum tomatoes, chopped (¾ cup)

¼ cup chopped onion

¼ cup chopped celery

2 teaspoons dried Italian seasoning, crushed

2 tablespoons olive oil

6 veal loin chops, cut 1 inch thick (about 3 pounds total)

2 cloves garlic, minced

½ teaspoon salt

½ teaspoon black pepper

2 teaspoons olive oil

1 tablespoon red wine vinegar

1 tablespoon tomato paste

1 teaspoon sugar

¼ cup sliced pitted kalamata olives

1 tablespoon pine nuts

1 tablespoon snipped fresh parsley

1 tablespoon drained capers

PREP:
25 minutes
GRILL:
20 minutes
MAKES:
8 servings

4
carbs per serving

Exchanges:
½ Vegetable
3 Very Lean Meat
1½ Fat

❶ For relish, in a large bowl combine eggplant, tomatoes, onion, celery, and ½ teaspoon of the Italian seasoning. Add the 2 tablespoons oil; toss to coat. Fold a 36×18-inch piece of heavy foil in half to make an 18-inch square. Place vegetables in center of foil. Bring up opposite edges of foil and seal with a double fold. Fold remaining edges together to completely enclose vegetables, leaving space for steam to build.

❷ Trim fat from chops. In a bowl combine the remaining 1½ teaspoons Italian seasoning, the garlic, salt, and pepper. Stir in the 2 teaspoons oil. Spoon mixture over both sides of chops; rub in with your fingers.

❸ Place foil packet on the rack of an uncovered grill directly over medium coals. Grill for 20 to 25 minutes or until vegetables are tender, turning packet occasionally. Grill chops on the rack next to packet for 12 to 15 minutes or until medium doneness (160°F), turning once halfway through grilling time.

❹ Meanwhile, in a bowl combine vinegar, tomato paste, and sugar. Stir in olives, pine nuts, parsley, and capers. Transfer vegetables from foil to a serving bowl. Stir in olive mixture. Thinly slice meat. Serve with vegetables.

Nutrition Facts per serving: 183 cal., 9 g total fat (2 g sat. fat), 79 mg chol., 307 mg sodium, 4 g carbo., 1 g fiber, 21 g pro.

VEAL CHOPS STUFFED WITH MUSHROOMS

PREP:
35 minutes
GRILL:
12 minutes
MAKES:
6 servings

4
carbs per
serving

Exchanges:
½ Vegetable
6½ Very Lean Meat
½ Fat

Nonstick cooking spray

8	ounces fresh mushrooms, finely chopped
2	tablespoons finely chopped shallots
2	tablespoons dried tart cherries, chopped
1	tablespoon dry sherry
¼	teaspoon salt
⅛	teaspoon black pepper
6	veal loin chops, cut 1 inch thick (about 3 pounds total)
1	tablespoon cooking oil
½	teaspoon salt
¼	teaspoon black pepper

1 For stuffing, coat an unheated large nonstick skillet with nonstick cooking spray. Preheat over medium heat. Add mushrooms and shallots to hot skillet. Cook about 5 minutes or until most of liquid evaporates, stirring frequently. Stir in cherries, dry sherry, the ¼ teaspoon salt, and the ⅛ teaspoon pepper. Cook for 2 to 3 minutes more or until all of the liquid evaporates. Cool slightly.

2 Trim fat from chops. Make a pocket in each chop by cutting horizontally from the fat side almost to the bone. Divide stuffing evenly among pockets. Secure with wooden toothpicks. Brush chops with oil; sprinkle with the ½ teaspoon salt and the ¼ teaspoon pepper.

3 Place chops on the rack of an uncovered grill directly over medium coals. Grill for 12 to 15 minutes or until medium doneness (160°F), turning once halfway through grilling time. Remove toothpicks before serving.

Nutrition Facts per serving: 303 cal., 10 g total fat (3 g sat. fat), 181 mg chol., 469 mg sodium, 4 g carbo., 0 g fiber, 47 g pro.

FISH & SEAFOOD

CATFISH & TURKEY SAUSAGE JAMBALAYA

PREP:
30 minutes
COOK:
10 minutes +
5 minutes +
5 minutes
STAND:
5 minutes
MAKES:
4 servings

30 carbs per serving

Exchanges:
1 Vegetable
1½ Starch
2 Lean Meat
½ Fat

8	ounces fresh or frozen skinless catfish fillets
1	teaspoon olive oil or cooking oil
4	ounces uncooked turkey hot Italian sausage links, cut into ½-inch pieces
1	medium onion, chopped
½	cup chopped green sweet pepper
1	stalk celery, chopped
3	cloves garlic, minced
1	14½-ounce can diced tomatoes, drained
1	14-ounce can reduced-sodium chicken broth
1½	cups instant brown rice
1½	teaspoons paprika
1	teaspoon dried oregano, crushed, or 1 tablespoon snipped fresh oregano
½	teaspoon dried thyme, crushed, or 1½ teaspoons snipped fresh thyme
⅛	to ¼ teaspoon cayenne pepper

1 Thaw fish, if frozen. Rinse fish; pat dry with paper towels. Cut fish into ¾-inch chunks. Set aside.

2 In a large saucepan heat oil over medium heat. Add sausage pieces; cook for 3 to 4 minutes or until browned. Add onion, sweet pepper, celery, and garlic; cook, stirring occasionally, about 10 minutes or until vegetables are tender and sausage is no longer pink.

3 Stir in tomatoes, chicken broth, uncooked rice, paprika, dried oregano (if using), dried thyme (if using), and cayenne pepper. Bring to boiling; reduce heat to medium-low. Cover and simmer for 5 minutes. Stir in catfish pieces, fresh oregano (if using), and fresh thyme (if using); cook about 5 minutes more or until liquid is nearly absorbed and rice is tender. Remove from heat. Cover and let stand for 5 minutes. Using a slotted spoon, spoon mixture into shallow bowls.

Nutrition Facts per serving: 267 cal., 9 g total fat (2 g sat. fat), 41 mg chol., 701 mg sodium, 30 g carbo., 4 g fiber, 18 g pro.

BROILED FISH WITH CITRUS-GRAPE SAUCE

1¼	pounds fresh or frozen grouper, halibut, or shark steaks, ¾ inch thick
	Nonstick cooking spray
½	teaspoon lemon-pepper seasoning
¼	cup thinly sliced green onions
½	teaspoon finely shredded orange peel
1¼	cups orange juice
1	tablespoon cornstarch
¼	teaspoon salt
3	oranges, peeled, sectioned, and seeded
1	cup seedless green grapes, halved

1 Thaw fish, if frozen. Coat the unheated rack of a broiler pan with nonstick cooking spray. Sprinkle both sides of fish with lemon-pepper seasoning. Place fish on prepared rack of broiler pan. Broil 4 inches from the heat for 4 minutes; turn fish. Broil 3 to 5 minutes more or until fish flakes easily when tested with a fork.

2 Meanwhile, for sauce, coat an unheated medium saucepan with nonstick cooking spray. Add green onions; cook and stir over medium heat until tender.

3 In a medium bowl stir together orange peel, orange juice, cornstarch, and salt. Add to green onions in saucepan. Cook and stir until mixture is thickened and bubbly. Cook and stir for 2 minutes more. Add orange sections and grapes. Heat through. Spoon sauce over fish.

Nutrition Facts per serving: 224 cal., 2 g total fat (0 g sat. fat), 52 mg chol., 329 mg sodium, 23 g carbo., 2 g fiber, 29 g pro.

START TO FINISH:
30 minutes
MAKES:
4 servings

23
carbs per serving

Exchanges:
1½ Fruit
4 Very Lean Meat

HONEY-GINGER HALIBUT WITH ORANGES

PREP:
25 minutes
MARINATE:
1 to 4 hours
BROIL:
8 minutes
MAKES:
4 servings

15
carbs per
serving

Exchanges:
1 Vegetable
½ Fruit
3½ Very Lean Meat
½ Other Carbo.

2	8-ounce fresh or frozen halibut steaks, 1 inch thick
2	medium oranges
	Orange juice (optional)
½	cup dry white wine or orange juice
2	tablespoons orange honey spread or honey
2	teaspoons grated fresh ginger
¼	teaspoon salt
¼	teaspoon coarsely ground black pepper
4	cups torn fresh spinach

1 Thaw fish, if frozen. Rinse fish; pat dry with paper towels. Place fish in resealable plastic bag set in shallow dish.

2 Over a bowl, peel and section oranges to catch juice. Reserve orange sections. Measure orange juice, adding additional orange juice if necessary to make ¼ cup. For marinade, in a small bowl stir together the ¼ cup orange juice, the wine or additional orange juice, honey spread, and ginger. Pour over fish. Seal bag; turn to coat fish. Marinate in refrigerator for at least 1 hour or up to 4 hours, turning bag occasionally.

3 Drain fish, reserving marinade. Pour marinade into a small saucepan. Bring to boiling. Boil, uncovered, for 2 minutes. Remove from heat. Cover; keep warm.

4 Place fish on the greased unheated rack of a broiler pan. Sprinkle with salt and pepper. Broil 4 inches from heat for 8 to 12 minutes or until fish flakes easily when tested with a fork, turning once halfway through broiling time. Cut each steak into two portions.

5 In a medium bowl drizzle ¼ cup of the hot marinade over spinach; toss gently to coat. Divide spinach mixture among 4 dinner plates. Top with fish, orange sections, and additional hot marinade.

Nutrition Facts per serving: 209 cal., 3 g total fat (0 g sat. fat), 36 mg chol., 232 mg sodium, 15 g carbo., 1 g fiber, 25 g pro.

HALIBUT VERACRUZ

4   fresh or frozen halibut, mahi mahi, grouper, or tuna steaks, 1 inch thick (about 1½ pounds total)

¼   teaspoon salt

⅛   teaspoon black pepper

1   14½-ounce can chopped tomatoes with green chile peppers, drained

¼   cup sliced green onions

1   tablespoon olive oil

2   cloves garlic, minced

1   teaspoon drained capers

1   teaspoon snipped fresh oregano or ½ teaspoon dried oregano, crushed

½   teaspoon snipped fresh thyme or ¼ teaspoon dried thyme, crushed

1 Thaw fish, if frozen. Rinse fish; pat dry with paper towels. Sprinkle fish with salt and pepper. In a small bowl combine drained tomatoes with green chile peppers, green onions, oil, garlic, capers, oregano, and thyme; set aside.

2 Tear a 36×18-inch piece of heavy-duty foil; fold in half to make an 18-inch square. Place fish steaks in center of foil. Top with tomato mixture. Bring up two opposite edges of foil; seal with a double fold. Fold remaining edges together to completely enclose fish, leaving space for steam to build.

3 Place foil packet on the rack of an uncovered grill directly over medium coals. Grill for 8 to 12 minutes or until fish flakes easily when tested with a fork.

Nutrition Facts per serving: 237 cal., 7 g total fat (1 g sat. fat), 54 mg chol., 672 mg sodium, 5 g carbo., 0 g fiber, 36 g pro.

PREP:
20 minutes
GRILL:
8 minutes
MAKES:
4 servings

5
carbs per serving

Exchanges:
1 Vegetable
4½ Very Lean Meat
1 Fat

SPICY GINGER FISH

PREP:
10 minutes
MICROWAVE:
4 minutes
MAKES:
4 servings

4   4-ounce fresh or frozen skinless sea bass fillets or other firm-fleshed white fish fillets, ¾ to 1 inch thick

⅔   cup thinly sliced green onions

4   teaspoons lemon juice or dry sherry

2   teaspoons grated fresh ginger

2   cloves garlic, minced

2   teaspoons fish sauce or reduced-sodium soy sauce

1   small fresh jalapeño chile pepper, seeded and finely chopped*

3

carbs per serving

❶ Thaw fish, if frozen. Rinse fish; pat dry with paper towels. In a small bowl stir together green onions, 2 teaspoons of the lemon juice or sherry, the ginger, and garlic.

❷ In a microwave-safe 2-quart square baking dish arrange fish fillets in a single layer, tucking under any thin edges. Spoon green onion mixture over fish. Cover dish with vented plastic wrap. Microwave on 100% power (high) for 4 to 6 minutes or until fish flakes easily when tested with a fork, giving the dish a half-turn halfway through cooking time.

❸ Using a slotted spatula, transfer fish to 4 dinner plates. In a small bowl stir together the fish sauce, chile pepper, and the remaining 2 teaspoons lemon juice or sherry; drizzle over fish.

Exchanges:
½ Vegetable
3 Very Lean Meat

***NOTE:** Because chile peppers contain volatile oils that can burn your skin and eyes, avoid direct contact with them as much as possible. When working with chile peppers, wear plastic or rubber gloves. If your bare hands do touch the peppers, wash your hands and nails well with soap and warm water.

Nutrition Facts per serving: 121 cal., 2 g total fat (1 g sat. fat), 46 mg chol., 312 mg sodium, 3 g carbo., 1 g fiber, 22 g pro.

GRILLED BASS WITH STRAWBERRY SALSA

4	4- to 5-ounce fresh or frozen sea bass or halibut steaks, 1 inch thick
1	small lime
¼	teaspoon salt
¼	teaspoon cayenne pepper
1	cup chopped fresh strawberries
¼	cup finely chopped seeded fresh poblano chile pepper (½ of a small)*
2	tablespoons snipped fresh cilantro
½	teaspoon cumin seeds, toasted**
⅛	teaspoon salt

PREP:
20 minutes
GRILL:
7 to 9 minutes per ½-inch thickness
MAKES:
4 servings

1 Thaw fish, if frozen. Rinse fish; pat dry with paper towels. Finely shred lime peel. Peel, section, and chop lime; set aside. In a small bowl combine lime peel, the ¼ teaspoon salt, and the cayenne pepper. Sprinkle evenly over both sides of each fish steak; rub in with your fingers.

2 Arrange medium-hot coals around a drip pan. Test for medium heat above pan. Place fish on the greased grill rack over drip pan. Cover and grill for 7 to 9 minutes per ½-inch thickness or until fish flakes easily when tested with a fork, gently turning once halfway through grilling time.

3 Meanwhile, in a medium bowl combine chopped lime, strawberries, chile pepper, cilantro, cumin seeds, and the ⅛ teaspoon salt. Serve with grilled fish.

7
carbs per serving

Exchanges:
3 Very Lean Meat
½ Other Carbo.

*NOTE: Because chile peppers contain volatile oils that can burn your skin and eyes, avoid direct contact with them as much as possible. When working with chile peppers, wear plastic or rubber gloves. If your bare hands do touch the peppers, wash your hands and nails well with soap and warm water.

**NOTE: To toast cumin seeds, in a small skillet heat cumin seeds over medium heat until fragrant, shaking skillet occasionally.

Nutrition Facts per serving: 137 cal., 3 g total fat (1 g sat. fat), 46 mg chol., 299 mg sodium, 7 g carbo., 1 g fiber, 22 g pro.

BAKED ORANGE ROUGHY WITH CITRUS SALSA

START TO FINISH:
30 minutes
OVEN:
450°F
MAKES:
4 servings

11
carbs per serving

Exchanges:
½ Fruit
3 Very Lean Meat
1½ Fat

4	5-ounce fresh or frozen orange roughy fillets or other white fish fillets, ½ to ¾ inch thick
¼	teaspoon salt
⅛	teaspoon black pepper
2	oranges, peeled and chopped
1	medium avocado, halved, pitted, peeled, and chopped
½	cup chopped, peeled jicama
½	of a small red onion, cut into thin wedges
1	tablespoon snipped fresh cilantro
1	tablespoon lime juice
½	of a small fresh jalapeño chile pepper, seeded and finely chopped*
⅛	teaspoon salt
	Lime wedges (optional)

1 Thaw fish, if frozen. Rinse fish; pat dry with paper towels. Sprinkle fish with the ¼ teaspoon salt and the pepper. Arrange fish in a single layer in a greased baking dish. Bake in a 450° oven for 6 to 9 minutes or until fish flakes easily when tested with a fork.

2 Meanwhile, for salsa, stir together oranges, avocado, jicama, red onion, cilantro, lime juice, chile pepper, and the ⅛ teaspoon salt. Spoon salsa over fish. If desired, serve with lime wedges.

*NOTE: Because chile peppers contain volatile oils that can burn your skin and eyes, avoid direct contact with them as much as possible. When working with chile peppers, wear plastic or rubber gloves. If your bare hands do touch the peppers, wash your hands and nails well with soap and warm water.

Nutrition Facts per serving: 198 cal., 8 g total fat (1 g sat. fat), 28 mg chol., 312 mg sodium, 11 g carbo., 4 g fiber, 22 g pro.

LEMON-THYME FISH KABOBS

12 ounces fresh or frozen skinless swordfish, tuna, or shark steaks, 1 inch thick

¼ cup lemon juice

2 tablespoons olive oil

½ teaspoon salt

½ teaspoon dried thyme, crushed, or 1 tablespoon snipped fresh thyme

⅛ teaspoon black pepper

¼ teaspoon lemon-pepper seasoning

12 medium fresh whole mushrooms

2 small zucchini or yellow summer squash, cut into 1-inch-thick slices

1 medium yellow, green, or red sweet pepper, cut into 1-inch pieces
Nonstick cooking spray

8 cherry tomatoes

3 cups hot cooked brown rice or orzo pasta (rosamarina) (optional)

1 Thaw fish, if frozen. For marinade, in a medium bowl combine lemon juice, 1 tablespoon of the oil, the salt, thyme, and black pepper. Rinse fish; pat dry with paper towels. Cut fish into 1-inch cubes. Add fish to marinade; toss gently to coat. Cover and marinate in the refrigerator for 30 minutes. If using wooden skewers, soak skewers in water for 30 minutes before grilling. Drain fish, discarding marinade.

2 In a large bowl combine the remaining 1 tablespoon oil and the lemon-pepper seasoning. Add mushrooms, zucchini, and sweet pepper; toss to coat. On eight 12-inch skewers, alternately thread fish cubes, mushrooms, squash, and sweet pepper, leaving a ¼-inch space between pieces.

3 Coat the unheated rack of a broiler pan with nonstick cooking spray. Place skewers on rack. Broil about 4 inches from the heat for 8 to 10 minutes or until fish flakes easily when tested with a fork, turning once halfway through broiling time. Place a cherry tomato on the end of each skewer for the last 2 minutes of broiling. If desired, serve the kabobs with hot cooked rice or orzo.

TO GRILL: Place skewers on the greased rack of an uncovered grill directly over medium coals. Grill for 8 to 12 minutes or until fish flakes easily when tested with a fork, turning once halfway through grilling time. Place a cherry tomato on the end of each skewer for the last 2 minutes of grilling.

Nutrition Facts per serving: 192 cal., 10 g total fat (2 g sat. fat), 32 mg chol., 369 mg sodium, 8 g carbo., 2 g fiber, 19 g pro.

PREP:
25 minutes
MARINATE:
30 minutes
BROIL:
8 minutes
MAKES:
4 servings

8
carbs per serving

Exchanges:
1½ Vegetable
2½ Very Lean Meat
1½ Fat

SESAME-SEARED TUNA

START TO FINISH:
15 minutes
MAKES:
4 servings

4   4-ounce fresh or frozen tuna fillets, about ¾ inch thick
     Nonstick cooking spray
⅓   cup bottled hoisin sauce
3   tablespoons orange juice
1   tablespoon sesame seeds, toasted

7
carbs per
serving

1 Thaw fish, if frozen. Rinse fish; pat dry with paper towels. Coat an unheated large nonstick skillet with nonstick cooking spray. Preheat over medium-high heat. Add fish; cook for 6 to 8 minutes or until fish flakes easily when tested with a fork (tuna can be slightly pink in the center), turning once.

2 Meanwhile, in a small saucepan stir together hoisin sauce and orange juice; heat through.

3 To serve, drizzle the hoisin mixture over fish. Sprinkle with sesame seeds.

Nutrition Facts per serving: 172 cal., 3 g total fat (0 g sat. fat), 51 mg chol., 313 mg sodium, 7 g carbo., 0 g fiber, 28 g pro.

Exchanges:
½ Other Carbo.
4 Very Lean Meat

TANGY THYME FISH

1 pound fresh or frozen salmon, sole, flounder, cod,
  or orange roughy fillets, ½ to ¾ inch thick

1 cup reduced-sodium chicken broth

¼ cup chopped onion

⅛ teaspoon black pepper

⅛ teaspoon dried thyme or marjoram, crushed, or ½ teaspoon
  snipped fresh thyme or marjoram

2 tablespoons cold water

1 teaspoon cornstarch

¼ cup bottled reduced-calorie buttermilk ranch salad dressing

2 tablespoons snipped fresh parsley

  Lemon slices (optional)

1 Thaw fish, if frozen. Rinse fish; pat dry with paper towels. Set aside.

2 In a large skillet combine chicken broth, onion, pepper, and dried thyme
(if using). Bring to boiling. Place fish in skillet, tucking under any thin edges.
Cover and simmer for 4 to 6 minutes per ½-inch thickness of fish or until
fish flakes easily when tested with a fork. Using a slotted spatula, transfer fish
to a serving platter. Cover and keep warm.

3 For sauce, bring liquid in skillet to boiling. Boil, uncovered, over
medium-high heat for 3 to 5 minutes or until reduced to about ½ cup. In
a small bowl combine cold water and cornstarch; stir into liquid in skillet.
Cook and stir until thickened and bubbly. Cook and stir for 2 minutes more.
Stir in fresh thyme (if using), salad dressing, and parsley. Serve the fish with
sauce. If desired, serve with lemon slices.

Nutrition Facts per serving: 248 cal., 15 g total fat (2 g sat. fat), 71 mg chol., 371 mg sodium, 3 g carbo.,
0 g fiber, 23 g pro.

**START TO
FINISH:**
25 minutes
MAKES:
4 servings

3
carbs per
serving

Exchanges:
3½ Very Lean Meat
1 Fat

SWEET 'N' HEAT-GLAZED SALMON

PREP:
30 minutes
BROIL:
8 minutes
MAKES:
4 servings

1½ cups apricot nectar

⅓ cup snipped dried apricots

2 tablespoons honey

2 tablespoons reduced-sodium soy sauce

1 tablespoon grated fresh ginger

2 cloves garlic, minced

¼ teaspoon ground cinnamon

⅛ teaspoon cayenne pepper

1 12-ounce fresh or frozen skinless salmon fillet, about 1 inch thick

30
carbs per serving

Exchanges:
1 Fruit
3 Lean Meat
1 Other Carbo.

❶ For glaze, in a medium saucepan stir together apricot nectar, apricots, honey, soy sauce, ginger, garlic, cinnamon, and cayenne pepper. Bring to boiling; reduce heat. Simmer, uncovered, about 20 minutes or until mixture is thickened and reduced by about half, stirring occasionally. Remove ¼ cup of the glaze to brush on fish; set aside the remaining glaze until ready to serve.

❷ Meanwhile, thaw fish, if frozen. Rinse fish; pat dry with paper towels. Place fish on the greased unheated rack of a broiler pan, tucking under any thin edges.

❸ Broil about 4 inches from the heat for 8 to 12 minutes or until fish flakes easily when tested with a fork, gently turning once and brushing occasionally with the ¼ cup glaze during the last 4 minutes of broiling. Discard remainder of glaze used as brush-on. Serve the fish with the reserved glaze.

Nutrition Facts per serving: 261 cal., 8 g total fat (1 g sat. fat), 52 mg chol., 332 mg sodium, 30 g carbo., 2 g fiber, 20 g pro.

SALMON WITH APRICOT SAUCE

4	4- to 5-ounce fresh or frozen salmon or halibut steaks, ¾ inch thick
4	fresh apricots or 8 dried apricot halves
½	cup apricot nectar
¼	cup apricot preserves
2	tablespoons sliced green onion
1½	teaspoons snipped fresh oregano or ½ teaspoon dried oregano, crushed
⅛	teaspoon salt
	Few drops bottled hot pepper sauce
1	tablespoon olive oil
1	to 2 teaspoons bottled hot pepper sauce
⅛	teaspoon black pepper

PREP:
25 minutes
GRILL:
6 minutes
MAKES:
4 servings

1 Thaw fish, if frozen. Pit and quarter fresh apricots; set aside. (Or halve the dried apricot halves; cover with boiling water. Let stand while preparing sauce and fish; drain well before using.)

2 For sauce, in a small saucepan combine apricot nectar, apricot preserves, green onion, oregano, and salt. Bring just to boiling, stirring frequently; reduce heat. Boil gently, uncovered, about 8 minutes or until sauce is slightly thickened. Remove from heat; reserve 2 tablespoons of the sauce to brush on fish. Stir apricots and few drops hot pepper sauce into the remaining sauce. Cover and keep warm.

3 Rinse fish; pat dry with paper towels. Combine olive oil and the 1 to 2 teaspoons hot pepper sauce. Brush both sides of the fish with oil mixture. Sprinkle with black pepper.

4 Place fish on the greased rack of an uncovered grill directly over medium coals. Grill for 6 to 9 minutes or until fish flakes easily when tested with a fork, turning once and brushing with the reserved 2 tablespoons sauce during the last 2 to 3 minutes of grilling time.

5 Transfer the fish to 4 dinner plates. Spoon the chunky apricot sauce over fish.

TO BROIL: Place fish on the greased unheated rack of a broiler pan. Broil about 4 inches from the heat for 6 to 9 minutes, turning once and brushing with the reserved sauce during the last 2 to 3 minutes of broiling time.

Nutrition Facts per serving: 254 cal., 7 g total fat (1 g sat. fat), 59 mg chol., 166 mg sodium, 23 g carbo., 1 g fiber, 23 g pro.

23
carbs per serving

Exchanges:
½ Fruit
3 Lean Meat
1 Other Carbo.

GRILLED SALMON
WITH ORANGE-PINEAPPLE SALSA

PREP:
30 minutes
CHILL:
8 to 24 hours
GRILL:
14 minutes
MAKES:
6 servings

11
carbs per serving

Exchanges:
½ Fruit
3½ Lean Meat
½ Fat

1	1½-pound fresh or frozen salmon fillet (with skin), about 1 inch thick
2	tablespoons sugar
2½	teaspoons finely shredded orange peel
1	teaspoon salt
¼	teaspoon black pepper
2	oranges, peeled, sectioned, and chopped
1	cup chopped fresh pineapple or canned pineapple tidbits (juice pack), drained
2	tablespoons snipped fresh cilantro
1	green onion, sliced
1	fresh jalapeño chile pepper, seeded and finely chopped*
	Nonstick cooking spray

1 Thaw fish, if frozen. Cut into 6 serving-size portions. Rinse fish; pat dry with paper towels. In a small bowl stir together sugar, 1½ teaspoons of the orange peel, the salt, and black pepper. Sprinkle sugar mixture evenly over salmon (not on skin side); rub in with your fingers. Place salmon, sugar sides up, in a glass baking dish. Cover dish and chill for at least 8 hours or up to 24 hours.

2 For salsa, in a small bowl combine the remaining 1 teaspoon orange peel, the chopped oranges, pineapple, cilantro, green onion, and chile pepper. Cover and chill until ready to serve or up to 24 hours.

3 Coat unheated grill rack with nonstick cooking spray. Arrange medium-hot coals around a drip pan. Test for medium heat above pan. Lift salmon pieces from dish; discard liquid in dish. Place salmon pieces, skin sides down, on grill rack over drip pan. Cover and grill for 14 to 18 minutes or until salmon flakes easily when tested with a fork.

4 To serve each piece, carefully slip a metal spatula between fish and skin; lift fish up and away from skin. Serve with salsa.

*NOTE: Because chile peppers contain volatile oils that can burn your skin and eyes, avoid direct contact with them as much as possible. When working with chile peppers, wear plastic or rubber gloves. If your bare hands do touch the peppers, wash your hands and nails well with soap and warm water.

Nutrition Facts per serving: 249 cal., 12 g total fat (2 g sat. fat), 66 mg chol., 457 mg sodium, 11 g carbo., 1 g fiber, 23 g pro.

GRILLED SALMON TACOS

1	pound fresh or frozen skinless salmon fillets
8	ounces medium round red or white potatoes, cubed
1½	teaspoons ground chipotle chile pepper
¾	teaspoon sugar
½	teaspoon salt
1	cup purchased green salsa
3	tablespoons lime juice
6	green onions, thinly sliced
½	cup snipped fresh cilantro
12	6-inch or sixteen 4-inch corn tortillas, warmed according to package directions
½	cup light dairy sour cream
	Lime wedges

1 Thaw fish, if frozen. In a covered small saucepan cook potatoes in enough boiling salted water to cover about 15 minutes or until tender. Drain and cool.

2 In a small bowl combine chipotle chile pepper, sugar, and ¼ teaspoon of the salt. Rinse fish; pat dry with paper towels. Measure thickness of fish. Sprinkle chile pepper mixture evenly over both sides of each fish fillet; rub in with your fingers. Place fish on the greased rack of an uncovered grill directly over medium coals. Grill for 4 to 6 minutes per ½-inch thickness or until fish flakes easily when tested with a fork, turning once halfway through grilling time. Cool slightly. Break fish into chunks.

3 In a medium bowl stir together green salsa, lime juice, and the remaining ¼ teaspoon salt. Add potatoes, fish, green onions, and cilantro; toss gently to coat.

4 Divide fish mixture among tortillas. Top with sour cream; fold tortillas. Serve with lime wedges.

Nutrition Facts per serving: 350 cal., 11 g total fat (3 g sat. fat), 51 mg chol., 416 mg sodium, 41 g carbo., 4 g fiber, 21 g pro.

PREP:
1 hour
GRILL:
4 to 6 minutes per ½-inch thickness
MAKES:
6 to 8 servings

41
carbs per serving

Exchanges:
2½ Starch
2 Lean Meat
1 Fat

APPLE-GLAZED SALMON

PREP:
20 minutes
BAKE:
8 minutes
OVEN:
400°F
MAKES:
4 servings

1	1½-pound fresh or frozen skinless salmon fillet, about 1 inch thick
2	teaspoons juniper berries, crushed (optional)
¼	cup dry vermouth or reduced-sodium chicken broth
1½	teaspoons snipped fresh thyme or ½ teaspoon dried thyme, crushed
1	teaspoon finely snipped fresh rosemary or ½ teaspoon dried rosemary, crushed
¼	cup apple jelly
	Salt
	Black pepper

14
carbs per
serving

Exchanges:
5 Very Lean Meat
1 Other Carbo.
½ Fat

1 Thaw fish, if frozen. For glaze, in a dry small saucepan cook juniper berries, if using, over medium-high heat about 1 minute or until toasted, shaking the saucepan frequently. Carefully add vermouth or chicken broth, thyme, and rosemary to saucepan. Bring to boiling. Stir in apple jelly; simmer about 1 minute or just until jelly is melted. Remove from heat.

2 Rinse fish; pat dry with paper towels. Cut fish into 4 serving-size pieces. Heat a very large nonstick skillet over high heat. Add fish to hot skillet. Cook about 2 minutes or until light brown on the bottom. If using an ovenproof skillet, turn fish with a large spatula. If using a skillet that is not ovenproof, transfer fish to a 2-quart rectangular baking dish, browned sides up. Sprinkle fish lightly with salt and pepper. Spoon the glaze over fish.

3 Bake in a 400° oven for 8 to 10 minutes or until fish flakes easily when tested with a fork.

Nutrition Facts per serving: 264 cal., 6 g total fat (1 g sat. fat), 88 mg chol., 266 mg sodium, 14 g carbo., 0 g fiber, 34 g pro.

SOY-LIME SCALLOPS WITH LEEKS

1	pound fresh or frozen sea scallops
¼	cup reduced-sodium soy sauce
¼	cup rice vinegar
4	baby leeks
8	medium green scallions, red scallions, or green onions
1	medium lime, halved

PREP:
10 minutes
MARINATE:
30 minutes
GRILL:
8 minutes
MAKES:
4 servings

1 Thaw scallops, if frozen. Rinse scallops; pat dry with paper towels. For marinade, in a small bowl combine soy sauce and rice vinegar; set aside.

2 Trim root ends and green tops of leeks. Rinse leeks thoroughly to remove any grit.

3 Place scallops, leeks, and scallions in a resealable plastic bag set in a shallow dish. Pour marinade over scallops and vegetables. Seal bag; turn to coat scallops and vegetables. Marinate in refrigerator for 30 minutes.

4 Remove scallops, leeks, and scallions from bag. Discard marinade. Place leeks, scallops, scallions, and lime halves (cut sides down) on the rack of an uncovered grill directly over medium coals. Grill for 8 to 10 minutes or until scallops are opaque, turning scallops and vegetables occasionally. Remove scallions from grill rack before they overbrown.

5 To serve, transfer leeks and scallions to 4 dinner plates. Top with scallops. Using grilling tongs, remove limes from grill and squeeze over scallops.

Nutrition Facts per serving: 130 cal., 1 g total fat (0 g sat. fat), 37 mg chol., 478 mg sodium, 9 g carbo., 1 g fiber, 20 g pro.

9
carbs per serving

Exchanges:
½ Vegetable
½ Very Lean Meat
½ Other Carbo

SEARED SCALLOPS WITH TROPICAL SALSA

8
carbs per serving

Exchanges:
½ Fruit
2 Very Lean Meat

12	ounces fresh or frozen sea scallops
¼	teaspoon salt
⅛	teaspoon black pepper
1	cup finely chopped strawberry papaya or papaya
½	cup finely chopped, seeded cucumber
1	small tomato, seeded and chopped
2	tablespoons snipped fresh cilantro
1	fresh jalapeño chile pepper, seeded and finely chopped*
4	teaspoons lime juice
1	teaspoon olive oil
	Nonstick cooking spray
1	clove garlic, minced

1 Thaw scallops, if frozen. Rinse scallops; pat dry with paper towels. Halve any large scallops. Lightly sprinkle with salt and black pepper.

2 Meanwhile, for salsa, in a small bowl stir together papaya, cucumber, tomato, cilantro, chile pepper, lime juice, and oil. Let stand at room temperature for at least 15 minutes to allow flavors to blend.

3 Coat an unheated large nonstick skillet with nonstick cooking spray. Preheat over medium heat. Cook garlic in hot skillet for 30 seconds. Add scallops. Cook and stir for 2 to 3 minutes or until scallops are opaque. Use a slotted spoon to remove scallops; drain on paper towels. Serve the scallops with salsa.

*NOTE: Because chile peppers contain volatile oils that can burn your skin and eyes, avoid direct contact with them as much as possible. When working with chile peppers, wear plastic or rubber gloves. If your bare hands do touch the peppers, wash your hands and nails well with soap and warm water.

Nutrition Facts per serving: 108 cal., 2 g total fat (0 g sat. fat), 28 mg chol., 286 mg sodium, 8 g carbo., 1 g fiber, 15 g pro.

SCALLOPS WITH ANISE-ORANGE TAPENADE

12   fresh or frozen sea scallops (about 1¼ pounds total)

⅓   cup pitted kalamata olives, coarsely chopped

1   green onion, sliced

½   teaspoon finely shredded orange peel

2   teaspoons orange juice

¼   teaspoon anise seeds, crushed

⅛   teaspoon cayenne pepper

    Nonstick cooking spray

    Finely shredded orange peel (optional)

1 Thaw scallops, if frozen. Rinse scallops; pat dry with paper towels. Set aside.

2 For tapenade, in a small bowl combine olives, green onion, the ½ teaspoon orange peel, the orange juice, anise seeds, and cayenne pepper.

3 Coat an unheated large nonstick skillet with nonstick cooking spray. Preheat over medium-high heat. Add scallops to skillet; cook for 3 to 6 minutes or until scallops are opaque, turning once.

4 Serve cooked scallops with tapenade. If desired, sprinkle with additional orange peel.

Nutrition Facts per serving: 145 cal., 3 g total fat (0 g sat. fat), 47 mg chol., 353 mg sodium, 5 g carbo., 1 g fiber, 24 g pro.

START TO FINISH:
20 minutes
MAKES:
4 servings

5

carbs per serving

Exchanges:
3½ Very Lean Meat
½ Fat

ZUCCHINI WITH SHRIMP

8
carbs per serving

Exchanges:
1½ Vegetable
1½ Very Lean Meat
1 Fat

8	ounces fresh or frozen peeled and deveined medium shrimp
5	medium zucchini (about 1¼ pounds)
8	ounces fresh asparagus, bias-cut into 1-inch pieces
	Nonstick cooking spray
1	fresh jalapeño chile pepper, seeded and finely chopped*
1	tablespoon grated fresh ginger
2	cloves garlic, minced
2	tablespoons snipped fresh cilantro
1	tablespoon sesame seeds, toasted
2	teaspoons toasted sesame oil
¼	teaspoon salt
¼	teaspoon black pepper

1 Thaw shrimp, if frozen. Rinse shrimp; pat dry with paper towels. Halve each zucchini lengthwise. Place each half, cut side down, on a cutting board and cut into long, thin strips. Set aside.

2 Place asparagus in a steamer basket over gently boiling water. Cover and steam for 2 minutes. Add zucchini and steam for 1 to 3 minutes more or just until vegetables are crisp-tender (do not overcook). Drain well; cover and keep warm.

3 Meanwhile, coat an unheated large nonstick skillet with nonstick cooking spray. Preheat over medium-high heat. Add chile pepper, ginger, and garlic to hot skillet; cook for 30 seconds. Add shrimp. Cook and stir for 2 to 3 minutes or until shrimp are opaque.

4 Stir cilantro, sesame seeds, sesame oil, salt, and black pepper into shrimp mixture. Add steamed asparagus and zucchini; toss gently to coat.

*NOTE: Because chile peppers contain volatile oils that can burn your skin and eyes, avoid direct contact with them as much as possible. When working with chile peppers, wear plastic or rubber gloves. If your bare hands do touch the peppers, wash your hands and nails well with soap and warm water.

Nutrition Facts per serving: 127 cal., 5 g total fat (1 g sat. fat), 86 mg chol., 246 mg sodium, 8 g carbo., 3 g fiber, 14 g pro.

SPICY JALAPEÑO-SHRIMP PASTA

12	ounces fresh or frozen peeled and deveined large shrimp
8	ounces dried linguine
	Nonstick cooking spray
1	or 2 fresh jalapeño chile peppers, seeded and finely chopped*
2	cloves garlic, minced
2	cups cherry tomatoes, halved or quartered, or chopped tomatoes
½	teaspoon salt
¼	teaspoon black pepper
	Finely shredded Parmesan cheese (optional)

1 Thaw shrimp, if frozen. Rinse shrimp; pat dry with paper towels. Meanwhile, cook linguine according to package directions.

2 Coat an unheated large nonstick skillet with nonstick cooking spray. Preheat over medium-high heat. Add chile pepper(s) and garlic to hot skillet; cook and stir for 1 minute. Add shrimp; cook and stir about 3 minutes more or until shrimp are opaque. Stir in tomatoes, salt, and black pepper; heat through.

3 Drain linguine; toss with shrimp mixture. If desired, sprinkle with Parmesan cheese.

*NOTE: Because chile peppers contain volatile oils that can burn your skin and eyes, avoid direct contact with them as much as possible. When working with chile peppers, wear plastic or rubber gloves. If your bare hands do touch the peppers, wash your hands and nails well with soap and warm water.

Nutrition Facts per serving: 321 cal., 3 g total fat (0 g sat. fat), 129 mg chol., 423 mg sodium, 48 g carbo., 3 g fiber, 25 g pro.

START TO FINISH:
30 minutes
MAKES:
4 servings

48
carbs per serving

Exchanges:
½ Vegetable
3 Starch
2 Very Lean Meat

GARLIC & HERB SHRIMP SAUTE

START TO FINISH:
25 minutes
MAKES:
4 servings

4
carbs per serving

1	pound fresh or frozen large shrimp in shells
	Nonstick cooking spray
⅓	cup thinly sliced leek or thinly sliced green onions
4	cloves garlic, minced
½	teaspoon dried basil, oregano, or tarragon, crushed, or 1½ teaspoons snipped fresh basil, oregano, or tarragon
2	tablespoons dry sherry or dry white wine
1	tablespoon lemon juice
¼	teaspoon salt
¼	teaspoon black pepper
1	tablespoon snipped fresh parsley

❶ Thaw shrimp, if frozen. Peel and devein shrimp, leaving tails intact (if desired). Rinse shrimp; pat dry with paper towels. Set aside.

❷ Coat an unheated large nonstick skillet with nonstick cooking spray. Preheat over medium heat. Add shrimp, leek or green onions, garlic, and herb. Cook and stir for 2 to 4 minutes or until shrimp are opaque. Carefully add sherry or white wine, lemon juice, salt, and pepper to skillet. Cook and stir just until heated through. Stir in parsley.

Nutrition Facts per serving: 112 cal., 2 g total fat (0 g sat. fat), 129 mg chol., 255 mg sodium, 4 g carbo., 0 g fiber, 18 g pro.

Exchanges:
2½ Very Lean Meat
½ Fat

CURRIED SHRIMP WITH CUCUMBER SAUCE

1	pound fresh or frozen large shrimp in shells
¼	cup plain low-fat yogurt
¼	cup light mayonnaise dressing or salad dressing
¼	cup finely chopped cucumber
1	to 2 teaspoons snipped fresh mint
⅛	teaspoon salt
1	tablespoon curry powder
¼	teaspoon salt
1	tablespoon cooking oil

START TO FINISH:
25 minutes
MAKES:
4 servings

1 Thaw shrimp, if frozen. For sauce, in a small bowl combine yogurt, mayonnaise dressing, cucumber, mint, and the ⅛ teaspoon salt. Set aside.

2 Peel and devein shrimp, leaving the tails intact (if desired). Rinse shrimp; pat dry with paper towels. In a small bowl combine curry powder and the ¼ teaspoon salt; sprinkle evenly over shrimp.

3 In a large nonstick skillet heat oil over medium-high heat. Add shrimp; cook for 2 to 3 minutes or until shrimp are opaque, turning once. Serve the shrimp with sauce.

Nutrition Facts per serving: 216 cal., 11 g total fat (2 g sat. fat), 178 mg chol., 487 mg sodium, 5 g carbo., 1 g fiber, 24 g pro.

5
carbs per serving

Exchanges:
3½ Very Lean Meat
2 Fat

CREOLE-STYLE SHRIMP & GRITS

START TO FINISH:
35 minutes
MAKES:
4 servings

25
carbs per serving

Exchanges:
2 Vegetable
1 Starch
2 Very Lean Meat
1 Fat

1	pound fresh or frozen medium shrimp in shells
½	cup quick-cooking yellow grits
12	ounces fresh asparagus, trimmed and bias-sliced into 2-inch pieces
1	medium red sweet pepper, cut into ½-inch squares
½	cup chopped onion
2	cloves garlic, minced
1	tablespoon olive oil
2	tablespoons all-purpose flour
2	teaspoons salt-free Creole seasoning
¾	cup reduced-sodium chicken broth
	Salt
	Black pepper

1 Thaw shrimp, if frozen. Peel and devein shrimp, leaving tails intact (if desired). Rinse shrimp; pat dry with paper towels. Prepare grits according to package directions. Cover and keep warm.

2 Meanwhile, in a large skillet cook asparagus, sweet pepper, onion, and garlic in hot oil for 4 to 5 minutes or just until vegetables are tender.

3 Stir flour and Creole seasoning into vegetable mixture. Add chicken broth. Cook and stir just until bubbly; reduce heat. Stir in shrimp. Cover and cook for 1 to 3 minutes or until shrimp are opaque, stirring once. Serve over grits. Season to taste with salt and black pepper.

Nutrition Facts per serving: 241 cal., 6 g total fat (1 g sat. fat), 129 mg chol., 387 mg sodium, 25 g carbo., 2 g fiber, 22 g pro.

ROCK LOBSTER TAILS

4	6-ounce fresh or frozen rock lobster tails
2	tablespoons olive oil
¼	teaspoon finely shredded lemon peel or lime peel (set aside)
3	teaspoons lemon juice or lime juice
2	cloves garlic, minced
1	teaspoon chili powder
¼	cup light mayonnaise dressing or salad dressing
½	teaspoon snipped fresh dill or ⅛ teaspoon dried dill
	Lemon or lime wedges (optional)

1 Thaw rock lobster tails, if frozen. Using kitchen shears or a large sharp knife, cut each lobster tail in half through center of hard top shell, meat of lobster tail, and undershell. Set lobster tails aside.

2 In a small bowl combine oil, 2 teaspoons of the lemon or lime juice, the garlic, and chili powder; brush on exposed lobster meat, reserving extra juice mixture.

3 Place lobster tails, cut sides down, on the rack of an uncovered grill directly over medium coals. Grill for 6 minutes. Turn; brush with remaining juice mixture. Grill for 5 to 8 minutes more or until lobster is opaque in the center. Do not overcook.

4 Meanwhile, for dill dipping sauce, in a small bowl combine mayonnaise dressing, dill, lemon or lime peel, and remaining 1 teaspoon lemon or lime juice. Serve lobster with dill dipping sauce. If desired, serve with lemon or lime wedges.

Nutrition Facts per serving: 280 cal., 11 g total fat (2 g sat. fat), 119 mg chol., 438 mg sodium, 7 g carbo., 0 g fiber, 35 g pro.

PREP:
15 minutes
GRILL:
6 minutes +
5 minutes
MAKES:
4 servings

7
carbs per
serving

Exchanges:
5 Very Lean Meat
½ Other Carbo.
1½ Fat

ASIAN-STYLE NOODLES WITH CLAMS

START TO FINISH:
30 minutes
MAKES:
4 servings

6   ounces dried whole wheat linguine
1   teaspoon toasted sesame oil
½   cup shredded fresh spinach
2   6-ounce cans chopped clams
2   teaspoons cornstarch
     Nonstick cooking spray
2   cups thin short strips red and/or yellow sweet peppers
1   tablespoon grated fresh ginger
1   clove garlic, minced
¼   teaspoon crushed red pepper
1   tablespoon reduced-sodium soy sauce

43
carbs per serving

Exchanges:
1 Vegetable
2½ Starch
3 Very Lean Meat

1 Cook linguine according to package directions. Drain. Return to pan. Stir in sesame oil; stir in spinach. Cover and keep warm.

2 Meanwhile, drain clams, reserving liquid. Measure ¾ cup clam liquid (if necessary, add enough water to clam liquid to equal ¾ cup). Stir liquid into cornstarch; set aside.

3 Coat an unheated large nonstick skillet with nonstick cooking spray. Preheat over medium-high heat. Add sweet peppers, ginger, garlic, and crushed red pepper. Cook and stir for 3 minutes. Stir in clam liquid mixture and soy sauce. Cook and stir over medium heat until bubbly; cook and stir for 1 minute more. Stir in clams. Cook and stir for 1 minute more or until clams are heated through.

4 Serve clam mixture over warm linguine mixture.

Nutrition Facts per serving: 316 cal., 4 g total fat (0 g sat. fat), 57 mg chol., 246 mg sodium, 43 g carbo., 2 g fiber, 29 g pro.

SOUPS & STEWS

ASIAN VEGETABLE, CHICKEN & SHRIMP SOUP

START TO FINISH:
30 minutes
MAKES:
6 servings

9
carbs per serving

Exchanges:
1 Vegetable
4 Very Lean Meat
½ Fat

8 ounces fresh or frozen peeled and deveined medium shrimp
   Nonstick cooking spray

12 ounces skinless, boneless chicken breast halves, cut into bite-size pieces

4 cups reduced-sodium chicken broth

2 cups water

8 ounces fresh bean sprouts, snipped

1 cup broccoli florets

½ of a 15-ounce jar (drained weight) straw mushrooms or one 8½-ounce jar (drained weight) whole mushrooms, drained

½ cup chopped red and/or green sweet pepper

4 green onions, diagonally sliced into 1-inch-long pieces

2 tablespoons reduced-sodium soy sauce
   Black pepper

1 Thaw shrimp, if frozen. Rinse shrimp; pat dry with paper towels. Set aside. Coat an unheated 4-quart Dutch oven with nonstick cooking spray. Preheat over medium heat. Add chicken to hot Dutch oven; cook and stir until no longer pink.

2 Add chicken broth and the water to Dutch oven. Bring to boiling. Add shrimp, bean sprouts, broccoli, mushrooms, sweet pepper, green onions, and soy sauce. Return to boiling; boil gently, uncovered, for 1 to 2 minutes or until shrimp are opaque and vegetables are just tender. Season to taste with black pepper.

Nutrition Facts per serving: 185 cal., 4 g total fat (1 g sat. fat), 90 mg chol., 807 mg sodium, 9 g carbo., 2 g fiber, 29 g pro.

MEXICAN CORN SOUP

1   16-ounce package frozen whole kernel corn, thawed
1   cup reduced-sodium chicken broth
1   4-ounce can diced green chile peppers
1   clove garlic, minced
1   tablespoon snipped fresh oregano or 1 teaspoon dried oregano, crushed
½   teaspoon salt
¼   teaspoon black pepper
2   cups fat-free milk
1   cup chopped cooked chicken (about 5 ounces)
1   cup chopped tomatoes
1   cup shredded Monterey Jack cheese (4 ounces)

1 In a blender combine half of the corn and the chicken broth. Cover; blend until nearly smooth.

2 In a large saucepan combine corn puree, remaining corn, undrained chile peppers, garlic, dried oregano (if using), salt, and black pepper. Bring to boiling; reduce heat. Simmer, uncovered, for 10 minutes, stirring occasionally.

3 Stir in milk, chicken, tomatoes, and fresh oregano (if using); heat just until boiling. Remove from heat. Stir in cheese until melted.

Nutrition Facts per serving: 222 cal., 8 g total fat (4 g sat. fat), 39 mg chol., 501 mg sodium, 22 g carbo., 2 g fiber, 17 g pro.

PREP:
20 minutes
COOK:
10 minutes
MAKES:
6 servings

22
carbs per serving

Exchanges:
½ Milk
1 Starch
1½ Lean Meat
½ Fat

CREOLE CHICKEN SOUP

START TO FINISH:
25 minutes
MAKES:
6 servings

7
carbs per serving

Exchanges:
1 Vegetable
2 Very Lean Meat
½ Fat

Nonstick cooking spray

12 ounces skinless, boneless chicken thighs, cut into 1-inch pieces

⅓ cup finely chopped cooked ham

1 cup coarsely chopped onion

¾ cup coarsely chopped green sweet pepper

3 cups reduced-sodium chicken broth

1 10-ounce can chopped tomatoes and green chile peppers

1 cup loose-pack frozen cut okra, thawed

1 tablespoon snipped fresh parsley

1 Coat an unheated Dutch oven with nonstick cooking spray. Preheat over medium-high heat. Add chicken and ham to hot Dutch oven. Cook and stir for 2 to 3 minutes or until chicken is browned.

2 Add onion and sweet pepper to Dutch oven; cook and stir about 2 minutes or until vegetables are nearly tender. Add chicken broth, undrained tomatoes and green chile peppers, and okra. Bring to boiling; reduce heat. Cover and simmer for 6 to 8 minutes or until chicken is no longer pink. Stir in parsley.

Nutrition Facts per serving: 121 cal., 3 g total fat (1 g sat. fat), 51 mg chol., 646 mg sodium, 7 g carbo., 2 g fiber, 15 g pro.

SPANISH CHICKEN STEW

1   pound skinless, boneless chicken thighs, cut into 1½-inch pieces
¼   teaspoon salt
¼   teaspoon black pepper
      Nonstick cooking spray
1   medium onion, thinly sliced
1   red sweet pepper, cut into thin bite-size strips
2   cloves garlic, minced
12   ounces red potatoes, cut into ½-inch wedges
1   cup reduced-sodium chicken broth
½   teaspoon dried savory, crushed, or 1½ teaspoons snipped fresh savory
¼   teaspoon dried thyme, crushed, or 1 teaspoon snipped fresh thyme
1   14½-ounce can diced tomatoes, undrained
3   tablespoons chopped pimiento-stuffed olives

1 Sprinkle chicken with salt and pepper. Coat an unheated 4-quart Dutch oven with nonstick cooking spray. Preheat over medium-high heat. Add chicken to hot Dutch oven; cook and stir until no longer pink.

2 Add onion and sweet pepper; cook and stir about 3 minutes or until crisp-tender. Add garlic; cook and stir for 30 seconds more. Add potatoes, chicken broth, dried savory (if using), and dried thyme (if using). Bring to boiling; reduce heat. Cover and simmer about 15 minutes or until chicken and potatoes are tender. Add undrained tomatoes. Return to boiling; reduce heat. Cover and simmer for 5 minutes. Stir in olives, fresh savory (if using), and fresh thyme (if using).

Nutrition Facts per serving: 258 cal., 5 g total fat (1 g sat. fat), 90 mg chol., 683 mg sodium, 24 g carbo., 3 g fiber, 26 g pro.

PREP:
15 minutes
COOK:
15 minutes +
5 minutes
MAKES:
4 servings

24
carbs per
serving

Exchanges:
1 Vegetable
1 Starch
3 Very Lean Meat
1 Fat

GINGER-CHICKEN NOODLE SOUP

PREP:
20 minutes
COOK:
*20 minutes +
8 minutes*
MAKES:
5 servings

1	tablespoon cooking oil
1	pound skinless, boneless chicken thighs, cut into 1-inch pieces
3	14-ounce cans reduced-sodium chicken broth
2	medium carrots, cut into thin bite-size sticks
1	cup water
2	tablespoons rice vinegar
1	tablespoon reduced-sodium soy sauce
2	to 3 teaspoons grated fresh ginger or ½ to ¾ teaspoon ground ginger
¼	teaspoon black pepper
2	ounces dried rice vermicelli noodles* or medium noodles
1	6-ounce package frozen pea pods, thawed and halved diagonally
	Reduced-sodium soy sauce (optional)

16
carbs per
serving

Exchanges:
1 Starch
3 Very Lean Meat
1 Fat

1 In a Dutch oven heat oil over medium heat. Cook chicken, half at a time, in hot oil just until browned. Drain off fat. Return all chicken to Dutch oven. Add chicken broth, carrots, the water, rice vinegar, the 1 tablespoon soy sauce, the ginger, and pepper. Bring to boiling; reduce heat. Cover and simmer for 20 minutes.

2 Return to boiling. Add noodles. Simmer, uncovered, for 8 to 10 minutes or until noodles are tender, adding pea pods for the last 1 to 2 minutes of cooking time. If desired, serve with additional soy sauce.

*NOTE: If desired, cut or break rice vermicelli noodles into 2-inch-long pieces.

Nutrition Facts per serving: 221 cal., 6 g total fat (1 g sat. fat), 72 mg chol., 805 mg sodium, 16 g carbo., 2 g fiber, 23 g pro.

GARDEN CHICKEN SOUP

Nonstick cooking spray

12 ounces packaged skinless, boneless chicken breast strips for stir-frying

3 cups reduced-sodium chicken broth

12 baby carrots (about 6 ounces with ½-inch tops) or 6 ounces packaged peeled baby carrots

2 medium onions, cut into thin wedges

2 cloves garlic, minced

1 tablespoon snipped fresh lemon thyme or thyme or 1 teaspoon dried thyme, crushed

1 large yellow summer squash, halved lengthwise and sliced (about 2 cups)

2 cups shredded fresh Swiss chard

1 Coat an unheated very large nonstick skillet with nonstick cooking spray. Preheat over medium-high heat. Add chicken to hot skillet; cook and stir about 3 minutes or until no longer pink.

2 Carefully add chicken broth, carrots, onions, garlic, and dried thyme (if using) to skillet. Bring to boiling; reduce heat. Cover and simmer for 5 minutes. Add yellow summer squash and Swiss chard. Cover and simmer about 3 minutes more or just until vegetables are tender. Stir in fresh thyme (if using).

Nutrition Facts per serving: 157 cal., 2 g total fat (0 g sat. fat), 49 mg chol., 544 mg sodium, 12 g carbo., 3 g fiber, 23 g pro.

START TO FINISH:
35 minutes
MAKES:
4 servings

12 carbs per serving

Exchanges:
2 Vegetable
3 Very Lean Meat

KALE, LENTIL & CHICKEN SOUP

PREP:
25 minutes
COOK:
10 minutes +
10 minutes +
5 minutes
MAKES:
6 servings

20
carbs per
serving

Exchanges:
1½ Vegetable
½ Starch
2 Very Lean Meat
½ Fat

Nonstick cooking spray
1   cup chopped onion
1   cup coarsely chopped carrots
2   cloves garlic, minced
6   cups reduced-sodium chicken broth
1   tablespoon snipped fresh basil or 1 teaspoon dried basil, crushed
4   cups coarsely chopped fresh kale (about 8 ounces)
¼   teaspoon salt
⅛   teaspoon black pepper
1½ cups cubed cooked chicken (about 8 ounces)
1   medium tomato, seeded and chopped
½   cup dry red lentils*

1 Coat an unheated large nonstick saucepan with nonstick cooking spray. Preheat over medium-low heat. Add onion, carrots, and garlic to hot saucepan. Cover and cook for 5 to 7 minutes or until vegetables are nearly tender, stirring occasionally.

2 Add chicken broth and dried basil (if using) to vegetable mixture. Bring to boiling; reduce heat. Cover and simmer for 10 minutes. Stir in kale, salt, and pepper. Return to boiling; reduce heat. Cover and simmer for 10 minutes.

3 Stir in chicken, tomato, red lentils, and fresh basil (if using). Cover and simmer for 5 to 10 minutes more or until kale and lentils are tender.

*NOTE: If you wish to substitute brown or yellow lentils for the red lentils, you'll need to increase the cooking time. Check the package directions for cooking times and add the lentils in step 2.

Nutrition Facts per serving: 179 cal., 3 g total fat (1 g sat. fat), 31 mg chol., 736 mg sodium, 20 g carbo., 5 g fiber, 18 g pro.

MEXICAN-STYLE TURKEY SOUP

Nonstick cooking spray

1   cup chopped onion

1   large red sweet pepper, chopped

1   teaspoon ground cumin

1   teaspoon chili powder

½   teaspoon paprika

5   cups reduced-sodium chicken broth

1½ cups peeled, cubed winter squash

1   large tomato, chopped

¼   teaspoon salt

¼   teaspoon black pepper

2   cups chopped cooked turkey or chicken (about 10 ounces)

1   cup loose-pack frozen whole kernel corn

2   tablespoons snipped fresh cilantro

1 Coat an unheated Dutch oven with nonstick cooking spray. Preheat over medium heat. Add onion and sweet pepper to hot Dutch oven. Cook about 5 minutes or until tender, stirring occasionally. Stir in cumin, chili powder, and paprika; cook and stir for 30 seconds.

2 Add chicken broth, squash, tomato, salt, and black pepper. Bring to boiling; reduce heat. Cover and simmer about 20 minutes or until squash is tender, stirring occasionally. Stir in turkey or chicken, corn, and cilantro; heat through.

Nutrition Facts per serving: 153 cal., 3 g total fat (1 g sat. fat), 35 mg chol., 615 mg sodium, 15 g carbo., 3 g fiber, 17 g pro.

PREP:
20 minutes
COOK:
20 minutes
MAKES:
6 servings

15
carbs per serving

Exchanges:
1 Vegetable
½ Starch
2 Very Lean Meat
½ Fat

BEEF & RUTABAGA STEW

PREP:
25 minutes
COOK:
*30 minutes +
1 hour*
MAKES:
6 servings

15
carbs per
serving

Exchanges:
2 Vegetable
2 Very Lean Meat
1½ Fat

12	ounces boneless beef chuck roast
2	tablespoons all-purpose flour
2	tablespoons olive oil or cooking oil
1	cup chopped onion
1	14-ounce can reduced-sodium beef broth
1	cup water
½	cup dry red wine
1	tablespoon Worcestershire sauce
10	cloves garlic
1	bay leaf
½	teaspoon dried thyme, crushed
¼	teaspoon black pepper
1	pound rutabaga, peeled and cut into ¾-inch cubes
6	ounces fresh green beans, trimmed and cut into 2½-inch pieces, or 1 cup loose-pack frozen cut green beans
1	tablespoon tomato paste

1 Trim fat from roast. Cut roast into ¾-inch cubes. Place flour in a resealable plastic bag. Add meat cubes, a few at a time, shaking to coat.

2 In a large saucepan or Dutch oven heat oil over medium heat. Add meat cubes and onion; cook for 4 to 5 minutes or until meat is brown. Drain off fat. Stir beef broth, the water, red wine, Worcestershire sauce, garlic, bay leaf, thyme, and black pepper into meat mixture in Dutch oven. Bring to boiling; reduce heat. Cover and simmer for 30 minutes.

3 Stir in rutabaga. Bring to boiling; reduce heat. Cover and simmer about 1 hour more or until meat and rutabaga are tender, adding fresh green beans for the last 20 minutes or frozen green beans for the last 10 minutes of cooking. Discard bay leaf. Stir in tomato paste.

Nutrition Facts per serving: 194 cal., 7 g total fat (1 g sat. fat), 34 mg chol., 212 mg sodium, 15 g carbo., 3 g fiber, 15 g pro.

BEEF SOUP WITH ROOT VEGETABLES

1½	pounds boneless beef round steak
	Nonstick cooking spray
3	14-ounce cans reduced-sodium beef broth
1	cup water
2	stalks celery, sliced
1	large onion, coarsely chopped
1	medium carrot, sliced
2	tablespoons snipped fresh thyme or 2 teaspoons dried thyme, crushed
2	teaspoons Worcestershire sauce
2	cloves garlic, minced
¼	teaspoon salt
¼	teaspoon black pepper
1	bay leaf
2	medium potatoes, peeled and cut into ¾-inch cubes
2	medium turnips, peeled and cut into ¾-inch cubes
1	large sweet potato, peeled and cut into ¾-inch cubes

1 Trim fat from steak. Cut steak into ¾-inch cubes. Coat an unheated 4-quart Dutch oven with nonstick cooking spray. Preheat over medium-high heat. Cook meat, half at a time, in hot pan until brown. Return all of the meat to the Dutch oven.

2 Add beef broth, the water, celery, onion, carrot, dried thyme (if using), Worcestershire sauce, garlic, salt, pepper, and bay leaf.

3 Bring to boiling; reduce heat. Cover and simmer about 1¼ hours or until meat is nearly tender. Discard bay leaf. Stir in potatoes, turnips, and sweet potato. Return to boiling; reduce heat. Cover and simmer about 15 minutes more or until meat and vegetables are tender. Stir in fresh thyme (if using).

Nutrition Facts per serving: 167 cal., 2 g total fat (1 g sat. fat), 37 mg chol., 453 mg sodium, 14 g carbo., 2 g fiber, 23 g pro.

PREP:
30 minutes
COOK:
1¼ hours +
15 minutes
MAKES:
8 servings

14
carbs per serving

Exchanges:
½ Vegetable
1 Starch
2½ Very Lean Meat

HEARTY BEEF STEW

PREP:
15 minutes
COOK:
*1 hour +
30 minutes*
MAKES:
6 servings

34

carbs per
serving

Exchanges:
2 Vegetable
1½ Starch
2 Lean Meat

1	pound boneless beef round steak
2	cups chopped onions
1	14-ounce can reduced-sodium beef broth
1	cup water
½	teaspoon salt
½	teaspoon dried thyme, crushed
¼	teaspoon black pepper
2	cloves garlic, minced
1	pound tiny new potatoes, quartered (3 cups)
1	pound carrots, sliced (3 cups)
8	ounces fresh mushrooms, quartered
1	14½-ounce can diced tomatoes, undrained
3	tablespoons tomato paste
1	cup loose-pack frozen peas, thawed

1 Trim fat from steak. Cut steak into 1-inch pieces. In a 4-quart Dutch oven combine meat, onions, beef broth, the water, salt, thyme, pepper, and garlic. Bring to boiling; reduce heat. Cover and simmer for 1 hour.

2 Stir in potatoes, carrots, and mushrooms. Return to boiling; reduce heat. Cover and simmer about 30 minutes more or until meat and vegetables are tender.

3 Stir in undrained tomatoes and tomato paste. Stir in peas; heat through.

Nutrition Facts per serving: 277 cal., 6 g total fat (2 g sat. fat), 45 mg chol., 517 mg sodium, 34 g carbo., 7 g fiber, 24 g pro.

GOULASH SOUP

2   tablespoons cooking oil

1   pound beef top round, cut into ½-inch cubes

1   medium onion, chopped

2   tablespoons all-purpose flour

1   tablespoon Hungarian paprika or paprika

2   cloves garlic, minced

3   14-ounce cans reduced-sodium chicken broth

1   14½-ounce can diced tomatoes, undrained

3   medium carrots, sliced

2   tablespoons tomato paste

1   bay leaf

½   teaspoon dried marjoram, crushed

½   teaspoon caraway seeds, crushed

½   teaspoon black pepper

2   medium potatoes, peeled and cubed

    Light dairy sour cream (optional)

1 In a 4- to 5-quart Dutch oven heat oil over medium-high heat. Add beef and onion; cook and stir about 5 minutes or until beef is brown and onion is tender.

2 Add flour, paprika, and garlic; cook, stirring constantly, for 3 minutes. Carefully stir in chicken broth, undrained tomatoes, carrots, tomato paste, bay leaf, marjoram, caraway seeds, and pepper. Bring to boiling; reduce heat. Cover and simmer for 50 minutes, stirring occasionally. Stir in potatoes. Cover and simmer for 25 to 30 minutes more or until potatoes and beef are tender. Discard bay leaf. If desired, top individual servings with sour cream.

Nutrition Facts per serving: 226 cal., 7 g total fat (1 g sat. fat), 42 mg chol., 675 mg sodium, 19 g carbo., 4 g fiber, 22 g pro.

PREP:
25 minutes
COOK:
50 minutes +
25 minutes
MAKES:
6 servings

19
carbs per serving

Exchanges:
1 Vegetable
1 Starch
2½ Very Lean Meat
1 Fat

SPICED PORK STEW

PREP:
40 minutes
BAKE:
*1 hour
20 minutes*
OVEN:
350°F
MAKES:
8 servings

22
carbs per
serving

Exchanges:
1½ Vegetable
1 Starch
1½ Medium-Fat Meat

3 tablespoons all-purpose flour

1 teaspoon ground cumin

2 pounds boneless pork shoulder, cut into ¾-inch pieces

1 medium onion, chopped

2 tablespoons cooking oil

2 14½-ounce cans diced tomatoes, undrained

⅓ cup water

1 teaspoon salt

1 teaspoon ground ginger

1 teaspoon ground cinnamon

½ teaspoon sugar

½ teaspoon black pepper

2 medium carrots, sliced

2 medium red potatoes, chopped

1 medium sweet potato, peeled and chopped

2 cups loose-pack frozen cut green beans

2 tablespoons snipped fresh cilantro or parsley

½ cup plain low-fat yogurt (optional)

❶ In a resealable plastic bag combine flour and cumin. Add pork pieces to plastic bag; shake to coat pork. In an oven-going 4- to 5-quart Dutch oven cook pork and onion, half at a time, in hot oil until meat is browned. Drain off fat. Return all pork and onion to the Dutch oven.

❷ Stir in undrained tomatoes, the water, salt, ginger, cinnamon, sugar, and pepper. Stir in carrots, red potatoes, sweet potato, and green beans. Bring mixture just to boiling.

❸ Cover and bake in a 350° oven about 1 hour and 20 minutes or until pork and vegetables are tender. Sprinkle individual servings with cilantro or parsley. If desired, serve with yogurt.

Nutrition Facts per serving: 245 cal., 9 g total fat (3 g sat. fat), 51 mg chol., 530 mg sodium, 22 g carbo., 3 g fiber, 17 g pro.

ASIAN PORK SOUP

Nonstick cooking spray

12 ounces lean boneless pork, cut into thin bite-size strips

2 cups sliced fresh shiitake mushrooms

2 cloves garlic, minced

3 14-ounce cans reduced-sodium chicken broth

2 tablespoons dry sherry

2 tablespoons reduced-sodium soy sauce

2 teaspoons grated fresh ginger or ½ teaspoon ground ginger

¼ teaspoon crushed red pepper

2 cups thinly sliced napa cabbage

1 green onion, thinly sliced

1 Coat an unheated large nonstick saucepan with nonstick cooking spray. Preheat saucepan over medium heat. Add pork to hot saucepan; cook for 2 to 3 minutes or until slightly pink in center. Remove from saucepan; set aside. Add mushrooms and garlic to saucepan; cook and stir until tender.

2 Stir in chicken broth, sherry, soy sauce, ginger, and crushed red pepper. Bring to boiling. Stir in pork, cabbage, and green onion; heat through.

Nutrition Facts per serving: 140 cal., 3 g total fat (1 g sat. fat), 31 mg chol., 691 mg sodium, 10 g carbo., 1 g fiber, 16 g pro.

START TO FINISH:
20 minutes
MAKES:
6 servings

10
carbs per serving

Exchanges:
1 Vegetable
2 Very Lean Meat
1 Fat

HARVEST PORK SOUP

PREP:
30 minutes
COOK:
10 minutes
MAKES:
6 servings

24

carbs per serving

Exchanges:
½ Vegetable
1½ Starch
1½ Very Lean Meat

10   ounces boneless pork loin chops, cut ¾ inch thick
      Nonstick cooking spray

3   14-ounce cans reduced-sodium beef broth or chicken broth

2   cups cubed, peeled sweet potatoes

1   cup sliced carrots

1   cup chopped onion

1   cup chopped, peeled turnip

½   cup sliced celery

½   cup quick-cooking barley

1   tablespoon snipped fresh oregano or 1 teaspoon dried oregano, crushed

1   tablespoon snipped fresh sage or ½ teaspoon dried sage, crushed

¼   teaspoon black pepper

1 Trim fat from chops. Cut chops into ¾-inch pieces. Coat an unheated 4-quart Dutch oven with nonstick cooking spray. Preheat over medium heat. Add pork to hot Dutch oven; cook for 4 to 5 minutes or until brown.

2 Add broth, sweet potatoes, carrots, onion, turnip, celery, barley, dried oregano (if using), dried sage (if using), and pepper. Bring to boiling; reduce heat. Cover and simmer for 10 to 12 minutes or until vegetables and barley are tender. Stir in fresh oregano (if using) and fresh sage (if using).

Nutrition Facts per serving: 183 cal., 3 g total fat (1 g sat. fat), 26 mg chol., 426 mg sodium, 24 g carbo., 4 g fiber, 15 g pro.

HOT 'N' SPICY FISH SOUP

3   6-ounce fresh or frozen halibut steaks, 1 inch thick

     Nonstick cooking spray

½   teaspoon cumin seeds

1   medium onion, chopped

4   to 5 teaspoons grated fresh ginger

2   fresh serrano chile peppers, seeded and finely chopped*

4   small plum tomatoes, chopped

1½ cups water

1   teaspoon ground coriander

½   teaspoon ground turmeric

½   teaspoon salt

     Fresh cilantro leaves (optional)

1 Thaw fish, if frozen. Rinse fish; pat dry with paper towels. Remove and discard skin and bones. Cut fish into 1-inch pieces; set aside.

2 Coat an unheated large nonstick saucepan with nonstick cooking spray. Preheat over medium heat. Add cumin seeds; cook and stir about 1 minute or until toasted. Add onion; cook and stir for 4 to 5 minutes or until tender. Add ginger and serrano pepper; cook and stir for 1 minute more. Add tomatoes; cook and stir for 2 to 3 minutes more or until tomatoes have softened. Stir in the water, coriander, turmeric, and salt. Bring just to boiling; reduce heat. Stir in fish. Cover and cook about 5 minutes or just until fish flakes easily when tested with a fork. If desired, garnish with cilantro. Serve immediately.

***NOTE:** Because chile peppers contain volatile oils that can burn your skin and eyes, avoid direct contact with them as much as possible. When working with chile peppers, wear plastic or rubber gloves. If your bare hands do touch the peppers, wash your hands and nails well with soap and warm water.

Nutrition Facts per serving: 164 cal., 3 g total fat (0 g sat. fat), 40 mg chol., 366 mg sodium, 5 g carbo., 1 g fiber, 27 g pro.

START TO FINISH:
35 minutes
MAKES:
4 servings

5

carbs per serving

Exchanges:
½ Vegetable
4 Very Lean Meat
½ Fat

SEAFOOD CIOPPINO

PREP:
35 minutes
STAND:
20 minutes
COOK:
20 minutes +
5 minutes
MAKES:
6 servings

24

carbs per
serving

Exchanges:
½ Vegetable
1½ Starch
4 Very Lean Meat
1 Fat

1 pound fresh or frozen firm white fish
(such as orange roughy or cod)

1 pound fresh or frozen monkfish

8 ounces fresh or frozen medium shrimp

2 dried pasilla chile peppers

¾ teaspoon chili powder

2 tablespoons olive oil

1 large onion, chopped

1 cup loose-pack frozen whole kernel corn

6 cloves garlic, minced

1 15- to 19-ounce can white kidney beans
(cannellini beans), rinsed and drained

1 14½-ounce can diced tomatoes, undrained

1 8-ounce bottle clam juice

1 cup dry white wine or reduced-sodium chicken broth

2 tablespoons canned diced green chile peppers

1 Thaw fish and shrimp, if frozen. Cut fish into 1-inch pieces. Peel and devein shrimp, leaving tails intact. Rinse fish and shrimp; pat dry.

2 In bowl cover pasilla peppers with boiling water. Let stand 20 minutes. Using a slotted spoon, remove peppers; reserve ¼ cup of the soaking liquid. Remove seeds and stems from peppers and discard. In a blender combine peppers and reserved liquid; cover and blend until smooth.

3 In a shallow bowl combine fish and shrimp. Combine ½ teaspoon salt and the chili powder; sprinkle over fish mixture. In a 4-quart Dutch oven heat 1 tablespoon of the oil over medium-high heat. Add half of the fish mixture; cook about 4 minutes or just until done, turning occasionally. Using a slotted spatula, transfer mixture to a bowl. Repeat with remaining fish mixture. (Add additional oil during cooking, if necessary.) Cover and chill.

4 In Dutch oven heat remaining oil. Add onion, corn, and garlic; cook and stir for 3 minutes. Stir in 1 cup water. Add pureed pepper mixture, white kidney beans, undrained tomatoes, clam juice, wine, green chile peppers, and ½ teaspoon salt. Bring to boiling; reduce heat. Cover and simmer for 20 minutes. Uncover; add fish mixture. Simmer for 5 minutes more.

Nutrition Facts per serving: 313 cal., 8 g total fat (1 g sat. fat), 78 mg chol., 812 mg sodium, 24 g carbo., 5 g fiber, 34 g pro.

SHRIMP & GREENS SOUP

12	ounces peeled and deveined fresh or frozen shrimp
1	large leek
	Nonstick cooking spray
2	cloves garlic, minced
3	14-ounce cans reduced-sodium chicken broth or vegetable broth
1	tablespoon snipped fresh parsley
1	teaspoon snipped fresh marjoram or thyme or ¼ teaspoon dried marjoram or dried thyme, crushed
¼	teaspoon lemon-pepper seasoning
3	cups shredded bok choy or fresh spinach leaves

1 Thaw shrimp, if frozen. Rinse shrimp; pat dry with paper towels. Set aside. Wash leek; trim roots from base. Cut leek in half lengthwise. Cut into thin slices (about ½ cup).

2 Coat an unheated large nonstick saucepan with nonstick cooking spray. Preheat over medium-high heat. Add leek and garlic to hot saucepan; cook about 2 minutes or until leek is tender. Carefully add chicken broth, parsley, marjoram or thyme, and lemon-pepper seasoning. Bring to boiling; add shrimp. Return to boiling; reduce heat.

3 Simmer, uncovered, for 2 minutes. Stir in the bok choy or spinach. Cook about 1 minute more or until bok choy or spinach is wilted.

Nutrition Facts per serving: 134 cal., 2 g total fat (0 g sat. fat), 129 mg chol., 947 mg sodium, 6 g carbo., 2 g fiber, 22 g pro.

START TO FINISH:
20 minutes
MAKES:
4 servings

6
carbs per serving

Exchanges:
1 Vegetable
3 Very Lean Meat

FENNEL-SHRIMP CHOWDER

12 ounces fresh or frozen peeled and deveined medium shrimp

1 small fennel bulb

12 ounces fresh asparagus

3 cups reduced-sodium chicken broth

1 cup chopped peeled potato

⅔ cup thinly sliced leek

⅛ teaspoon salt

⅛ teaspoon black pepper

¾ cup finely chopped red sweet pepper

1 cup fat-free half-and-half

2 tablespoons cornstarch

24
carbs per
serving

Exchanges:
2 Vegetable
1 Starch
2½ Very Lean Meat

① Thaw shrimp, if frozen. Rinse shrimp; pat dry with paper towels. Set aside. Cut off and discard upper stalks of fennel, reserving some feathery leaves for garnish. Remove wilted outer layer of stalks and cut off a thin slice from base. Finely chop fennel bulb. Snap off and discard woody bases from asparagus. Scrape off scales. Cut asparagus into 1-inch-long pieces.

② In a large saucepan combine chopped fennel, chicken broth, potato, leek, salt, and black pepper. Bring to boiling; reduce heat. Cover and simmer for 8 minutes. Add shrimp, asparagus, and sweet pepper. Bring to boiling.

③ In a small bowl combine half-and-half and cornstarch; add to shrimp mixture. Cook and stir until thickened and bubbly. Cook and stir about 2 minutes more or until shrimp are opaque. Garnish individual servings with fennel leaves.

Nutrition Facts per serving: 200 cal., 2 g total fat (0 g sat. fat), 97 mg chol., 717 mg sodium, 24 g carbo., 8 g fiber, 20 g pro.

TUSCAN BEAN SOUP WITH SPINACH

8 ounces dry white kidney beans (cannellini beans)
   or Great Northern beans (about 1½ cups)

1 pound crosscut beef shanks (1 to 1½ inches thick)

1 tablespoon olive oil

3 medium onions, chopped

3 medium carrots, chopped

1 cup fennel wedges or chopped celery

4 cloves garlic, minced

12 ounces smoked ham hocks

1 tablespoon instant beef bouillon granules

1 bay leaf

1 14½-ounce can diced tomatoes, undrained

4 cups torn fresh spinach leaves

2 teaspoons snipped fresh thyme

2 teaspoons snipped fresh rosemary

PREP:
30 minutes
STAND:
1 hour
COOK:
*1½ hours +
30 minutes*
MAKES:
10 servings

22 carbs per serving

Exchanges:
1½ Vegetable
1 Starch
1 Lean Meat

1 Rinse beans. In a 4½- to 6-quart Dutch oven combine beans and 6 cups water. Bring to boiling; reduce heat. Simmer, uncovered, for 2 minutes. Remove from heat. Cover and let stand for 1 hour. (Or place beans in water in Dutch oven. Cover and let soak in a cool place for 6 to 8 hours or overnight.) Drain; set aside. Sprinkle beef with ¼ teaspoon salt and ¼ teaspoon black pepper. In a 4½- to 6-quart Dutch oven heat oil over medium-high heat. Add beef; cook about 5 minutes or until brown, turning once. Transfer beef to a plate. Reserve 1 tablespoon of the drippings in Dutch oven.

2 Add onions, carrots, fennel, and garlic to Dutch oven. Cover and cook about 10 minutes or until vegetables are tender, stirring occasionally. Return beef to Dutch oven; add 6 cups water. Stir in drained beans, ham hocks, bouillon granules, bay leaf, and ½ teaspoon salt. Bring to boiling; reduce heat. Cover and simmer for 1½ hours. Stir in undrained tomatoes. Return to boiling; reduce heat. Cover and simmer about 30 minutes more or until beans and meats are tender.

3 Remove ham hocks and beef; let stand until cool enough to handle. Remove meat from bones. Cut meat into bite-size pieces; return to soup. Discard bones and bay leaf. Skim off fat. Stir in spinach, thyme, and rosemary. Heat through.

Nutrition Facts per serving: 169 cal., 3 g total fat (1 g sat. fat), 14 mg chol., 608 mg sodium, 22 g carbo., 8 g fiber, 13 g pro.

PROVENÇAL VEGETABLE STEW

START TO FINISH:
35 minutes
OVEN:
400°F
MAKES:
4 servings

40
carbs per
serving

Exchanges:
2½ Vegetable
1½ Starch
½ Fat

4	½-inch-thick slices baguette-style French bread
3	tablespoons finely shredded Romano or Parmesan cheese
2	baby eggplants or 1 very small eggplant (about 8 ounces)
	Nonstick cooking spray
1	large zucchini, quartered lengthwise and cut into ½-inch-thick slices
1	large yellow summer squash, quartered lengthwise and cut into ½-inch-thick slices
4	cloves garlic, minced
1½	cups low-sodium tomato juice
1	tablespoon snipped fresh basil or 1 teaspoon dried basil, crushed
1	teaspoon snipped fresh rosemary or thyme or ¼ teaspoon dried rosemary or thyme, crushed
1	15- to 19-ounce can white kidney beans (cannellini beans) or Great Northern beans, rinsed and drained
1	large tomato, chopped
¼	teaspoon black pepper
1	tablespoon white or regular balsamic vinegar

❶ For croutons, sprinkle bread slices with 1 tablespoon of the cheese. Place bread on a baking sheet. Bake in a 400° oven for 6 to 8 minutes or until toasted. Set aside.

❷ Meanwhile, peel eggplant, if desired. Cut eggplant into ¾-inch cubes (you should have about 2 cups). Coat an unheated large nonstick saucepan with nonstick cooking spray. Preheat over medium heat. Add eggplant, zucchini, yellow squash, and garlic to hot saucepan. Cook and stir about 5 minutes or until vegetables are nearly tender. Add tomato juice, dried basil (if using), and dried rosemary or thyme (if using).

❸ Bring to boiling; reduce heat. Simmer, uncovered, for 5 minutes. Stir in beans. Simmer, uncovered, for 2 to 3 minutes more or until vegetables are tender. Stir in tomato, fresh basil (if using), fresh rosemary or thyme (if using), and pepper. Heat through. Remove from heat; stir in balsamic vinegar.

❹ To serve, ladle vegetable mixture into bowls. Top each serving with a crouton and sprinkle with some of the remaining 2 tablespoons cheese.

Nutrition Facts per serving: 207 cal., 2 g total fat (1 g sat. fat), 3 mg chol., 437 mg sodium, 40 g carbo., 9 g fiber, 13 g pro.

BLACK BEAN-TORTILLA SOUP

Nonstick cooking spray

1 cup chopped onion

1 tablespoon cumin seeds

4 cloves garlic, minced

2 14-ounce cans reduced-sodium chicken broth (3½ cups)

3 medium tomatoes, chopped (about 2 cups)

1½ cups loose-pack frozen whole kernel corn

1 4-ounce can diced green chile peppers

1 15-ounce can black beans, rinsed and drained

¼ to ½ cup snipped fresh cilantro

2 cups coarsely crushed tortilla chips

Shredded Monterey Jack cheese (optional)

1 Coat an unheated large nonstick saucepan with nonstick cooking spray. Preheat over medium heat. Add onion, cumin seeds, and garlic to hot saucepan. Cook and stir about 5 minutes or until tender. Carefully add chicken broth, tomatoes, corn, and undrained chile peppers. Bring to boiling; reduce heat. Cover and simmer about 5 minutes or until corn is tender. Stir in black beans and cilantro; heat through.

2 Divide crushed tortilla chips among 6 soup bowls; ladle soup over chips. If desired, garnish individual servings with cheese.

Nutrition Facts per serving: 171 cal., 4 g total fat (1 g sat. fat), 0 mg chol., 601 mg sodium, 31 g carbo., 6 g fiber, 9 g pro.

START TO FINISH:
30 minutes
MAKES:
6 servings

31
carbs per serving

Exchanges:
1 Vegetable
1½ Starch
½ Very Lean Meat
½ Fat

TOMATO-VEGETABLE SOUP

PREP:
40 minutes
COOK:
*15 minutes +
10 minutes*
MAKES:
*8 side-dish
servings*

16
carbs per
serving

Exchanges:
1½ Vegetable
½ Starch

2 leeks

   Nonstick cooking spray

3 cloves garlic, minced

8 cups water

1 14½-ounce can stewed tomatoes, undrained

4 stalks celery, sliced

3 medium carrots, thinly sliced

1 medium red apple, cored and coarsely chopped

1 medium sweet potato, peeled and cut into ½-inch cubes

4 teaspoons instant vegetable bouillon granules or vegetable
   bouillon cubes (to make 4 cups broth)

2 cups shredded cabbage

1 cup cut fresh green beans

¼ teaspoon salt

¼ teaspoon black pepper

½ cup snipped fresh parsley

2 tablespoons lemon juice

1 Wash leeks; trim roots from bases. Cut off and discard green parts. Thinly slice white parts. Coat an unheated 4-quart Dutch oven with nonstick cooking spray. Preheat over medium heat. Add leeks and garlic to hot Dutch oven; cook and stir about 3 minutes or until nearly tender. Carefully add the water, undrained tomatoes, celery, carrots, apple, sweet potato, and bouillon granules or cubes. Bring to boiling; reduce heat. Cover and simmer for 15 minutes.

2 Add cabbage, green beans, salt, and pepper. Return to boiling; reduce heat. Cover and simmer about 10 minutes more or until vegetables are tender. Stir in parsley and lemon juice.

Nutrition Facts per serving: 76 cal., 1 g total fat (0 g sat. fat), 0 mg chol., 710 mg sodium, 16 g carbo., 4 g fiber, 2 g pro.

ROASTED TOMATO & VEGETABLE SOUP

Nonstick cooking spray

1	medium onion, chopped
1	stalk celery, sliced
1	medium carrot, chopped
2	cloves garlic, minced
3	14-ounce cans reduced-sodium chicken broth
2	cups cut-up, peeled, and seeded butternut squash
1	14½-ounce can fire-roasted diced tomatoes or one 14½-ounce can diced tomatoes, undrained
1	15- to 19-ounce can white kidney beans (cannellini beans), rinsed and drained
1	small zucchini, halved lengthwise and sliced
1	cup small broccoli and/or cauliflower florets
1	tablespoon snipped fresh oregano or 2 teaspoons dried oregano, crushed
¼	teaspoon salt
¼	teaspoon black pepper

Freshly shredded Parmesan cheese (optional)

1 Coat an unheated 4-quart Dutch oven with nonstick cooking spray. Preheat over medium heat. Add onion, celery, carrot, and garlic to hot Dutch oven. Cook and stir for 5 minutes.

2 Stir in chicken broth, butternut squash, and undrained tomatoes. Bring to boiling; reduce heat. Cover and simmer for 20 minutes. Add white kidney beans, zucchini, broccoli and/or cauliflower, oregano, salt, and pepper; cook for 5 minutes more. If desired, sprinkle individual servings with Parmesan cheese.

Nutrition Facts per serving: 77 cal., 0 g total fat (0 g sat. fat), 0 mg chol., 641 mg sodium, 16 g carbo., 4 g fiber, 6 g pro.

PREP:
30 minutes
COOK:
20 minutes +
5 minutes
MAKES:
8 side-dish servings

16
carbs per serving

Exchanges:
1 Vegetable
½ Starch

ACORN SQUASH BISQUE

PREP:
30 minutes
BAKE:
50 minutes
COOL:
10 minutes
OVEN:
325°F
MAKES:
8 first-course servings

17
carbs per serving

Exchanges:
1 Starch

2 medium acorn squash (about 2½ pounds total)
  Nonstick cooking spray
½ cup chopped onion
1 14-ounce can reduced-sodium chicken broth
¼ cup water
2 tablespoons packed brown sugar
¼ teaspoon salt
¼ teaspoon ground cinnamon
⅛ to ¼ teaspoon white pepper or black pepper
¼ cup half-and-half or light cream
  Pumpkin seeds (optional)
  Ground cinnamon (optional)

❶ Wash and halve squash; remove seeds. Place squash halves, cut sides down, in a 3-quart rectangular baking dish. Bake in a 325° oven for 50 to 60 minutes or until tender. Let squash cool about 10 minutes or until cool enough to handle. Using a spoon, remove squash pulp from shells. Discard shells.

❷ Coat an unheated large nonstick saucepan with nonstick cooking spray. Preheat over medium heat. Add onion to hot saucepan; cook until tender, stirring frequently. Add squash pulp, chicken broth, and the water. Cook over medium-high heat just until mixture reaches boiling, stirring frequently. Stir in brown sugar, salt, the ¼ teaspoon cinnamon, and the pepper. Remove from heat; cool slightly.

❸ Place half of the squash mixture in a blender or food processor. Cover and blend or process until smooth. Pour pureed squash into a medium bowl. Repeat with remaining squash mixture. Return all squash mixture to saucepan. Stir in half-and-half; heat through, stirring often. If desired, garnish individual servings with pumpkin seeds and sprinkle with additional cinnamon.

TO MAKE AHEAD: Prepare as directed, except do not heat through after adding half-and-half. Let stand at room temperature for 30 minutes. Transfer soup to a storage container. Cover and chill for up to 48 hours. To serve, spoon soup into a medium saucepan. Cook over medium heat just until heated through, stirring often.

Nutrition Facts per serving: 79 cal., 1 g total fat (1 g sat. fat), 3 mg chol., 201 mg sodium, 17 g carbo., 2 g fiber, 2 g pro.

MEATLESS
MAIN DISHES

SPINACH-FETA BAKE

PREP:
20 minutes
BAKE:
30 minutes
OVEN:
350°F
MAKES:
6 servings

9
carbs per
serving

Exchanges:
1½ Vegetable
2 Lean Meat
½ Fat

Nonstick cooking spray
¾ cup chopped onion
3 cloves garlic, minced
2 10-ounce packages frozen chopped spinach, thawed and well drained
1 cup low-fat cottage cheese, drained
1 cup crumbled feta cheese (4 ounces)
2 slightly beaten eggs or ½ cup refrigerated or frozen egg product, thawed
1 tablespoon snipped fresh oregano or 1 teaspoon dried oregano, crushed
¼ teaspoon coarsely ground black pepper
¼ cup finely shredded Parmesan cheese (1 ounce)
2 tablespoons fine dry bread crumbs

1 Lightly coat a 9-inch pie plate with nonstick cooking spray; set aside. Coat an unheated medium nonstick saucepan with nonstick cooking spray. Preheat over medium heat. Add onion and garlic to hot pan; cook until onion is tender, stirring occasionally. Remove from heat.

2 Stir spinach, drained cottage cheese, feta cheese, eggs, oregano, and pepper into onion mixture. Spoon the spinach mixture into the prepared pie plate.

3 In a small bowl combine Parmesan cheese and bread crumbs; sprinkle over spinach mixture. Bake in a 350° oven for 30 to 35 minutes or until a knife inserted near center comes out clean.

Nutrition Facts per serving: 173 cal., 8 g total fat (5 g sat. fat), 96 mg chol., 700 mg sodium, 9 g carbo., 3 g fiber, 14 g pro.

VEGETABLE-POLENTA LASAGNA

1½ cups cornmeal

1¼ teaspoons salt

Nonstick cooking spray

1 small onion, thinly sliced

4 cups fresh mushrooms, halved

¼ teaspoon black pepper

3 medium green sweet peppers, roasted and chopped*

3 medium red sweet peppers, roasted and chopped*

1¼ cups purchased marinara sauce

1 cup shredded mozzarella cheese (4 ounces)

PREP:
25 minutes
CHILL:
1 hour
BAKE:
30 minutes +
10 minutes
OVEN:
350°F
MAKES:
8 servings

1 For polenta, in a medium saucepan bring 2½ cups water to boiling. In a medium bowl combine 1½ cups cold water, the cornmeal, and 1 teaspoon of the salt. Slowly add cornmeal mixture to boiling water, stirring constantly. Cook and stir until mixture returns to boiling; reduce heat to low. Cook about 10 minutes or until mixture is very thick, stirring occasionally. Pour the hot mixture into a 3-quart rectangular baking dish. Cool slightly. Cover and refrigerate about 1 hour or until firm.

2 Coat an unheated large nonstick skillet with nonstick cooking spray. Preheat over medium heat. Add onion to hot skillet; cook and stir for 3 to 4 minutes or until tender. Add mushrooms, the remaining ¼ teaspoon salt, and the black pepper. Cook and stir about 5 minutes or until mushrooms are tender. Remove from heat; stir in the green and red roasted sweet peppers.

3 Spread the marinara sauce over chilled polenta. Top with the vegetable mixture; sprinkle with cheese. Cover; bake in a 350° oven for 30 minutes. Bake, uncovered, for 10 to 15 minutes more or until edges are bubbly.

*NOTE: To roast sweet peppers, quarter the peppers lengthwise; remove and discard stems, seeds, and membranes. Place peppers, cut sides down, on a foil-lined baking sheet. Roast in a 450°F oven for 15 to 20 minutes or until skins are blistered and bubbly. Fold up foil on baking sheet around peppers to form a packet; seal. Let stand for 20 minutes or until cool enough to handle. Using the tip of a sharp knife, loosen the edges of skins from peppers; gently and slowly pull off the skin in strips. Chop peppers. (Or substitute three 7-ounce jars or two 12-ounce jars roasted red sweet peppers, drained and chopped, for the green and red sweet peppers.)

Nutrition Facts per serving: 186 cal., 4 g total fat (2 g sat. fat), 9 mg chol., 623 mg sodium, 31 g carbo., 5 g fiber, 8 g pro.

31
carbs per serving

Exchanges:
1½ Vegetable
1 Starch
½ Medium-Fat Meat
½ Other Carbo.

PUMPKIN & SAGE RISOTTO

6 cups reduced-sodium chicken broth
½ cup canned pumpkin
1 tablespoon olive oil
1 small onion, finely chopped
3 cups cubed, peeled pumpkin or butternut squash
2 cups Arborio rice
⅓ cup dry white wine or reduced-sodium chicken broth
½ cup grated Parmesan cheese (2 ounces)
2 teaspoons snipped fresh sage or ½ teaspoon dried sage, crushed
Black pepper
Hot cooked broccoli (optional)

57
carbs per serving

Exchanges:
1½ Vegetable
3½ Starch
½ Fat

❶ In a large saucepan stir together the 6 cups chicken broth and canned pumpkin. Bring to boiling; reduce heat. Simmer until needed.

❷ Meanwhile, in a 4-quart Dutch oven heat oil over medium heat. Add onion; cook about 5 minutes or until tender. Add fresh pumpkin or squash; cook and stir for 2 minutes. Add uncooked rice. Cook and stir for 2 minutes more.

❸ Slowly add wine or additional chicken broth to the rice mixture; cook until wine is evaporated. Slowly add 2 cups of the chicken broth mixture, stirring constantly. Continue to cook and stir until liquid is absorbed. Add the remaining chicken broth mixture, ¾ cup at a time, stirring constantly until the chicken broth mixture is absorbed. (This should take about 30 minutes.)

❹ Stir Parmesan cheese and sage into rice mixture. Season to taste with pepper. If desired, serve the rice mixture over broccoli.

Nutrition Facts per serving: 333 cal., 5 g total fat (2 g sat. fat), 7 mg chol., 781 mg sodium, 57 g carbo., 2 g fiber, 12 g pro.

STIR-FRIED VEGETABLES
IN THAI PEANUT SAUCE

½ cup reduced-sodium chicken broth

1 fresh jalapeño chile pepper, seeded and finely chopped*

1 clove garlic, minced

¼ cup peanut butter

2 tablespoons rice vinegar

2 tablespoons reduced-sodium soy sauce

Nonstick cooking spray

1 teaspoon toasted sesame oil

2 medium carrots, cut into thin bite-size strips

1 small onion, cut into thin wedges

2 cups shredded napa cabbage

1 small cucumber, seeded and cut into thin bite-size strips

1 tablespoon snipped fresh Thai basil or mint, or
1 teaspoon dried basil or mint, crushed

3 cups hot cooked brown or jasmine rice

¼ cup coarsely chopped unsalted dry-roasted peanuts (optional)

START TO FINISH:
25 minutes
MAKES:
4 servings

44
carbs per serving

Exchanges:
2 Vegetable
2 Starch
1 High-Fat Meat

❶ For sauce, in a small saucepan stir together chicken broth, chile pepper, and garlic. Bring to boiling; reduce heat. Cover and simmer about 2 minutes or until chile pepper is tender. Add peanut butter; stir until combined. Remove from heat. Stir in rice vinegar and soy sauce; set aside.

❷ Coat an unheated wok or large nonstick skillet with nonstick cooking spray; add sesame oil. Heat over medium-high heat. Add carrots and onion; cook and stir about 4 minutes or until vegetables are crisp-tender.

❸ Add the sauce, cabbage, cucumber, and basil or mint. Reduce heat to medium-low. Cook and stir for 1 to 2 minutes or until heated through. Serve immediately over hot cooked rice. If desired, sprinkle individual servings with peanuts.

*NOTE: Because chile peppers contain volatile oils that can burn your skin and eyes, avoid direct contact with them as much as possible. When working with chile peppers, wear plastic or rubber gloves. If your bare hands do touch the peppers, wash your hands and nails well with soap and warm water.

Nutrition Facts per serving: 309 cal., 11 g total fat (2 g sat. fat), 0 mg chol., 472 mg sodium, 44 g carbo., 5 g fiber, 10 g pro.

TWO-BEAN BURRITOS

START TO FINISH:
30 minutes
OVEN:
350°F
MAKES:
8 servings

62
carbs per serving

Exchanges:
3 Starch
½ Very Lean Meat
1 Other Carbo.
½ Fat

8   8-inch spinach flour tortillas
1   15-ounce can black beans, rinsed and drained
1   8¾-ounce can whole kernel corn, rinsed and drained
1   medium mango, chopped
⅓   cup chopped red sweet pepper
¼   cup snipped fresh cilantro
2   tablespoons lime juice
1   fresh jalapeño chile pepper, seeded and finely chopped*
    Nonstick cooking spray
½   cup chopped onion
1   16-ounce can vegetarian refried beans
½   cup purchased salsa

1 Wrap the tortillas in foil. Heat in a 350° oven about 10 minutes or until warm.

2 Meanwhile, in a medium bowl combine half of the black beans, the corn, mango, sweet pepper, cilantro, lime juice, and chile pepper. Set aside until ready to serve.

3 Coat an unheated large nonstick skillet with nonstick cooking spray. Preheat over medium heat. Add onion to hot skillet; cook about 5 minutes or until tender. Stir in the remaining black beans, the refried beans, and salsa; heat through.

4 Divide the refried bean mixture among the warm tortillas; roll up. Top individual servings with corn mixture.

*NOTE: Because chile peppers contain volatile oils that can burn your skin and eyes, avoid direct contact with them as much as possible. When working with chile peppers, wear plastic or rubber gloves. If your bare hands do touch the peppers, wash your hands and nails well with soap and warm water.

Nutrition Facts per serving: 339 cal., 5 g total fat (1 g sat. fat), 0 mg chol., 845 mg sodium, 62 g carbo., 10 g fiber, 14 g pro.

SPICY VEGETABLE ENCHILADAS

8	7- or 8-inch whole wheat or flour tortillas
	Nonstick cooking spray
2	medium carrots, thinly sliced
1	large zucchini or yellow summer squash, quartered lengthwise and sliced
2	teaspoons ancho chili powder or chili powder
1	teaspoon ground cumin
1	15-ounce can no-salt-added black beans, rinsed and drained
1	14½-ounce can Mexican-style stewed tomatoes, undrained
⅔	cup shredded Monterey Jack cheese
	Dash bottled hot pepper sauce

PREP:
25 minutes
BAKE:
15 minutes
OVEN:
350°F
MAKES:
8 servings

1 Wrap tortillas tightly in foil. Bake in a 350° oven for 10 minutes to soften. Lightly coat a 2-quart rectangular baking dish with nonstick cooking spray; set aside.

2 Meanwhile, coat an unheated large nonstick skillet or wok with nonstick cooking spray. Preheat over medium heat. Add carrots; cook and stir for 2 minutes. Add zucchini or summer squash, chili powder, and cumin; cook and stir for 2 to 3 minutes or until vegetables are crisp-tender. Remove wok or skillet from heat. Stir in drained beans, half of the undrained tomatoes, ⅓ cup of the cheese, and hot pepper sauce.

3 Spoon about ½ cup of the vegetable mixture onto each tortilla near an edge; roll up tortillas. Arrange filled tortillas, seam sides down, in prepared baking dish. Lightly coat tops of tortillas with nonstick cooking spray.

4 Bake, uncovered, in the 350° oven for 15 to 17 minutes or until mixture is heated through and tortillas are crisp.

5 Meanwhile, in a small saucepan heat remaining undrained tomatoes. Spoon over enchiladas; top with remaining ⅓ cup cheese.

Nutrition Facts per serving: 248 cal., 6 g total fat (2 g sat. fat), 8 mg chol., 633 mg sodium, 40 g carbo., 6 g fiber, 10 g pro.

40
carbs per serving

Exchanges:
1 Vegetable
2 Starch
½ Very Lean Meat
1 Fat

ITALIAN BEANS WITH PESTO

PREP:
15 minutes
COOK:
15 minutes
CHILL:
*4 hours to
3 days*
MAKES:
4 servings

47
carbs per
serving

Exchanges:
½ Vegetable
3 Starch
1 Very Lean Meat
1 Fat

1   14-ounce can reduced-sodium chicken broth or vegetable broth
¾   cup bulgur
1   medium red sweet pepper, chopped
⅓   cup refrigerated basil pesto
¼   cup thinly sliced green onions
2   tablespoons balsamic vinegar
2   cups cooked or canned red kidney beans, pinto beans,
     Christmas lima beans, and/or other beans*
     Black pepper
     Whole wheat flour tortillas and/or salad greens (optional)

1 In a large saucepan combine broth and bulgur. Bring to boiling; reduce heat. Cover and simmer about 15 minutes or until bulgur is tender. Remove from heat. Stir in sweet pepper, basil pesto, green onions, and balsamic vinegar. Stir in beans. Season with black pepper. Transfer to an airtight storage container. Cover and chill for at least 4 hours or up to 3 days.

2 If desired, roll up bean mixture in tortillas or serve on salad greens.

*NOTE: To cook dry beans, rinse ¾ cup dry beans. In a large saucepan, combine rinsed beans and 5 cups water. Bring to boiling; reduce heat. Simmer, uncovered, for 2 minutes. Remove from heat. Cover and let stand for 1 hour. Drain; rinse beans and return to saucepan. Add 5 cups fresh water. Bring to boiling; reduce heat. Cover and simmer for 1¼ to 1½ hours or until beans are tender; drain.

Nutrition Facts per serving: 333 cal., 11 g total fat (2 g sat. fat), 3 mg chol., 426 mg sodium, 47 g carbo., 11 g fiber, 15 g pro.

BEAN QUESADILLAS
WITH TOMATILLO SALSA

8 ounces fresh tomatillos, husked, stems removed, and cut into quarters (about 8)

1 small red onion, cut up

¼ cup fresh cilantro leaves

1 fresh jalapeño chile pepper, seeded and cut up*

1 tablespoon lime juice

¼ teaspoon salt

Nonstick cooking spray

1 16-ounce can fat-free refried beans

½ teaspoon ground cumin

½ teaspoon chili powder

6 10-inch flour tortillas

1½ cups fresh corn kernels, cooked (about 3 medium ears), or 1½ cups loose-pack frozen whole kernel corn, thawed

2 cups shredded reduced-fat cheddar cheese (8 ounces)

1 For salsa, in a food processor combine tomatillos, red onion, cilantro, chile pepper, lime juice, and salt. Cover and process with several on-off turns until desired consistency. Set aside.

2 Coat 2 large cookie sheets with nonstick cooking spray. In a medium bowl stir together refried beans, cumin, and chili powder.

3 Place tortillas on work surface. Spread one half of each tortilla with about ¼ cup of the refried bean mixture. Sprinkle beans with corn; sprinkle with 1½ cups of the cheese.

4 Lift the unspread side of each tortilla up and over the spread side; press lightly. Place on cookie sheets; sprinkle tops with the remaining ½ cup cheese.

5 Bake in a 350° oven about 5 minutes or until cheese melts. Cut into wedges and serve with salsa.

***NOTE:** Because chile peppers contain volatile oils that can burn your skin and eyes, avoid direct contact with them as much as possible. When working with chile peppers, wear plastic or rubber gloves. If your bare hands do touch the peppers, wash your hands and nails well with soap and warm water.

Nutrition Facts per serving: 380 cal., 11 g total fat (5 g sat. fat), 27 mg chol., 847 mg sodium, 48 g carbo., 7 g fiber, 19 g pro.

PREP:
15 minutes
BAKE:
5 minutes
OVEN:
350°F
MAKES:
6 servings

48
carbs per serving

Exchanges:
1 Vegetable
2½ Starch
1½ Lean Meat
1½ Fat

HERB- & BEAN-STUFFED TOMATOES

PREP:
25 minutes
BAKE:
20 minutes
OVEN:
350°F
MAKES:
4 servings

25
carbs per
serving

Exchanges:
1½ Vegetable
1 Starch
½ Very Lean Meat
2 Fat

4	large red and/or yellow tomatoes
1½	cups soft bread crumbs (2 slices)
¾	cup canned white kidney beans (cannellini beans), rinsed and drained
¼	cup pine nuts, toasted
2	tablespoons grated Parmesan cheese
1	tablespoon finely shredded fresh basil or ½ teaspoon dried basil, crushed
1	tablespoon olive oil
2	cloves garlic, minced
⅛	teaspoon salt
⅛	teaspoon black pepper
2	teaspoons snipped fresh thyme or ½ teaspoon dried thyme, crushed
2	teaspoons butter or margarine, melted

1 Cut off ½ inch from the top of each tomato. Finely chop enough of the tomato tops to equal 1 cup; set aside. Remove and discard the seeds from tomatoes.

2 In a large bowl stir together the chopped tomato, ¾ cup of the bread crumbs, the beans, pine nuts, Parmesan cheese, basil, oil, garlic, salt, and pepper. Spoon the bean mixture into the tomatoes. Place the stuffed tomatoes in a 2-quart square baking dish.

3 In a small bowl stir together the remaining ¾ cup bread crumbs and the thyme. Sprinkle over tomatoes. Drizzle with melted butter.

4 Bake, uncovered, in a 350° oven about 20 minutes or until crumbs are golden brown and tomatoes are heated through.

Nutrition Facts per serving: 220 cal., 12 g total fat (4 g sat. fat), 10 mg chol., 327 mg sodium, 25 g carbo., 5 g fiber, 9 g pro.

WHITE BEAN MOUSSAKA

1   large eggplant (about 1½ pounds), peeled (if desired)
     and cut crosswise into ¼-inch-thick slices

     Nonstick cooking spray

1   medium onion, chopped

2   cloves garlic, minced

2   19-ounce cans white kidney beans (cannellini beans),
     rinsed and drained

1   14½-ounce can diced tomatoes, undrained

2   tablespoons tomato paste

½   teaspoon ground cinnamon

⅛   teaspoon black pepper

1   tablespoon butter

2   tablespoons all-purpose flour

1½   cups fat-free milk

⅛   teaspoon ground nutmeg

2¼   cups soft bread crumbs (3 slices)

2   tablespoons olive oil

PREP:
40 minutes
BAKE:
30 minutes
OVEN:
350°F
MAKES:
8 servings

38 carbs per serving

Exchanges:
1 Vegetable
2 Starch
1 Fat

1 Coat each eggplant slice on both sides with nonstick cooking spray. Arrange in a single layer on an extra-large baking sheet. Broil 4 to 5 inches from the heat for 4 to 6 minutes or just until tender; turn once.

2 For bean mixture, coat an unheated large nonstick skillet with nonstick cooking spray. Preheat over medium heat. Add onion and garlic to skillet. Cook for 4 to 5 minutes or just until tender, stirring frequently. Add white kidney beans, undrained tomatoes, tomato paste, cinnamon, and pepper. Bring to boiling; reduce heat. Simmer, uncovered, for 10 to 15 minutes or until slightly thickened, stirring occasionally.

3 For sauce, in a medium saucepan melt butter over medium heat. Stir in flour and ¼ teaspoon salt. Stir in milk. Cook and stir over medium heat until thickened and bubbly. Remove from heat; stir in nutmeg.

4 Coat a 3-quart rectangular baking dish with nonstick cooking spray. Arrange half of the eggplant in the prepared dish. Spread bean mixture over the eggplant; top with remaining eggplant. Pour sauce on top, spreading evenly to cover. In a bowl combine bread crumbs and oil. Sprinkle over sauce. Bake in a 350° oven for 30 to 35 minutes or until heated through and bread crumbs are golden brown.

Nutrition Facts per serving: 245 cal., 6 g total fat (1 g sat. fat), 5 mg chol., 559 mg sodium, 38 g carbo., 9 g fiber, 9 g pro.

INDIAN LENTILS & SPINACH

PREP:
20 minutes
COOK:
30 minutes
MAKES:
6 servings

33
carbs per
serving

Exchanges:
1½ Vegetable
1½ Starch
1 Very Lean Meat

Nonstick cooking spray

1½ cups coarsely chopped red, green, and/or yellow sweet pepper

½ cup coarsely chopped onion

2 cloves garlic, minced

½ teaspoon curry powder

1½ cups dry brown or yellow lentils, rinsed and drained

1 14-ounce can vegetable broth

1 cup water

¼ teaspoon black pepper

6 cups fresh baby spinach

2 tablespoons snipped fresh mint (optional)

Plain fat-free yogurt (optional)

1 Coat an unheated large nonstick saucepan with nonstick cooking spray. Preheat over medium heat. Add sweet pepper, onion, garlic, and curry powder to hot saucepan; cook for 1 minute.

2 Stir in lentils, vegetable broth, the water, and black pepper. Bring to boiling; reduce heat. Cover and simmer about 30 minutes or until lentils are tender and most of the liquid is absorbed.

3 Transfer mixture to a large serving bowl. Add spinach and stir mixture until spinach is wilted. If desired, serve with mint and yogurt.

Nutrition Facts per serving: 192 cal., 1 g total fat (0 g sat. fat), 0 mg chol., 298 mg sodium, 33 g carbo., 16 g fiber, 15 g pro.

CURRIED LENTILS & VEGETABLES

3	cups water
1½	cups dry brown or yellow lentils, rinsed and drained
1	cup chopped carrot
1	cup chopped onion
⅔	cup chopped celery
4	teaspoons curry powder
1	teaspoon grated fresh ginger or ¼ teaspoon ground ginger
1	clove garlic, minced
½	teaspoon salt
1	cup plain low-fat yogurt
1	cup chopped tomato
2	tablespoons snipped fresh parsley or cilantro

1 In a large saucepan combine the water, lentils, carrot, onion, celery, curry powder, ginger, garlic, and salt. Bring to boiling; reduce heat. Cover and simmer for 20 to 25 minutes or until lentils are tender and liquid is absorbed.

2 In a small bowl stir together yogurt, tomato, and parsley or cilantro. Serve the lentil mixture with yogurt mixture.

Nutrition Facts per serving: 333 cal., 2 g total fat (1 g sat. fat), 4 mg chol., 382 mg sodium, 57 g carbo., 25 g fiber, 25 g pro.

PREP:
15 minutes
COOK:
20 minutes
MAKES:
4 servings

57
carbs per serving

Exchanges:
2½ Vegetable
3 Starch
1 Very Lean Meat

CARAMELIZED ONIONS & CAVATELLI

START TO FINISH:
30 minutes
MAKES:
4 servings

63
carbs per serving

Exchanges:
2 Vegetable
3½ Starch
1½ Fat

10	ounces dried cavatelli (3½ cups) or other medium-size pasta
1	tablespoon olive oil
2	medium onions, sliced
1	teaspoon sugar
2	small zucchini, halved lengthwise and sliced
4	cloves garlic, minced
2	tablespoons water
1	to 2 tablespoons balsamic vinegar
1	tablespoon snipped fresh thyme or 1 teaspoon dried thyme, crushed
¼	cup pine nuts or chopped walnuts, toasted

1 Cook pasta according to package directions, except omit any oil or salt. Drain. Return pasta to hot saucepan; cover and keep warm.

2 Meanwhile, in a heavy large nonstick skillet heat oil over medium-low heat. Add onions to skillet; cover and cook for 13 to 15 minutes or until onions are tender. Sprinkle with sugar. Cook and stir, uncovered, over medium-high heat for 4 to 5 minutes more or until onion is golden brown.

3 Add zucchini and garlic to onions in skillet. Cook and stir for 2 minutes. Stir in the water, balsamic vinegar, and dried thyme (if using). Cook for 2 to 3 minutes more or until zucchini is crisp-tender, stirring occasionally.

4 Add zucchini mixture, nuts, and fresh thyme (if using) to cooked pasta; gently toss to combine.

Nutrition Facts per serving: 383 cal., 10 g total fat (1 g sat. fat), 0 mg chol., 77 mg sodium, 63 g carbo., 3 g fiber, 13 g pro.

HERBED PASTA PRIMAVERA

6	ounces dried whole wheat penne pasta
1	cup water
1	tablespoon cornstarch
2	teaspoons instant chicken bouillon granules
	Nonstick cooking spray
8	ounces packaged peeled baby carrots, halved lengthwise
1½	cups fresh green beans bias-sliced into 2-inch pieces
2	medium leeks, halved lengthwise and cut into ¼-inch-thick slices
1	clove garlic, minced
8	ounces baby pattypan squash
2	tablespoons water
1	tablespoon snipped fresh basil or 1 teaspoon dried basil, crushed
2	teaspoons snipped fresh dill or ½ teaspoon dried dill
¼	cup chopped almonds, toasted
	Cracked black pepper

START TO FINISH:
40 minutes
MAKES:
4 servings

48
carbs per serving

Exchanges:
2 Vegetable
2½ Starch
½ Fat

1 Cook penne according to package directions; drain. Return penne to hot saucepan; cover and keep warm.

2 Meanwhile, for sauce, in a small bowl combine the 1 cup water, the cornstarch, and bouillon granules; set aside.

3 Coat an unheated wok or large nonstick skillet with nonstick cooking spray. Preheat wok or skillet over medium-high heat. Cook and stir carrots in hot wok or skillet for 5 minutes. Add green beans, leeks, and garlic. Cook and stir for 2 minutes more. Stir in squash and the 2 tablespoons water. Cover and cook for 3 to 4 minutes or until vegetables are crisp-tender. Push vegetables from center of wok or skillet.

4 Stir sauce; add to center of wok or skillet. Cook and stir until thickened and bubbly. Add basil and dill. Stir all ingredients together to coat with sauce. Cook and stir for 1 to 2 minutes more or until heated through.

5 To serve, spoon the vegetable mixture over penne. Sprinkle with almonds and pepper. Serve immediately.

Nutrition Facts per serving: 258 cal., 5 g total fat (0 g sat. fat), 0 mg chol., 485 mg sodium, 48 g carbo., 8 g fiber, 10 g pro.

MUSHROOM & ASPARAGUS FETTUCCINE

START TO FINISH:
25 minutes
MAKES:
4 servings

54
carbs per
serving

Exchanges:
1½ Vegetable
3 Starch
1 Fat

8   ounces dried whole wheat fettuccine or linguine

8   ounces fresh asparagus, trimmed and cut into 1½-inch-long pieces
    Nonstick cooking spray

3   cups sliced fresh cremini, shiitake, or button mushrooms

1   medium leek, thinly sliced, or ½ cup chopped onion

3   cloves garlic, minced

⅓   cup vegetable broth

¼   cup evaporated fat-free milk

1   tablespoon finely shredded fresh basil or 1 teaspoon dried basil, crushed

1   tablespoon snipped fresh oregano or 1 teaspoon dried oregano, crushed

¼   teaspoon salt

⅛   teaspoon black pepper

1   cup chopped plum tomatoes

¼   cup pine nuts, toasted
    Finely shredded Parmesan cheese (optional)

1 Cook fettuccine or linguine according to package directions, adding asparagus for the last 1 to 2 minutes of the cooking time; drain. Return pasta mixture to saucepan; cover and keep warm.

2 Meanwhile, coat an unheated large nonstick skillet with nonstick cooking spray. Preheat over medium-high heat. Add mushrooms, leek or onion, and garlic to hot skillet. Cover and cook for 4 to 5 minutes or until tender, stirring occasionally. Stir in vegetable broth, evaporated milk, dried basil (if using), dried oregano (if using), salt, and pepper. Bring to boiling. Boil gently, uncovered, for 4 to 5 minutes or until mixture is slightly thickened. Stir in tomatoes, fresh basil (if using), and fresh oregano (if using); heat through.

3 Spoon mushroom mixture over pasta mixture; gently toss to coat. Sprinkle with pine nuts and, if desired, Parmesan cheese. Serve immediately.

Nutrition Facts per serving: 319 cal., 8 g total fat (1 g sat. fat), 1 mg chol., 255 mg sodium, 54 g carbo., 3 g fiber, 15 g pro.

WHEAT FETTUCCINE WITH ARUGULA

8   ounces dried whole wheat fettuccine

2   cloves garlic, minced

1   tablespoon olive oil

¼   cup reduced-sodium chicken broth

3   tablespoons balsamic vinegar

¼   teaspoon salt

⅛   teaspoon crushed red pepper

8   cups torn arugula

2   medium tomatoes, coarsely chopped

⅓   cup finely shredded Parmesan cheese

¼   cup pine nuts, toasted

1 Cook fettuccine according to package directions; drain. Return fettuccine to hot saucepan; cover and keep warm.

2 Meanwhile, in a 12-inch skillet cook garlic in hot oil for 1 minute. Stir in chicken broth, balsamic vinegar, salt, and crushed red pepper. Bring to boiling; remove skillet from heat. Stir in cooked fettuccine, arugula, and tomatoes.

3 To serve, divide the pasta mixture among 4 dinner plates. Sprinkle with Parmesan cheese and pine nuts. Serve immediately.

Nutrition Facts per serving: 347 cal., 11 g total fat (3 g sat. fat), 5 mg chol., 312 mg sodium, 52 g carbo., 1 g fiber, 15 g pro.

START TO FINISH:
25 minutes
MAKES:
4 servings

52
carbs per serving

Exchanges:
3 Vegetable
2½ Starch
½ Lean Meat
1 Fat

GARDEN VEGETABLES LASAGNA

PREP:
45 minutes
BAKE:
55 minutes
STAND:
10 minutes
OVEN:
375°F
MAKES:
8 servings

31
carbs per
serving

Exchanges:
1½ Vegetable
1½ Starch
3 Very Lean Meat
½ Fat

	Nonstick cooking spray
9	dried lasagna noodles
6	cups broccoli florets
1	red sweet pepper, cut into bite-size strips
1	medium zucchini, sliced (1¼ cups)
1	medium yellow summer squash, sliced (about 1¼ cups)
2	slightly beaten eggs or ½ cup refrigerated or frozen egg product, thawed
1	16-ounce carton low-fat cottage cheese
1	15-ounce carton fat-free ricotta cheese
½	cup snipped fresh basil or 1 tablespoon dried basil, crushed
1	tablespoon snipped fresh thyme or 1 teaspoon dried thyme, crushed
3	cloves garlic, minced
½	teaspoon salt
¼	teaspoon black pepper
¼	teaspoon bottled hot pepper sauce
2	cups shredded part-skim mozzarella cheese (8 ounces)

1 Lightly coat a 3-quart rectangular baking dish with nonstick cooking spray; set aside. In a Dutch oven cook lasagna noodles in a large amount of boiling water for 10 to 12 minutes or until tender but still firm. Drain noodles; rinse with cold water. Drain well.

2 Meanwhile, place a steamer basket in a Dutch oven. Add water to just below the bottom of the steamer basket. Bring to boiling. Add broccoli, sweet pepper, zucchini, and yellow summer squash. Reduce heat. Cover and steam for 6 to 8 minutes or until vegetables are crisp-tender. Remove from heat.

3 In a large bowl combine eggs, cottage cheese, ricotta cheese, basil, thyme, garlic, salt, black pepper, and hot pepper sauce.

4 Layer 3 of the cooked noodles in prepared baking dish. Spread with one-third of the ricotta cheese mixture. Top with one-third of the vegetable mixture and ⅔ cup of the mozzarella cheese. Repeat layers twice.

5 Bake, covered, in a 375° oven for 55 to 60 minutes or until heated through. Uncover; let stand on a wire rack for 10 minutes before serving.

Nutrition Facts per serving: 294 cal., 7 g total fat (4 g sat. fat), 86 mg chol., 718 mg sodium, 31 g carbo., 3 g fiber, 26 g pro.

SPINACH LASAGNA ROLLS
WITH SWISS CHEESE SAUCE

8	dried lasagna noodles
2	slightly beaten egg whites
1	15-ounce carton light ricotta cheese
1	10-ounce package frozen chopped spinach, thawed and well drained
6	ounces reduced-fat Swiss cheese, finely chopped
½	cup grated Parmesan cheese (2 ounces)
¼	teaspoon ground nutmeg (optional)
	Nonstick cooking spray
1½	cups sliced fresh mushrooms
½	cup thinly sliced green onions
1	12-ounce can (1½ cups) evaporated fat-free milk
2	tablespoons all-purpose flour
¼	teaspoon salt
	Paprika

PREP:
40 minutes
BAKE:
35 minutes
OVEN:
350°F
MAKES:
8 servings

27
carbs per serving

Exchanges:
1 Vegetable
1½ Starch
2 Lean Meat

1 Cook lasagna noodles according to package directions, except omit any oil or salt; drain. Rinse with cold water; drain again. Place noodles in a single layer on a sheet of foil; set aside.

2 For filling, in a large bowl combine egg whites, ricotta cheese, spinach, half of the Swiss cheese, the Parmesan cheese, and, if desired, nutmeg.

3 Lightly coat a 2-quart rectangular baking dish with nonstick cooking spray; set aside. Spread about ⅓ cup of the filling on each lasagna noodle. Starting from a short end, roll up each noodle. Place the lasagna rolls, seam sides down, in the prepared baking dish; set aside.

4 For sauce, coat an unheated medium nonstick saucepan with nonstick cooking spray. Preheat over medium-high heat. Add mushrooms and green onions; cook and stir about 3 minutes or until vegetables are tender. In a medium bowl stir together ¼ cup of the evaporated milk and the flour until smooth; stir in the remaining evaporated milk and the salt. Stir the milk mixture into the mushroom mixture. Cook and stir until thickened and bubbly. Remove from heat. Stir in the remaining Swiss cheese until melted. Pour the sauce over the lasagna rolls.

5 Cover and bake in a 350° oven about 35 minutes or until lasagna rolls are heated through. Sprinkle with paprika.

Nutrition Facts per serving: 250 cal., 6 g total fat (3 g sat. fat), 27 mg chol., 383 mg sodium, 27 g carbo., 2 g fiber, 21 g pro.

LASAGNA WITH ZUCCHINI & WALNUTS

PREP:
35 minutes
BAKE:
20 minutes +
20 minutes
STAND:
15 minutes
OVEN:
375°F
MAKES:
6 servings

39
carbs per serving

Exchanges:
2 Vegetable
2 Starch
1 Medium-Fat Meat
1 Fat

2	medium zucchini
1	teaspoon olive oil
	Nonstick cooking spray
2	large carrots, finely chopped
2	cups finely chopped onions
4	cloves garlic, minced
1	25- to 26-ounce jar chunky tomato pasta sauce (about 2½ cups)
1	tablespoon snipped fresh basil or 1 teaspoon dried basil, crushed
⅛	teaspoon black pepper
1	cup shredded mozzarella cheese (4 ounces)
⅓	cup finely shredded Parmesan cheese
6	no-boil lasagna noodles
¼	cup chopped walnuts

1 Trim ends off zucchini. Thinly slice zucchini lengthwise. (You should have a total of 9 long slices, each about ⅛ inch thick.) Lightly grease a baking sheet. Place zucchini slices on baking sheet; brush lightly with oil. Broil 3 to 4 inches from heat about 5 minutes or until crisp-tender, turning once. Let cool before handling.

2 Coat an unheated large nonstick saucepan with nonstick cooking spray. Preheat over medium-high heat. Add carrots, onions, and garlic to hot saucepan; cook and stir about 5 minutes or until tender. Add pasta sauce, basil, and pepper. Bring to boiling; reduce heat. Cover and simmer for 10 minutes, stirring occasionally. In a small bowl combine mozzarella and Parmesan cheeses; set aside.

3 Grease a 2-quart square baking dish; arrange 2 lasagna noodles in the dish. Spread with one-third of the pasta sauce mixture. Sprinkle with one-third of the nuts. Top with one-third of the zucchini; sprinkle with one-third of the cheese mixture. Repeat layering, alternating direction of the zucchini in each layer and finishing with the zucchini; set remaining cheese mixture aside.

4 Cover and bake in a 375° oven for 20 minutes. Uncover and sprinkle with remaining cheese mixture. Bake, uncovered, about 20 minutes more or until heated through. Let stand for 15 minutes before serving.

Nutrition Facts per serving: 315 cal., 13 g total fat (4 g sat. fat), 21 mg chol., 628 mg sodium, 39 g carbo., 5 g fiber, 13 g pro.

GARDEN-STYLE RAVIOLI

1   9-ounce package refrigerated light cheese ravioli
    Nonstick cooking spray
1   medium red sweet pepper, cut into long, thin strips
1   medium green sweet pepper, cut into long, thin strips
1   medium carrot, cut into long, thin strips
1   small onion, chopped
3   cloves garlic, minced
1   medium tomato, chopped
¼   cup reduced-sodium chicken broth or vegetable broth
1   tablespoon snipped fresh tarragon or 1 teaspoon dried tarragon, crushed, or 3 tablespoons snipped fresh basil or 2 teaspoons dried basil, crushed

1 Cook ravioli according to package directions, except omit any oil or salt. Drain. Return pasta to hot saucepan; cover and keep warm.

2 Meanwhile, coat an unheated large nonstick skillet with nonstick cooking spray. Preheat over medium-high heat. Add sweet peppers, carrot, onion, and garlic to hot skillet; cook and stir about 5 minutes or until vegetables are tender. Stir in tomato, broth, and tarragon or basil. Cook and stir about 2 minutes more or until heated through.

3 Add vegetable mixture to the cooked ravioli; gently toss to combine.

Nutrition Facts per serving: 248 cal., 6 g total fat (3 g sat. fat), 26 mg chol., 380 mg sodium, 38 g carbo., 2 g fiber, 13 g pro.

START TO FINISH:
30 minutes
MAKES:
4 servings

38
carbs per serving

Exchanges:
1 Vegetable
2 Starch
1 Lean Meat

NUTTY ORZO & VEGETABLES

START TO FINISH:
25 minutes
MAKES:
4 servings

2	cups loose-pack frozen mixed vegetables
½	cup dried orzo pasta (rosamarina)
1	15-ounce can garbanzo beans (chickpeas), rinsed and drained
1	14½-ounce can no-salt-added diced tomatoes, undrained
1⅓	cups purchased light spaghetti sauce
1	tablespoon snipped fresh thyme or 1 teaspoon dried thyme, crushed
¼	cup chopped cashews or slivered almonds, toasted
¼	cup shredded reduced-fat mozzarella cheese (1 ounce)

67

carbs per serving

❶ In a large saucepan cook the frozen vegetables and pasta according to pasta package directions, except omit any oil or salt. Drain. Return pasta mixture to hot saucepan.

❷ Stir in garbanzo beans, undrained tomatoes, spaghetti sauce, and thyme. Bring to boiling; reduce heat. Cover and simmer for 5 minutes.

❸ Stir in cashews or almonds. Sprinkle individual servings with cheese.

Nutrition Facts per serving: 379 cal., 7 g total fat (2 g sat. fat), 3 mg chol., 453 mg sodium, 67 g carbo., 12 g fiber, 16 g pro.

Exchanges:
3 Vegetable
3½ Starch
½ Fat

UDON NOODLES WITH BOK CHOY & TOFU

6   ounces udon noodles

¼   cup reduced-sodium soy sauce

2   tablespoons honey

1   tablespoon oyster sauce

1   tablespoon balsamic vinegar

2   teaspoons cornstarch

1   teaspoon toasted sesame oil

     Nonstick cooking spray

1   tablespoon grated fresh ginger

2   cloves garlic, minced

1   medium red sweet pepper, cut into thin bite-size strips

6   green onions, cut into 1-inch-long pieces

6   cups sliced bok choy

1   12-ounce package extra-firm tofu (fresh bean curd), drained and cut into ½-inch cubes

1   8-ounce can sliced water chestnuts, drained

START TO FINISH:
30 minutes
MAKES:
6 servings

42
carbs per serving

Exchanges:
1½ Vegetable
2 Starch
½ Medium-Fat Meat
½ Other Carbo.

1 Cook udon noodles according to package directions; drain. Return noodles to hot saucepan; cover and keep warm.

2 Meanwhile, for sauce, in a small bowl stir together soy sauce, honey, oyster sauce, balsamic vinegar, cornstarch, and sesame oil; set aside.

3 Coat an unheated wok or large nonstick skillet with nonstick cooking spray. Preheat over medium-high heat. Add ginger and garlic to hot wok or skillet; cook for 15 seconds. Add sweet pepper and green onions. Cook and stir about 2 minutes or until sweet pepper is crisp-tender. Remove vegetables. Add bok choy, half at a time; cook and stir about 3 minutes or until crisp-tender. Remove bok choy. Add tofu; cook and stir for 4 minutes. Push tofu from center of wok or skillet.

4 Stir sauce; add to center of wok or skillet. Cook and stir until slightly thickened. Return all vegetables to wok or skillet. Add cooked noodles and water chestnuts. Stir all ingredients together to coat with sauce; heat through. Serve immediately.

Nutrition Facts per serving: 266 cal., 6 g total fat (1 g sat. fat), 0 mg chol., 551 mg sodium, 42 g carbo., 4 g fiber, 13 g pro.

TABBOULEH-STYLE COUSCOUS WITH TOFU

30
carbs per
serving

Exchanges:
2 Starch
1 Medium-Fat Meat
½ Fat

1⅓	cups reduced-sodium chicken broth or vegetable broth
1	cup quick-cooking couscous
2	tablespoons olive oil
1	16-ounce package extra-firm tofu (fresh bean curd), drained and cut into ½-inch cubes
⅔	cup sliced green onions
2	cloves garlic, minced
1½	cups chopped tomatoes
¼	cup snipped fresh basil or 1 tablespoon dried basil, crushed
¼	cup lemon juice
1	tablespoon snipped fresh mint
¼	teaspoon black pepper
½	cup crumbled feta cheese (2 ounces)

1 In a medium saucepan bring broth to boiling. Stir in couscous. Remove saucepan from heat. Cover and let stand about 5 minutes or until liquid is absorbed.

2 Meanwhile, in a large nonstick skillet heat 1 tablespoon of the oil over medium-high heat. Add tofu, green onions, and garlic. Cook for 8 to 10 minutes or until tofu is light brown, turning carefully. (If necessary to prevent overbrowning, reduce heat to medium.)

3 In a large bowl combine the cooked couscous, tofu mixture, the remaining 1 tablespoon oil, the tomatoes, basil, lemon juice, mint, and pepper; gently toss to coat. Sprinkle with feta cheese.

Nutrition Facts per serving: 264 cal., 10 g total fat (3 g sat. fat), 8 mg chol., 257 mg sodium, 30 g carbo., 3 g fiber, 14 g pro.

MAIN-DISH SALADS

SESAME CHICKEN SALAD

7
carbs per serving

Exchanges:
1½ Vegetable
2½ Very Lean Meat
½ Fat

Nonstick cooking spray

4   skinless, boneless chicken breast halves (1 to 1½ pounds total)

Salt

Black pepper

1   10-ounce package torn Italian-style or European-style salad greens

1   14- or 15-ounce can whole baby corn,
    drained and halved crosswise

½   cup coarsely shredded carrot

¼   cup sliced radishes

½   of a large red onion, halved and thinly sliced

½   cup orange juice

¼   cup rice vinegar or white vinegar

1   tablespoon salad oil

1   teaspoon toasted sesame oil

¼   teaspoon salt

¼   teaspoon black pepper

1½   teaspoons sesame seeds, toasted*

1 Lightly coat an unheated large nonstick skillet with nonstick cooking spray. Preheat over medium heat. Sprinkle chicken lightly with salt and pepper. Add to hot skillet. Cook for 10 to 12 minutes or until no longer pink (170°F), turning once halfway through cooking time. Remove from skillet to a cutting board. Cut into bite-size strips; set aside to cool slightly.

2 Divide salad greens among 6 dinner plates. Arrange chicken, whole baby corn, carrot, radishes, and red onion over greens.

3 For dressing, in a screw-top jar combine orange juice, rice vinegar, salad oil, sesame oil, the ¼ teaspoon salt, and the ¼ teaspoon pepper. Cover and shake well. Pour dressing over salads. Sprinkle with sesame seeds.

*NOTE: To toast sesame seeds, in a small nonstick skillet cook and stir sesame seeds over medium heat about 1 minute or just until golden brown. Watch closely so the seeds don't burn. Remove from heat and transfer to a bowl to cool completely.

Nutrition Facts per serving: 154 cal., 5 g total fat (1 g sat. fat), 44 mg chol., 286 mg sodium, 7 g carbo., 2 g fiber, 19 g pro.

POTPOURRI CHICKEN SALAD

3 cups chopped cooked chicken breast (about 1 pound)

1½ cups finely chopped celery

½ cup finely chopped onion

½ cup water chestnuts, drained and finely chopped

¼ cup pitted ripe olives, finely chopped

¼ cup shelled sunflower seeds

1 cup low-fat mayonnaise dressing

2 tablespoons Dijon-style mustard

8 cups torn mixed salad greens

PREP:
30 minutes
CHILL:
2 to 24 hours
MAKES:
8 servings

1 In a large bowl combine chicken breast, celery, onion, water chestnuts, olives, and sunflower seeds. Add mayonnaise dressing and Dijon-style mustard; mix well. Cover and chill for at least 2 hours or up to 24 hours.

2 Serve chicken mixture over salad greens.

Nutrition Facts per serving: 196 cal., 10 g total fat (2 g sat. fat), 39 mg chol., 440 mg sodium, 13 g carbo., 2 g fiber, 17 g pro.

13
carbs per serving

Exchanges:
1½ Vegetable
2 Very Lean Meat
½ Other Carbo.
1½ Fat

GRILLED CAJUN CHICKEN SALAD

PREP:
30 minutes
GRILL:
12 minutes
MAKES:
6 servings

6
carbs per serving

Exchanges:
1 Vegetable
2½ Very Lean Meat
1½ Fat

¼ cup cider vinegar

4 tablespoons salad oil

1 tablespoon water

2 teaspoons sugar

2 teaspoons snipped fresh thyme or ½ teaspoon dried thyme, crushed

1¼ teaspoons onion powder

½ teaspoon cayenne pepper

¼ teaspoon garlic powder

¼ teaspoon dry mustard

½ teaspoon black pepper

¼ teaspoon salt

4 skinless, boneless chicken breast halves (1 to 1½ pounds total)

6 cups torn mixed salad greens

1 medium carrot, shredded

1 small red sweet pepper, cut into bite-size strips

1 green onion, sliced

1 For dressing, in a screw-top jar combine cider vinegar, 3 tablespoons of the salad oil, the water, sugar, thyme, ¼ teaspoon of the onion powder, ¼ teaspoon of the cayenne pepper, the garlic powder, and the mustard. Cover and shake well. Chill until serving time.

2 In a small bowl combine remaining 1 tablespoon salad oil, remaining 1 teaspoon onion powder, remaining ¼ teaspoon cayenne pepper, the black pepper, and salt. Brush chicken with all of the oil mixture.

3 Place chicken on the rack of an uncovered grill directly over medium coals. Grill for 12 to 15 minutes or until chicken is tender and no longer pink (170°F), turning once halfway through grilling time.

4 To serve, in a large serving bowl combine salad greens, carrot, red sweet pepper, and green onion. Cut chicken into bite-size pieces. Add chicken and dressing to salad. Toss to coat.

Nutrition Facts per serving: 190 cal., 10 g total fat (2 g sat. fat), 44 mg chol., 152 mg sodium, 6 g carbo., 2 g fiber, 19 g pro.

GRILLED CHICKEN & RICE SALAD

1   recipe Thyme Vinaigrette
12   ounces skinless, boneless chicken breast halves or thighs
1   cup loose-pack frozen French-cut green beans
2   cups cooked brown rice and wild rice blend, chilled
1   14-ounce can artichoke hearts, drained and quartered
1   cup shredded red cabbage
½   cup shredded carrot
1   green onion, sliced
     Lettuce leaves (optional)

PREP:
20 minutes
GRILL:
12 minutes
MAKES:
4 servings

1 Measure 2 tablespoons of the Thyme Vinaigrette to use as brush-on; set aside the remaining vinaigrette until ready to serve. Brush chicken with all of the 2 tablespoons vinaigrette.

2 Place chicken on the rack of an uncovered grill directly over medium coals. Grill for 12 to 15 minutes or until chicken is tender and no longer pink (170°F), turning once halfway through grilling time. Cut chicken into bite-size strips.

3 Meanwhile, rinse green beans with cool water for 30 seconds; drain well. In a large bowl toss together beans, cooked rice, artichoke hearts, cabbage, carrot, and green onion. Pour the remaining vinaigrette over rice mixture; toss gently to coat.

4 If desired, arrange lettuce leaves on 4 dinner plates. Top with the rice mixture and chicken.

29 carbs per serving

Exchanges:
1 Vegetable
1½ Starch
3 Very Lean Meat
1 Fat

THYME VINAIGRETTE: In a screw-top jar combine ¼ cup white wine vinegar; 2 tablespoons olive oil; 2 tablespoons water; 1 tablespoon grated Parmesan cheese; 2 teaspoons snipped fresh thyme or ½ teaspoon dried thyme, crushed; 1 clove garlic, minced; ¼ teaspoon salt; and ¼ teaspoon black pepper. Cover and shake well.

TO BROIL: Place chicken on the unheated rack of a broiler pan. Broil 4 to 5 inches from the heat for 12 to 15 minutes or until tender and no longer pink (170°F), turning once halfway through broiling time.

Nutrition Facts per serving: 305 cal., 8 g total fat (1 g sat. fat), 50 mg chol., 541 mg sodium, 29 g carbo., 6 g fiber, 26 g pro.

NORTHWEST CHICKEN SALAD

PREP:
30 minutes
MARINATE:
30 minutes
GRILL:
12 minutes
MAKES:
4 servings

14
carbs per
serving

Exchanges:
2 Vegetable
½ Fruit
3½ Very Lean Meat
1½ Fat

½ cup pear nectar
¼ cup raspberry vinegar
2 tablespoons salad oil
2 teaspoons dried basil, crushed, or 2 tablespoons snipped fresh basil
2 teaspoons Dijon-style mustard
2 teaspoons toasted sesame oil
⅛ teaspoon black pepper
4 skinless, boneless chicken breast halves (1 to 1½ pounds)
20 thick fresh asparagus spears, trimmed
6 cups torn mixed salad greens
12 fresh strawberries, hulled and halved
¼ cup chopped sweet onion
   Pecan halves, toasted (optional)

1 For vinaigrette, in a screw-top jar combine pear nectar, raspberry vinegar, salad oil, basil, mustard, toasted sesame oil, and pepper. Cover and shake well.

2 Place chicken in a resealable plastic bag set into a shallow bowl. Reserve half of the vinaigrette for dressing. Pour remaining vinaigrette over chicken in bag. Seal bag; turn to coat chicken. Marinate in the refrigerator for 30 minutes.

3 Drain chicken, reserving marinade. Brush asparagus with reserved marinade. Place chicken and asparagus on the rack of an uncovered grill directly over medium coals. Grill for 12 to 15 minutes or until chicken and asparagus are tender and chicken is no longer pink (170°F), turning and brushing once with marinade halfway through grilling time. Discard any remaining marinade.

4 To serve, divide greens among 4 dinner plates. Slice chicken into strips; arrange on greens. Top with asparagus, strawberries, and onion. Drizzle with reserved vinaigrette. If desired, sprinkle with pecans.

Nutrition Facts per serving: 272 cal., 11 g total fat (2 g sat. fat), 66 mg chol., 133 mg sodium, 14 g carbo., 3 g fiber, 29 g pro.

ASIAN CHICKEN SALAD

4   skinless, boneless chicken breast halves (1 to 1½ pounds total)

3   tablespoons reduced-sodium soy sauce

2   teaspoons grated fresh ginger

5   cups torn mixed salad greens

3   cups assorted fresh vegetables
     (such as fresh pea pods, halved crosswise; red sweet pepper
     strips; shredded carrot; and/or bite-size cucumber strips)

1   cup coarsely chopped red cabbage

¼   cup sliced green onions

1   recipe Asian Salad Dressing

2   teaspoons sesame seeds, toasted

1 Place chicken on the unheated greased rack of a broiler pan. In a small bowl combine soy sauce and ginger; brush some of the mixture onto one side of each chicken breast half. Broil chicken, brushed sides up, 4 inches from heat for 12 to 15 minutes or until chicken is tender and no longer pink (170°F), turning and brushing once with the remaining soy mixture halfway through broiling time. Discard any remaining soy mixture. Remove from heat; cool slightly. Cut chicken into bite-size strips. Set aside.

2 In a large bowl toss together salad greens, assorted fresh vegetables, red cabbage, and green onions.

3 Shake Asian Salad Dressing well; pour about ½ cup of the dressing over salad. Toss lightly to coat. Divide salad among 6 dinner plates. Top salads with chicken strips; pour remaining dressing over chicken. Sprinkle with sesame seeds. Serve immediately.

ASIAN SALAD DRESSING: In a screw-top jar combine ⅓ cup unsweetened pineapple juice, ¼ cup rice vinegar or white vinegar, 3 tablespoons salad oil, 1 tablespoon reduced-sodium soy sauce, 2 teaspoons sugar, 1½ teaspoons toasted sesame oil, and ¼ teaspoon black pepper. Cover and shake well.

Nutrition Facts per serving: 221 cal., 10 g total fat (2 g sat. fat), 44 mg chol., 439 mg sodium, 10 g carbo., 2 g fiber, 20 g pro.

START TO FINISH:
35 minutes
MAKES:
6 servings

10
carbs per serving

Exchanges:
2 Vegetable
2½ Very Lean Meat
2 Fat

JAMAICAN CHICKEN SALAD

START TO FINISH:
25 minutes
MAKES:
6 servings

½ cup bottled fat-free honey-mustard salad dressing

1 teaspoon finely shredded lime peel

4 skinless, boneless chicken breast halves (1 to 1½ pounds total)

1 to 2 teaspoons Homemade Jamaican Jerk Seasoning
or purchased Jamaican jerk seasoning

Nonstick cooking spray

9 cups torn mixed salad greens

2 large fresh mangoes, seeded, peeled, and sliced,
or 12 chilled bottled mango slices in light syrup, drained

20

carbs per
serving

Exchanges:
1½ Vegetable
½ Fruit
2½ Very Lean Meat
½ Other Carbo.

1 For dressing, in a small bowl stir together honey-mustard dressing and lime peel. If necessary, stir in enough water to make drizzling consistency. Cover and chill dressing until ready to serve.

2 Sprinkle chicken with Homemade Jamaican Jerk Seasoning. Coat an unheated large nonstick skillet with nonstick cooking spray. Preheat over medium heat. Add chicken to hot skillet; cook about 12 minutes or until golden brown and no longer pink (170°F), turning once halfway through cooking time. Thinly bias-slice chicken.

3 Divide salad greens among 6 dinner plates. Arrange warm chicken and mango on greens; drizzle with dressing.

HOMEMADE JAMAICAN JERK SEASONING: In a small bowl combine 2 teaspoons onion powder; 1 teaspoon sugar; 1 teaspoon crushed red pepper; 1 teaspoon dried thyme, crushed; ½ teaspoon salt; ½ teaspoon ground cloves; and ½ teaspoon ground cinnamon. Store in a covered container for up to 6 months. Makes about 6½ teaspoons.

Nutrition Facts per serving: 173 cal., 2 g total fat (0 g sat. fat), 44 mg chol., 327 mg sodium, 20 g carbo., 3 g fiber, 19 g pro.

MANGO-STEAK SALAD
WITH CILANTRO DRESSING

12 ounces beef flank steak or boneless beef top sirloin steak, cut 1 inch thick

⅛ teaspoon salt

⅛ teaspoon black pepper

⅓ cup lime juice

2 tablespoons olive oil

2 tablespoons snipped fresh cilantro

1 tablespoon honey

2 cloves garlic, minced

8 cups torn romaine leaves

5 ounces jicama, peeled and cut into thin bite-size strips (1 cup)

1 medium mango, seeded, peeled, and sliced

1 small red onion, cut into thin wedges

1 Trim fat from steak. If using flank steak, score both sides of steak in a diamond pattern by making shallow diagonal cuts at 1-inch intervals. Sprinkle with salt and pepper.

2 Place steak on the rack of an uncovered grill directly over medium coals. Grill until medium doneness (160°F), turning once halfway through grilling time. Allow 17 to 21 minutes for flank steak or 18 to 22 minutes for top sirloin steak. Thinly slice steak diagonally across the grain.

3 Meanwhile, for dressing, in a small bowl whisk together lime juice, oil, cilantro, honey, and garlic.

4 To serve, divide romaine among 6 dinner plates. Top with steak slices, jicama, mango, and red onion. Drizzle the dressing over salads.

TO BROIL: Place steak on the unheated rack of a broiler pan. Broil 3 to 4 inches from the heat until medium doneness (160°F), turning once halfway through broiling time. Allow 15 to 18 minutes for flank steak or 20 to 22 minutes for sirloin steak.

Nutrition Facts per serving: 195 cal., 9 g total fat (2 g sat. fat), 23 mg chol., 87 mg sodium, 17 g carbo., 3 g fiber, 14 g pro.

PREP:
25 minutes
GRILL:
17 minutes
MAKES:
6 servings

17
carbs per serving

Exchanges:
1½ Vegetable
½ Fruit
1½ Lean Meat
1 Fat

HOT ITALIAN BEEF SALAD

START TO FINISH:
20 minutes
MAKES:
4 servings

1   12-ounce beef top round steak, cut 1 inch thick
     Nonstick cooking spray

1   medium red or green sweet pepper, seeded
     and cut into bite-size strips

½   cup bottled fat-free Italian salad dressing

6   cups torn mixed salad greens

¼   cup finely shredded Parmesan cheese (1 ounce)
     Coarsely ground black pepper

6

carbs per
serving

1 Trim fat from steak. Thinly slice steak across the grain into bite-size strips.

2 Coat an unheated large nonstick skillet with nonstick cooking spray. Preheat over medium-high heat. Add steak and sweet pepper to hot skillet. Cook and stir for 3 to 5 minutes or until steak is desired doneness and sweet pepper is crisp-tender; drain. Add dressing to skillet. Cook and stir until heated through.

3 Divide the salad greens among 4 dinner plates. Top with the beef mixture. Sprinkle with Parmesan cheese and black pepper. Serve immediately.

Nutrition Facts per serving: 146 cal., 4 g total fat (2 g sat. fat), 52 mg chol., 410 mg sodium, 6 g carbo., 1 g fiber, 22 g pro.

Exchanges:
2 Vegetable
2½ Very Lean Meat

STIR-FRIED BEEF & APPLE SALAD

¼ cup rice vinegar

1 tablespoon salad oil

2 teaspoons snipped fresh chives

2 teaspoons reduced-sodium soy sauce

1 teaspoon honey or packed brown sugar

⅛ teaspoon ground cinnamon

   Dash salt

8 ounces beef top round steak

   Nonstick cooking spray

1 teaspoon toasted sesame oil

1 medium red apple, cored and thinly sliced

½ teaspoon coarsely cracked black pepper

6 cups torn mixed salad greens

START TO FINISH:
20 minutes
MAKES:
4 servings

9

carbs per serving

1 For dressing, in a screw-top jar combine rice vinegar, salad oil, chives, soy sauce, honey or brown sugar, cinnamon, and salt. Cover and shake well. Set aside.

2 Trim fat from steak. Cut steak into thin bite-size strips. Coat an unheated large nonstick skillet with nonstick cooking spray. Add sesame oil to skillet. Preheat skillet over medium-high heat. Add meat. Cook and stir in hot oil for 2 to 3 minutes or until meat is slightly pink in center. Add apple slices; cook and stir about 1 minute more or just until heated through. Sprinkle meat mixture with pepper.

3 To serve, divide salad greens among 4 dinner plates. Arrange meat mixture on top of greens. Shake dressing; drizzle over salads.

Nutrition Facts per serving: 185 cal., 10 g total fat (3 g sat. fat), 33 mg chol., 164 mg sodium, 9 g carbo., 2 g fiber, 14 g pro.

Exchanges:
½ Vegetable
½ Fruit
2 Lean Meat
1 Fat

STEAK SALAD WITH BUTTERMILK DRESSING

START TO FINISH:
30 minutes
MAKES:
4 servings

17
carbs per serving

Exchanges:
3 Vegetable
2 Lean Meat
½ Fat

8   cups torn mixed salad greens

2   medium carrots, cut into thin bite-size strips

1   medium yellow sweet pepper, cut into thin bite-size strips

1   cup cherry and/or pear-shaped tomatoes, halved

8   ounces boneless beef top sirloin steak
    Nonstick cooking spray

¼   cup finely shredded fresh basil or 1 tablespoon dried basil, crushed

1   recipe Buttermilk Dressing
    Whole cherry or pear-shaped tomatoes (optional)

1 Arrange salad greens, carrots, sweet pepper, and halved tomatoes on 4 dinner plates. Set aside. Trim fat from meat. Cut meat across the grain into thin bite-size strips.

2 Coat an unheated large nonstick skillet with nonstick cooking spray. Preheat over medium-high heat. Add meat and dried basil (if using). Cook and stir for 2 to 3 minutes or until meat is slightly pink in the center. Remove from heat. Stir in fresh basil (if using).

3 To serve, spoon the warm meat mixture over greens mixture. Drizzle with Buttermilk Dressing. If desired, garnish with whole tomatoes.

BUTTERMILK DRESSING: In a small bowl combine ½ cup plain low-fat yogurt; ⅓ cup buttermilk or sour milk;* 3 tablespoons freshly grated Parmesan cheese; 3 tablespoons finely chopped red onion; 3 tablespoons light mayonnaise dressing or salad dressing; 2 tablespoons snipped fresh parsley; 1 tablespoon white wine vinegar or lemon juice; 1 clove garlic, minced; ¼ teaspoon salt; and ⅛ teaspoon black pepper. Cover and chill for at least 30 minutes or until ready to serve.

*NOTE: To make ⅓ cup sour milk, place 1 teaspoon lemon juice or vinegar in a glass measuring cup. Add enough milk to make ⅓ cup liquid; stir. Let the mixture stand for 5 minutes before using.

Nutrition Facts per serving: 226 cal., 10 g total fat (4 g sat. fat), 32 mg chol., 387 mg sodium, 17 g carbo., 4 g fiber, 19 g pro.

MEDITERRANEAN BEEF SALAD
WITH LEMON VINAIGRETTE

1	pound boneless beef top sirloin steak, cut 1 inch thick
¼	teaspoon salt
⅛	teaspoon black pepper
4	cups torn romaine leaves
½	of a small red onion, thinly sliced and separated into rings
1	cup halved cherry or grape tomatoes
½	cup crumbled feta cheese (2 ounces)
1	recipe Lemon Vinaigrette

1 Trim fat from steak. Sprinkle steak with salt and pepper. Place steak on the unheated rack of a broiler pan. Broil 3 to 4 inches from the heat until desired doneness, turning once halfway through broiling time. Allow 15 to 17 minutes for medium-rare doneness (145°F) or 20 to 22 minutes for medium doneness (160°F). Thinly slice steak.

2 Divide romaine among 4 dinner plates. Top with sliced meat, red onion, halved tomatoes, and feta cheese. Drizzle with Lemon Vinaigrette.

LEMON VINAIGRETTE: In a screw-top jar combine ¼ cup olive oil; ½ teaspoon finely shredded lemon peel; 3 tablespoons lemon juice; 1 tablespoon snipped fresh oregano or 1 teaspoon dried oregano, crushed; and 2 cloves garlic, minced. Cover and shake well. Season to taste with salt and black pepper.

Nutrition Facts per serving: 198 cal., 7 g total fat (3 g sat. fat), 81 mg chol., 365 mg sodium, 5 g carbo., 2 g fiber, 27 g pro.

PREP:
20 minutes
BROIL:
15 minutes
MAKES:
4 servings

5
carbs per serving

Exchanges:
1 Vegetable
3½ Very Lean Meat
1 Fat

SAUTEED PORK & PEAR SALAD

START TO FINISH:
30 minutes
MAKES:
4 servings

25
carbs per
serving

Exchanges:
1½ Vegetable
1 Fruit
2 Very Lean Meat
2 Fat

8	ounces boneless pork top loin roast or pork tenderloin
½	teaspoon black pepper
½	teaspoon dried sage, crushed, or 1½ teaspoons snipped fresh sage
	Nonstick cooking spray
¼	cup coarsely chopped hazelnuts or almonds, toasted
½	cup unsweetened pineapple juice
1	tablespoon olive oil
1	tablespoon honey
2	teaspoons Dijon-style mustard
6	cups torn mixed salad greens
2	medium pears, cored and sliced

1 Trim fat from pork. Cut pork across the grain into thin bite-size strips. Sprinkle with pepper and sage. Coat an unheated large nonstick skillet with nonstick cooking spray. Preheat over medium-high heat. Add pork. Cook and stir for 2 to 3 minutes or until meat is slightly pink in the center. Add nuts. Cook and stir for 30 seconds more. Remove meat mixture. Cover and keep warm.

2 For dressing, in the same skillet combine pineapple juice, oil, honey, and Dijon-style mustard. Cook and stir just until bubbly, scraping up any crusty browned bits from bottom of the skillet.

3 Divide salad greens among 4 shallow bowls or dinner plates. Arrange pears on greens. Top with pork mixture. Drizzle with dressing. Serve immediately.

Nutrition Facts per serving: 260 cal., 12 g total fat (2 g sat. fat), 31 mg chol., 92 mg sodium, 25 g carbo., 4 g fiber, 15 g pro.

SALMON PINWHEEL SALAD

1   1½-pound fresh or frozen skinless salmon fillet, ½ to ¾ inch thick
    Salt
    Black pepper
½   cup dry white wine or water
¼   teaspoon salt
¼   teaspoon black pepper
1   bay leaf
1   10-ounce package torn mixed salad greens
2   medium oranges, peeled and sectioned
1   cup thinly sliced cucumber
¼   cup sliced almonds, toasted
1   recipe Creamy Orange Dressing

PREP:
25 minutes
CHILL:
2 to 24 hours
MAKES:
6 servings

11 carbs per serving

Exchanges:
1 Vegetable
½ Fruit
3 Lean Meat

1 Thaw fish, if frozen. Rinse fish; pat dry with paper towels. Cut fillet lengthwise into 6 even strips. Lightly season with salt and pepper. Starting with the thick end of each strip, roll into pinwheels. Secure each pinwheel with a wooden toothpick or wooden skewer.

2 In a large skillet combine white wine or the water, the ¼ teaspoon salt, the ¼ teaspoon pepper, and the bay leaf; bring to boiling. Add salmon. Return to boiling; reduce heat. Cover and simmer for 6 to 8 minutes or just until fish flakes easily when tested with a fork, turning once. Using a slotted spoon, remove salmon from cooking liquid. Discard cooking liquid. Cover and chill salmon in the refrigerator for at least 2 hours or up to 24 hours.

3 To serve, arrange salad greens, orange sections, cucumber slices, and almonds in 6 salad bowls. Top each with a salmon roll. Spoon Creamy Orange Dressing over salad mixture in bowls.

CREAMY ORANGE DRESSING: In a small bowl stir together ½ cup light dairy sour cream, ½ teaspoon finely shredded orange peel, 2 tablespoons orange juice, 2 teaspoons sugar, and ½ teaspoon poppy seeds. Stir in enough additional orange juice, 1 teaspoon at a time, to make desired consistency.

Nutrition Facts per serving: 238 cal., 9 g total fat (2 g sat. fat), 67 mg chol., 190 mg sodium, 11 g carbo., 3 g fiber, 26 g pro.

TUNA SALAD NIÇOISE

PREP:
30 minutes
BROIL:
8 minutes
MAKES:
4 servings

1   pound fresh or frozen tuna steaks, 1 inch thick
3   tablespoons sherry vinegar
2   tablespoons finely chopped shallots
1   tablespoon Dijon-style mustard
2   tablespoons olive oil
1   anchovy fillet, rinsed and mashed
    Salt
    Black pepper
8   ounces tiny new potatoes, quartered
6   ounces fresh green beans
6   cups butterhead (Bibb or Boston) lettuce leaves
¾   cup thinly sliced radishes
½   cup niçoise olives or ripe olives, pitted (optional)

18
carbs per serving

Exchanges:
2 Vegetable
½ Starch
3½ Very Lean Meat
1 Fat

1 Thaw fish, if frozen. Rinse fish; pat dry with paper towels. For dressing, in a small bowl combine sherry vinegar and shallots. Whisk in Dijon-style mustard. Add oil in a thin, steady stream, whisking constantly. Stir in the anchovy; season to taste with salt and pepper. Remove 1 tablespoon of the dressing for brushing tuna steaks; set aside remaining dressing.

2 Brush all of the 1 tablespoon dressing over both sides of tuna steaks. Place tuna steaks on the unheated greased rack of a broiler pan. Broil about 4 inches from the heat for 8 to 12 minutes or until fish flakes easily when tested with a fork, gently turning once halfway through broiling time. Cut fish into slices.

3 Meanwhile, in a covered medium saucepan cook potatoes in enough boiling water to cover for 7 minutes. Add green beans; cook about 2 minutes more or until potatoes are tender. Drain and cool slightly.

4 To serve, arrange fish, potatoes, green beans, lettuce leaves, radishes, and olives (if desired) on 4 dinner plates. Serve with remaining dressing.

TO GRILL: Place fish on the greased rack of an uncovered grill directly over medium coals. Grill for 8 to 12 minutes or until fish flakes easily when tested with a fork, gently turning once halfway through grilling time. Cut fish into slices.

Nutrition Facts per serving: 270 cal., 8 g total fat (1 g sat. fat), 51 mg chol., 339 mg sodium, 18 g carbo., 4 g fiber, 31 g pro.

SPINACH-PASTA SALAD WITH SHRIMP

1   cup dried medium shell pasta or elbow macaroni,
    cooked according to package directions and drained

1   pound frozen cooked shrimp, thawed, or 1 pound cooked deli shrimp

1   cup chopped red sweet pepper

1/3 cup bottled creamy onion or Caesar salad dressing

2   tablespoons snipped fresh dill (optional)

1/4 teaspoon salt

1/8 teaspoon black pepper

1   6-ounce package fresh baby spinach

4   ounces goat cheese, sliced, or feta cheese, crumbled

1 In an extra-large bowl combine cooked pasta, shrimp, and sweet pepper. Drizzle with salad dressing; sprinkle with dill (if desired), salt, and pepper. Toss to coat. Divide spinach among 6 dinner plates. Top with shrimp mixture and cheese.

Nutrition Facts per serving: 247 cal., 10 g total fat (4 g sat. fat), 156 mg chol., 509 mg sodium, 17 g carbo., 2 g fiber, 23 g pro.

START TO FINISH:
25 minutes
MAKES:
6 servings

17
carbs per serving

Exchanges:
1 Vegetable
1 Starch
2½ Very Lean Meat
1 Fat

GRILLED TOMATO & MOZZARELLA SALAD

PREP:
30 minutes
GRILL:
5 minutes +
2 minutes
MAKES:
4 servings

1   tablespoon balsamic vinegar or red wine vinegar
1   tablespoon olive oil or salad oil
1   tablespoon water
¼   teaspoon salt
⅛   teaspoon black pepper
1   medium yellow summer squash, bias-cut into ¼-inch-thick slices
2   large red and/or yellow tomatoes, cut into ½-inch-thick slices
4   cups torn mixed salad greens
8   ounces part-skim mozzarella cheese, thinly sliced and cut into triangles
     Black pepper
2   tablespoons assorted snipped fresh herbs (such as oregano, basil, thyme, and/or sage)

8 carbs per serving

Exchanges:
2 Vegetable
2 Lean Meat
1 Fat

1 For dressing, in a screw-top jar combine balsamic or red wine vinegar, oil, the water, salt, and the ⅛ teaspoon pepper. Cover and shake well; set aside.

2 Place squash slices on the greased rack of an uncovered grill directly over medium coals. Grill for 5 to 6 minutes or until crisp-tender, turning once halfway through grilling time. Add tomato slices to rack; grill for 2 to 4 minutes or until heated through but still slightly firm, turning once halfway through grilling time.

3 Divide greens among 4 dinner plates. Top with grilled tomato slices, squash, and cheese. Sprinkle with additional pepper. Drizzle dressing over vegetables. Sprinkle with snipped fresh herbs.

Nutrition Facts per serving: 202 cal., 13 g total fat (6 g sat. fat), 36 mg chol., 504 mg sodium, 8 g carbo., 2 g fiber, 15 g pro.

SANDWICHES & WRAPS

11

TEX-MEX SLOPPY JOES

26
carbs per serving

1	pound uncooked ground chicken breast or turkey breast
2	medium onions, chopped
1	medium green sweet pepper, chopped
½	cup loose-pack frozen whole kernel corn
2	large cloves garlic, minced
1	fresh jalapeño chile pepper, seeded (if desired) and finely chopped*
1	teaspoon chili powder
1	teaspoon ground cumin
1	teaspoon dried oregano, crushed, or 1 tablespoon snipped fresh oregano
¾	cup ketchup
4	teaspoons Worcestershire sauce
8	whole wheat hamburger buns
	Dill pickle slices (optional)

1 In a large nonstick skillet combine ground chicken breast, onions, sweet pepper, corn, garlic, chile pepper, chili powder, cumin, and oregano. Cook over medium heat until chicken is no longer pink and onions are tender, stirring frequently. Stir in ketchup and Worcestershire sauce; heat through.

2 Divide mixture among buns. If desired, top with pickle slices.

*NOTE: Because chile peppers contain volatile oils that can burn your skin and eyes, avoid direct contact with them as much as possible. When working with chile peppers, wear plastic or rubber gloves. If your bare hands do touch the peppers, wash your hands and nails well with soap and warm water.

Nutrition Facts per serving: 208 cal., 6 g total fat (0 g sat. fat), 0 mg chol., 453 mg sodium, 26 g carbo., 4 g fiber, 13 g pro.

Exchanges:
½ Vegetable
1½ Starch
1½ Very Lean Meat
½ Fat

GRILLED TURKEY BURGERS

½ cup finely shredded carrot

¼ cup thinly sliced green onions

2 tablespoons fine dry bread crumbs

2 tablespoons fat-free milk

¼ teaspoon dried Italian seasoning, crushed

¼ teaspoon garlic salt

⅛ teaspoon black pepper

12 ounces uncooked ground turkey or chicken

¼ cup Dijon-style mustard

½ teaspoon curry powder

4 whole wheat hamburger buns, split and toasted

Lettuce leaves (optional)

Sliced tomato (optional)

1 In a medium bowl stir together carrot, green onions, bread crumbs, milk, Italian seasoning, garlic salt, and pepper. Add ground turkey; mix well. Form the turkey mixture into four ½-inch-thick patties.

2 Place patties on the greased rack of an uncovered grill directly over medium coals. Grill for 11 to 13 minutes or until patties are done (165°F),* turning once halfway through grilling time.

3 Meanwhile, in a small bowl stir together mustard and curry powder. Spread buns with mustard mixture. Top with burgers and, if desired, lettuce and tomato.

TO BROIL: Place patties on the unheated greased rack of a broiler pan. Broil 4 to 5 inches from the heat for 11 to 13 minutes or until patties are done (165°F),* turning once halfway through broiling time.

*NOTE: The internal color of a burger is not a reliable doneness indicator. A turkey or chicken patty cooked to 165°F is safe, regardless of color. To measure the doneness of a patty, insert an instant-read thermometer through the side of the patty to a depth of 2 to 3 inches.

Nutrition Facts per serving: 287 cal., 11 g total fat (3 g sat. fat), 68 mg chol., 470 mg sodium, 26 g carbo., 3 g fiber, 21 g pro.

PREP:
15 minutes
GRILL:
11 minutes
MAKES:
4 servings

26 carbs per serving

Exchanges:
½ Vegetable
1½ Starch
2 Medium-Fat Meat

TURKEY & CRANBERRY SANDWICHES
WITH CURRY DRESSING

START TO FINISH:
15 minutes
MAKES:
4 servings

34
carbs per serving

Exchanges:
2 Starch
1½ Lean Meat
1 Fat

- 3 tablespoons light mayonnaise dressing or salad dressing
- ½ teaspoon curry powder
- ⅓ cup canned whole cranberry sauce
- 8 thin slices firm-textured whole wheat bread
- 8 ounces thinly sliced smoked turkey breast
- 1 cup watercress, tough stems removed, or spinach leaves

❶ For dressing, in a small bowl stir together the mayonnaise dressing and curry powder. Set aside.

❷ Snip any large pieces in the cranberry sauce. Spread one side of 4 of the bread slices with cranberry sauce. Divide and arrange turkey and watercress atop the cranberry sauce. Spread dressing on one side of the remaining 4 slices bread. Place bread slices, dressing sides down, on top of turkey and watercress.

Nutrition Facts per serving: 255 cal., 7 g total fat (1 g sat. fat), 28 mg chol., 908 mg sodium, 34 g carbo., 4 g fiber, 17 g pro.

ASIAN CHICKEN WRAPS

1   2- to 2¼-pound deli-roasted chicken

8   8- to 10-inch flour tortillas

½   cup bottled hoisin sauce

¼   cup finely chopped peanuts

¼   cup finely chopped green onions

½   cup shredded daikon, well drained

3   tablespoons reduced-sodium soy sauce

3   tablespoons Chinese black vinegar or rice vinegar

1   tablespoon water

1   teaspoon chili oil or toasted sesame oil

1 Remove skin from chicken and discard. Remove chicken from bones and shred chicken; set aside.

2 Spread one side of each tortilla with hoisin sauce; sprinkle with peanuts and green onions. Top with shredded chicken and shredded daikon. Roll up tortillas; halve each roll crosswise.

3 For dipping sauce, in a small bowl combine soy sauce, vinegar, the water, and chili or sesame oil. Serve with chicken wraps.

Nutrition Facts per serving: 292 cal., 11 g total fat (2 g sat. fat), 63 mg chol., 621 mg sodium, 22 g carbo., 1 g fiber, 25 g pro.

START TO FINISH:
30 minutes
MAKES:
8 servings

22

carbs per serving

Exchanges:
1½ Starch
3 Lean Meat

CHICKEN FOCACCIA SANDWICHES

START TO FINISH:
15 minutes
MAKES:
6 servings

1	8-inch tomato or onion Italian flatbread (focaccia) or 1 loaf sourdough bread
⅓	cup light mayonnaise dressing or salad dressing
1	cup lightly packed fresh basil leaves
2	cups sliced or shredded cooked chicken
½	of a 7-ounce jar roasted red sweet peppers, drained and cut into strips (about ½ cup)

27 carbs per serving

1 Using a long serrated knife, cut bread in half horizontally. Spread cut sides of bread halves with mayonnaise dressing.

2 Layer basil leaves, chicken, and roasted sweet peppers between bread halves. Cut into six pieces.

Nutrition Facts per serving: 263 cal., 10 g total fat (2 g sat. fat), 51 mg chol., 341 mg sodium, 27 g carbo., 1 g fiber, 19 g pro.

Exchanges:
2 Starch
2 Very Lean Meat
1 Fat

TURKEY-TOMATO WRAPS

1   7-ounce container hummus

3   8- to 10-inch tomato-basil flour tortillas or whole wheat tortillas

8   ounces thinly sliced, cooked peppered turkey breast

6   romaine leaves, ribs removed

3   small tomatoes, thinly sliced

3   thin slices red onion, separated into rings

1 Spread hummus evenly over tortillas. Layer turkey breast, romaine, tomatoes, and red onion on tortillas. Roll up each tortilla into a spiral. Cut each roll in half.

TO MAKE AHEAD: Prepare as directed. Wrap in plastic wrap and chill for up to 4 hours.

Nutrition Facts per serving: 236 cal., 6 g total fat (1 g sat. fat), 32 mg chol., 458 mg sodium, 29 g carbo., 4 g fiber, 19 g pro.

START TO FINISH:
20 minutes

MAKES:
6 servings

29
carbs per serving

Exchanges:
1 Vegetable
1½ Starch
2 Lean Meat

GRILLED ASIAN BURGERS

PREP:
15 minutes
GRILL:
10 minutes
MAKES:
4 servings

25
carbs per
serving

Exchanges:
½ Vegetable
1½ Starch
2 Medium-Fat Meat

½ cup finely chopped fresh mushrooms

¼ cup thinly sliced green onions

2 tablespoons fine dry bread crumbs

2 tablespoons fat-free milk

2 teaspoons reduced-sodium soy sauce

¼ teaspoon black pepper

12 ounces lean ground beef

4 whole wheat hamburger buns, split and toasted

Asian hot mustard (optional)

Sliced tomato (optional)

Shredded Chinese cabbage (optional)

1 In a medium bowl stir together mushrooms, green onions, bread crumbs, milk, soy sauce, and pepper. Add the ground beef; mix well. Form meat mixture into four ½-inch-thick patties.

2 Place patties on the rack of an uncovered grill directly over medium coals. Grill for 10 to 13 minutes or until meat is done (160°F),* turning once halfway through grilling time.

3 If desired, spread buns with hot mustard. Top buns with patties and, if desired, tomatoes and Chinese cabbage.

TO BROIL: Place patties on the unheated rack of a broiler pan. Broil 3 to 4 inches from the heat for 10 to 12 minutes or until meat is done (160°F),* turning once halfway through broiling time.

*NOTE: The internal color of a burger is not a reliable doneness indicator. A beef, veal, lamb, or pork patty cooked to 160°F is safe, regardless of color. To measure the doneness of a patty, insert an instant-read thermometer through the side of the patty to a depth of 2 to 3 inches.

Nutrition Facts per serving: 281 cal., 11 g total fat (4 g sat. fat), 54 mg chol., 439 mg sodium, 25 g carbo., 2 g fiber, 20 g pro.

ROAST BEEF SANDWICHES
WITH HORSERADISH SLAW

⅓ cup light dairy sour cream

2 tablespoons snipped fresh chives

2 tablespoons spicy brown mustard

1 teaspoon prepared horseradish

½ teaspoon sugar

¼ teaspoon salt

1 cup packaged shredded broccoli (broccoli slaw mix)

8 ounces thinly sliced cooked roast beef

8 ½-inch-thick slices sourdough bread, toasted

START TO FINISH:
15 minutes
MAKES:
4 servings

❶ In a medium bowl combine sour cream, chives, brown mustard, horseradish, sugar, and salt. Add shredded broccoli; toss to coat.

❷ To assemble, divide roast beef among 4 of the bread slices. Top with broccoli mixture and remaining bread slices. If desired, secure sandwiches with toothpicks.

Nutrition Facts per serving: 303 cal., 10 g total fat (4 g sat. fat), 51 mg chol., 616 mg sodium, 30 g carbo., 2 g fiber, 22 g pro.

30
carbs per serving

Exchanges:
½ Vegetable
2 Starch
2 Lean Meat
½ Fat

LAMB & BULGUR BURGERS

PREP:
20 minutes
BAKE:
20 minutes
OVEN:
350°F
MAKES:
6 servings

32

carbs per serving

Exchanges:
2 Starch
2 Medium-Fat Meat

1	6-ounce carton plain low-fat yogurt
2	teaspoons snipped fresh dill or ½ teaspoon dried dill
¾	cup water
½	cup bulgur
½	teaspoon salt
¼	cup finely chopped onion
3	tablespoons snipped fresh parsley
2	cloves garlic, minced
1	teaspoon ground coriander
1	teaspoon snipped fresh thyme or ¼ teaspoon dried thyme, crushed
⅛	teaspoon black pepper
12	ounces lean ground lamb
½	of a medium cucumber, cut lengthwise into thin ribbons
6	sandwich rolls or whole wheat hamburger buns, split
	Tomato slices (optional)

❶ For sauce, in a small bowl stir together yogurt and dill. Cover and chill until ready to serve.

❷ In a small saucepan bring the water to boiling. Stir in bulgur and ¼ teaspoon of the salt. Reduce heat to low. Cover and cook for 10 minutes. Remove from heat. Let stand, covered, for 5 minutes.

❸ Meanwhile, in a large bowl combine onion, parsley, garlic, coriander, thyme, pepper, and the remaining ¼ teaspoon salt. Stir in cooked bulgur and lamb; mix well. Shape meat mixture into six ½-inch-thick patties. Place in a shallow baking pan. Bake in a 350° oven for 20 to 25 minutes or until meat is done (160°F).*

❹ To serve, arrange the cucumber ribbons on bottoms of rolls. Add patties, sauce, tomato slices (if desired), and roll tops.

*NOTE: The internal color of a burger is not a reliable doneness indicator. A lamb, beef, veal, or pork patty cooked to 160°F is safe, regardless of color. To measure the doneness of a patty, insert an instant-read thermometer through the side of the patty to a depth of 2 to 3 inches.

Nutrition Facts per serving: 290 cal., 11 g total fat (4 g sat. fat), 40 mg chol., 447 mg sodium, 32 g carbo., 4 g fiber, 17 g pro.

SEASONED TUNA SANDWICHES

2   6-ounce cans solid white tuna (water pack), drained
2   tablespoons olive oil
2   teaspoons lemon juice
1   teaspoon capers, drained
⅛   teaspoon black pepper
2   tablespoons fat-free mayonnaise dressing or salad dressing
8   slices whole wheat bread
4   lettuce leaves (optional)
4   tomato slices

1 In a small bowl combine tuna, oil, lemon juice, capers, and pepper.

2 To assemble, spread mayonnaise dressing on 4 of the bread slices. Top with lettuce leaves (if desired), tomato slices, and tuna mixture. Top with remaining bread slices.

Nutrition Facts per serving: 309 cal., 11 g total fat (2 g sat. fat), 36 mg chol., 669 mg sodium, 26 g carbo., 2 g fiber, 25 g pro.

START TO FINISH:
15 minutes
MAKES:
4 servings

26
carbs per serving

Exchanges:
2 Starch
3 Very Lean Meat
1 Fat

HOT APPLE & CHEESE SANDWICHES

START TO FINISH:
25 minutes
MAKES:
4 servings

1   medium apple or pear

4   whole wheat English muffins, split

2   tablespoons Dijon-style mustard

4   slices Canadian-style bacon

4   slices Swiss cheese

1 Core apple or pear and thinly slice crosswise to form rings. Spread cut sides of muffin halves with mustard.

2 To assemble, top each of 4 of the muffin halves with a slice of bacon, 1 or 2 apple or pear rings, and a slice of cheese. Top with remaining muffin halves, cut sides down.

3 Heat a large nonstick skillet or griddle. Place sandwiches in skillet or on griddle. Cook over medium-low heat for 9 to 10 minutes or until sandwiches are golden brown and cheese starts to melt, turning once.

Nutrition Facts per serving: 303 cal., 11 g total fat (6 g sat. fat), 40 mg chol., 851 mg sodium, 34 g carbo., 3 g fiber, 20 g pro.

34
carbs per
serving

Exchanges:
2 Starch
2 Medium-Fat Meat

EGG-VEGETABLE SALAD WRAPS

6	hard-cooked eggs, chopped
½	cup chopped cucumber
½	cup chopped yellow summer squash or zucchini
¼	cup shredded carrot
2	tablespoons chopped red onion
¼	cup low-fat mayonnaise dressing
2	tablespoons Dijon-style mustard
1	tablespoon fat-free milk
1	teaspoon snipped fresh tarragon or basil or ¼ teaspoon dried tarragon or basil, crushed
¼	teaspoon salt
⅛	teaspoon paprika
6	leaf lettuce leaves
6	6- to 7-inch whole wheat flour tortillas
2	plum tomatoes, thinly sliced

1 In a large bowl combine eggs, cucumber, yellow summer squash or zucchini, carrot, and red onion. For dressing, in a small bowl stir together mayonnaise dressing, Dijon mustard, milk, tarragon or basil, salt, and paprika. Pour the dressing over egg mixture; toss gently to coat.

2 For each sandwich, place a lettuce leaf on a tortilla. Place 3 or 4 tomato slices on top of the lettuce, slightly off center. Spoon about ½ cup of the egg mixture on top of the tomato slices. Roll up tortilla. If necessary, secure with toothpicks. Cut the tortilla rolls in half crosswise.

Nutrition Facts per serving: 196 cal., 8 g total fat (2 g sat. fat), 212 mg chol., 596 mg sodium, 21 g carbo., 2 g fiber, 10 g pro.

START TO FINISH:
35 minutes
MAKES:
6 servings

21
carbs per serving

Exchanges:
1 Vegetable
1 Starch
1 Medium-Fat Meat
½ Fat

ZUCCHINI-CARROT BURGERS

START TO FINISH:
25 minutes
MAKES:
4 servings

41
carbs per serving

Exchanges:
1½ Vegetable
2 Starch
2 Fat

1   slightly beaten egg or ¼ cup refrigerated or frozen egg product, thawed

1   tablespoon olive oil

1   teaspoon dried oregano, crushed

1   cup crushed stone-ground wheat crackers (about 22)

1   cup finely shredded zucchini

1   cup finely shredded carrots

¼   cup chopped green onions

½   cup plain low-fat yogurt

2   cloves garlic, minced

½   teaspoon finely shredded lemon peel

2   large whole wheat pita bread rounds, halved crosswise

1   cup shredded leaf lettuce

1   small tomato, thinly sliced

½   of a small cucumber, thinly sliced

1 In a medium bowl combine egg, 1 teaspoon of the oil, and the oregano. Add crushed crackers, zucchini, carrots, and green onions; mix well. Form the vegetable mixture into four patties, each about 3½ inches in diameter.

2 In a large nonstick skillet heat the remaining 2 teaspoons oil over medium heat. Add patties to skillet. Cook for 5 to 7 minutes or until patties are golden brown, turning once halfway through cooking time.

3 Meanwhile, for sauce, in a small bowl combine yogurt, garlic, and lemon peel.

4 To serve, place each vegetable patty in a pita bread half. Add lettuce, tomato, cucumber, and sauce.

Nutrition Facts per serving: 284 cal., 10 g total fat (2 g sat. fat), 55 mg chol., 378 mg sodium, 41 g carbo., 6 g fiber, 10 g pro.

COOKING
FOR TWO

12

271

SPICED BREAKFAST POPOVERS

PREP:
15 minutes
BAKE:
35 minutes
OVEN:
400°F
MAKES:
2 popovers

31
carbs per
popover

Exchanges:
½ Fruit
1 Starch
½ Other Carbo.
1 Fat

Nonstick cooking spray
1   egg
⅓   cup fat-free milk
1   teaspoon cooking oil
⅓   cup all-purpose flour
     Dash salt
1   recipe Orange Cream
1   cup halved or quartered strawberries

1 For popovers, generously coat the bottoms and sides of two 6-ounce custard cups with nonstick cooking spray. Place the custard cups in a shallow baking pan; set aside.

2 In a small bowl combine egg, milk, and oil. Beat with a wire whisk or rotary beater. Add flour and salt; beat until smooth. Pour batter into prepared custard cups, filling each half full. Bake in a 400° oven about 35 minutes or until popovers are firm.

3 Remove popovers from oven and immediately prick each popover with a fork to let steam escape. (For crisper popovers, turn off oven; return popovers to the oven for 5 to 10 minutes or until desired crispness is reached.) Remove popovers from cups.

4 To serve, split warm popovers in half crosswise; top with Orange Cream and strawberries.

ORANGE CREAM: In a small bowl combine ¼ cup fat-free dairy sour cream, 1½ teaspoons packed brown sugar, ⅛ teaspoon finely shredded orange peel, 2 teaspoons orange juice, and dash ground cinnamon. Cover and refrigerate until ready to serve or up to 24 hours.

Nutrition Facts per popover: 202 cal., 5 g total fat (1 g sat. fat), 109 mg chol., 170 mg sodium, 31 g carbo., 2 g fiber, 8 g pro.

TEX-MEX SPINACH OMELET

4   eggs or 1 cup refrigerated or frozen egg product, thawed
1   tablespoon snipped fresh cilantro
     Dash salt
     Dash ground cumin
     Nonstick cooking spray
1   ounce Monterey Jack cheese with jalapeño chile peppers,
     reduced-fat cheddar cheese, or reduced-fat Swiss cheese,
     shredded (¼ cup)
¾   cup fresh baby spinach leaves
1   recipe Corn-Pepper Relish

START TO FINISH: *25 minutes*
MAKES: *2 servings*

8 carbs per serving

1 In a medium bowl combine eggs, cilantro, salt, and cumin. Beat with a wire whisk or rotary beater until frothy.

2 Coat an unheated 10-inch nonstick skillet with flared sides with nonstick cooking spray. Preheat skillet over medium heat. Pour egg mixture into hot skillet. Cook, without stirring, for 2 to 3 minutes or until egg mixture begins to set. Run a spatula around edge of skillet, lifting egg mixture so that the uncooked portion flows underneath. Continue cooking and lifting edge until egg mixture is cooked through but is still glossy and moist. Remove from heat.

3 Sprinkle with cheese. Top with three-fourths of the spinach and half of the Corn-Pepper Relish. Using the spatula, lift and fold an edge of the omelet partially over filling. Top with remaining spinach and relish.

CORN-PEPPER RELISH: In a small bowl combine ¼ cup chopped red sweet pepper; ¼ cup loose-pack frozen whole kernel corn, thawed; 2 tablespoons chopped red onion; and 1 tablespoon snipped fresh cilantro.

Nutrition Facts per serving: 230 cal., 14 g total fat (6 g sat. fat), 435 mg chol., 298 mg sodium, 8 g carbo., 1 g fiber, 17 g pro.

Exchanges:
½ Vegetable
½ Starch
2½ Medium-Fat Meat

SOUTHWESTERN BREAKFAST TOSTADAS

START TO FINISH:
20 minutes
MAKES:
2 servings

2	6-inch corn tortillas
½	cup canned black beans, rinsed and drained
2	eggs or ½ cup refrigerated or frozen egg product, thawed
1	tablespoon fat-free milk
⅛	teaspoon black pepper
	Dash salt
	Nonstick cooking spray
½	cup chopped tomato
2	tablespoons crumbled queso fresco or shredded Monterey Jack cheese
2	teaspoons snipped fresh cilantro
	Purchased chunky salsa (optional)

24
carbs per
serving

Exchanges:
1½ Starch
1½ Medium-Fat Meat

❶ Warm tortillas according to package directions. Meanwhile, in a small bowl use a potato masher or fork to slightly mash beans; set aside. In another small bowl or 1-cup glass measure combine eggs, milk, pepper, and salt. Beat with a wire whisk or rotary beater.

❷ Lightly coat an unheated medium nonstick skillet with nonstick cooking spray. Preheat over medium heat. Pour egg mixture into hot skillet. Cook, without stirring, until egg mixture begins to set. Run a spatula around edge of skillet, lifting egg mixture so that the uncooked portion flows underneath. Continue cooking about 2 minutes more or until egg mixture is cooked through but is still glossy and moist. Remove from heat.

❸ Spread tortillas with mashed beans. Divide cooked egg mixture between tortillas. Top with tomato, cheese, and cilantro. If desired, top with salsa. Serve immediately.

Nutrition Facts per serving: 215 cal., 8 g total fat (3 g sat. fat), 219 mg chol., 409 mg sodium, 24 g carbo., 5 g fiber, 15 g pro.

EGG & POTATO CASSEROLE

Nonstick cooking spray

⅔ cup loose-pack frozen diced hash brown potatoes with onion and peppers

⅓ cup loose-pack frozen cut broccoli or frozen cut asparagus

2 tablespoons finely chopped Canadian-style bacon or lean cooked ham

2 tablespoons evaporated fat-free milk

2 teaspoons all-purpose flour

3 slightly beaten eggs or ¾ cup refrigerated or frozen egg product, thawed

3 tablespoons shredded reduced-fat cheddar cheese

1 teaspoon snipped fresh basil or ¼ teaspoon dried basil, crushed

⅛ teaspoon black pepper

Dash salt

1 Lightly coat two 10-ounce individual casseroles with nonstick cooking spray. Arrange hash brown potatoes and broccoli in bottoms of casseroles; top with Canadian-style bacon. In a small bowl gradually stir evaporated milk into flour. Stir in eggs, half of the cheese, the basil, pepper, and salt. Pour egg mixture over vegetables.

2 Bake in a 350° oven for 25 to 30 minutes or until a knife inserted near the centers comes out clean. Sprinkle with the remaining cheese. Let stand for 5 minutes before serving.

Nutrition Facts per serving: 238 cal., 11 g total fat (4 g sat. fat), 333 mg chol., 583 mg sodium, 16 g carbo., 1 g fiber, 18 g pro.

PREP:
15 minutes
BAKE:
25 minutes
STAND:
5 minutes
OVEN:
350°F
MAKES:
2 servings

16
carbs per
serving

Exchanges:
1 Starch
2 Medium-Fat Meat

SHORTCUT CHICKEN MOLE

START TO FINISH:
20 minutes
MAKES:
2 servings

¾ cup quick-cooking rice

Nonstick cooking spray

1 medium red and/or yellow sweet pepper, cut into bite-size pieces

½ of a small onion, cut into thin wedges

6 ounces cooked chicken, cut into bite-size strips

1 cup purchased salsa

1 tablespoon unsweetened cocoa powder

½ teaspoon ground cumin

Fresh herb sprigs (optional)

41 carbs per serving

❶ Cook rice according to package directions; keep warm.

❷ Meanwhile, coat an unheated large nonstick skillet with nonstick cooking spray. Preheat over medium heat. Add sweet pepper and onion to hot skillet. Cook and stir for 3 to 5 minutes or until crisp-tender. Add chicken, salsa, cocoa powder, and cumin to skillet. Heat through, stirring gently. Serve chicken with hot cooked rice. If desired, garnish with fresh herb sprigs.

Nutrition Facts per serving: 354 cal., 7 g total fat (2 g sat. fat), 76 mg chol., 356 mg sodium, 41 g carbo., 3 g fiber, 30 g pro.

Exchanges:
2 Vegetable
2 Starch
3 Very Lean Meat
1 Fat

APPLE-GLAZED CHICKEN WITH SPINACH

¼ cup apple jelly

1 tablespoon reduced-sodium soy sauce

2 teaspoons snipped fresh thyme or ½ teaspoon dried thyme, crushed

½ teaspoon finely shredded lemon peel

½ teaspoon grated fresh ginger

2 skinless, boneless chicken breast halves (8 to 10 ounces total)

⅛ teaspoon salt

⅛ teaspoon black pepper

Nonstick cooking spray

1 medium apple, peeled, cored, and chopped

¼ cup sliced onion

1 clove garlic, minced

6 cups packaged prewashed fresh spinach

1 For glaze, in a small microwave-safe bowl combine apple jelly, soy sauce, thyme, lemon peel, and ginger. Microwave, uncovered, on 100% power (high) for 60 to 90 seconds or just until jelly is melted, stirring once. Reserve 2 tablespoons of the glaze.

2 Season chicken with salt and pepper. Place chicken on the unheated rack of a broiler pan. Broil 4 to 5 inches from the heat for 12 to 15 minutes or until chicken is tender and no longer pink, turning once halfway through the broiling time and brushing with the remaining glaze during the last 5 minutes of broiling. Discard remainder of the glaze used as a brush-on.

3 Meanwhile, coat an unheated large nonstick saucepan with nonstick cooking spray. Preheat over medium heat. Add apple, onion, and garlic to hot saucepan; cook and stir for 3 minutes. Stir in the reserved 2 tablespoons glaze; bring to boiling. Add spinach; toss just until wilted.

4 To serve, slice each chicken breast half crosswise into 6 to 8 pieces. Divide spinach mixture between 2 dinner plates. Top with sliced chicken.

Nutrition Facts per serving: 300 cal., 2 g total fat (1 g sat. fat), 66 mg chol., 579 mg sodium, 42 g carbo., 4 g fiber, 30 g pro.

START TO FINISH:
30 minutes
MAKES:
2 servings

42
carbs per serving

Exchanges:
2 Vegetable
½ Fruit
4 Very Lean Meat
1½ Other Carbo.

CHICKEN WITH PEAR, SAGE & CHEESE

START TO FINISH:
25 minutes
MAKES:
2 servings

14
carbs per serving

Exchanges:
1 Fruit
4 Very Lean Meat
½ High-Fat Meat

2	skinless, boneless chicken breast halves (8 to 10 ounces total)
¼	teaspoon salt
⅛	teaspoon black pepper
	Nonstick cooking spray
2	thin slices Emmentaler or Gruyère cheese (about 1½ ounces total)
1	small pear, cored and cut into thin slices
¼	cup apple juice or apple cider
1	tablespoon finely snipped fresh sage or 1 teaspoon dried sage, crushed

1 Place each chicken piece between 2 pieces of plastic wrap. Using the flat side of a meat mallet, lightly pound to ¼-inch thickness. Remove plastic wrap. Sprinkle chicken with salt and pepper.

2 Coat an unheated medium nonstick skillet with nonstick cooking spray. Preheat over medium heat. Add chicken; cook for 4 to 6 minutes or until chicken is tender and no longer pink, turning once halfway through cooking time. Transfer to 2 dinner plates; top with cheese. Cover and keep warm.

3 In the same skillet cook and stir pear slices for 2 to 3 minutes or just until tender. Add apple juice and sage. Bring to boiling, scraping up any crusty browned bits from bottom of skillet. To serve, spoon the pear mixture over chicken.

Nutrition Facts per serving: 261 cal., 8 g total fat (4 g sat. fat), 85 mg chol., 409 mg sodium, 14 g carbo., 2 g fiber, 33 g pro.

CHEESY GRITS & SAUSAGE

2 cups water

½ cup quick-cooking grits

2 ounces uncooked bulk turkey sausage, cooked and drained

1 tablespoon sliced green onion

2 teaspoons finely chopped, seeded fresh jalapeño chile pepper*

¼ teaspoon garlic salt

Dash black pepper

2 tablespoons shredded reduced-fat cheddar cheese

START TO FINISH:
25 minutes
MAKES:
2 servings

1 In a medium saucepan bring the water to boiling. Slowly add grits, stirring constantly. Return to boiling; reduce heat. Cook and stir for 5 to 7 minutes or until the water is absorbed and mixture is thickened.

2 Stir in cooked turkey sausage, green onion, chile pepper, garlic salt, and black pepper. Spoon into serving dishes. Sprinkle with cheese.

*NOTE: Because chile peppers contain volatile oils that can burn your skin and eyes, avoid direct contact with them as much as possible. When working with chile peppers, wear plastic or rubber gloves. If your bare hands do touch the peppers, wash your hands and nails well with soap and warm water.

Nutrition Facts per serving: 226 cal., 7 g total fat (2 g sat. fat), 42 mg chol., 444 mg sodium, 30 g carbo., 2 g fiber, 12 g pro.

30
carbs per serving

Exchanges:
2 Starch
1 Medium-Fat Meat

WARM SAUSAGE & POTATO SALAD

23
carbs per serving

Exchanges:
½ Vegetable
1½ Starch
2 Lean Meat

10 ounces small new potatoes, cleaned and quartered
1 small leek, rinsed well
    Nonstick cooking spray
6 ounces light smoked turkey sausage, cut into ½-inch-thick slices
½ of a small green sweet pepper, chopped
2 tablespoons red wine vinegar
1 tablespoon water
1 tablespoon whole-grain mustard
½ teaspoon snipped fresh thyme or ¼ teaspoon dried thyme, crushed

1 In a covered medium saucepan cook potatoes in a small amount of boiling salted water for 12 to 15 minutes or until tender. Drain; set aside.

2 Meanwhile, slice white portion and about 1 inch of the green portion of the leek; separate green leek pieces from the white and set both portions aside.

3 Coat an unheated large nonstick skillet with nonstick cooking spray. Preheat over medium heat. Cook sausage in hot skillet for 2 to 3 minutes. Stir in the white part of leek and the sweet pepper. Cook and stir for 2 to 3 minutes more. Stir in vinegar, the water, mustard, and thyme. Stir in green portion of leek. Cook and stir for 1 minute. Add cooked potatoes; gently toss to coat. Serve warm.

Nutrition Facts per serving: 237 cal., 9 g total fat (3 g sat. fat), 45 mg chol., 772 mg sodium, 23 g carbo., 2 g fiber, 17 g pro.

LEMON PEPPER STEAK

10	ounces beef flank steak
1	tablespoon snipped fresh oregano or 1 teaspoon dried oregano, crushed
2	cloves garlic, minced
1	teaspoon finely shredded lemon peel
1	teaspoon olive oil or cooking oil
¼	teaspoon coarsely ground black pepper

1 Trim fat from steak. In a small bowl combine oregano, garlic, lemon peel, oil, and pepper. Using your fingers, rub mixture onto both sides of steak.

2 Place steak on unheated rack of a broiler pan. Broil 3 to 4 inches from heat for 15 to 18 minutes or until medium doneness (160°F), turning once halfway through broiling time. Cover and let stand for 5 minutes before slicing. To serve, thinly slice steak diagonally across the grain.

Nutrition Facts per serving: 247 cal., 12 g total fat (4 g sat. fat), 57 mg chol., 76 mg sodium, 2 g carbo., 0 g fiber, 31 g pro.

PREP:
10 minutes
BROIL:
15 minutes
STAND:
5 minutes
MAKES:
2 servings

2
carbs per serving

Exchanges:
4½ Very Lean Meat

TOMATO-HERBED STEAK

START TO FINISH:
15 minutes
MAKES:
2 servings

1   8-ounce beef top loin steak, cut ¾ inch thick
⅛   teaspoon salt
⅛   teaspoon black pepper
     Nonstick cooking spray
¼   cup sliced green onions
1   teaspoon snipped fresh basil or ½ teaspoon dried basil, crushed
½   cup chopped tomato

3 carbs per serving

❶ Cut steak in half. Sprinkle steak with salt and pepper. Coat an unheated heavy medium skillet with nonstick cooking spray. Preheat skillet over medium-high heat. Add steaks; reduce heat to medium. Cook until desired doneness. Allow 10 to 13 minutes for medium-rare doneness (145°F) to medium doneness (160°F), turning once halfway through cooking time. Remove steaks from skillet and keep warm.

❷ Add green onions and basil to hot skillet. Cook and stir about 2 minutes or until green onions are tender. Stir in tomato; heat through. Serve tomato mixture over steaks.

Nutrition Facts per serving: 170 cal., 6 g total fat (2 g sat. fat), 66 mg chol., 207 mg sodium, 3 g carbo., 1 g fiber, 25 g pro.

Exchanges:
½ Vegetable
3½ Very Lean Meat
1 Fat

BEEF & BOK CHOY

START TO FINISH:
25 minutes
MAKES:
2 servings

2   teaspoons toasted sesame oil

6   ounces beef sirloin, trimmed of fat and very thinly sliced

½   teaspoon red chile pepper paste

3   cups sliced bok choy

1   clove garlic, minced

1½   teaspoons reduced-sodium soy sauce

1   teaspoon sesame seeds, toasted

1 In a large nonstick skillet heat 1 teaspoon of the sesame oil over medium-high heat. Cook and stir beef and chile paste in hot oil about 3 minutes or until beef is desired doneness. Remove skillet from heat. Reduce heat to medium. Remove beef from skillet with a slotted spoon, reserving liquid in skillet; keep beef warm.

2 Add remaining 1 teaspoon sesame oil to skillet. Return skillet to heat. Add bok choy and garlic; cook and stir for 2 to 3 minutes or until bok choy is crisp-tender. Transfer to serving dish. Top with warm beef mixture. Drizzle with soy sauce and sprinkle with toasted sesame seeds.

Nutrition Facts per serving: 179 cal., 9 g total fat (2 g sat. fat), 52 mg chol., 271 mg sodium, 4 g carbo., 1 g fiber, 20 g pro.

4

carbs per serving

Exchanges:
1 Vegetable
2½ Lean Meat
½ Fat

BEEF & ASPARAGUS SAUTE

START TO FINISH:
25 minutes
MAKES:
2 servings

20
carbs per
serving

Exchanges:
1 Vegetable
1 Starch
3 Very Lean Meat
1 Fat

6   ounces fresh asparagus

8   ounces lean beef sirloin or tenderloin,
      trimmed of fat and very thinly sliced

¼   teaspoon salt

⅛   teaspoon black pepper

      Nonstick cooking spray

¼   cup coarsely shredded carrot

½   teaspoon dried herbes de Provence, crushed

¼   cup dry Marsala

⅛   teaspoon grated lemon peel

¾   cup hot cooked brown rice

1 Snap off and discard fibrous stem ends of asparagus. Bias-cut asparagus into 2-inch-long pieces; rinse and drain well. Set aside. Sprinkle beef with salt and pepper.

2 Coat an unheated large nonstick skillet with nonstick cooking spray. Preheat over medium-high heat. Cook and stir beef in hot skillet for 3 minutes. Add asparagus, carrot, and herbes de Provence; cook and stir for 2 minutes more. Add Marsala and lemon peel; reduce heat.

3 Cook, uncovered, for 3 to 5 minutes more or until beef is cooked through and asparagus is crisp-tender. Serve over hot cooked rice.

Nutrition Facts per serving: 257 cal., 5 g total fat (2 g sat. fat), 54 mg chol., 368 mg sodium, 20 g carbo., 3 g fiber, 27 g pro.

LAMB CHOPS WITH GINGER-DIJON SAUCE

6   ounces fingerling potatoes and/or tiny Yukon gold potatoes

1   teaspoon grated fresh ginger

1   teaspoon snipped fresh tarragon or ¼ teaspoon dried tarragon, crushed

¼   teaspoon black pepper

4   lamb rib chops, cut 1 inch thick and, if desired, frenched (about 1 pound total)

¼   teaspoon salt

2   teaspoons cooking oil

⅓   cup Riesling wine

1   to 2 teaspoons Dijon-style mustard

PREP:
15 minutes
COOK:
25 minutes
MAKES:
2 servings

1 Halve any large potatoes to make potatoes of similar size. In a small saucepan cook potatoes in a small amount of lightly salted boiling water for 10 to 13 minutes or just until tender. Drain well and set aside. Meanwhile, in a small bowl combine ginger, tarragon, and ⅛ teaspoon of the pepper; set aside.

2 Trim fat from chops; sprinkle chops with salt and the remaining ⅛ teaspoon pepper. In a large skillet heat oil over medium heat. Add chops and potatoes to skillet. Cook for 9 to 11 minutes or until chops are medium doneness (160°F), turning chops once halfway through cooking time and turning potatoes occasionally to brown evenly. Remove chops and potatoes from skillet; keep warm.

3 Remove skillet from heat. Drain off fat. For sauce, carefully pour wine into skillet; return to heat and stir to scrape up any browned bits. Add ginger mixture. Simmer and stir about 2 minutes or until liquid is reduced by half. Stir in mustard. Return to a simmer.

4 Place chops and potatoes on 2 warm dinner plates and top with the sauce.

Nutrition Facts per serving: 276 cal., 13 g total fat (4 g sat. fat), 64 mg chol., 417 mg sodium, 12 g carbo., 1 g fiber, 21 g pro.

12 carbs per serving

Exchanges:
1 Starch
2½ Very Lean Meat
1 Fat

PORK MEDALLIONS
WITH CRANBERRY & FIG CHUTNEY

START TO FINISH:
20 minutes
MAKES:
2 servings

22
carbs per serving

Exchanges:
1 Fruit
2½ Very Lean Meat
½ Other Carbo.

½ cup fresh cranberries or ¼ cup canned whole cranberry sauce

¼ cup apple juice or apple cider

2 tablespoons snipped dried figs

1 tablespoon packed brown sugar or granulated sugar

½ teaspoon snipped fresh rosemary or ¼ teaspoon dried rosemary, crushed

¼ teaspoon salt

⅛ teaspoon black pepper

6 ounces pork tenderloin

Nonstick cooking spray

Hot cooked long grain and wild rice (optional)

1 For chutney, in a heavy small saucepan stir together cranberries or cranberry sauce, apple juice, figs, sugar, rosemary, salt, and pepper. Bring to boiling; reduce heat. Simmer, uncovered, for 5 to 8 minutes or until chutney reaches desired consistency, stirring occasionally. Set aside.

2 Meanwhile, trim fat from pork. Cut pork crosswise into 6 pieces, each about 1 inch thick. Press each piece with palm of your hand to an even thickness. Coat an unheated large nonstick skillet with nonstick cooking spray. Preheat over medium-high heat. Cook pork in hot skillet for 2 to 3 minutes or until pork is slightly pink in center and juices run clear, turning once halfway through cooking time.

3 To serve, divide pork between 2 dinner plates. If desired, serve with long grain and wild rice. Spoon some of the warm chutney over pork. Pass remaining chutney.

Nutrition Facts per serving: 184 cal., 3 g total fat (1 g sat. fat), 55 mg chol., 334 mg sodium, 22 g carbo., 3 g fiber, 18 g pro.

PORK CHOPS & CHERRIES

2   boneless pork sirloin chops, cut ¾ inch thick (about 10 ounces total)

¼   teaspoon black pepper

⅛   teaspoon salt

        Nonstick cooking spray

½   cup cranberry juice, apple juice, or apple cider

1½   teaspoons spicy brown mustard

¾   teaspoon cornstarch

½   cup pitted and halved fresh dark sweet cherries or frozen
        unsweetened pitted dark sweet cherries, thawed and halved

1 Sprinkle pork chops with pepper and salt. Coat an unheated large nonstick skillet with nonstick cooking spray. Preheat over medium-high heat. Add pork chops to skillet. Cook for 8 to 10 minutes or until pork is slightly pink in the center and juices run clear (160°F), turning once halfway through cooking time. Remove chops; cover and keep warm.

2 In a small bowl stir together cranberry juice, mustard, and cornstarch; add to skillet. Cook and stir over medium heat until thickened and bubbly. Cook and stir for 2 minutes more. Stir in cherries. Serve cherry mixture over pork chops.

Nutrition Facts per serving: 262 cal., 8 g total fat (3 g sat. fat), 88 mg chol., 263 mg sodium, 16 g carbo., 1 g fiber, 30 g pro.

16
carbs per
serving

Exchanges:
1 Fruit
4 Very Lean Meat
1½ Fat

SALMON WITH COUSCOUS

2	4-ounce fresh or frozen salmon fillets, about 1 inch thick
¼	teaspoon lemon-pepper seasoning or black pepper
½	to 1 teaspoon reduced-sodium soy sauce
1	small orange, thinly sliced
1	cup small broccoli florets
½	cup reduced-sodium chicken broth
⅓	cup water
1	clove garlic, minced
⅛	teaspoon salt
½	cup quick-cooking regular or whole wheat couscous

47

carbs per
serving

Exchanges:
1 Vegetable
½ Fruit
2½ Starch
3 Very Lean Meat
½ Fat

1 Thaw fish, if frozen. Rinse fish; pat dry with paper towels. Sprinkle fish with lemon-pepper seasoning or pepper.

2 Place the fish in a lightly greased nonstick baking pan, tucking under any thin edges. Drizzle with soy sauce. Arrange orange slices on top of fish. Cover and bake in a 450° oven for 8 to 12 minutes or until fish flakes easily when tested with a fork.

3 Meanwhile, in a medium saucepan combine broccoli, chicken broth, the water, garlic, and salt. Bring just to boiling; reduce heat. Cover and simmer about 3 minutes or just until broccoli is crisp-tender. Stir in couscous. Remove saucepan from heat. Cover; let stand for 5 minutes.

4 To serve, spoon couscous mixture onto a serving platter. Arrange the orange-topped fish on top of couscous mixture.

Nutrition Facts per serving: 386 cal., 8 g total fat (1 g sat. fat), 62 mg chol., 552 mg sodium, 47 g carbo., 5 g fiber, 31 g pro.

FIERY SOUTHWESTERN SEAFOOD SKEWERS

8	ounces fresh or frozen medium or large shrimp in shells and/or sea scallops
1	medium zucchini or yellow summer squash, halved lengthwise and sliced ¾ inch thick
½	of a medium red sweet pepper, cut into 1-inch pieces
1	small onion, cut into 4 wedges
1	tablespoon canned chipotle chile pepper in adobo sauce, mashed*
2	teaspoons lime juice
2	teaspoons cooking oil
1	teaspoon packed brown sugar
1	clove garlic, minced
¼	teaspoon salt
¼	teaspoon ground cumin
1	tablespoon snipped fresh cilantro
	Lime wedges (optional)

PREP:
25 minutes
GRILL:
8 minutes
MAKES:
2 servings

10
carbs per serving

Exchanges:
1½ Vegetable
2 Lean Meat
1 Fat

1 Thaw shrimp and/or scallops, if frozen. Peel and devein shrimp. Rinse shrimp and/or scallops; pat dry with paper towels. On 4 long metal skewers, alternately thread shrimp and/or scallops, zucchini, sweet pepper, and onion, leaving a ¼-inch space between pieces.

2 For sauce, in a small bowl combine chipotle chile pepper, lime juice, oil, brown sugar, garlic, salt, and cumin. Brush over kabobs.

3 Place kabobs on the rack of an uncovered grill directly over medium coals. Grill for 8 to 10 minutes or until shrimp and/or scallops are opaque and vegetables are crisp-tender, turning once halfway through grilling time. Sprinkle kabobs with cilantro. If desired, serve with lime wedges.

*NOTE: Because chile peppers contain volatile oils that can burn your skin and eyes, avoid direct contact with them as much as possible. When working with chile peppers, wear plastic or rubber gloves. If your bare hands do touch the peppers, wash your hands and nails well with soap and warm water.

Nutrition Facts per serving: 147 cal., 6 g total fat (1 g sat. fat), 119 mg chol., 470 mg sodium, 10 g carbo., 3 g fiber, 15 g pro.

ROASTED MANGO WITH COCONUT TOPPING

PREP:
10 minutes
BAKE:
10 minutes
OVEN:
425°F
MAKES:
2 servings

1   ripe medium mango, seeded, peeled, and cubed
1   tablespoon flaked coconut
1   teaspoon finely shredded orange peel
1   teaspoon finely chopped crystallized ginger

1 Divide mango cubes between two 6-ounce custard cups. In a small bowl combine coconut, orange peel, and crystallized ginger. Sprinkle over mango cubes.

2 Bake in a 425° oven about 10 minutes or just until topping begins to brown.

Nutrition Facts per serving: 89 cal., 2 g total fat (1 g sat. fat), 0 mg chol., 14 mg sodium, 20 g carbo., 2 g fiber, 1 g pro.

20
carbs per
serving

Exchanges:
1½ Fruit

BERRY CHEESECAKE DESSERT

¼ of an 8-ounce tub (¼ cup) fat-free cream cheese

¼ cup light ricotta cheese

1 tablespoon sugar

¼ teaspoon finely shredded orange peel

2 teaspoons orange juice

1½ cups fresh raspberries, blueberries, and/or sliced strawberries

2 gingersnaps or chocolate wafer cookies, broken

1 In a medium mixing bowl combine cream cheese, ricotta cheese, sugar, orange peel, and orange juice. Beat with an electric mixer on medium speed until smooth. Cover and chill for at least 4 hours or up to 24 hours.

2 To serve, spoon the fruit into dessert dishes. Top with the cream cheese mixture and sprinkle with the broken cookies.

Nutrition Facts per serving: 138 cal., 2 g total fat (1 g sat. fat), 12 mg chol., 74 mg sodium, 21 g carbo., 7 g fiber, 8 g pro.

PREP:
15 minutes
CHILL:
4 to 24 hours
MAKES:
2 servings

21
carbs per
serving

Exchanges:
½ Fruit
½ Medium-Fat Meat
1 Other Carbo.

ALMOND PANNA COTTA
WITH BLUEBERRY SAUCE

PREP:
20 minutes
CHILL:
8 hours
MAKES:
2 servings

1	teaspoon unflavored gelatin
2	tablespoons cold water
1	cup milk
4½	teaspoons sugar
1	or 2 drops almond extract
1	cup fresh or frozen blueberries
1	tablespoon sugar
2	teaspoons orange juice
¼	teaspoon cornstarch
¼	teaspoon vanilla

33

carbs per
serving

Exchanges:
½ Milk
1 Fruit
1 Other Carbo.
½ Fat

1 For panna cotta, in a small saucepan sprinkle gelatin over the cold water. Let stand for 3 minutes to soften. Cook and stir over medium heat until gelatin is dissolved. Stir in milk and the 4½ teaspoons sugar. Cook and stir just until milk is heated through and sugar is dissolved. Stir in almond extract. Pour into two 6-ounce custard cups or disposable plastic cups. Cover and chill for at least 8 hours or until firm.

2 For sauce, in another small saucepan combine blueberries, the 1 tablespoon sugar, the orange juice, and cornstarch. Cook and stir over medium heat until slightly thickened and bubbly. Cook and stir for 2 minutes more. Stir in vanilla. Transfer to a bowl. Cover and chill until ready to serve.

3 To serve, spoon the sauce into 2 dessert dishes. Run a small knife around the edge of each panna cotta; unmold onto sauce.

Nutrition Facts per serving: 183 cal., 3 g total fat (2 g sat. fat), 9 mg chol., 65 mg sodium, 33 g carbo., 2 g fiber, 5 g pro.

SLOW COOKER

SPINACH, CHICKEN & WILD RICE SOUP

PREP:
15 minutes
COOK:
7 to 8 hours (low) or 3½ to 4 hours (high)
MAKES:
6 servings

3　cups water

1　14-ounce can reduced-sodium chicken broth

1　10¾-ounce can reduced-fat and reduced-sodium condensed cream of chicken soup

⅔　cup wild rice, rinsed and drained

½　teaspoon dried thyme, crushed

¼　teaspoon black pepper

3　cups chopped cooked chicken or turkey (about 1 pound)

2　cups shredded fresh spinach

19
carbs per serving

❶ In a 3½- or 4-quart slow cooker combine the water, chicken broth, cream of chicken soup, uncooked wild rice, thyme, and pepper.

❷ Cover and cook on low-heat setting for 7 to 8 hours or on high-heat setting for 3½ to 4 hours. Just before serving, stir in chicken or turkey and spinach.

Nutrition Facts per serving: 233 cal., 6 g total fat (2 g sat. fat), 66 mg chol., 405 mg sodium, 19 g carbo., 2 g fiber, 25 g pro.

Exchanges:
½ Vegetable
1 Starch
3 Very Lean Meat
1 Fat

CHICKEN WITH SOURDOUGH STUFFING

6	cups cubed (1-inch cubes) crusty, rustic-style, open-textured sourdough bread
1⅓	cups chopped tomatoes
1	cup finely chopped carrots
½	cup reduced-sodium chicken broth
1½	teaspoons dried thyme, crushed
¼	teaspoon coarsely ground black pepper
6	small whole chicken leg quarters (drumstick and thigh), skinned
⅓	cup thinly sliced leek or chopped onion

1 For stuffing, in a large bowl combine bread cubes, tomatoes, and carrots. In a small bowl combine chicken broth, thyme, and pepper. Drizzle bread cube mixture with broth mixture, lightly tossing to mix. (Stuffing will not be completely moistened.)

2 Place chicken in a 4- to 5-quart slow cooker. Add leek or onion. Lightly pack stuffing on top of chicken and leek.

3 Cover and cook on low-heat setting for 6 to 6½ hours or on high-heat setting for 3 to 3½ hours.

Nutrition Facts per serving: 270 cal., 6 g total fat (1 g sat. fat), 104 mg chol., 379 mg sodium, 22 g carbo., 2 g fiber, 30 g pro.

PREP:
20 minutes
COOK:
6 to 6½ hours (low) or 3 to 3½ hours (high)
MAKES:
6 servings

22
carbs per serving

Exchanges:
½ Vegetable
1½ Starch
3½ Very Lean Meat
½ Fat

CHICKEN & BEAN BURRITOS

PREP:
5 minutes
COOK:
*5 to 6 hours
(low) or 2½ to
3 hours (high)*
MAKES:
12 servings

2	pounds skinless, boneless chicken breast halves
1	15-ounce can pinto beans in chili sauce
1	16-ounce bottle (1⅔ cups) salsa with chipotle chile peppers
12	8-inch whole wheat or plain flour tortillas, warmed*
1	cup shredded reduced-fat Monterey Jack cheese (4 ounces)
	Shredded lettuce (optional)
	Chopped tomatoes (optional)
	Light dairy sour cream (optional)

34

carbs per
serving

1 In a 3½-quart slow cooker combine chicken and undrained beans. Pour salsa over all.

2 Cover and cook on low-heat setting for 5 to 6 hours or on high-heat setting for 2½ to 3 hours.

3 Using a slotted spoon, transfer chicken to a cutting board. Using 2 forks, gently separate the chicken into thin shreds. Using a potato masher, mash beans slightly in cooker. Return chicken to slow cooker, stirring to mix.

4 Divide chicken mixture evenly among the warmed tortillas. Top with cheese. Fold bottom edge of each tortilla up and over filling; fold in opposite sides just until they meet. Roll up from the bottom. If necessary, secure with toothpicks. If desired, serve with lettuce, tomatoes, and/or sour cream.

Exchanges:
2 Starch
3 Very Lean Meat
½ Fat

***NOTE:** To warm tortillas, wrap them in white microwave-safe paper towels; microwave on 100% power (high) for 15 to 30 seconds or until tortillas are softened. (Or wrap tortillas in foil. Heat in a 350°F oven for 10 to 15 minutes or until warmed.)

Nutrition Facts per serving: 293 cal., 6 g total fat (2 g sat. fat), 50 mg chol., 707 mg sodium, 34 g carbo., 5 g fiber, 26 g pro.

GREEK CHICKEN WITH COUSCOUS

2	pounds skinless, boneless chicken breast halves
2	14½-ounce cans diced tomatoes with basil, oregano, and garlic, undrained
1½	cups water
2	6-ounce packages couscous with toasted pine nut mix
½	cup crumbled feta cheese (2 ounces)
½	cup pitted kalamata olives, coarsely chopped (optional)

1 Cut chicken into ½-inch pieces. Place chicken in a 3½- or 4-quart slow cooker. Add undrained tomatoes and the water.

2 Cover and cook on low-heat setting for 5 to 6 hours or on high-heat setting for 2½ to 3 hours. Stir in couscous. Cover and let stand for 5 minutes. Fluff couscous mixture with a fork.

3 Serve couscous mixture with feta cheese. If desired, pass olives.

Nutrition Facts per serving: 271 cal., 4 g total fat (2 g sat. fat), 59 mg chol., 861 mg sodium, 31 g carbo., 2 g fiber, 28 g pro.

PREP:
15 minutes
COOK:
5 to 6 hours (low) or 2½ to 3 hours (high)
STAND:
5 minutes
MAKES:
10 servings

31
carbs per serving

Exchanges:
½ Vegetable
2 Starch
3 Very Lean Meat

ROSEMARY CHICKEN & ARTICHOKES

PREP:
15 minutes
COOK:
*5 to 6 hours
(low) or 2½ to
3 hours (high)
plus 30 minutes
(high)*
MAKES:
6 servings

8

carbs per
serving

Exchanges:
1½ Vegetable
3 Very Lean Meat
½ Fat

1	medium onion, chopped
⅓	cup reduced-sodium chicken broth
1	tablespoon quick-cooking tapioca
6	cloves garlic, minced
2	to 3 teaspoons finely shredded lemon peel
2	teaspoons snipped fresh rosemary or 1 teaspoon dried rosemary, crushed
¾	teaspoon black pepper
2½	to 3 pounds chicken thighs, skinned
½	teaspoon salt
1	8- or 9-ounce package frozen artichoke hearts, thawed
1	medium red sweet pepper, cut into strips
3	cups hot cooked brown rice (optional)
	Snipped fresh parsley (optional)

1 In a 3½- or 4-quart slow cooker combine onion, chicken broth, tapioca, garlic, 1 teaspoon of the lemon peel, the rosemary, and ½ teaspoon of the black pepper. Add chicken. Sprinkle chicken with salt and the remaining ¼ teaspoon black pepper.

2 Cover and cook on low-heat setting for 5 to 6 hours or on high-heat setting for 2½ to 3 hours.

3 If using low-heat setting, turn to high-heat setting. Add thawed artichokes and sweet pepper strips. Cover and cook for 30 minutes more. To serve, sprinkle with remaining 1 to 2 teaspoons lemon peel. If desired, serve with hot cooked rice; sprinkle rice with parsley.

Nutrition Facts per serving: 168 cal., 4 g total fat (1 g sat. fat), 89 mg chol., 328 mg sodium, 8 g carbo., 3 g fiber, 23 g pro.

BARBECUE-STYLE CHICKEN

- 2 medium unpeeled potatoes, cut into ½-inch pieces
- 1 large green sweet pepper, cut into strips
- 1 medium onion, sliced
- 1 tablespoon quick-cooking tapioca
- 2 pounds chicken drumsticks or thighs, skinned
- 1 8-ounce can tomato sauce
- 2 tablespoons packed brown sugar
- 1 tablespoon Worcestershire sauce
- 1 tablespoon yellow mustard
- 1 clove garlic, minced
- ¼ teaspoon salt

1 In a 3½- or 4-quart slow cooker place potatoes, sweet pepper, and onion. Sprinkle tapioca over vegetables. Place chicken on top of the vegetables. For sauce, in a small bowl stir together tomato sauce, brown sugar, Worcestershire sauce, mustard, garlic, and salt. Pour sauce over chicken.

2 Cover and cook on low-heat setting for 10 to 12 hours or on high-heat setting for 5 to 6 hours.

3 Transfer chicken and vegetables to a large serving bowl. Skim fat from sauce. Spoon sauce over chicken and vegetables.

Nutrition Facts per serving: 267 cal., 4 g total fat (1 g sat. fat), 98 mg chol., 594 mg sodium, 27 g carbo., 2 g fiber, 29 g pro.

PREP:
25 minutes
COOK:
10 to 12 hours (low) or 5 to 6 hours (high)
MAKES:
4 or 5 servings

27
carbs per serving

Exchanges:
1 Vegetable
1 Starch
3½ Very Lean Meat
½ Other Carbo.

SESAME-GINGER TURKEY WRAPS

PREP:
20 minutes
COOK:
6 to 7 hours (low) or 3 to 3½ hours (high)
STAND:
5 minutes
MAKES:
12 servings

20
carbs per serving

Exchanges:
1 Vegetable
1 Starch
2 Lean Meat

Nonstick cooking spray
3 turkey thighs, skinned (3½ to 4 pounds total)
1 cup bottled sesame-ginger stir-fry sauce
¼ cup water
1 16-ounce package shredded broccoli (broccoli slaw mix)
12 8-inch flour tortillas, warmed*
¾ cup sliced green onions

1 Lightly coat a 3½- or 4-quart slow cooker with nonstick cooking spray. Place turkey thighs in slow cooker. In a small bowl stir together stir-fry sauce and the water. Pour over turkey.

2 Cover and cook on low-heat setting for 6 to 7 hours or on high-heat setting for 3 to 3½ hours.

3 Remove turkey from slow cooker; cool slightly. Remove turkey from bones; discard bones. Using 2 forks, separate turkey into shreds. Place broccoli in sauce mixture in slow cooker. Stir to coat; cover and let stand for 5 minutes. Using a slotted spoon, remove broccoli from slow cooker.

4 To assemble, place some of the turkey on each tortilla. Top with broccoli and green onions. Spoon sauce from slow cooker on top of green onions. Roll up and serve immediately.

*NOTE: To warm tortillas, wrap them in white microwave-safe paper towels; microwave on 100% power (high) for 15 to 30 seconds or until tortillas are softened. (Or wrap tortillas in foil. Heat in a 350°F oven for 10 to 15 minutes or until warmed.)

Nutrition Facts per serving: 207 cal., 5 g total fat (1 g sat. fat), 67 mg chol., 422 mg sodium, 20 g carbo., 2 g fiber, 20 g pro.

SAUSAGE & TORTELLINI SOUP

2   14½-ounce cans Italian-style stewed tomatoes, undrained

3   cups water

2   cups loose-pack frozen cut green beans or Italian-style green beans

1   10½-ounce can condensed French onion soup

8   ounces smoked turkey sausage, halved lengthwise and
     cut into ½-inch-thick slices

2   cups packaged shredded cabbage with carrot (coleslaw mix)

1   9-ounce package refrigerated cheese-filled tortellini
     Shaved or shredded Parmesan cheese

1 In a 4- to 5-quart slow cooker combine undrained tomatoes, the water, frozen green beans, French onion soup, and turkey sausage.

2 Cover and cook on low-heat setting for 8 to 10 hours or on high-heat setting for 4 to 5 hours.

3 If using low-heat setting, turn to high-heat setting. Stir cabbage and tortellini into soup. Cover and cook for 15 minutes more. Serve with Parmesan cheese.

Nutrition Facts per serving: 176 cal., 5 g total fat (1 g sat. fat), 28 mg chol., 717 mg sodium, 23 g carbo., 2 g fiber, 9 g pro.

PREP:
10 minutes
COOK:
*8 to 10 hours
(low) or 4 to
5 hours (high)
plus 15 minutes
(high)*
MAKES:
*10 to
12 servings*

23 carbs per serving

Exchanges:
1 Vegetable
1 Starch
½ Very Lean Meat
1 Fat

BRISKET IN ALE

PREP:
25 minutes
COOK:
*10 to 12 hours
(low) or 5 to
6 hours (high)*
MAKES:
10 servings

8

carbs per
serving

Exchanges:
4 Very Lean Meat
½ Other Carbo.
1 Fat

1	3- to 4-pound fresh beef brisket
2	medium onions, thinly sliced and separated into rings
1	bay leaf
1	12-ounce can beer
¼	cup chili sauce
2	tablespoons packed brown sugar
1	clove garlic, minced
½	teaspoon dried thyme, crushed
¼	teaspoon salt
¼	teaspoon black pepper
2	tablespoons cornstarch
2	tablespoons cold water

1 Trim fat from brisket. If necessary, cut brisket to fit into a 3½- to 6-quart slow cooker. In slow cooker place onions, bay leaf, and brisket. In a medium bowl combine beer, chili sauce, brown sugar, garlic, thyme, salt, and pepper; pour over brisket. Cover; cook on low-heat setting for 10 to 12 hours or on high-heat setting for 5 to 6 hours.

2 Using a slotted spoon, transfer brisket and onions to a serving platter; keep warm. Discard bay leaf.

3 For gravy, skim fat from cooking liquid. Measure 2½ cups of the cooking liquid; discard remaining liquid. In a medium saucepan stir together cornstarch and the cold water; stir in the cooking liquid. Cook and stir until thickened and bubbly; cook and stir for 2 minutes more. Pass gravy with meat.

Nutrition Facts per serving: 227 cal., 7 g total fat (2 g sat. fat), 78 mg chol., 242 mg sodium, 8 g carbo., 1 g fiber, 30 g pro.

BEEF ROAST WITH TOMATO-WINE GRAVY

1   2- to 2½-pound boneless beef chuck pot roast
      Nonstick cooking spray

2   medium turnips, peeled and cut into 1-inch pieces (2 cups)

3   medium carrots, cut into ½-inch pieces (1½ cups)

1   15-ounce can tomato sauce

¼   cup dry red wine or reduced-sodium beef broth

3   tablespoons quick-cooking tapioca

¼   teaspoon salt

⅛   teaspoon ground allspice

⅛   teaspoon black pepper

1   pound winter squash, peeled, seeded, and cut into thin wedges
      or 1½- to 2-inch pieces (2 cups)

1 Trim fat from roast. If necessary, cut roast to fit into a 3½- to 6-quart slow cooker. Coat an unheated large nonstick skillet with nonstick cooking spray. Preheat skillet over medium heat. Brown roast on all sides in hot skillet.

2 Meanwhile, in the slow cooker stir together turnips, carrots, tomato sauce, red wine or beef broth, tapioca, salt, allspice, and pepper. Place roast on top of vegetables. Place squash on roast. Cover and cook on low-heat setting for 10 to 12 hours or high-heat setting for 5 to 6 hours.

3 Transfer roast and vegetables to a warm serving platter. Skim fat from tomato sauce mixture in slow cooker. Pass tomato sauce mixture with roast.

Nutrition Facts per serving: 270 cal., 6 g total fat (2 g sat. fat), 89 mg chol., 576 mg sodium, 18 g carbo., 3 g fiber, 34 g pro.

PREP:
30 minutes
COOK:
*10 to 12 hours
(low) or 5 to
6 hours (high)*
MAKES:
6 servings

18
carbs per
serving

Exchanges:
1 Vegetable
1 Starch
4 Very Lean Meat
½ Fat

SOUTHWESTERN SHREDDED BEEF SANDWICHES

PREP:
25 minutes
COOK:
*10 to 12 hours
(low) or 5 to
6 hours (high)*
MAKES:
16 servings

34
carbs per
serving

Exchanges:
2 Starch
3 Lean Meat

1	3- to 3½-pound boneless beef chuck pot roast
1	tablespoon ground cumin
1	tablespoon chili powder
¼	teaspoon salt
⅛	teaspoon black pepper
1	cup coarsely chopped onion
1	14½-ounce can stewed tomatoes, undrained
1	7-ounce can chopped green chile peppers or two 4-ounce cans chopped green chile peppers
2	tablespoons chopped pickled jalapeño chile peppers* (optional)
¼	cup snipped fresh cilantro
2	cups shredded reduced-fat cheddar or Monterey Jack cheese (8 ounces)
16	onion or kaiser rolls, split and toasted
	Lettuce leaves (optional)

1 Trim fat from roast. In a small bowl combine cumin, chili powder, salt, and black pepper. Sprinkle evenly over roast; rub in with your fingers. If necessary, cut roast to fit into a 4- or 4½-quart slow cooker. Place roast in slow cooker. Add onion, undrained tomatoes, green chile peppers, and, if desired, jalapeño chile peppers.

2 Cover and cook on low-heat setting for 10 to 12 hours or on high-heat setting for 5 to 6 hours. Transfer roast to a cutting board, reserving juices in slow cooker. Using 2 forks, gently separate the meat into thin shreds. Return meat to slow cooker; heat through. Stir in cilantro.

3 To serve, sprinkle cheese over bottoms of onion or kaiser rolls. Using a slotted spoon, place about ½ cup of the meat mixture on top of cheese on each bun. If desired, add a lettuce leaf to each. Replace roll tops.

*NOTE: Because chile peppers contain volatile oils that can burn your skin and eyes, avoid direct contact with them as much as possible. When working with chile peppers, wear plastic or rubber gloves. If your bare hands do touch the peppers, wash your hands and nails well with soap and warm water.

Nutrition Facts per serving: 338 cal., 9 g total fat (3 g sat. fat), 60 mg chol., 591 mg sodium, 34 g carbo., 2 g fiber, 28 g pro.

**MEDITERRANEAN BEEF SALAD
WITH LEMON VINAIGRETTE**
Recipe on page 251

SAUTEED PORK & PEAR SALAD
Recipe on page 252

EGG·VEGETABLE SALAD WRAPS
Recipe on page 269

SHORTCUT CHICKEN MOLE
Recipe on page 276

SALMON WITH COUSCOUS
Recipe on page 288

BARBECIE-STYLE CHICKEN
Recipe on page 299

**SOUTHWESTERN
SHREDDED BEEF SANDWICHES**
Recipe on page 304

HUNGARIAN GOULASH
Recipe on page 321

SAUCY CHICKEN PARMESAN
Recipe on page 343

FAST FAJITA ROLL-UPS
Recipe on page 347

**FRUIT CUPS
WITH STRAWBERRY DRESSING**
Recipe on page 355

VEGETABLE KABOBS
Recipe on page 366

OVEN·ROASTED VEGETABLES
Recipe on page 368

DREAM CREAM PUFFS
Recipe on page 380

LEMON·ROSEMARY CAKE
Recipe on page 386

MOCHA MERINGUE STARS
Recipe on page 399

HUNGARIAN GOULASH

3	cups chopped onions
1½	cups coarsely chopped green sweet peppers
3	cloves garlic, minced
3	pounds beef stew meat, cut into 1-inch cubes
1	6-ounce can tomato paste
½	cup water
4	teaspoons Hungarian paprika or regular paprika
¼	teaspoon salt
¼	teaspoon black pepper
6	cups hot cooked noodles

PREP:
20 minutes
COOK:
10 to 12 hours (low) or 5 to 6 hours (high)
MAKES:
10 servings

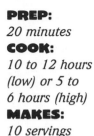

1 In a 3½- or 4-quart slow cooker combine onions, sweet peppers, and garlic. Top with meat. In a small bowl combine tomato paste, the water, paprika, salt, and black pepper. Pour over meat.

2 Cover and cook on low-heat setting for 10 to 12 hours or on high-heat setting for 5 to 6 hours.

3 Serve over hot cooked noodles.

Nutrition Facts per serving: 340 cal., 7 g total fat (2 g sat. fat), 112 mg chol., 170 mg sodium, 34 g carbo., 3 g fiber, 35 g pro.

34
carbs per serving

Exchanges:
½ Vegetable
2 Starch
4 Very Lean Meat
½ Fat

COWBOY BEEF

PREP:
10 minutes
COOK:
10 to 12 hours (low) or 5 to 6 hours (high)
MAKES:
6 servings

1   2- to 2½-pound boneless beef chuck pot roast
1   15-ounce can chili beans with chili gravy
1   11-ounce can whole kernel corn with sweet peppers, drained
1   10-ounce can chopped tomatoes and green chile peppers, undrained
1   to 2 teaspoons finely chopped canned chipotle chile peppers in adobo sauce*

23

carbs per serving

❶ Trim fat from roast. If necessary, cut roast to fit into a 3½- or 4-quart slow cooker. Place meat in the slow cooker. In a medium bowl combine undrained beans, drained corn, undrained tomatoes, and chipotle peppers. Pour bean mixture over roast in slow cooker.

❷ Cover and cook on low-heat setting for 10 to 12 hours or on high-heat setting for 5 to 6 hours.

❸ Transfer roast to a cutting board. Slice roast and arrange in a shallow serving bowl. Using a slotted spoon, spoon bean mixture over meat. Drizzle some of the cooking liquid over all.

*NOTE: Because chile peppers contain volatile oils that can burn your skin and eyes, avoid direct contact with them as much as possible. When working with chile peppers, wear plastic or rubber gloves. If your bare hands do touch the peppers, wash your hands and nails well with soap and warm water.

Nutrition Facts per serving: 307 cal., 7 g total fat (2 g sat. fat), 89 mg chol., 655 mg sodium, 23 g carbo., 5 g fiber, 37 g pro.

Exchanges:
1 Vegetable
1 Starch
4½ Very Lean Meat
1 Fat

MUSHROOM-SAUCED POT ROAST

1   1½-pound boneless beef chuck eye roast, eye of round roast, or round rump roast

4   medium unpeeled potatoes, quartered (about 1½ pounds)

1   16-ounce package frozen tiny whole carrots

1   4-ounce can mushroom stems and pieces, drained

½   teaspoon dried tarragon or basil, crushed

⅛   teaspoon salt

1   10¾-ounce can condensed golden mushroom soup

PREP:
20 minutes
COOK:
10 to 12 hours (low) or 5 to 6 hours (high)
MAKES:
6 servings

1 Trim fat from roast. If necessary, cut roast to fit into a 3½- to 4½-quart slow cooker. In the slow cooker combine potatoes, frozen carrots, mushrooms, tarragon, and salt. Place roast on top of vegetables. Pour soup over roast.

2 Cover and cook on low-heat setting for 10 to 12 hours or on high-heat setting for 5 to 6 hours.

Nutrition Facts per serving: 288 cal., 6 g total fat (2 g sat. fat), 68 mg chol., 640 mg sodium, 30 g carbo., 5 g fiber, 28 g pro.

30
carbs per serving

Exchanges:
1 Vegetable
1½ Starch
3 Very Lean Meat
1 Fat

BEEF & BEAN RAGOUT

PREP:
10 minutes
COOK:
*8 to 10 hours
(low) or 4 to
5 hours (high)*
MAKES:
6 servings

1   pound beef stew meat, cut into 1-inch cubes

1   16-ounce can kidney beans, rinsed and drained

1   15-ounce can tomato sauce with onion and garlic

1   14½-ounce can Italian-style stewed tomatoes, undrained

½   of a 28-ounce package frozen loose-pack diced hash brown
    potatoes with onion and peppers (about 4 cups)

1 In a 3½- or 4-quart slow cooker combine stew meat, kidney beans, tomato sauce, undrained tomatoes, and frozen hash brown potatoes.

2 Cover and cook on low-heat setting for 8 to 10 hours or on high heat setting for 4 to 5 hours.

Nutrition Facts per serving: 247 cal., 4 g total fat (1 g sat. fat), 45 mg chol., 634 mg sodium, 31 g carbo., 6 g fiber, 23 g pro.

31
carbs per
serving

Exchanges:
1 Vegetable
1½ Starch
2½ Very Lean Meat
½ Fat

BEEF STEW WITH RAVIOLI

3	medium carrots, cut into ½-inch-thick slices
1	medium onion, chopped
1½	cups fresh mushrooms, halved
2	cloves garlic, minced
2	tablespoons snipped fresh basil or 1 teaspoon dried basil, crushed
1	tablespoon snipped fresh oregano or ½ teaspoon dried oregano, crushed
3	tablespoons quick-cooking tapioca
1	pound beef stew meat, cut into 1-inch cubes
2	cups water
1	14½-ounce can diced tomatoes, undrained
1	8-ounce can tomato sauce
½	cup dry red wine or water
1½	teaspoons instant beef bouillon granules
1	9-ounce package refrigerated light cheese-filled ravioli

PREP:
25 minutes
COOK:
7 to 9 hours (low) or 3½ to 4½ hours (high) plus 20 minutes (high)
MAKES:
8 servings

27

carbs per serving

1 In a 3½- or 4-quart slow cooker place carrots, onion, mushrooms, garlic, and, if using, dried basil and dried oregano. Sprinkle tapioca over vegetables. Add meat. Stir in the 2 cups water, the undrained tomatoes, tomato sauce, wine or additional water, and bouillon granules.

2 Cover and cook on low-heat setting for 7 to 9 hours or on high-heat setting for 3½ to 4½ hours.

3 If using low-heat setting, turn to high-heat setting. Stir in ravioli. Cover and cook for 20 minutes more. If using, stir in fresh basil and oregano.

Nutrition Facts per serving: 243 cal., 5 g total fat (2 g sat. fat), 47 mg chol., 578 mg sodium, 27 g carbo., 1 g fiber, 20 g pro.

Exchanges:
1 Vegetable
1½ Starch
2 Lean Meat

CINCINNATI-STYLE CHILI CASSEROLE

PREP:
25 minutes
COOK:
*8 to 10 hours
(low) or 4 to
5 hours (high)*
MAKES:
16 servings

33
carbs per
serving

Exchanges:
½ Vegetable
2 Starch
1½ Lean Meat

2	pounds lean ground beef
2	cups chopped onions
1	26-ounce jar garlic pasta sauce
1	15-ounce can red kidney beans, rinsed and drained
½	cup water
2	tablespoons chili powder
2	tablespoons semisweet chocolate pieces
1	tablespoon vinegar
1	teaspoon ground cinnamon
1	teaspoon instant beef bouillon granules
¼	teaspoon cayenne pepper
¼	teaspoon ground allspice
1	pound dried cut ziti or gemelli
	Shredded cheddar cheese (optional)

1 In a 12-inch skillet cook ground beef and onions until meat is brown. Drain off fat. Transfer meat mixture to a 4- to 5-quart slow cooker. Stir in pasta sauce, kidney beans, the water, chili powder, chocolate pieces, vinegar, cinnamon, bouillon granules, cayenne pepper, and allspice.

2 Cover and cook on low-heat setting for 8 to 10 hours or on high-heat setting for 4 to 5 hours.

3 Before serving, cook pasta according to package directions; drain well. Add pasta to meat mixture in slow cooker; toss gently to combine. If desired, sprinkle with cheese.

Nutrition Facts per serving: 257 cal., 7 g total fat (2 g sat. fat), 36 mg chol., 277 mg sodium, 33 g carbo., 4 g fiber, 17 g pro.

PORK ROAST & HARVEST VEGETABLES

1	1½- to 2-pound boneless pork shoulder roast
	Nonstick cooking spray
2	cups parsnips cut into ½-inch pieces
1½	cups carrots cut into ½-inch pieces
1	large green sweet pepper, cut into wedges
1	cup celery cut into ½-inch pieces
3	tablespoons quick-cooking tapioca
1	6-ounce can frozen apple juice concentrate, thawed
¼	cup water
1	teaspoon instant beef bouillon granules
¼	teaspoon ground cinnamon
¼	teaspoon black pepper

1 Trim fat from roast. If necessary, cut roast to fit into a 3½- to 5-quart slow cooker. Coat an unheated large nonstick skillet with nonstick cooking spray. Preheat over medium heat. Brown roast on all sides in hot skillet. In the slow cooker combine parsnips, carrots, sweet pepper, and celery. Sprinkle with tapioca.

2 In a small bowl combine apple juice concentrate, the water, bouillon granules, cinnamon, and black pepper. Pour over vegetables. Place roast on top of vegetables.

3 Cover and cook on low-heat setting for 10 to 12 hours or on high-heat setting for 5 to 6 hours. Transfer meat and vegetables to a serving platter. Strain cooking juices; skim off fat. Drizzle some of the cooking juices over meat; pass remaining juices.

Nutrition Facts per serving: 278 cal., 7 g total fat (2 g sat. fat), 73 mg chol., 269 mg sodium, 29 g carbo., 4 g fiber, 24 g pro.

PREP:
30 minutes
COOK:
10 to 12 hours (low) or 5 to 6 hours (high)
MAKES:
6 servings

29 carbs per serving

Exchanges:
1 Vegetable
1 Fruit
3 Very Lean Meat
½ Other Carbo.

ASIAN PORK WRAPS

PREP:
15 minutes
COOK:
*8 to 10 hours
(low) or 4 to
5 hours (high)*
MAKES:
12 servings

1	3-pound boneless pork shoulder roast
1	teaspoon ground ginger
½	teaspoon garlic powder
1	16-ounce package frozen stir-fry vegetables
1	8½-ounce jar plum sauce or hoisin sauce
½	cup reduced-sodium chicken broth
12	8-inch whole wheat flour tortillas, warmed*
2	cups shredded or coarsely chopped napa cabbage

37

carbs per
serving

Exchanges:
½ Vegetable
2 Starch
3 Lean Meat

❶ Remove string from roast, if present. Trim fat from roast. Sprinkle ginger and garlic powder evenly over roast; rub in with your fingers. If necessary, cut roast to fit into a 3½- or 4-quart slow cooker.

❷ Place roast in the slow cooker. Add frozen vegetables and half of the plum sauce or hoisin sauce. Pour chicken broth over vegetables.

❸ Cover and cook on low-heat setting for 8 to 10 hours or on high-heat setting for 4 to 5 hours.

❹ Transfer roast to a cutting board. Using 2 forks, gently separate the meat into thin shreds. Place shredded meat in a large bowl. Using a slotted spoon, transfer vegetables to the same bowl; discard cooking juices. Stir the remaining plum sauce or hoisin sauce into pork and vegetables. Arrange some of the meat mixture along the center of each tortilla. Top with shredded cabbage. Fold bottom edges of tortillas up and over the meat mixture. Fold opposite sides in until they meet. Roll up from bottom. If necessary, secure with toothpicks.

*NOTE: To warm tortillas, wrap them in white microwave-safe paper towels; microwave on 100% power (high) for 15 to 30 seconds or until tortillas are softened. (Or wrap tortillas in foil. Heat in a 350°F oven for 10 to 15 minutes or until warmed.)

Nutrition Facts per serving: 345 cal., 9 g total fat (3 g sat. fat), 73 mg chol., 608 mg sodium, 37 g carbo., 3 g fiber, 28 g pro.

MEDITERRANEAN LAMB PITAS

1   2-pound portion boneless lamb leg roast
    Nonstick cooking spray
1   15-ounce can garbanzo beans (chickpeas), rinsed and drained
¾   cup dry red wine
½   of a 6-ounce can (⅓ cup) tomato paste
¼   cup water
1   cup chopped onion
4   cloves garlic, minced
½   teaspoon ground allspice
½   teaspoon dried mint, crushed
¼   teaspoon salt
¼   teaspoon black pepper
6   large whole wheat or white pita bread rounds, halved crosswise
    Lettuce leaves and/or thinly sliced cucumber
1   6-ounce carton plain low-fat yogurt
¼   teaspoon ground cumin
1   medium tomato, chopped

PREP:
25 minutes
COOK:
8 to 10 hours (low) or 4 to 5 hours (high) plus 15 minutes
MAKES:
12 servings

28
carbs per serving

Exchanges:
1½ Starch
2 Very Lean Meat
½ Other Carbo.
½ Fat

1 Trim fat from roast. If necessary, cut roast to fit into a 3½- or 4-quart slow cooker. Coat an unheated large nonstick skillet with nonstick cooking spray. Preheat over medium heat. Brown roast on all sides in hot skillet. Drain off fat.

2 Meanwhile, in the slow cooker combine drained garbanzo beans, wine, tomato paste, the water, onion, garlic, allspice, mint, salt, and pepper. Place roast over bean mixture.

3 Cover and cook on low-heat setting for 8 to 10 hours or on high-heat setting for 4 to 5 hours. Using a slotted spoon, transfer roast to a cutting board. Using 2 forks, gently separate the meat into thin shreds. Return meat to cooker. Cover and cook for 15 minutes more. Using a slotted spoon, remove meat and beans.

4 To serve, open each pita bread half to form a large pocket. Line pitas with lettuce and/or cucumber. In a small bowl combine yogurt and cumin. Spoon meat mixture into pitas. Top meat mixture with yogurt mixture. Sprinkle with tomato.

Nutrition Facts per serving: 243 cal., 4 g total fat (1 g sat. fat), 48 mg chol., 395 mg sodium, 28 g carbo., 4 g fiber, 22 g pro.

RED BEANS OVER SPANISH RICE

PREP:
25 minutes
STAND:
1 hour
COOK:
10 to 11 hours (low) or 5 to 5½ hours (high)
MAKES:
8 servings

52
carbs per serving

Exchanges:
3 Starch
1 Very Lean Meat

2   cups dry red beans or dry red kidney beans
5   cups water
    Nonstick cooking spray
4   cups water
2½ cups chopped onions
6   cloves garlic, minced
1   tablespoon ground cumin
1   6¾-ounce package Spanish rice mix
    Lime wedges (optional)

1 Rinse beans. In a large saucepan combine the 5 cups water and beans. Bring to boiling; reduce heat. Simmer, uncovered, for 2 minutes. Remove from heat. Cover and let stand for 1 hour. (Or in a saucepan combine the 5 cups water and dry beans. Cover and let soak in a cool place for 6 to 8 hours or overnight.) Drain and rinse beans.

2 Lightly coat a 3½- or 4-quart slow cooker with nonstick cooking spray. In the slow cooker combine drained beans, the 4 cups water, onions, garlic, and cumin.

3 Cover and cook on low-heat setting for 10 to 11 hours or on high-heat setting for 5 to 5½ hours.

4 Prepare rice mix according to package directions. Using a slotted spoon, remove beans from slow cooker. Serve beans over cooked rice. If desired, spoon some of the cooking liquid from the slow cooker over beans; squeeze lime wedges over beans and rice.

Nutrition Facts per serving: 260 cal., 1 g total fat (0 g sat. fat), 0 mg chol., 343 mg sodium, 52 g carbo., 13 g fiber, 14 g pro.

CAJUN-SEASONED VEGETARIAN GUMBO

2   15-ounce cans black beans, rinsed and drained

1   28-ounce can diced tomatoes, undrained

1   16-ounce package frozen loose-pack pepper stir-fry vegetables
(yellow, green, and red sweet peppers and onions)

2   cups frozen cut okra

2   to 3 teaspoons Cajun seasoning

3   cups hot cooked brown rice (optional)

1 In a 3½- to 4½-quart slow cooker combine drained beans, undrained tomatoes, frozen stir-fry vegetables, okra, and Cajun seasoning.

2 Cover and cook on low-heat setting for 6 to 8 hours or on high-heat setting for 3 to 4 hours. If desired, serve over hot cooked brown rice.

Nutrition Facts per serving: 153 cal., 0 g total fat (0 g sat. fat), 0 mg chol., 639 mg sodium, 31 g carbo., 10 g fiber, 12 g pro.

PREP:
10 minutes
COOK:
*6 to 8 hours
(low) or 3 to
4 hours (high)*
MAKES:
6 servings

31
carbs per
serving

Exchanges:
2 Vegetable
1 Starch
1 Very Lean Meat

BARLEY-VEGETABLE SOUP

PREP:
20 minutes
COOK:
*8 to 9 hours
(low) or 4 to
4½ hours (high)*
MAKES:
*8 side-dish
servings*

20

carbs per
serving

Exchanges:
2 Vegetable
½ Starch

4	cups low-sodium tomato juice
2	14-ounce cans reduced-sodium chicken broth
2½	cups chopped zucchini
1½	cups coarsely chopped yellow and/or red sweet peppers
1	cup chopped onion
½	cup regular barley
¼	teaspoon salt
¼	teaspoon black pepper
3	cloves garlic, minced

1 In a 3½- to 5-quart slow cooker combine tomato juice, chicken broth, zucchini, sweet peppers, onion, barley, salt, black pepper, and garlic.

2 Cover and cook on low-heat setting for 8 to 9 hours or on high-heat setting for 4 to 4½ hours.

Nutrition Facts per serving: 100 cal., 0 g total fat (0 g sat. fat), 0 mg chol., 385 mg sodium, 20 g carbo., 4 g fiber, 4 g pro.

VEGETABLE & GARBANZO CURRY

3	cups cauliflower florets
1	cup loose-pack frozen cut green beans
1	cup sliced carrots
½	cup chopped onion
1	15-ounce can garbanzo beans (chickpeas), rinsed and drained
1	14-ounce can vegetable broth
2	to 3 teaspoons curry powder
1	14-ounce can light coconut milk
¼	cup shredded fresh basil leaves

1 In a 3½- or 4-quart slow cooker combine cauliflower, green beans, carrots, onion, and drained garbanzo beans. Stir in vegetable broth and curry powder.

2 Cover and cook on low-heat setting for 5 to 6 hours or on high-heat setting for 2½ to 3 hours. Stir in coconut milk and basil.

Nutrition Facts per serving: 219 cal., 7 g total fat (4 g sat. fat), 0 mg chol., 805 mg sodium, 32 g carbo., 9 g fiber, 8 g pro.

PREP:
15 minutes
COOK:
5 to 6 hours (low) or 2½ to 3 hours (high)
MAKES:
4 to 6 side-dish servings

32
carbs per serving

Exchanges:
1½ Vegetable
1 Starch
½ Very Lean Meat
½ Other Carbo.
1 Fat

EGGPLANT SAUCE WITH WHOLE WHEAT PASTA

PREP:
15 minutes
COOK:
3 to 4 hours (low)
MAKES:
10 side-dish servings

36
carbs per serving

Exchanges:
1 Vegetable
1½ Starch
½ Other Carbo.

Nonstick cooking spray

1 medium eggplant, cut into 1-inch pieces (5½ cups)

1 large onion, cut into thin wedges

1 2¼-ounce can sliced pitted ripe olives, drained

1 28-ounce jar roasted garlic pasta sauce

12 ounces dried whole wheat penne or rotini pasta

Shredded Parmesan cheese (optional)

1 Coat a 3½- or 4-quart slow cooker with nonstick cooking spray. In the slow cooker combine eggplant, onion, and olives. Stir in pasta sauce.

2 Cover and cook on low-heat setting for 3 to 4 hours. Cook pasta according to package directions; drain. Serve sauce over hot cooked pasta. If desired, sprinkle with Parmesan cheese.

Nutrition Facts per serving: 182 cal., 2 g total fat (0 g sat. fat), 0 mg chol., 308 mg sodium, 36 g carbo., 6 g fiber, 7 g pro.

KIDS' FAVORITES

14

TRIPLE-GRAIN FLAPJACKS

START TO FINISH:
30 minutes
MAKES:
8 to 10 servings (2 pancakes per serving)

38
carbs per serving

Exchanges:
1½ Starch
1 Other Carbo.
1 Fat

1½ cups all-purpose flour

½ cup yellow cornmeal

2½ teaspoons baking powder

½ teaspoon salt

½ cup regular rolled oats

3 tablespoons packed brown sugar

1 egg or ¼ cup refrigerated or frozen egg product, thawed

1¾ cups fat-free milk

¼ cup plain low-fat yogurt

3 tablespoons cooking oil

½ cup dried blueberries or currants (optional)

Nonstick cooking spray

Pure maple syrup or reduced-calorie maple-flavored syrup (optional)

1 In a large bowl stir together flour, cornmeal, baking powder, and salt. In a blender or food processor combine oats and brown sugar. Cover and blend or process until oats are coarsely ground. Stir oat mixture into flour mixture. Make a well in the center of flour mixture.

2 In a medium bowl combine egg, milk, yogurt, and oil; beat with a fork until combined. Add the egg mixture all at once to flour mixture. Stir just until moistened (batter should be lumpy and thin). Let stand for 10 minutes to thicken slightly, stirring once or twice. If desired, gently fold in blueberries.

3 Lightly coat an unheated nonstick griddle or heavy skillet with nonstick cooking spray. Preheat over medium heat. For each pancake, pour about ¼ cup batter onto the hot griddle or skillet. Cook over medium heat for 1½ to 2 minutes or until pancakes have bubbly surfaces and edges are slightly dry. Turn pancakes; cook for 1½ to 2 minutes more or until golden brown. If desired, serve with maple syrup.

Nutrition Facts per serving: 248 cal., 7 g total fat (1 g sat. fat), 28 mg chol., 263 mg sodium, 38 g carbo., 2 g fiber, 8 g pro.

CHUNKY APPLE-PUMPKIN MUFFINS

Nonstick cooking spray

1	cup all-purpose flour
⅔	cup whole wheat flour
1½	teaspoons baking powder
1	teaspoon pumpkin pie spice
½	teaspoon salt
¾	cup canned pumpkin
½	cup applesauce
2	slightly beaten eggs or ½ cup refrigerated or frozen egg product, thawed
⅓	cup packed brown sugar
¼	cup fat-free milk
2	tablespoons cooking oil
½	cup finely chopped cooking apple

1 Lightly coat twelve 2½-inch muffin cups with nonstick cooking spray; set aside. In a large bowl combine all-purpose flour, whole wheat flour, baking powder, pumpkin pie spice, and salt. Make a well in the center of flour mixture.

2 In a medium bowl combine pumpkin, applesauce, eggs, brown sugar, milk, and oil. Add egg mixture all at once to flour mixture. Stir just until moistened (batter should be lumpy). Gently fold in apple.

3 Spoon batter into the prepared muffin cups, filling each about three-fourths full. Bake in a 375° oven for 20 to 25 minutes or until golden brown. Cool in pan on a wire rack for 5 minutes. Remove from muffin cups. Serve warm.

Nutrition Facts per muffin: 131 cal., 3 g total fat (1 g sat. fat), 35 mg chol., 145 mg sodium, 23 g carbo., 2 g fiber, 3 g pro.

PREP:
20 minutes
BAKE:
20 minutes
COOL:
5 minutes
OVEN:
375°F
MAKES:
12 muffins

23
carbs per muffin

Exchanges:
1 Starch
½ Other Carbo.
½ Fat

BREAKFAST PIZZA

PREP:
25 minutes
BAKE:
10 minutes
OVEN:
375°F
MAKES:
8 servings

28
carbs per
serving

Exchanges:
2 Starch
1½ Medium-Fat Meat

Nonstick cooking spray

1½ cups loose-pack frozen diced hash brown potatoes with onion and peppers

1 clove garlic, minced

6 slightly beaten eggs or 1½ cups refrigerated or frozen egg product, thawed

⅓ cup fat-free milk

1 tablespoon snipped fresh basil or 1 teaspoon dried basil, crushed

½ teaspoon salt

¼ teaspoon black pepper

1 tablespoon olive oil

1 14-ounce Italian bread shell (Boboli)

1 cup shredded mozzarella cheese (4 ounces)

2 plum tomatoes, halved lengthwise and sliced

¼ cup shredded fresh basil (optional)

1 Coat an unheated large nonstick skillet with nonstick cooking spray. Preheat over medium heat. Add potatoes and garlic. Cook and stir about 4 minutes or until the vegetables are tender.

2 In a small bowl stir together eggs, milk, the snipped or dried basil, the salt, and black pepper. Add oil to skillet; add egg mixture. Cook, without stirring, until mixture begins to set on the bottom and around the edge. Using a large spatula, lift and fold partially cooked egg mixture so that the uncooked portion flows underneath. Continue cooking and folding until egg mixture is cooked through but is still glossy and moist. Remove from heat.

3 To assemble pizza, place the bread shell on a large baking sheet or a 12-inch pizza pan. Sprinkle half of the cheese over the bread shell. Top with egg mixture, tomatoes, and the remaining cheese.

4 Bake in a 375° oven about 10 minutes or until cheese is melted. If desired, sprinkle with the shredded basil. Cut into wedges to serve.

Nutrition Facts per serving: 265 cal., 11 g total fat (3 g sat. fat), 170 mg chol., 565 mg sodium, 28 g carbo., 2 g fiber, 15 g pro.

VEGGIE-FILLED BAKED OMELETS

Nonstick cooking spray

3 cups chopped broccoli, chopped red or green sweet pepper, sliced fresh mushrooms, thinly sliced zucchini, and/or chopped tomato

⅓ cup chopped onion

2 teaspoons snipped fresh basil or ½ teaspoon dried basil, crushed

½ teaspoon salt

⅛ teaspoon black pepper

3 tablespoons canned tomato sauce

10 egg whites

5 eggs

¼ cup water

¼ cup shredded mozzarella cheese (1 ounce)

2 tablespoons Parmesan cheese

Canned tomato sauce, warmed (optional)

PREP:
30 minutes
BAKE:
7 minutes
OVEN:
400°F
MAKES:
6 servings

5
carbs per serving

Exchanges:
1 Vegetable
2 Very Lean Meat

1 Lightly coat a 15×10×1-inch baking pan with nonstick cooking spray; set aside.

2 Coat an unheated large nonstick skillet with nonstick cooking spray. Preheat over medium heat. Add broccoli, onion, and dried basil (if using) to hot skillet. Cook and stir for 5 to 8 minutes or until vegetables are crisp-tender. Stir in fresh basil (if using), ¼ teaspoon of the salt, and the black pepper. Remove from heat. Stir in the 3 tablespoons tomato sauce. Cover and keep warm.

3 In a medium mixing bowl combine egg whites, eggs, the water, and remaining ¼ teaspoon salt. Beat with a rotary beater until combined but not frothy. Place the prepared baking pan on an oven rack. Carefully pour the egg mixture into the pan. Bake in a 400° oven about 7 minutes or until egg mixture is set but still has a glossy surface.

4 Meanwhile, in a small bowl combine mozzarella cheese and Parmesan cheese; set aside.

5 Cut the baked omelet into six 5-inch squares. Using a large spatula, lift each omelet square from baking pan; invert onto warm serving plate. Divide warm vegetable mixture among omelet squares. Top with cheese mixture. Fold each omelet square diagonally in half, forming a triangle. If desired, drizzle with additional tomato sauce. Serve immediately.

Nutrition Facts per serving: 130 cal., 6 g total fat (2 g sat. fat), 180 mg chol., 452 mg sodium, 5 g carbo., 1 g fiber, 14 g pro.

SUNRISE SMOOTHIE

PREP:
15 minutes
FREEZE:
1 hour
MAKES:
*6 (5-ounce)
servings*

2   medium bananas, sliced

1   cup orange juice

1   cup plain fat-free yogurt

1   cup fresh or unsweetened frozen strawberries

6   to 8 ice cubes

1 Place banana slices on a baking sheet. Freeze for 1 hour.

2 In a blender combine orange juice, yogurt, strawberries, and frozen bananas. Cover and blend until pureed. With machine running, add ice through feed tube, one cube at a time, until desired consistency.

Nutrition Facts per serving: 84 cal., 0 g total fat (0 g sat. fat), 1 mg chol., 32 mg sodium, 18 g carbo., 2 g fiber, 3 g pro.

18
carbs per
serving

Exchanges:
1 Fruit

FAMILY-STYLE CHILI

8	ounces lean ground beef
1	cup chopped onion
½	cup chopped celery
½	cup chopped green sweet pepper
2	cloves garlic, minced
1	15-ounce can red kidney beans, rinsed and drained (optional)
1	15-ounce can tomato puree
1	11½-ounce can tomato juice
½	cup water
2	teaspoons chili powder
1	teaspoon sugar (optional)
½	teaspoon dried basil, crushed, or 1½ teaspoons snipped fresh basil
¼	teaspoon salt
	Shredded reduced-fat cheddar cheese (optional)

1 In a large saucepan combine ground beef, onion, celery, sweet pepper, and garlic. Cook over medium-high heat until meat is brown and onion is tender. Drain off fat.

2 Stir in the kidney beans (if using), tomato puree, tomato juice, the water, chili powder, sugar (if desired), dried basil (if using), and salt. Bring to boiling; reduce heat. Cover and simmer for 25 to 30 minutes or until the vegetables are tender. Stir in fresh basil (if using). If desired, top individual servings with cheese.

Nutrition Facts per serving: 167 cal., 6 g total fat (2 g sat. fat), 36 mg chol., 509 mg sodium, 16 g carbo., 3 g fiber, 13 g pro

PREP:
25 minutes
COOK:
25 minutes
MAKES:
4 servings

16
carbs per serving

Exchanges:
1 Vegetable
½ Starch
2 Very Lean Meat
1 Fat

SPUD-FILLED SOUP

PREP:
25 minutes
COOK:
25 minutes
MAKES:
4 servings

4   medium unpeeled round red, white, or yellow potatoes, cut into bite-size pieces (about 1¼ pounds)

½   cup sliced carrot

½   cup sliced celery

2   tablespoons butter or margarine

2   tablespoons all-purpose flour

½   teaspoon salt

⅛   teaspoon ground white pepper

1½   cups fat-free milk

1   14-ounce can reduced-sodium chicken broth

     Fat-free milk (optional)

¼   cup shredded reduced-fat cheddar cheese

33
carbs per serving

Exchanges:
1½ Starch
½ Milk
1½ Fat

❶ In a covered large saucepan cook potatoes in a large amount of boiling salted water for 5 minutes. Add carrot and celery. Cook about 10 minutes more or until vegetables are tender; drain. Transfer 1 cup of the vegetable mixture to a small bowl; set remaining vegetable mixture aside. Using a potato masher, mash the 1 cup vegetables until nearly smooth. Set mashed vegetable mixture aside.

❷ In the same saucepan melt butter. Stir in flour, the ½ teaspoon salt, and the ⅛ teaspoon white pepper. Add the 1½ cups milk all at once. Cook and stir until slightly thickened and bubbly.

❸ Stir in the reserved cooked vegetables, mashed vegetable mixture, and chicken broth. Cook and stir over medium heat until heated through. If necessary, stir in additional milk to reach desired consistency. If desired, sprinkle with shredded cheese.

Nutrition Facts per serving: 236 cal., 8 g total fat (4 g sat. fat), 23 mg chol., 701 mg sodium, 33 g carbo., 3 g fiber, 9 g pro.

SAUCY CHICKEN PARMESAN

4	skinless, boneless chicken breast halves (1 to 1½ pounds total)
	Nonstick cooking spray
1	slightly beaten egg white
1	tablespoon water
¾	cup cornflakes, crushed (about ⅓ cup)
2	tablespoons grated Parmesan cheese
¼	teaspoon dried Italian seasoning, basil, or oregano, crushed, or 1 teaspoon snipped fresh basil or oregano
⅛	teaspoon black pepper
1⅓	cups purchased spaghetti sauce
4	ounces dried spaghetti, fettuccine, or other pasta, cooked according to package directions and drained
	Grated Parmesan cheese (optional)
	Fresh herb sprigs (optional)

PREP:
20 minutes
BAKE:
15 minutes
OVEN:
400°F
MAKES:
4 servings

37
carbs per serving

Exchanges:
½ Vegetable
1 Starch
4 Very Lean Meat
1½ Other Carbo.

1 Place each piece of chicken between 2 pieces of plastic wrap. Using the flat side of a meat mallet, lightly pound to flatten slightly (about ½ inch thick). Remove plastic wrap.

2 Lightly coat a shallow baking pan with nonstick cooking spray; set aside. In a shallow dish combine egg white and the water. In another shallow dish combine crushed cornflakes, the 2 tablespoons Parmesan cheese, the Italian seasoning, and pepper. Dip chicken pieces, one at a time, into egg mixture; coat with crumb mixture. Place coated chicken pieces in prepared baking pan.

3 Bake in a 400° oven about 15 minutes or until chicken is tender and no longer pink (170°F).

4 Meanwhile, in a small saucepan warm spaghetti sauce over low heat. Divide pasta among 4 dinner plates. Place chicken on top of pasta. Spoon spaghetti sauce over chicken. If desired, sprinkle with additional Parmesan cheese. If desired, garnish with fresh herb sprigs.

Nutrition Facts per serving: 312 cal., 3 g total fat (1 g sat. fat), 68 mg chol., 566 mg sodium, 37 g carbo., 3 g fiber, 34 g pro.

DIZZY SPIRAL SANDWICH

START TO FINISH:
15 minutes
MAKES:
1 serving

1 slice reduced-fat American cheese, quartered

1 ounce very thinly sliced cooked chicken, turkey, or lean beef

1 7- to 8-inch flour tortilla

2 teaspoons honey mustard

¼ cup shredded carrot

2 teaspoons dried tart cherries or raisins

1 Layer cheese and chicken on tortilla. Spread the mustard on chicken. Top with carrot and cherries. Tightly roll up tortilla. Cut in half.

Nutrition Facts per serving: 227 cal., 7 g total fat (3 g sat. fat), 35 mg chol., 495 mg sodium, 25 g carbo., 2 g fiber, 15 g pro.

25
carbs per
serving

Exchanges:
½ Vegetable
1½ Starch
1½ Lean Meat

CHAMPION CHICKEN POCKETS

¼ cup plain low-fat yogurt

¼ cup bottled reduced-fat ranch salad dressing

1½ cups chopped cooked chicken or turkey (about 8 ounces)

½ cup chopped broccoli

¼ cup shredded carrot

¼ cup chopped pecans or walnuts (optional)

2 6- to 7-inch whole wheat pita bread rounds, halved crosswise

1 In a small bowl stir together yogurt and ranch salad dressing.

2 In a medium bowl combine chicken, broccoli, carrot, and, if desired, nuts. Pour yogurt mixture over chicken; toss to coat. Spoon chicken mixture into pita halves.

TO MAKE AHEAD: Prepare as directed. Wrap each sandwich tightly in plastic wrap. Chill for up to 24 hours.

Nutrition Facts per serving: 231 cal., 8 g total fat (1 g sat. fat), 53 mg chol., 392 mg sodium, 21 g carbo., 3 g fiber, 20 g pro.

START TO FINISH:
15 minutes
MAKES:
4 servings

21
carbs per serving

Exchanges:
½ Vegetable
1 Starch
2 Lean Meat
½ Fat

TURKEY & TOMATO WRAPS

START TO FINISH:
15 minutes
MAKES:
*2 servings
(4 wraps per
serving)*

4   butterhead (Bibb or Boston) lettuce leaves

4   ounces very thinly sliced cooked turkey breast

2   teaspoons honey mustard or low-fat mayonnaise dressing

1   small plum tomato, halved and very thinly sliced

1 Place lettuce leaves on a flat surface. Cut leaves in half lengthwise and remove center vein.

2 Place ½ ounce of the turkey on each leaf half just below the center. Spread honey mustard or mayonnaise dressing over turkey. Top with tomato slices. Roll up, starting from a short side. Secure with toothpicks.

Nutrition Facts per serving: 70 cal., 2 g total fat (0 g sat. fat), 22 mg chol., 676 mg sodium, 6 g carbo., 0 g fiber, 10 g pro.

6
carbs per
serving

Exchanges:
1 Vegetable
2 Very Lean Meat

FAST FAJITA ROLL-UPS

12	ounces beef flank steak or sirloin steak or skinless, boneless chicken breast halves
4	8-inch whole wheat, spinach, or flour tortillas
	Nonstick cooking spray
⅓	cup finely chopped onion
⅓	cup finely chopped green sweet pepper
½	cup chopped tomato
2	tablespoons bottled reduced-fat Italian salad dressing
½	cup shredded reduced-fat cheddar cheese (2 ounces)
¼	cup purchased salsa or bottled taco sauce
¼	cup light dairy sour cream (optional)

1 If desired, partially freeze beef for easier slicing. If using beef, trim fat from meat. Cut beef or chicken into bite-size strips.

2 Wrap tortillas tightly in foil. Heat in a 350° oven about 10 minutes or until heated through.

3 Meanwhile, coat an unheated 12-inch nonstick skillet with nonstick cooking spray. Preheat over medium-high heat. Add meat, onion, and sweet pepper to hot skillet. Cook and stir for 2 to 3 minutes or until desired doneness for steak or until chicken is no longer pink. Remove from heat. Drain well. Stir in tomato and salad dressing.

4 To serve, fill warm tortillas with meat mixture. Roll up tortillas. Serve with cheese, salsa or taco sauce, and, if desired, sour cream.

Nutrition Facts per serving: 337 cal., 11 g total fat (5 g sat. fat), 45 mg chol., 664 mg sodium, 30 g carbo., 3 g fiber, 27 g pro.

START TO FINISH:
20 minutes
OVEN:
350°F
MAKES:
4 servings

30
carbs per serving

Exchanges:
½ Vegetable
2 Starch
3 Very Lean Meat

DELI-STYLE SUBMARINES

START TO FINISH:
20 minutes
MAKES:
8 servings

- 1 16-ounce loaf French bread
- ½ of an 8-ounce container light dairy sour cream ranch dip
- ¾ cup shredded carrot (1 large)
- 1 cup shredded lettuce
- ¾ cup shredded, seeded cucumber (½ of a medium)
- 8 ounces thinly sliced assorted deli meats (such as roast beef, ham, and/or turkey)
- 4 ounces thinly sliced mozzarella or provolone cheese

1 Slice French bread in half lengthwise. Spread cut sides of bread with dip. Layer carrot, lettuce, cucumber, meat, and cheese on bottom portion of bread. Replace top portion of bread. Cut into 8 pieces. If necessary, secure each piece with a toothpick.

TO MAKE AHEAD: Prepare as directed. Wrap whole sandwich tightly in plastic wrap. Chill for up to 4 hours. Slice and serve as directed.

Nutrition Facts per serving: 250 cal., 6 g total fat (3 g sat. fat), 24 mg chol., 743 mg sodium, 34 g carbo., 2 g fiber, 14 g pro.

34 carbs per serving

Exchanges:
½ Vegetable
2 Starch
1½ Lean Meat

CHEESY HAM QUESADILLAS

¾   cup shredded Swiss, Monterey Jack, or cheddar cheese (3 ounces)

4   7- to 8-inch whole wheat, spinach, tomato, or plain flour tortillas

3   ounces thinly sliced cooked ham

⅔   cup chopped tomato

2   tablespoons sliced green onion tops (optional)

1 Sprinkle cheese onto one half of each tortilla. Top with ham, tomato, and, if desired, green onion tops. Fold tortillas in half, pressing together gently.

2 In a 10-inch skillet cook quesadillas, 2 at a time, over medium heat for 3 to 4 minutes or until lightly browned, turning once. Cut into wedges and serve immediately.

Nutrition Facts per serving: 260 cal., 10 g total fat (5 g sat. fat), 31 mg chol., 699 mg sodium, 29 g carbo., 3 g fiber, 13 g pro.

START TO FINISH:
20 minutes
MAKES:
4 servings

29
carbs per
serving

Exchanges:
2 Starch
1 Lean Meat
1 Fat

TUNA & CHEESE SUBS

START TO FINISH:
20 minutes
MAKES:
4 servings

⅓   cup low-fat mayonnaise dressing

1½   teaspoons yellow mustard

¼   teaspoon dried dill or ½ teaspoon snipped fresh dill

Dash black pepper

1   12-ounce can tuna (water pack), drained and flaked

½   cup chopped carrot, celery, or red sweet pepper

4   frankfurter buns, split

½   cup shredded reduced-fat cheddar cheese (2 ounces)

29 carbs per serving

❶ In a medium bowl stir together mayonnaise dressing, mustard, dill, and black pepper. Stir in tuna and carrot; set aside.

❷ Using a fork, hollow out the tops and bottoms of frankfurter buns, leaving ¼-inch-thick shells. Sprinkle cheese into hollowed-out bun bottoms. Spoon tuna mixture over cheese. Add bun tops.

TO MAKE AHEAD: Prepare as directed. Wrap each sandwich tightly in plastic wrap. Chill for up to 24 hours.

Nutrition Facts per serving: 307 cal., 7 g total fat (3 g sat. fat), 39 mg chol., 858 mg sodium, 29 g carbo., 2 g fiber, 29 g pro.

Exchanges:
2 Starch
3 Very Lean Meat
1 Fat

CRUNCHY PB&A WRAP

⅓   cup peanut butter

4   7- to 8-inch flour tortillas

1   cup chopped apple

¼   cup low-fat granola

1 Spread peanut butter over tortillas. Sprinkle with apple and granola. Tightly roll up tortillas. Cut each in half.

Nutrition Facts per serving: 254 cal., 14 g total fat (3 g sat. fat), 0 mg chol., 234 mg sodium, 28 g carbo., 3 g fiber, 8 g pro.

START TO FINISH:
10 minutes
MAKES:
4 servings

28
carbs per serving

Exchanges:
½ Fruit
1½ Starch
½ High-Fat Meat
1½ Fat

FIESTA CHEESE TOSTADAS

START TO FINISH:
30 minutes
OVEN:
400°F
MAKES:
6 servings

6	6- to 7-inch corn tortillas
2	teaspoons cooking oil or olive oil
1	cup canned vegetarian refried beans
⅓	cup bottled picante sauce or purchased salsa
1	medium red, yellow, or green sweet pepper, cut into thin bite-size strips
⅓	cup loose-pack frozen whole kernel corn, thawed and drained
¾	cup shredded reduced-fat cheddar cheese (3 ounces)
1	cup shredded lettuce
	Light dairy sour cream (optional)
	Chopped tomato (optional)

22

carbs per
serving

Exchanges:
½ Vegetable
1½ Starch
½ Lean Meat
½ Fat

❶ Place tortillas in a single layer on an ungreased extra-large baking sheet. Brush the top side of each tortilla with a little of the oil. Bake, uncovered, in a 400° oven for 5 minutes. Remove from oven.

❷ Meanwhile, in a small bowl stir together refried beans and picante sauce or salsa. Spread bean mixture evenly over the tortillas. Top with sweet pepper strips and corn. Sprinkle with cheese.

❸ Bake for 7 to 8 minutes more or until cheese is melted and filling is heated through. Top with lettuce. If desired, garnish with sour cream and chopped tomato.

Nutrition Facts per serving: 168 cal., 6 g total fat (2 g sat. fat), 10 mg chol., 440 mg sodium, 22 g carbo., 4 g fiber, 8 g pro.

TURKEY TACO SALAD

Nonstick cooking spray
12 ounces uncooked ground turkey
1 cup loose-pack frozen whole kernel corn
1 cup purchased salsa
¼ cup water
4 to 6 cups shredded lettuce
¼ cup shredded reduced-fat cheddar cheese (1 ounce)
1 cup broken purchased baked tortilla chips

1 Coat an unheated large nonstick skillet with nonstick cooking spray. Preheat over medium heat. Cook ground turkey in hot skillet about 5 minutes or until no longer pink. Drain off fat. Stir in corn, salsa, and the water. Bring to boiling; reduce heat. Cover and simmer for 2 to 3 minutes to blend flavors.

2 Line 4 salad bowls or plates with shredded lettuce. Top with hot turkey mixture. Sprinkle with cheese and broken tortilla chips. Serve immediately.

Nutrition Facts per serving: 275 cal., 9 g total fat (3 g sat. fat), 59 mg chol., 676 mg sodium, 29 g carbo., 3 g fiber, 23 g pro.

TURKEY-BEAN TACO SALAD: Prepare as directed, except stir in one 15-ounce can pinto beans, rinsed and drained, with with corn.

Nutrition Facts per serving: 348 cal., 9 g total fat (3 g sat. fat), 58 mg chol., 941 mg sodium, 44 g carbo., 7 g fiber, 27 g pro.

Exchanges: 1½ Vegetable, 2½ Starch, 2 Lean Meat

START TO FINISH:
25 minutes
MAKES:
4 servings

29
carbs per serving

Exchanges:
1½ Vegetable
1½ Starch
2 Lean Meat

TERRIFIC TORTELLINI SALAD

PREP:
20 minutes
CHILL:
2 to 24 hours
MAKES:
8 side-dish servings

1	9-ounce package refrigerated light cheese tortellini or ravioli
3	cups broccoli florets
1	cup crinkle-cut or sliced carrots
¼	cup sliced green onions
½	cup bottled reduced-fat ranch salad dressing
1	large tomato, chopped
1	cup fresh pea pods, halved
	Fat-free milk (optional)

22 carbs per serving

1 In a large saucepan cook pasta according to package directions, adding the broccoli and carrots for the last 3 minutes of cooking time. Drain. Rinse with cold water. Drain again.

2 In a large bowl combine cooked pasta mixture and green onions; drizzle with dressing. Gently toss to coat. Cover and chill for at least 2 hours or up to 24 hours.

3 Before serving, gently stir tomato and pea pods into pasta mixture. If necessary, stir in a little milk to moisten.

Nutrition Facts per serving: 145 cal., 5 g total fat (1 g sat. fat), 17 mg chol., 344 mg sodium, 22 g carbo., 3 g fiber, 6 g pro.

Exchanges:
1½ Vegetable
1 Starch
½ Fat

FRUIT CUPS WITH STRAWBERRY DRESSING

2   cups cut-up strawberries and/or whole raspberries

¼   cup frozen orange juice concentrate, thawed

2   teaspoons sugar

2   kiwifruits, peeled and thinly sliced

1   orange, peeled and sectioned

2   bananas, sliced

1   medium peach, plum, or nectarine, sliced

1   small apple or pear, cored and sliced

1 For dressing, in a blender or food processor place half of the berries, the orange juice concentrate, and sugar. Cover and blend or process until smooth; set aside. If using strawberries, slice remaining berries.

2 In a large bowl combine kiwifruits , orange sections, banana slices, peach slices, apple slices, and remaining berries. Serve fruit in bowls with dressing.

Nutrition Facts per serving: 120 cal., 1 g total fat (0 g sat. fat), 0 mg chol., 4 mg sodium, 29 g carbo., 4 g fiber, 2 g pro.

START TO FINISH:
25 minutes
MAKES:
6 side-dish servings

29
carbs per serving

Exchanges:
2 Fruit

BURST-OF-ORANGE BUTTERNUT SQUASH

PREP:
25 minutes
BAKE:
25 minutes
OVEN:
425°F
MAKES:
4 side-dish servings

Nonstick cooking spray

1   pound butternut squash, peeled, seeded, and cut into ½-inch pieces

⅓   cup orange juice

1   tablespoon pure maple syrup or maple-flavored syrup

¼   teaspoon salt

⅛   teaspoon black pepper (optional)

Dash ground cinnamon

1   tablespoon butter or margarine

15 carbs per serving

1 Lightly coat a 2-quart rectangular baking dish with nonstick cooking spray. Place squash in prepared baking dish. In a small bowl combine orange juice, maple syrup, salt, pepper (if desired), and cinnamon. Drizzle over squash; toss to coat. Dot with butter.

2 Bake, uncovered, in a 425° oven about 25 minutes or until squash is tender, stirring twice.

Nutrition Facts per serving: 91 cal., 3 g total fat (2 g sat. fat), 8 mg chol., 182 mg sodium, 15 g carbo., 2 g fiber, 2 g pro.

Exchanges:
1 Starch
½ Fat

VEGGIE MASH

3   medium baking potatoes (1 pound), peeled and cubed

1   cup coarsely chopped cauliflower

½   cup sliced carrot or coarsely chopped cauliflower

¼   cup light dairy sour cream

¼   teaspoon salt

      Salt

      Black pepper

2   tablespoons finely shredded Parmesan cheese

1 In a covered medium saucepan cook potatoes, cauliflower, and carrot in enough boiling salted water to cover for 15 to 20 minutes or until tender. Drain. Mash with a potato masher or beat with an electric mixer on low speed. Add sour cream and the ¼ teaspoon salt. Mash or beat until combined. Season to taste with additional salt and pepper. Top individual servings with Parmesan cheese.

Nutrition Facts per serving: 113 cal., 4 g total fat (2 g sat. fat), 11 mg chol., 303 mg sodium, 13 g carbo., 2 g fiber, 6 g pro.

START TO FINISH:
30 minutes
MAKES:
6 side-dish servings

13
carbs per serving

Exchanges:
1 Vegetable
½ Starch
1 Fat

EASY CHEESY BROCCOLI & RICE

START TO FINISH:
15 minutes
MAKES:
6 side-dish servings

1   10-ounce package frozen chopped broccoli
1   cup instant rice
1   cup water
¼   teaspoon salt
1   cup shredded reduced-fat cheddar or Swiss cheese (4 ounces)

1 In a medium saucepan combine frozen broccoli, uncooked rice, the water, and salt. Bring to boiling, stirring frequently to break up frozen broccoli.

2 Remove from heat. Cover and let stand for 5 minutes. Return saucepan to burner on low heat. Add cheese, stirring just until cheese is melted.

Nutrition Facts per serving: 132 cal., 4 g total fat (3 g sat. fat), 13 mg chol., 270 mg sodium, 16 g carbo., 1 g fiber, 7 g pro.

16
carbs per
serving

Exchanges:
½ Vegetable
1 Starch
½ Medium-Fat Meat

OAT & NUT CRUNCH MIX

4   cups sweetened oat square cereal
      or brown sugar-flavored oat biscuit cereal

½   cup sliced almonds

2   tablespoons butter or margarine, melted

½   teaspoon apple pie spice

      Dash salt

1   cup dried cherries and/or golden raisins

1 In a 15×10×1-inch baking pan combine cereal and almonds. In a small bowl stir together melted butter, apple pie spice, and salt. Drizzle butter mixture over cereal mixture; toss to coat.

2 Bake in a 300° oven about 20 minutes or until almonds are toasted, stirring once during baking. Cool in pan on a wire rack for 20 minutes. Stir in dried cherries or raisins. Cool completely. Store in a tightly covered container at room temperature for up to 1 week.

Nutrition Facts per serving: 83 cal., 3 g total fat (1 g sat. fat), 3 mg chol., 63 mg sodium, 12 g carbo., 1 g fiber, 2 g pro.

PREP:
10 minutes
BAKE:
20 minutes
COOL:
20 minutes
OVEN:
300°F
MAKES:
*20 servings
(¼ cup
per serving)*

12
carbs per
serving

Exchanges:
1 Starch

CHEESY CHILI POPCORN

START TO FINISH:
10 minutes
MAKES:
10 servings (about ¾ cup per serving)

8   cups popped popcorn

2   tablespoons butter or margarine, melted

1   teaspoon chili powder

⅛   teaspoon garlic powder

2   tablespoons grated Parmesan cheese

1 Place popcorn in a large bowl. In a small bowl stir together butter, chili powder, and garlic powder. Drizzle over popcorn; toss to coat. Sprinkle with Parmesan cheese; toss to coat. Store in a tightly covered container at room temperature for up to 3 days.

Nutrition Facts per serving: 51 cal., 3 g total fat (2 g sat. fat), 7 mg chol., 46 mg sodium, 5 g carbo., 1 g fiber, 1 g pro.

5 carbs per serving

Exchanges:
½ Starch
½ Fat

SIDES

RICE PILAF WITH TOASTED PECANS

Nonstick cooking spray

2 cloves garlic, minced

2½ cups reduced-sodium chicken broth

1 cup long grain rice

1½ cups sliced fresh mushrooms

½ cup thinly sliced green onions

¼ cup chopped red sweet pepper

2 teaspoons finely shredded lemon peel

⅛ teaspoon black pepper

2 tablespoons chopped pecans, toasted

27
carbs per serving

Exchanges:
½ Vegetable
1½ Starch
½ Fat

❶ Coat an unheated large nonstick saucepan with nonstick cooking spray. Preheat over medium heat. Cook garlic in hot pan for 30 seconds. Add chicken broth and uncooked rice. Bring to boiling; reduce heat. Cover and simmer for 10 minutes.

❷ Add mushrooms, green onions, sweet pepper, lemon peel, and black pepper. Cover and cook for 10 to 15 minutes more or until liquid is absorbed and rice is tender. Stir in toasted pecans.

Nutrition Facts per serving: 147 cal., 2 g total fat (0 g sat. fat), 0 mg chol., 242 mg sodium, 27 g carbo., 1 g fiber, 4 g pro.

BROCCOLI WITH LEMON & DILL

Nonstick cooking spray

½ cup chopped onion or leek (white part only)

1 clove garlic, minced

½ cup reduced-sodium chicken broth

1½ pounds broccoli, cut into spears

1 tablespoon lemon juice

1 teaspoon all-purpose flour

2 tablespoons snipped fresh dill or 1 teaspoon dried dill

¼ teaspoon salt

⅛ teaspoon black pepper

1 Coat an unheated large nonstick saucepan with nonstick cooking spray. Preheat over medium heat. Cook and stir onion or leek and garlic in hot pan about 3 minutes or until tender. Add chicken broth; bring to boiling. Add broccoli and return to boiling; reduce heat. Cover and cook for 8 to 10 minutes or until broccoli is tender. Transfer vegetables to a serving platter, reserving broth in pan (add additional broth, if necessary, to measure ½ cup).

2 In small bowl combine lemon juice and flour; add to broth in saucepan. Cook and stir until thickened and bubbly; cook and stir for 1 minute more. Add dill, salt, and pepper. Spoon sauce over vegetables and toss to coat.

Nutrition Facts per serving: 33 cal., 0 g total fat (0 g sat. fat), 0 mg chol., 119 mg sodium, 7 g carbo., 2 g fiber, 2 g pro.

START TO FINISH:
25 minutes
MAKES:
6 to 8 servings

7
carbs per serving

Exchanges:
1½ Vegetable

ROMA-STYLE SPINACH

START TO FINISH:
15 minutes
MAKES:
4 servings

Nonstick cooking spray

¼ cup golden raisins

2 tablespoons pine nuts or chopped walnuts

1 large clove garlic, minced

¼ teaspoon salt

Dash cayenne pepper

12 cups torn fresh spinach (1 pound)

1 tablespoon finely shredded Parmesan cheese

13 carbs per serving

❶ Coat an unheated very large nonstick skillet with nonstick cooking spray. Preheat over medium heat. Add raisins, nuts, garlic, salt, and cayenne pepper to hot skillet. Cook and stir about 1 minute or until garlic is light brown.

❷ Add spinach; toss to coat. Cook and stir for 1 to 2 minutes or just until spinach is wilted and heated through. Sprinkle with Parmesan cheese.

Nutrition Facts per serving: 84 cal., 3 g total fat (1 g sat. fat), 1 mg chol., 239 mg sodium, 13 g carbo., 3 g fiber, 5 g pro.

Exchanges:
1½ Vegetable
½ Fruit
½ Fat

LEMON DILL POTATOES

4   large baking potatoes (about 8 ounces each)

⅓   cup light dairy sour cream

2   tablespoons butter or margarine, melted

4   teaspoons lemon juice

1   tablespoon snipped fresh dill or ¾ teaspoon dried dill

½   teaspoon salt

⅛   teaspoon black pepper

   Fat-free milk (optional)

1 Scrub potatoes thoroughly with a brush. Pat dry with paper towels. Prick potatoes with a fork. Bake in a 425° oven for 40 to 60 minutes or until tender. (Or microwave the potatoes, uncovered, on 100% power [high] for 13 to 17 minutes or until almost tender, rearranging once. Let stand for 5 minutes.)

2 Cut potatoes in half lengthwise. Gently scoop out each potato half, leaving a thin shell. In a large mixing bowl combine potato pulp, sour cream, 1 tablespoon of the butter, the lemon juice, dill, salt, and pepper. Beat with an electric mixer on low speed until smooth. (If necessary, stir in 1 to 2 tablespoons milk to reach desired consistency.) Divide mixture among the 8 shells. Place in a 3-quart rectangular baking dish. Drizzle potatoes with remaining 1 tablespoon melted butter.

3 Bake in a 425° oven for 20 to 25 minutes or until light brown.

TO MAKE AHEAD: Prepare as directed through step 2. Cover and chill for up to 24 hours. Bake, covered, in a 425° oven for 20 minutes. Uncover and bake for 10 to 15 minutes more or until heated through.

Nutrition Facts per serving: 125 cal., 4 g total fat (2 g sat. fat), 12 mg chol., 191 mg sodium, 20 g carbo., 2 g fiber, 3 g pro.

PREP:
20 minutes
BAKE:
40 minutes +
20 minutes
OVEN:
425°F
MAKES:
8 servings

20
carbs per serving

Exchanges:
1 Starch
1 Fat

VEGETABLE KABOBS

PREP:
20 minutes
COOK:
8 minutes
GRILL:
10 minutes
MAKES:
8 servings

2	medium potatoes, quartered
2	small red onions, each cut into 4 wedges, or 8 red boiling onions
8	baby squash (such as zucchini and/or yellow summer squash)
8	medium fresh mushrooms
8	miniature sweet peppers or 1 or 2 small red and/or orange sweet peppers, cut into 1-inch pieces
¼	cup bottled oil-and-vinegar salad dressing
2	teaspoons snipped fresh rosemary or ½ teaspoon dried rosemary, crushed
⅛	teaspoon salt
⅛	teaspoon black pepper

9
carbs per
serving

Exchanges:
1 Vegetable
½ Starch
½ Fat

1 In a covered medium saucepan cook potatoes and onions in a small amount of lightly salted boiling water over medium heat for 8 to 10 minutes or until nearly tender, adding the squash and mushrooms for the last 1 minute of cooking time. Drain well. Cool slightly. If using wooden skewers, soak in water for 30 minutes before grilling.

2 On eight 10-inch skewers, alternately thread potatoes, onions, squash, mushrooms, and sweet peppers, leaving a ¼-inch space between pieces. In a small bowl combine salad dressing, rosemary, salt, and black pepper; brush over vegetables.

3 Place kabobs on the rack of an uncovered grill directly over medium coals. Grill for 10 to 12 minutes or until vegetables are tender and lightly browned, turning and brushing occasionally with dressing mixture.

TO BROIL: Place kabobs on the greased unheated rack of a broiler pan. Broil 3 to 4 inches from the heat for 10 to 12 minutes or until vegetables are tender and lightly browned, turning and brushing occasionally with dressing mixture.

Nutrition Facts per serving: 75 cal., 4 g total fat (1 g sat. fat), 0 mg chol., 145 mg sodium, 9 g carbo., 1 g fiber, 2 g pro.

ROSEMARY GRILLED SWEET POTATO SLICES

1½ pounds sweet potatoes, peeled and cut lengthwise into ½-inch-thick slices

1 cup water

4 teaspoons Dijon-style mustard

4 teaspoons honey

4 teaspoons olive oil

2 teaspoons snipped fresh rosemary or ½ teaspoon dried rosemary, crushed

⅛ teaspoon black pepper

1 In a microwave-safe baking dish combine sweet potatoes and the water. Cover with vented plastic wrap. Microwave on 100% power (high) for 10 to 12 minutes or until sweet potatoes are nearly tender, rearranging sweet potatoes once halfway through cooking. Drain well.

2 Meanwhile, in a small bowl combine mustard, honey, olive oil, rosemary, and pepper; set aside.

3 Place sweet potatoes on the greased rack of an uncovered grill directly over medium-hot coals. Grill for 3 to 4 minutes or until sweet potatoes are golden brown, carefully turning once with a metal spatula. Brush with half of the mustard mixture. Grill for 2 to 3 minutes more or just until potatoes are tender, turning and brushing once with remaining mustard mixture.

TO BROIL: Place sweet potatoes on the greased unheated rack of a broiler pan. Broil 3 to 4 inches from the heat for 3 to 4 minutes, carefully turning once with a metal spatula. Brush with half of the mustard mixture. Broil for 2 to 3 minutes more, turning and brushing once with remaining mustard mixture.

Nutrition Facts per serving: 197 cal., 5 g total fat (1 g sat. fat), 0 mg chol., 44 mg sodium, 36 g carbo., 4 g fiber, 2 g pro.

PREP:
15 minutes
MICROWAVE:
10 minutes
GRILL:
5 minutes
MAKES:
4 servings

36 carbs per serving

Exchanges:
2½ Starch

OVEN-ROASTED VEGETABLES

PREP:
15 minutes
BAKE:
*30 minutes +
5 minutes*
OVEN:
425°F
MAKES:
6 servings

15
carbs per
serving

Exchanges:
1 Vegetable
½ Starch
½ Fat

2 medium sweet potatoes and/or white potatoes, peeled and cut into 1-inch cubes

2 carrots, cut into 1-inch pieces, or 1 cup packaged peeled baby carrots

1 medium parsnip, peeled and cut into 1-inch pieces

1 medium red onion, cut into thin wedges (optional)

1 tablespoon olive oil

3 cloves garlic, minced

1 teaspoon desired dried herbs (such as marjoram, thyme, rosemary, and/or oregano), crushed

¼ teaspoon salt

⅛ teaspoon black pepper

Fresh herb sprig (optional)

1 In a 13×9×2-inch baking pan arrange potatoes, carrots, parsnip, and, if desired, red onion. In a small bowl combine oil, garlic, desired dried herbs, salt, and pepper. Drizzle oil mixture over vegetables; toss to coat. Cover with foil.

2 Bake in a 425° oven for 30 minutes. Remove foil; stir vegetables. Bake, uncovered, for 5 to 10 minutes more or until vegetables are tender. If desired, garnish with fresh herb sprig.

Nutrition Facts per serving: 83 cal., 2 g total fat (0 g sat. fat), 0 mg chol., 110 mg sodium, 15 g carbo., 3 g fiber, 1 g pro.

GLAZED CARROTS & PARSNIPS

1   pound small carrots, cut into ½-inch-wide strips
8   ounces small parsnips, peeled and cut into ½-inch-wide strips
¼   cup water
1   tablespoon butter
1   tablespoon honey
2   whole star anise
½   teaspoon salt
⅛   teaspoon black pepper

1 In a large skillet combine carrots, parsnips, the water, butter, honey, star anise, salt, and pepper. Bring just to boiling; reduce heat to medium-low. Cook, uncovered, for 7 to 10 minutes or until vegetables are crisp-tender, stirring occasionally. Increase heat to medium. Cook for 3 to 5 minutes or until vegetables are light brown, stirring gently. Discard star anise.

Nutrition Facts per serving: 121 cal., 3 g total fat (2 g sat. fat), 8 mg chol., 242 mg sodium, 23 g carbo., 5 g fiber, 2 g pro.

START TO FINISH:
25 minutes
MAKES:
4 servings

23
carbs per serving

Exchanges:
1½ Vegetable
1 Other Carbo.
½ Fat

ITALIAN-STYLE VEGETABLES

PREP:
15 minutes
CHILL:
4 to 24 hours
MAKES:
5 or 6 servings

1   10-ounce package frozen lima beans
1   8-ounce package frozen sugar snap peas or one 9-ounce
      package frozen Italian green beans
1   6-ounce jar marinated artichoke hearts
1   tablespoon snipped fresh dill or 1 teaspoon dried dill
⅛   teaspoon crushed red pepper
      Romaine leaves
1   green onion, thinly sliced
      Lemon wedges (optional)

17
carbs per
serving

1 In a covered medium saucepan cook lima beans and snap peas or Italian green beans in a small amount of boiling water for 5 to 8 minutes or until crisp-tender; drain. Rinse with cold water; drain again.

2 In a medium bowl combine lima bean mixture, undrained artichoke hearts, dill, and crushed red pepper. Cover and chill for at least 4 hours or up to 24 hours.

3 To serve, place the romaine leaves in a salad bowl. Spoon lima bean mixture over romaine leaves. Sprinkle with sliced green onion. If desired, serve with lemon wedges.

Exchanges:
½ Vegetable
1 Starch
½ Fat

Nutrition Facts per serving: 114 cal., 4 g total fat (1 g sat. fat), 0 mg chol., 48 mg sodium, 17 g carbo., 6 g fiber, 5 g pro.

BASIL BEETS & ONION

4   medium fresh beets (about 1 pound)

½   teaspoon fennel seeds

5   whole black peppercorns

⅓   cup chopped red onion

2   tablespoons snipped fresh basil or 2 teaspoons dried basil, crushed

2   tablespoons white wine vinegar

1   tablespoon chopped shallot

1   tablespoon olive oil

¼   teaspoon salt

1 Cut off all but 1 inch of the fresh beet stems and roots; wash. Do not peel. In a covered large saucepan cook beets, fennel seeds, and peppercorns in a large amount of boiling water for 35 to 45 minutes or until tender. Drain; discard fennel seeds and peppercorns. Cool slightly. Slip skins off beets and discard. Dice beets.

2 In a medium bowl combine diced beets, red onion, basil, vinegar, shallot, oil, and salt. Serve warm or chilled.

Nutrition Facts per serving: 57 cal., 3 g total fat (0 g sat. fat), 0 mg chol., 162 mg sodium, 7 g carbo., 2 g fiber, 1 g pro.

PREP:
20 minutes
COOK:
35 minutes
MAKES:
5 servings

7
carbs per
serving

Exchanges:
1½ Vegetable
½ Fat

POTATO-FENNEL SALAD

PREP:
25 minutes
CHILL:
2 to 24 hours
MAKES:
4 to 6 servings

1	cup water
¼	teaspoon salt
12	ounces tiny new potatoes, quartered
12	ounces fresh asparagus, trimmed and cut into 1-inch-long pieces
1	medium fennel bulb, thinly sliced (1 cup)
¼	cup fat-free mayonnaise dressing or salad dressing
¼	cup plain fat-free yogurt
2	green onions, thinly sliced
1	tablespoon white wine vinegar
2	teaspoons snipped fresh fennel leaves
⅛	teaspoon coarsely ground black pepper

23
carbs per
serving

Exchanges:
1½ Vegetable
1 Starch

1 In a large saucepan bring the water and salt to boiling. Add potatoes. Cover and cook for 8 minutes. Add asparagus and fennel. Cover and cook for 4 to 6 minutes more or just until potatoes are tender and asparagus and fennel are crisp-tender; drain. Arrange vegetables in a shallow serving dish. Cover and chill for at least 2 hours or up to 24 hours.

2 For dressing, in a small bowl stir together mayonnaise dressing, yogurt, green onions, vinegar, fennel leaves, and pepper. Cover and chill for at least 2 hours or up to 24 hours.

3 To serve, spoon the dressing over vegetables; toss gently to coat.

Nutrition Facts per serving: 122 cal., 1 g total fat (0 g sat. fat), 0 mg chol., 322 mg sodium, 23 g carbo., 5 g fiber, 6 g pro.

MELON & WATERCRESS SALAD

4 cups watercress sprigs

1½ cups arugula leaves

3 cups assorted melon balls
(such as watermelon, cantaloupe, and/or honeydew)

2 medium oranges, peeled and sectioned

½ of a medium red onion, cut into thin slices

¼ cup pecan or walnut halves, lightly toasted

2 to 4 tablespoons thinly sliced fresh mint leaves

⅓ cup Citrus Vinaigrette

1 Line 4 salad plates with watercress sprigs and arugula leaves. Arrange melon balls, orange sections, red onion slices, toasted nuts, and mint on top of greens.

2 Drizzle Citrus Vinaigrette over salads.

CITRUS VINAIGRETTE: In a small bowl combine ¼ cup lemon juice; 2 tablespoons frozen orange juice concentrate, thawed; 1 tablespoon finely shredded orange peel; 1 teaspoon Dijon-style mustard; and ½ teaspoon sugar. Slowly beat or whisk in ¼ cup olive oil until slightly thickened. Cover and refrigerate for up to 2 weeks.

Nutrition Facts per serving: 190 cal., 12 g total fat (1 g sat. fat), 0 mg chol., 48 mg sodium, 20 g carbo., 4 g fiber, 3 g pro.

START TO FINISH:
20 minutes
MAKES:
4 servings

20
carbs per serving

Exchanges:
1½ Vegetable
1 Fruit
2 Fat

HONEY-MUSTARD FRUIT SLAW

PREP:
20 minutes
CHILL:
2 to 24 hours
MAKES:
4 servings

14
carbs per
serving

Exchanges:
1½ Vegetable
½ Fruit
1½ Fat

1½ cups shredded green cabbage

1 cup shredded carrot

⅔ cup coarsely chopped apple or pear

4 teaspoons salad oil

4 teaspoons Dijon-style mustard or coarse-grain brown mustard

1 tablespoon lemon juice

1 tablespoon honey

2 small cloves garlic, minced

2 tablespoons chopped peanuts or cashews

1 In a medium bowl toss together cabbage, carrot, and apple or pear; set aside.

2 For dressing, in a small screw-top jar combine salad oil, mustard, lemon juice, honey, and garlic. Cover and shake well. Pour dressing over cabbage mixture; toss gently to coat. Cover and chill for at least 2 hours or up to 24 hours.

3 To serve, sprinkle the cabbage mixture with peanuts or cashews.

Nutrition Facts per serving: 122 cal., 7 g total fat (1 g sat. fat), 0 mg chol., 64 mg sodium, 14 g carbo., 3 g fiber, 2 g pro.

DESSERTS

CHERRY COBBLER WITH CORN BREAD BISCUITS

PREP:
30 minutes
BAKE:
15 minutes
OVEN:
400°F
MAKES:
4 servings

23
carbs per
serving

Exchanges:
1 Fruit
½ Starch
1 Fat

1	14- to 16-ounce package frozen unsweetened pitted dark sweet cherries
¼	cup cold water or orange juice
2	teaspoons cornstarch
3	tablespoons all-purpose flour
2	tablespoons cornmeal
1	tablespoon sugar
¾	teaspoon baking powder
⅛	teaspoon salt
⅛	teaspoon ground allspice or nutmeg
4	teaspoons butter
1	egg white or 2 tablespoons refrigerated or frozen egg product, thawed
2	tablespoons fat-free milk
	Low-fat ice cream (optional)

1 For filling, in a medium saucepan combine cherries, the water or orange juice, and cornstarch. Let stand for 20 minutes.

2 Meanwhile, for biscuit topping, in a medium bowl stir together flour, cornmeal, sugar, baking powder, salt, and allspice or nutmeg. Using a pastry blender, cut in the butter until mixture resembles coarse crumbs. Make a well in the center of the cornmeal mixture. Set aside.

3 Cook and stir the filling over medium heat until thickened and bubbly. Divide fruit mixture among four 10-ounce custard cups or individual baking dishes.

4 In a small bowl beat egg white and milk with a fork until well mixed. Add the milk mixture all at once to the cornmeal mixture. Using a fork, stir just until moistened. Immediately spoon a mound of the biscuit topping on top of the hot filling in each custard cup or baking dish.

5 Bake in a 400° oven about 15 minutes or until a toothpick inserted in topping comes out clean. Serve warm. If desired, serve with ice cream.

Nutrition Facts per serving: 141 cal., 5 g total fat (2 g sat. fat), 11 mg chol., 165 mg sodium, 23 g carbo., 2 g fiber, 3 g pro.

PINEAPPLE-PEAR CRISP

5	medium pears (about 1¾ pounds)
¼	teaspoon ground cinnamon
1¼	cups chopped fresh pineapple
⅔	cup rolled oats
¼	cup chopped hazelnuts (filberts) or pecans
2	tablespoons packed brown sugar
1	tablespoon whole wheat flour or all-purpose flour
1	teaspoon grated fresh ginger or ¼ teaspoon ground ginger
¼	teaspoon ground nutmeg
2	tablespoons butter, melted
	Vanilla low-fat frozen yogurt or ice cream (optional)

1 If desired, peel pears. Core and halve pears lengthwise. Arrange pear halves, cut sides up, in a 2-quart rectangular baking dish. Sprinkle with cinnamon. Top with pineapple.

2 In a medium bowl combine oats, hazelnuts or pecans, brown sugar, flour, ginger, and nutmeg. Stir in melted butter until well mixed. Sprinkle oat mixture over fruit.

3 Bake in a 375° oven for 25 to 30 minutes or until pears are tender. If desired, serve with frozen yogurt or ice cream.

Nutrition Facts per serving: 135 cal., 5 g total fat (2 g sat. fat), 7 mg chol., 26 mg sodium, 22 g carbo., 3 g fiber, 2 g pro.

PREP:
25 minutes
BAKE:
25 minutes
OVEN:
375°F
MAKES:
10 servings

22
carbs per
serving

Exchanges:
1 Fruit
½ Other Carbo.
1 Fat

SWEET POTATO BREAD PUDDING

PREP:
15 minutes
BAKE:
30 minutes
OVEN:
325°F
MAKES:
9 servings

26

carbs per serving

Exchanges:
1 Starch
½ Lean Meat
½ Other Carbo.
½ Fat

2   eggs

2   egg whites

1   cup fat-free milk or vanilla-flavored soy milk

1   cup mashed cooked sweet potato*

¼   cup packed brown sugar

1   teaspoon ground cinnamon

⅛   teaspoon ground nutmeg

3   cups dry whole-grain or raisin bread cubes (4 slices)**

⅓   cup golden raisins or snipped dried apricots

¼   cup chopped pecans, toasted

1 In a medium bowl beat together whole eggs, egg whites, and milk. Whisk in sweet potato, brown sugar, cinnamon, and nutmeg.

2 In a 2-quart square baking dish combine bread cubes, raisins or apricots, and pecans. Pour egg mixture over bread mixture. Lightly press with the back of a spoon to thoroughly moisten bread.

3 Bake in a 325° oven for 30 to 35 minutes or until a knife inserted near center comes out clean. Serve warm.

*NOTE: For 1 cup mashed cooked sweet potato, peel and quarter one 11- to 12-ounce sweet potato. In a small covered saucepan cook sweet potato in enough boiling water to cover about 25 minutes or until tender; drain and mash.

**NOTE: To dry bread cubes, spread in a single layer in a 15×10×1-inch baking pan. Bake in a 300°F oven for 10 to 15 minutes or until dry, stirring twice; cool. Bread will continue to dry and crisp as it cools. (Or instead of baking, let bread cubes stand, loosely covered, at room temperature for 8 to 12 hours.)

Nutrition Facts per serving: 147 cal., 4 g total fat (1 g sat. fat), 48 mg chol., 89 mg sodium, 26 g carbo., 4 g fiber, 6 g pro.

CHOCOLATE SOUFFLÉS

⅔ cup granulated sugar

⅓ cup unsweetened cocoa powder

1 tablespoon all-purpose flour

⅛ teaspoon salt

½ cup fat-free milk

2 egg yolks

4 egg whites

1 teaspoon vanilla

⅛ teaspoon cream of tartar

   Sifted powdered sugar (optional)

PREP:
30 minutes
BAKE:
25 minutes
OVEN:
350°F
MAKES:
8 servings

1 Place eight 6-ounce ramekins in a shallow baking pan; set aside.

2 In a small saucepan stir together ⅓ cup of the granulated sugar, the cocoa powder, flour, and salt. Gradually stir in milk. Cook and stir over medium-high heat until thickened and bubbly. Reduce heat; cook and stir for 1 minute more. Remove from heat. In a small bowl slightly beat egg yolks. Slowly add chocolate mixture to egg yolks, stirring constantly.

3 In a large mixing bowl combine egg whites, vanilla, and cream of tartar. Beat with an electric mixer on high speed until soft peaks form (tips curl). Gradually add remaining ⅓ cup granulated sugar, beating on high speed until stiff peaks form (tips stand straight). Stir about one-fourth of the egg whites into chocolate mixture to lighten. Gently fold chocolate mixture into egg white mixture. Spoon into ramekins.

4 Bake in a 350° oven about 25 minutes or until knife inserted near centers comes out clean. If desired, sprinkle with powdered sugar. Serve immediately.

Nutrition Facts per serving: 102 cal., 2 g total fat (1 g sat. fat), 52 mg chol., 74 mg sodium, 20 g carbo., 1 g fiber, 4 g pro.

20 carbs per serving

Exchanges:
½ Very Lean Meat
1½ Other Carbo.

DREAM CREAM PUFFS

PREP:
25 minutes
BAKE:
30 minutes
OVEN:
400°F
MAKES:
8 servings

Nonstick cooking spray

½   cup water

2   tablespoons butter

½   cup all-purpose flour

2   eggs

1   4-serving-size package sugar-free instant chocolate pudding mix

2   cups fat-free milk

⅛   teaspoon peppermint extract

Sifted powdered sugar or unsweetened cocoa powder (optional)

13

carbs per
serving

Exchanges:
1 Other Carbo.
½ Fat

1 Lightly coat a baking sheet with nonstick cooking spray; set aside.

2 In a small saucepan combine the water and butter. Bring to boiling. Add flour all at once, stirring vigorously. Cook and stir until mixture forms a ball. Remove from heat. Cool for 10 minutes. Add eggs, one at a time, beating well with a wooden spoon after each addition. Drop mixture in 8 mounds, 3 inches apart, on the prepared baking sheet.

3 Bake in a 400° oven about 30 minutes or until golden brown. Transfer cream puffs to a wire rack; cool. Cut tops from cream puffs; remove soft dough from insides.

4 Meanwhile, for filling, prepare pudding mix according to package directions, using the fat-free milk. Stir in peppermint extract. Cover surface with plastic wrap. Chill until ready to serve.

5 To serve, spoon about ¼ cup of the filling into the bottom half of each cream puff. Replace tops. If desired, sprinkle with powdered sugar or cocoa powder.

MOCHA CREAM PUFFS: Prepare as directed, except omit peppermint extract. Add 2 teaspoons instant espresso powder or instant coffee crystals with the milk when preparing the pudding.

Nutrition Facts per serving: 112 cal., 4 g total fat (2 g sat. fat), 62 mg chol., 231 mg sodium, 13 g carbo., 0 g fiber, 5 g pro.

MOCHA CUSTARDS

2¼ cups fat-free milk

⅓ cup sugar

3 tablespoons unsweetened cocoa powder

1 tablespoon instant coffee crystals

3 slightly beaten eggs or ¾ cup refrigerated or frozen egg product, thawed

1½ teaspoons vanilla

Frozen light whipped dessert topping, thawed (optional)

PREP:
20 minutes
BAKE:
30 minutes
COOL:
15 minutes
OVEN:
325°F
MAKES:
6 servings

1 In a medium saucepan combine milk, sugar, cocoa powder, and coffee crystals. Cook and stir just until cocoa and coffee are dissolved.

2 In a medium bowl gradually whisk hot milk mixture into eggs. Add vanilla. Place six 6-ounce custard cups in a 3-quart rectangular baking dish. Place baking dish on an oven rack. Pour egg mixture into the custard cups. Carefully pour boiling water around the custard cups into the baking dish to a depth of about 1 inch.

3 Bake in a 325° oven for 30 to 35 minutes or until a knife inserted near the centers comes out clean. Remove the custard cups from baking dish. Cool on wire rack for 15 minutes. Serve warm. (Or to serve chilled, cool on wire rack for 1 hour. Chill for at least 2 hours or up to 24 hours.) If desired, serve with whipped topping.

Nutrition Facts per serving: 125 cal., 3 g total fat (1 g sat. fat), 108 mg chol., 76 mg sodium, 17 g carbo., 0 g fiber, 7 g pro.

17
carbs per serving

Exchanges:
½ Milk
½ Medium-Fat Meat
½ Other Carbo.

BLUEBERRY-MANGO UPSIDE-DOWN CAKE

PREP:
35 minutes
STAND:
30 minutes
BAKE:
35 minutes
COOL:
5 minutes
OVEN:
350°F
MAKES:
12 servings

25 carbs per serving

Exchanges:
½ Starch
1 Other Carbo.
1 Fat

2	egg whites
1⅓	cups whole wheat pastry flour or whole wheat flour
2	teaspoons baking powder
1	teaspoon finely shredded orange peel
½	teaspoon ground ginger
3	tablespoons packed brown sugar
2	tablespoons butter, melted
1	tablespoon water
2	cups peeled, pitted, and sliced fresh mangoes or peaches
½	cup fresh blueberries
½	cup granulated sugar
¼	cup butter, softened
1	teaspoon vanilla
⅔	cup fat-free milk
	Vanilla frozen yogurt (optional)

1 Place egg whites in a medium mixing bowl. Let stand at room temperature for 30 minutes. In a small bowl stir together whole wheat flour, baking powder, orange peel, and ginger; set aside.

2 Grease a 9×1½-inch round baking pan. In a small bowl stir together brown sugar, the 2 tablespoons melted butter, and the water. Spread in prepared pan. Arrange mango or peach slices over brown sugar mixture. Sprinkle with blueberries.

3 Beat egg whites with an electric mixer on high speed until soft peaks form (tips curl). Gradually add ¼ cup of the granulated sugar, beating until stiff peaks form (tips stand straight). Set aside.

4 In a large mixing bowl beat the ¼ cup butter with an electric mixer on medium speed for 30 seconds. Beat in the remaining ¼ cup granulated sugar and the vanilla. Alternately add the flour mixture and milk to the beaten mixture, beating on low speed just until combined. Fold egg white mixture into batter; spoon over fruit in baking pan, spreading evenly.

5 Bake in a 350° oven for 35 to 40 minutes or until a toothpick inserted near the center comes out clean. Cool cake in pan on a wire rack for 5 minutes.

6 Loosen side by running a knife around cake; invert onto serving plate. Cut into wedges. Serve warm. If desired, serve with frozen yogurt.

Nutrition Facts per serving: 162 cal., 6 g total fat (4 g sat. fat), 17 mg chol., 147 mg sodium, 25 g carbo., 2 g fiber, 3 g pro.

GINGERBREAD

Nonstick cooking spray

1½ cups all-purpose flour

¼ cup sugar

1 teaspoon ground ginger

1 teaspoon ground cinnamon

½ teaspoon baking powder

½ teaspoon baking soda

¼ teaspoon salt

½ cup water

⅓ cup full-flavored molasses

3 tablespoons butter, melted

2 egg whites

Frozen light whipped dessert topping, thawed (optional)

PREP:
15 minutes
BAKE:
20 minutes
COOL:
10 minutes
OVEN:
350°F
MAKES:
9 servings

28 carbs per serving

Exchanges:
2 Other Carbo.
½ Fat

1 Lightly coat an 8×8×2-inch baking pan with nonstick cooking spray; dust lightly with flour. Set aside.

2 In a large mixing bowl combine the 1½ cups flour, the sugar, ginger, cinnamon, baking powder, baking soda, and salt. Add the water, molasses, butter, and egg whites. Beat with an electric mixer on low to medium speed until combined. Beat on high speed for 2 minutes. Spread into prepared pan.

3 Bake in a 350° oven about 20 minutes or until a toothpick inserted near the center comes out clean. Cool in pan on a wire rack for 10 minutes. Remove cake from pan. Serve warm. If desired, serve with whipped topping.

Nutrition Facts per serving: 163 cal., 4 g total fat (3 g sat. fat), 11 mg chol., 216 mg sodium, 28 g carbo., 1 g fiber, 3 g pro.

CARROT SNACK CAKE

PREP:
15 minutes
BAKE:
30 minutes
OVEN:
350°F
MAKES:
12 servings

21
carbs per
serving

Exchanges:
½ Starch
1 Other Carbo.
1 Fat

Nonstick cooking spray
1   cup all-purpose flour
¾   cup sugar
1½   teaspoons apple pie spice
½   teaspoon baking powder
½   teaspoon baking soda
⅛   teaspoon salt
1   cup finely shredded carrot
⅓   cup cooking oil
¼   cup fat-free milk
3   egg whites

1 Lightly coat an 8×8×2-inch baking pan with nonstick cooking spray. Set aside.

2 In a large bowl combine flour, sugar, apple pie spice, baking powder, baking soda, and salt. Add carrot, oil, and milk. Stir to moisten. In a medium mixing bowl beat egg whites with an electric mixer on medium to high speed until stiff peaks form (tips stand straight). Fold egg whites into carrot mixture.

3 Pour batter into prepared pan. Bake in a 350° oven for 30 to 35 minutes or until a toothpick inserted near the center comes out clean. Cool completely in pan on a wire rack.

Nutrition Facts per serving: 146 cal., 6 g total fat (1 g sat. fat), 0 mg chol., 110 mg sodium, 21 g carbo., 1 g fiber, 2 g pro.

MOCHA CAKE WITH BERRIES

Nonstick cooking spray

¾ cup sugar

½ cup water

1 tablespoon instant espresso coffee powder
or 2 tablespoons instant coffee powder

3 ounces bittersweet or semisweet chocolate, chopped

2 egg yolks

1 teaspoon vanilla

½ cup unsweetened cocoa powder

⅓ cup all-purpose flour

¼ teaspoon baking powder

5 egg whites

1½ cups fresh raspberries, blackberries, and/or blueberries

½ of an 8-ounce container frozen light whipped dessert topping, thawed

1 Lightly coat a 9-inch springform pan with nonstick cooking spray; set aside. In a medium saucepan stir together sugar, the water, and espresso powder. Cook and stir over medium-low heat until the sugar dissolves and mixture almost boils. Stir in the chocolate until melted. Remove from heat. In a small bowl slightly beat egg yolks. Gradually stir the chocolate mixture into egg yolks; stir in vanilla (mixture may appear slightly grainy). Set aside.

2 In a medium bowl stir together cocoa powder, flour, and baking powder. Stir in chocolate-egg yolk mixture until smooth. In a large mixing bowl beat egg whites with an electric mixer on medium speed until stiff peaks form (tips stand straight). Stir a small amount of the beaten egg whites into the chocolate mixture to lighten. Fold chocolate mixture into remaining egg whites. Spread in the prepared pan.

3 Bake in a 350° oven about 30 minutes or until top springs back when lightly touched. Cool in pan on a wire rack for 10 minutes. Loosen and remove side of pan. Cool completely. (Cake may fall slightly during cooling.)

4 To serve, cut cake into wedges. Top with berries and whipped topping.

Nutrition Facts per serving: 152 cal., 5 g total fat (3 g sat. fat), 34 mg chol., 31 mg sodium, 24 g carbo., 2 g fiber, 4 g pro.

PREP:
25 minutes
BAKE:
30 minutes
COOL:
10 minutes
OVEN:
350°F
MAKES:
12 servings

24
carbs per serving

Exchanges:
1½ Other Carbo.
1 Fat

LEMON-ROSEMARY CAKE

PREP:
30 minutes
BAKE:
25 minutes
COOL:
10 minutes
OVEN:
350°F
MAKES:
8 servings

31
carbs per serving

Exchanges:
2 Other Carbo.
1 Fat

Nonstick cooking spray
1   cup all-purpose flour
1   teaspoon snipped fresh rosemary
1   teaspoon baking powder
¼   teaspoon baking soda
⅛   teaspoon salt
⅔   cup granulated sugar
2   egg yolks
3   tablespoons cooking oil
⅓   cup lemon low-fat yogurt
2   teaspoons finely shredded lemon peel
2   egg whites
1   recipe Lemon Glaze
    Fresh strawberries, quartered (optional)
    Lemon slices, cut into sixths (optional)
    Sifted powdered sugar

1 Lightly coat an 8×1½-inch round cake pan with nonstick cooking spray; set aside. In a small bowl stir together flour, rosemary, baking powder, baking soda, and salt.

2 In a large mixing bowl combine granulated sugar, egg yolks, and oil; beat with an electric mixer on high speed for 2 minutes. Add yogurt and lemon peel. Beat until combined. Add flour mixture. Beat just until combined.

3 Thoroughly wash beaters. In medium mixing bowl beat egg whites until stiff peaks form (tips stand straight). Stir one-third of the stiffly beaten egg whites into batter to lighten. Fold in remaining egg whites. Spread in prepared pan.

4 Bake in a 350° oven for 25 to 28 minutes or until the top springs back when lightly touched.

5 Cool in pan on a wire rack for 10 minutes. Use tines of a fork to pierce cake. Slowly drizzle Lemon Glaze over cake. Cool completely. Invert to remove from pan; turn cake top side up. If desired, top individual servings with strawberries and garnish with lemon pieces. Sprinkle with powdered sugar.

LEMON GLAZE: In a small bowl stir together 3 tablespoons lemon juice and 2 tablespoons sifted powdered sugar.

Nutrition Facts per serving: 197 cal., 7 g total fat (1 g sat. fat), 54 mg chol., 149 mg sodium, 31 g carbo., 0 g fiber, 4 g pro.

TIRAMISU

2   8-ounce cartons fat-free or light dairy sour cream
2   8-ounce packages reduced-fat cream cheese (Neufchâtel), softened
⅔   cup sugar
¼   cup fat-free milk
½   teaspoon vanilla
½   cup strong coffee
2   tablespoons coffee liqueur or strong coffee
2   3-ounce packages ladyfingers, split
2   tablespoons sifted unsweetened cocoa powder

1 In a large mixing bowl combine sour cream, cream cheese, sugar, milk, and vanilla. Beat with an electric mixer on high speed until smooth. In a small bowl combine the ½ cup coffee and the coffee liqueur or additional coffee.

2 Layer 1 package of the ladyfingers, cut sides up, in a 2-quart rectangular baking dish. Brush with half of the coffee mixture. Spread with half of the cream cheese mixture. Repeat with remaining ladyfingers, coffee mixture, and cream cheese mixture.

3 Sprinkle with cocoa powder. Cover and chill for at least 4 hours or up to 24 hours.

Nutrition Facts per serving: 186 cal., 8 g total fat (5 g sat. fat), 67 mg chol., 182 mg sodium, 22 g carbo., 0 g fiber, 5 g pro.

PREP:
30 minutes
CHILL:
4 to 24 hours
MAKES:
15 servings

22
carbs per serving

Exchanges:
1½ Other Carbo.
1½ Fat

BANANA CREAM TARTS WITH RASPBERRIES

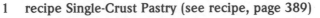

PREP:
30 minutes
BAKE:
8 minutes +
5 minutes
OVEN:
450°F
MAKES:
10 servings

16
carbs per
serving

Exchanges:
1 Other Carbo.
1½ Fat

1   recipe Single-Crust Pastry (see recipe, page 389)

1   8-ounce carton light dairy sour cream

1   medium banana, mashed (⅓ cup), or ⅓ cup mashed fresh mango

1   teaspoon granulated sugar or granulated heat-stable sugar substitute (Splenda®) (optional)

1   cup fresh raspberries, banana slices, and/or kiwifruit slices

1 Divide Single-Crust Pastry into 10 portions. On a lightly floured surface, use your hands to slightly flatten one portion. Roll dough from center to edges into a circle about 3½ inches in diameter. Line a 3-inch individual tart pan with pastry. Press pastry into fluted side of tart pan; trim edge. Prick bottom of pastry. Line with a double thickness of foil. Repeat with remaining portions of pastry.

2 Place pastry-lined tart pans on a very large baking sheet. Bake in a 450° oven for 8 minutes; remove foil. Bake for 5 to 6 minutes more or until tart shells are golden brown. Cool in pans on a wire rack. Remove tart shells from pans.

3 For filling, in a medium bowl stir together sour cream and mashed banana or mango. If desired, sweeten with sugar or sugar substitute.

4 Divide filling mixture among tart shells; top with raspberries, banana slices, and/or kiwifruit slices.

Nutrition Facts per serving: 157 cal., 9 g total fat (3 g sat. fat), 7 mg chol., 73 mg sodium, 16 g carbo., 2 g fiber, 3 g pro.

FRESH FRUIT TART

1   recipe Single-Crust Pastry

1   8-ounce carton fat-free or light dairy sour cream

2   tablespoons sugar

⅓   cup shredded coconut, toasted

2   to 3 cups assorted fresh fruit (such as sliced peaches, sliced strawberries, blueberries, raspberries, pitted dark sweet cherries, sliced bananas, and/or sliced mango)

PREP:
30 minutes
BAKE:
10 minutes
OVEN:
450°F
MAKES:
12 servings

❶ On a lightly floured surface, flatten the ball of Single-Crust Pastry with your hands. Roll dough from center to edges into a circle about 12 inches in diameter. To transfer pastry, wrap it around the rolling pin. Unroll pastry into a 9-inch tart pan with a removable bottom. Ease pastry into tart pan, being careful not to stretch pastry. Press pastry into fluted side of tart pan. Trim pastry even with edge of tart pan. Prick bottom and side of pastry generously with a fork.

❷ Bake in a 450° oven for 10 to 12 minutes or until pastry is golden brown. Cool in pan on a wire rack. Remove side of pan. In a small bowl stir together sour cream and sugar; spread over cooled crust.

17
carbs per
serving

❸ To serve, sprinkle with half of the coconut; arrange fruit on top. Sprinkle with remaining coconut.

SINGLE-CRUST PASTRY: In a large bowl stir together 1¼ cups all-purpose flour and ¼ teaspoon salt. Using a pastry blender, cut in ⅓ cup shortening until pieces are pea-size. Sprinkle 1 tablespoon cold water over part of the mixture; toss gently with a fork. Push moistened dough to the side of the bowl. Repeat moistening flour mixture, using 1 tablespoon cold water at a time, until all of the flour mixture is moistened (4 to 5 tablespoons cold water total). Form dough into a ball.

Exchanges:
1 Other Carbo.
1 Fat

TO MAKE AHEAD: Prepare as directed through step 2. Cover and chill for up to 2 hours. Serve as directed in step 3.

Nutrition Facts per serving: 138 cal., 7 g total fat (3 g sat. fat), 2 mg chol., 86 mg sodium, 17 g carbo., 1 g fiber, 2 g pro.

COUNTRY PEAR TART

PREP:
40 minutes
BAKE:
40 minutes
OVEN:
375°F
MAKES:
10 servings

29
carbs per serving

Exchanges:
1 Fruit
½ Starch
½ Other Carbo.
1 Fat

⅓ cup dried tart cherries
3 tablespoons brandy or apple juice
2 tablespoons granulated sugar
1 tablespoon cornstarch
¼ teaspoon ground cinnamon
4 cups sliced, peeled pears (about 1½ pounds)
1 teaspoon finely shredded lemon peel
1 teaspoon vanilla
All-purpose flour
1 recipe Browned Butter Pastry
1 tablespoon sliced almonds
Fat-free milk
Granulated sugar or coarse sugar (optional)

1 In a small saucepan combine dried cherries and brandy or apple juice. Heat over low heat just until liquid is hot but not boiling; set aside to cool and plump cherries. In a large bowl stir together the 2 tablespoons granulated sugar, the cornstarch, and cinnamon. Gently stir in the cherries with any remaining soaking liquid, the pears, lemon peel, and vanilla.

2 Line a large baking sheet with foil; sprinkle lightly with flour. Place Browned Butter Pastry on baking sheet; roll from center to the edges into a circle about 13 inches in diameter. Place pear mixture in center of crust, leaving a 2-inch border. Fold border up over pear mixture, pleating pastry as necessary to fit. Sprinkle center with sliced almonds.

3 Brush top and side of crust with milk. If desired, sprinkle lightly with additional granulated sugar or coarse sugar. Bake in a 375° oven for 40 to 45 minutes or until crust is golden brown. Serve warm or cool.

BROWNED BUTTER PASTRY: In a small saucepan heat and stir 2 tablespoons butter over medium heat until light brown; set aside to cool slightly. In a medium bowl stir together 1¼ cups whole wheat pastry flour or whole wheat flour, 1 tablespoon granulated sugar, and ¼ teaspoon salt. Using a pastry blender, cut in 2 tablespoons shortening and the browned butter until mixture resembles crumbs. Sprinkle 1 tablespoon cold water over part of the mixture; toss gently with a fork. Push moistened dough to side of bowl. Repeat moistening flour mixture, using 1 tablespoon cold water at a time, until all of the flour mixture is moistened (4 to 5 tablespoons cold water total). Form dough into a ball.

Nutrition Facts per serving: 183 cal., 6 g total fat (2 g sat. fat), 6 mg chol., 79 mg sodium, 29 g carbo., 4 g fiber, 3 g pro.

LATTICE-TOPPED APPLES

2 pounds cooking apples
(such as Granny Smith, Cortland, or Jonathan)

3 tablespoons sugar

1 teaspoon ground cinnamon

1 tablespoon cornstarch

½ cup all-purpose flour

¼ cup whole wheat pastry flour or whole wheat flour

2 tablespoons toasted wheat germ

⅛ teaspoon ground nutmeg

3 tablespoons butter

2 to 3 tablespoons cold water

Fat-free milk

PREP:
30 minutes
BAKE:
40 minutes
OVEN:
375°F
MAKES:
8 servings

26 carbs per serving

❶ If desired, peel apples. Core and slice apples (you should have about 6 cups). Place apple slices in a 2-quart rectangular baking dish. In a small bowl combine sugar and cinnamon; set aside 1 teaspoon of the sugar mixture. Stir cornstarch into remaining sugar mixture. Sprinkle cornstarch mixture over apples; toss to combine.

❷ In a medium bowl stir together all-purpose flour, whole wheat pastry flour, wheat germ, and nutmeg. Using a pastry blender, cut in butter until mixture resembles coarse crumbs. Sprinkle 1 tablespoon of the cold water over part of the flour mixture; toss gently with a fork. Push moistened dough to side of bowl. Repeat moistening flour mixture, using 1 tablespoon of the cold water at a time, until all of the flour mixture is moistened. Form dough into a ball.

❸ On a lightly floured surface, flatten dough. Roll dough from center to edges into a 10×5-inch rectangle. Cut pastry lengthwise into 9 strips, each about ½ inch wide. Carefully place 4 of the pastry strips lengthwise over apples; place remaining strips crosswise over apples, spacing strips evenly to form a lattice-style crust. Trim pastry as needed. Tuck ends of pastry into the dish. Brush pastry with milk and sprinkle with reserved sugar mixture.

❹ Bake in a 375° oven for 40 to 45 minutes or until apples are tender. Serve warm or at room temperature.

Nutrition Facts per serving: 152 cal., 5 g total fat (2 g sat. fat), 12 mg chol., 48 mg sodium, 26 g carbo., 3 g fiber, 2 g pro.

Exchanges:
1 Fruit
1 Other Carbo.
½ Fat

MARINATED STRAWBERRIES

PREP:
15 minutes
CHILL:
*20 minutes to
4 hours*
MAKES:
6 servings

4   cups fresh strawberries (2 pints)
2   tablespoons sugar
2   tablespoons balsamic vinegar
2   tablespoons finely shredded fresh mint
1   tablespoon lemon juice
3   cups vanilla low-fat or fat-free frozen yogurt

1 Remove stems from strawberries; halve or, if large, quarter berries lengthwise. In a medium bowl combine strawberries, sugar, balsamic vinegar, mint, and lemon juice. Cover and chill for at least 20 minutes or up to 4 hours.

2 To serve, spoon the strawberry mixture over scoops of frozen yogurt.

Nutrition Facts per serving: 157 cal., 3 g total fat (2 g sat. fat), 15 mg chol., 86 mg sodium, 30 g carbo., 2 g fiber, 5 g pro.

**30
carbs per
serving**

Exchanges:
1 Starch
1 Fruit

SUMMER BERRIES
WITH ALMOND-SOUR CREAM SAUCE

4 cups fresh blackberries, raspberries, blueberries, and/or halved strawberries

¾ cup light dairy sour cream

½ to ¾ teaspoon almond extract

1 to 2 teaspoons sugar or sugar substitute equal to 1 to 2 teaspoons sugar

1 Divide berries among 6 dessert dishes. Set aside.

2 In a small bowl combine sour cream and almond extract. Stir in sugar or sugar substitute. Spoon mixture evenly over berries.

Nutrition Facts per serving: 86 cal., 3 g total fat (2 g sat. fat), 10 mg chol., 21 mg sodium, 12 g carbo., 5 g fiber, 3 g pro.

START TO FINISH:
10 minutes
MAKES:
6 servings

12
carbs per serving

Exchanges:
1 Fruit
½ Fat

HONEY-APRICOT FROZEN YOGURT

PREP:
35 minutes
FREEZE:
4 hours +
6 hours
STAND:
20 minutes
MAKES:
12 (¹/₂-cup)
servings

18
carbs per serving

3   cups pitted and finely chopped fresh apricots* or nectarines
1   32-ounce carton vanilla low-fat yogurt
2   tablespoons honey
    Sliced fresh apricots and/or nectarines (optional)

❶ In a large food processor combine half of the chopped apricots or nectarines, the yogurt, and honey. Cover and process until smooth. (If using a smaller food processor, do this step in two batches.)

❷ Pour apricot mixture into a 2-quart freezer container. Stir in remaining chopped apricots or nectarines. Cover and freeze about 4 hours or until firm.

❸ Chill the mixer bowl for a heavy stand electric mixer. Spoon the frozen mixture into the chilled mixer bowl. Beat with the electric mixer on medium speed until slightly fluffy, starting slowly and gradually increasing the speed. Return mixture to freezer container. Cover and freeze about 6 hours or until firm.

❹ Let frozen yogurt stand at room temperature for 20 minutes before serving. If desired, serve with sliced apricots and/or nectarines.

***NOTE:** If fresh apricots aren't available, use three 15-ounce cans unpeeled apricot halves in light syrup, drained.*

Exchanges:
¹/₂ Milk
¹/₂ Other Carbo.

Nutrition Facts per serving: 93 cal., 1 g total fat (1 g sat. fat), 4 mg chol., 50 mg sodium, 18 g carbo., 1 g fiber, 4 g pro.

FRESH BERRY NAPOLEONS

8	sheets frozen phyllo dough, thawed
	Nonstick cooking spray
2	tablespoons coarse sugar
1½	cups fresh blueberries
3	tablespoons orange juice
¼	teaspoon finely shredded orange peel
2	tablespoons sugar
1	teaspoon butter (no substitutes)
2	teaspoons cornstarch
2	teaspoons cold water
2	cups mixed fresh berries, such as blueberries, blackberries, red raspberries, and/or sliced strawberries
1	teaspoon water
⅓	cup frozen light whipped dessert topping
	Mint sprigs (optional)

1 Place 1 sheet of phyllo on a work surface. (Cover remaining sheets to prevent them from drying out.) Lightly coat phyllo sheet with cooking spray. Top with another sheet of phyllo; coat with cooking spray. Lightly sprinkle with some of the coarse sugar. Repeat layering with remaining phyllo sheets, cooking spray, and coarse sugar. Cut stack crosswise into six strips. Cut each strip crosswise into three rectangles, each about 2x3 inches. Place stacks on ungreased cookie sheets. (There will be 2 extra stacks.) Bake in a 350°F oven 10 to 12 minutes or until golden. Transfer to a wire rack to cool.

2 For blueberry curd, combine 1½ cups blueberries, orange juice, and orange peel in a saucepan. Bring to boiling; reduce heat. Simmer, covered, for 5 minutes. Remove from heat; cool slightly. Transfer blueberry mixture to a blender or food processor. Cover and blend or process until smooth. Return to saucepan. Stir in 2 tablespoons sugar and butter.

3 In a bowl combine cornstarch and 2 teaspoons cold water. Add to blueberry mixture in saucepan. Cook and stir over medium heat until thickened and bubbly. Cook and stir 2 minutes more. Remove from heat; transfer to a bowl. Cover surface with plastic wrap and chill for 2 hours or overnight.

4 To serve, stir together 1 tablespoon blueberry curd and 1 teaspoon water in a bowl; set aside. Divide remaining blueberry curd in half. Place 1 phyllo stack on each of 8 dessert plates. Spoon half of the blueberry curd atop phyllo stacks; top with fruit. Spoon remaining blueberry curd atop fruit; top with another phyllo stack and some of the whipped topping. Drizzle with reserved blueberry curd. If desired, garnish with mint sprigs. Makes 8 servings

Nutrition Facts per cookie: 99 cal., 2 g total fat (1 g sat. fat), 1 mg chol., 50 mg sodium, 21 g carbo., 2 g dietary fiber, 1 g protein

PREP:
45 minutes
CHILL:
2 hours
BAKE:
10 minutes

21
carbs per serving

Exchanges:
1 Other Carbo.,
.5 Fruit

CHOCOLATE CHIP-YOGURT DROPS

PREP:
20 minutes
BAKE:
9 minutes
per batch
OVEN:
375°F
MAKES:
about
60 cookies

11
carbs per
cookie

Exchanges:
½ Other Carbo.
½ Fat

1	cup rolled oats
½	cup butter, softened
1	cup packed brown sugar
1	teaspoon baking soda
¼	teaspoon salt
1	cup plain low-fat yogurt
2	eggs or ½ cup refrigerated or frozen egg product, thawed
1	teaspoon vanilla
2½	cups all-purpose flour
1	cup miniature semisweet chocolate pieces (6 ounces)

1 Place oats in a shallow baking pan. Bake in a 375° oven about 10 minutes or until toasted, stirring once. Transfer oats to a food processor or blender. Cover and process or blend oats until ground; set aside.

2 In a large mixing bowl beat butter with an electric mixer on medium to high speed for 30 seconds. Add brown sugar, baking soda, and salt; beat until combined. Beat in yogurt, eggs, and vanilla until combined. Beat in as much of the flour as you can with the mixer. Using a wooden spoon, stir in any remaining flour and the oats. Stir in chocolate pieces.

3 Drop dough by rounded teaspoons 2 inches apart on ungreased cookie sheets. Bake in the 375° oven for 9 to 11 minutes or until bottoms are browned. Transfer to a wire rack and let cool.

Nutrition Facts per cookie: 71 cal., 3 g total fat (1 g sat. fat), 12 mg chol., 49 mg sodium, 11 g carbo., 0 g fiber, 1 g pro.

BROWNIE COOKIES

1	cup all-purpose flour
¼	teaspoon baking soda
¼	cup butter
⅔	cup granulated sugar
⅓	cup unsweetened cocoa powder
¼	cup packed brown sugar
¼	cup buttermilk or sour milk*
1	teaspoon vanilla
	Nonstick cooking spray
1	tablespoon sifted powdered sugar

1 In a small bowl stir together flour and baking soda; set aside. In a medium saucepan melt butter; remove from heat. Stir in granulated sugar, cocoa powder, and brown sugar. Stir in buttermilk and vanilla. Stir in flour mixture just until combined. Cover and chill dough for 1 hour. (Dough will be stiff.)

2 Lightly coat cookie sheets with nonstick cooking spray. Drop chilled dough by rounded teaspoons onto cookie sheets.

3 Bake in a 350° oven for 8 to 10 minutes or until edges are set. Cool on cookie sheets for 1 minute. Transfer to a wire rack and let cool. Sprinkle with powdered sugar.

*NOTE: To make ¼ cup sour milk, place ¾ teaspoon lemon juice or vinegar in a glass measuring cup. Add enough milk to make ¼ cup total liquid; stir. Let mixture stand for 5 minutes before using.

Nutrition Facts per cookie: 73 cal., 2 g total fat (1 g sat. fat), 6 mg chol., 38 mg sodium, 12 g carbo., 0 g fiber, 1 g pro.

PREP:
20 minutes
CHILL:
1 hour
BAKE:
8 minutes per batch
OVEN:
350°F
MAKES:
24 cookies

12
carbs per cookie

Exchanges:
1 Other Carbo.

COCOA-NUTMEG SNICKERSTICKS

PREP:
30 minutes
CHILL:
2 hours
BAKE:
8 minutes
per batch
OVEN:
375°F
MAKES:
48 cookies

8
carbs per
cookie

Exchanges:
½ Other Carbo.
½ Fat

⅓	cup butter, softened
1	cup sugar
1	teaspoon baking powder
½	teaspoon ground nutmeg
¼	teaspoon baking soda
⅓	cup fat-free dairy sour cream*
1	egg or ¼ cup refrigerated or frozen egg product, thawed
1	teaspoon vanilla
2	cups all-purpose flour
2	tablespoons sugar
1½	teaspoons unsweetened cocoa powder

1 In a large mixing bowl beat butter with an electric mixer on medium to high speed for 30 seconds. Add the 1 cup sugar, the baking powder, nutmeg, and baking soda; beat until combined. Beat in the sour cream, egg, and vanilla until combined. Beat in as much of the flour as you can with the mixer. Using a wooden spoon, stir in any remaining flour. Cover and chill about 2 hours or until dough is easy to handle.

2 In a shallow dish combine the 2 tablespoons sugar and the cocoa powder. Roll dough into 1-inch balls; shape into 3-inch-long logs. Roll logs in cocoa mixture to lightly coat. Place 1½ inches apart on ungreased cookie sheets.

3 Bake in a 375° oven for 8 to 10 minutes or until edges are lightly golden brown. Transfer cookies to a wire rack and let cool.

*NOTE: Stir the fat-free sour cream in the carton before measuring.

TO STORE: Place cooled cookies in a freezer container. Seal, label, and freeze for up to 3 months.

Nutrition Facts per cookie: 50 cal., 2 g total fat (1 g sat. fat), 8 mg chol., 32 mg sodium, 8 g carbo., 0 g fiber, 1 g pro.

MOCHA MERINGUE STARS

⅓ cup sifted powdered sugar

2 tablespoons unsweetened cocoa powder

1 tablespoon cornstarch

1 teaspoon instant espresso coffee powder or 2 teaspoons instant coffee powder

3 egg whites

½ teaspoon vanilla

¼ cup granulated sugar

⅓ cup semisweet chocolate pieces

1 teaspoon shortening

PREP:
25 minutes
BAKE:
1 hour
OVEN:
250°F
MAKES:
24 cookies

1 Line a cookie sheet with parchment paper or foil; set aside. In a small bowl stir together powdered sugar, cocoa powder, cornstarch, and espresso powder; set aside.

2 In a medium mixing bowl beat egg whites and vanilla with an electric mixer on high speed until foamy. Gradually add the granulated sugar, 1 tablespoon at a time, beating until stiff peaks form (tips stand straight). Gradually fold in the cocoa powder mixture.

3 Transfer the mixture to a pastry bag fitted with a large star tip. Pipe twenty-four 2-inch stars onto the prepared cookie sheet. (Or drop mixture by rounded teaspoons onto the prepared cookie sheet.) Bake in a 250° oven for 1 hour. Cool on cookie sheet on wire rack. Remove from parchment paper.

4 In a small saucepan combine chocolate pieces and shortening. Cook and stir over low heat until chocolate is melted. Drizzle the melted chocolate over cookies.

Nutrition Facts per cookie: 32 cal., 1 g total fat (0 g sat. fat), 0 mg chol., 7 mg sodium, 5 g carbo., 0 g fiber, 1 g pro.

5
carbs per
cookie

Exchanges:
½ Starch

LUNCH BOX OATMEAL COOKIES

PREP:
25 minutes
BAKE:
7 minutes
per batch
OVEN:
375°F
MAKES:
about
40 cookies

9
carbs per cookie

Exchanges:
½ Other Carbo.
½ Fat

½ cup butter, softened
½ cup reduced-fat peanut butter
⅓ cup granulated sugar
⅓ cup packed brown sugar
½ teaspoon baking soda
2 egg whites
½ teaspoon vanilla
1 cup all-purpose flour
1 cup quick-cooking rolled oats

1 In a large mixing bowl combine butter and peanut butter. Beat with an electric mixer on medium to high speed about 30 seconds or until combined.

2 Add granulated sugar, brown sugar, and baking soda. Beat until combined, scraping side of bowl occasionally. Beat in egg whites and vanilla until combined. Beat in as much of the flour as you can with the mixer. Using a wooden spoon, stir in any remaining flour. Stir in oats.

3 Drop dough by rounded teaspoons 2 inches apart on ungreased cookie sheets. Bake in a 375° oven for 7 to 8 minutes or until edges are golden brown. Cool on cookie sheets for 1 minute. Transfer to a wire rack and let cool.

Nutrition Facts per cookie: 76 cal., 4 g total fat (2 g sat. fat), 7 mg chol., 69 mg sodium, 9 g carbo., 1 g fiber, 2 g pro.

VANILLA BEAN BISCOTTI

- 1   vanilla bean, split, or 2 teaspoons vanilla
- 3   cups all-purpose flour
- 1   tablespoon baking powder
- ¼   teaspoon salt
- 3   eggs
- ¾   cup sugar
- ½   cup butter, melted and cooled

1 Grease a very large cookie sheet; set aside. Scrape seeds from vanilla bean, if using; set aside.

2 In a medium bowl combine flour, baking powder, and salt; set aside. In a large mixing bowl beat eggs with an electric mixer on high speed for 1 minute. Gradually beat in sugar, beating on high speed for 1 minute. Add butter and vanilla seeds or vanilla; beat on low speed until combined. Beat in as much of the flour mixture as you can with the mixer. Using a wooden spoon, stir in any remaining flour mixture.

3 Divide dough into thirds. On a lightly floured surface, roll each third into a 14-inch-long roll. Arrange rolls 2½ inches apart on the prepared cookie sheet; flatten each roll slightly to a 1½-inch width.

4 Bake in a 325° oven about 25 minutes or until firm and lightly browned. Cool on cookie sheet on a wire rack for 15 minutes.

5 Transfer rolls to a large cutting board. Using a serrated knife, cut each roll diagonally into slices about ½ inch thick. Arrange slices, cut sides down, on cookie sheet.

6 Bake slices in the 325° oven for 10 minutes. Turn slices and bake about 10 minutes more or until crisp and lightly browned. Cool on the cookie sheet on a wire rack.

Nutrition Facts per cookie: 63 cal., 2 g total fat (1 g sat. fat), 19 mg chol., 62 mg sodium, 9 g carbo., 0 g fiber, 1 g pro.

PREP:
30 minutes
BAKE:
25 minutes +
10 minutes +
10 minutes
COOL:
15 minutes
OVEN:
325°F
MAKES:
48 cookies

9

carbs per cookie

Exchanges:
½ Other Carbo.
½ Fat

INDEX

METRIC INFORMATION

The charts on this page provide a guide for converting measurements from the U.S. customary system, which is used throughout this book, to the metric system.

Product Differences

Most of the ingredients called for in the recipes in this book are available in most countries. However, some are known by different names. Here are some common American ingredients and their possible counterparts:

- **All-purpose flour** is enriched, bleached or unbleached white household flour. When self-rising flour is used in place of all-purpose flour in a recipe that calls for leavening, omit the leavening agent (baking soda or baking powder) and salt.
- **Baking soda** is bicarbonate of soda.
- **Cornstarch** is cornflour.
- **Golden raisins** are sultanas.
- **Green, red, or yellow sweet peppers** are capsicums or bell peppers.
- **Light-colored corn syrup** is golden syrup.
- **Powdered sugar** is icing sugar.
- **Sugar** (white) is granulated, fine granulated, or castor sugar.
- **Vanilla** or vanilla extract is vanilla essence.

Volume and Weight

The United States traditionally uses cup measures for liquid and solid ingredients. The chart below shows the approximate imperial and metric equivalents. If you are accustomed to weighing solid ingredients, the following approximate equivalents will be helpful.

- 1 cup butter, castor sugar, or rice = 8 ounces = $1/2$ pound = 250 grams
- 1 cup flour = 4 ounces = $1/4$ pound = 125 grams
- 1 cup icing sugar = 5 ounces = 150 grams

Canadian and U.S. volume for a cup measure is 8 fluid ounces (237 ml), but the standard metric equivalent is 250 ml.

1 British imperial cup is 10 fluid ounces.

In Australia, 1 tablespoon equals 20 ml, and there are 4 teaspoons in the Australian tablespoon.

Spoon measures are used for smaller amounts of ingredients. Although the size of the tablespoon varies slightly in different countries, for practical purposes and for recipes in this book, a straight substitution is all that's necessary. Measurements made using cups or spoons always should be level unless stated otherwise.

Common Weight Range Replacements

Imperial / U.S.	Metric
$1/2$ ounce	15 g
1 ounce	25 g or 30 g
4 ounces ($1/4$ pound)	115 g or 125 g
8 ounces ($1/2$ pound)	225 g or 250 g
16 ounces (1 pound)	450 g or 500 g
$1^1/4$ pounds	625 g
$1^1/2$ pounds	750 g
2 pounds or $2^1/4$ pounds	1,000 g or 1 Kg

Oven Temperature Equivalents

Fahrenheit Setting	Celsius Setting*	Gas Setting
300°F	150°C	Gas Mark 2 (very low)
325°F	160°C	Gas Mark 3 (low)
350°F	180°C	Gas Mark 4 (moderate)
375°F	190°C	Gas Mark 5 (moderate)
400°F	200°C	Gas Mark 6 (hot)
425°F	220°C	Gas Mark 7 (hot)
450°F	230°C	Gas Mark 8 (very hot)
475°F	240°C	Gas Mark 9 (very hot)
500°F	260°C	Gas Mark 10 (extremely hot)
Broil	Broil	Grill

*Electric and gas ovens may be calibrated using Celsius. However, for an electric oven, increase Celsius setting 10 to 20 degrees when cooking above 160°C. For convection or forced air ovens (gas or electric), lower the temperature setting 25°F/10°C when cooking at all heat levels.

Baking Pan Sizes

Imperial / U.S.	Metric
$9 \times 1^1/2$-inch round cake pan	22- or 23×4-cm (1.5 L)
$9 \times 1^1/2$-inch pie plate	22- or 23×4-cm (1 L)
8×8×2-inch square cake pan	20×5-cm (2 L)
9×9×2-inch square cake pan	22- or 23×4.5-cm (2.5 L)
$11 \times 7 \times 1^1/2$-inch baking pan	28×17×4-cm (2 L)
2-quart rectangular baking pan	30×19×4.5-cm (3 L)
13×9×2-inch baking pan	34×22×4.5-cm (3.5 L)
15×10×1-inch jelly roll pan	40×25×2-cm
9×5×3-inch loaf pan	23×13×8-cm (2 L)
2-quart casserole	2 L

U.S. / Standard Metric Equivalents

$1/8$ teaspoon = 0.5 ml	
$1/4$ teaspoon = 1 ml	
$1/2$ teaspoon = 2 ml	
1 teaspoon = 5 ml	
1 tablespoon = 15 ml	
2 tablespoons = 25 ml	
$1/4$ cup = 2 fluid ounces = 50 ml	
$1/3$ cup = 3 fluid ounces = 75 ml	
$1/2$ cup = 4 fluid ounces = 125 ml	
$2/3$ cup = 5 fluid ounces = 150 ml	
$3/4$ cup = 6 fluid ounces = 175 ml	
1 cup = 8 fluid ounces = 250 ml	
2 cups = 1 pint = 500 ml	
1 quart = 1 litre